Snow White with the Red Hair

SORATA AKIDUKI

3

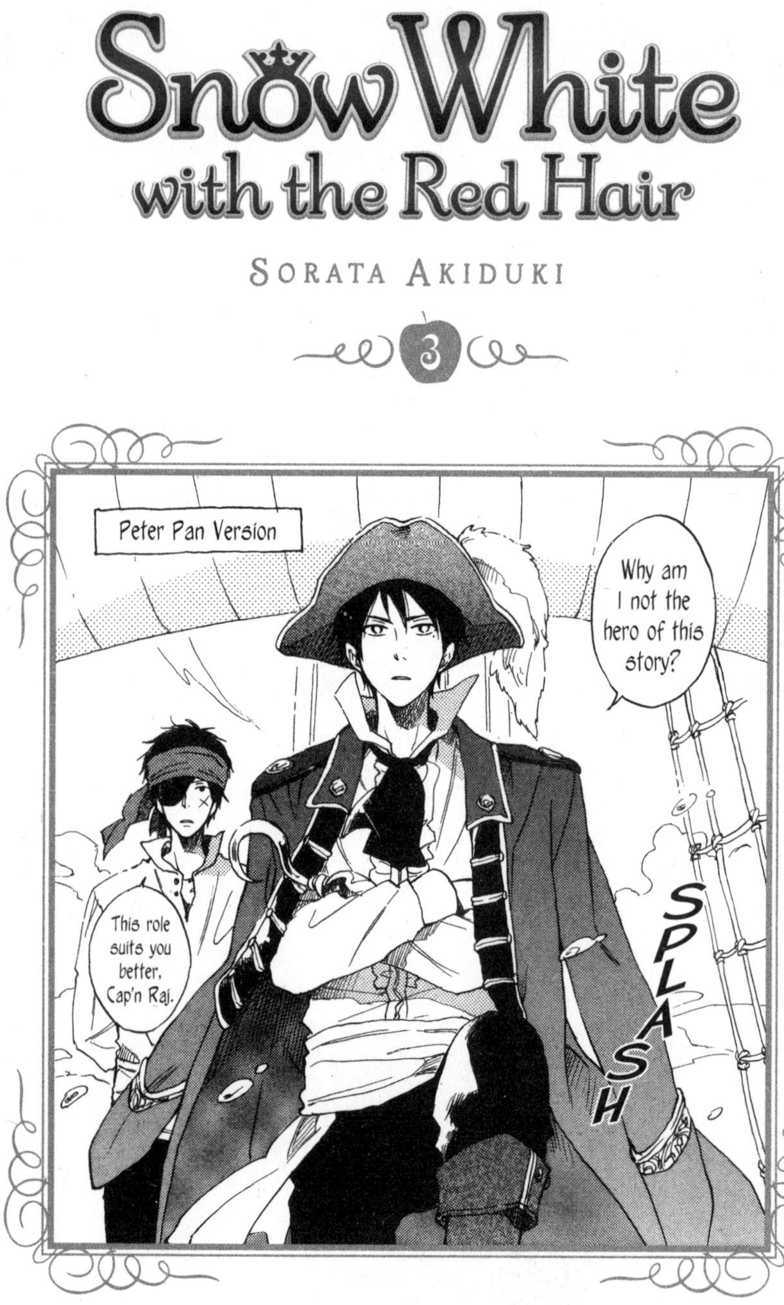
Why am I not the hero of this story?
Peter Pan Version
SPLASH
This role suits you better, Cap'n Raj.

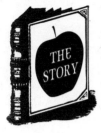

THE STORY

Shirayuki was born with beautiful hair as red as apples, but when her rare hair earns her unwanted attention from the notorious prince Raj, she's forced to flee her home. A young man named Zen helps her in the forest of the neighboring kingdom, Clarines, and it turns out he is that kingdom's second prince! Shirayuki decides to accompany Zen back to Wistal, the capital city of Clarines.

Shirayuki has met all manner of people since becoming a court herbalist, and her relationship with Zen continues to grow. But when Izana—the crown prince of Clarines and Zen's older brother—returns home, he has a thing or two to say about his little brother's new friend...

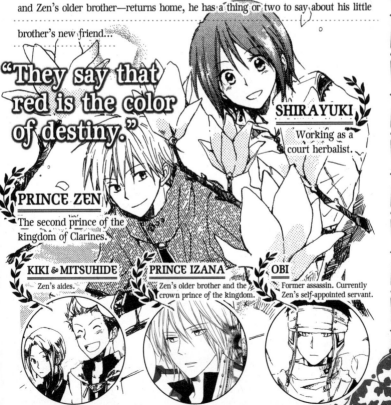

"They say that red is the color of destiny."

SHIRAYUKI
Working as a court herbalist.

PRINCE ZEN
The second prince of the kingdom of Clarines.

KIKI & MITSUHIDE
Zen's aides.

PRINCE IZANA
Zen's older brother and the crown prince of the kingdom.

OBI
Former assassin. Currently Zen's self-appointed servant.

Upon returning to the palace, Izana learns of Zen's deepening relationship with Shirayuki. Izana's mere presence puts Zen on edge.

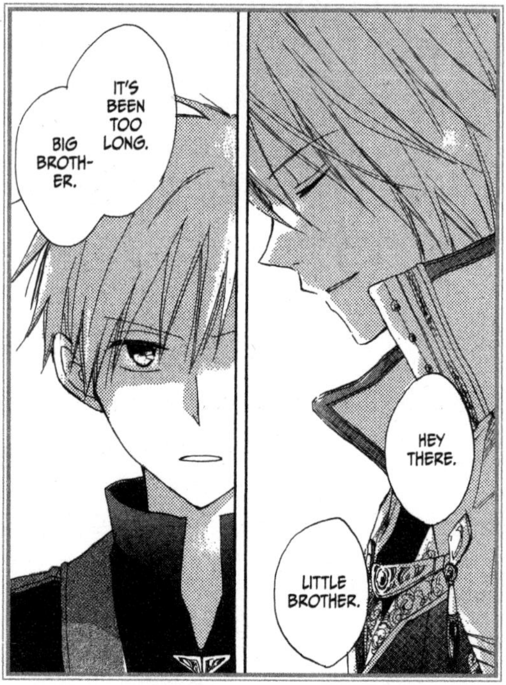
HEY THERE.
LITTLE BROTHER.
IT'S BEEN TOO LONG.
BIG BROTHER.

Izana asks Shirayuki, "Is there something about you that Zen really needs in his life?" She's left speechless.

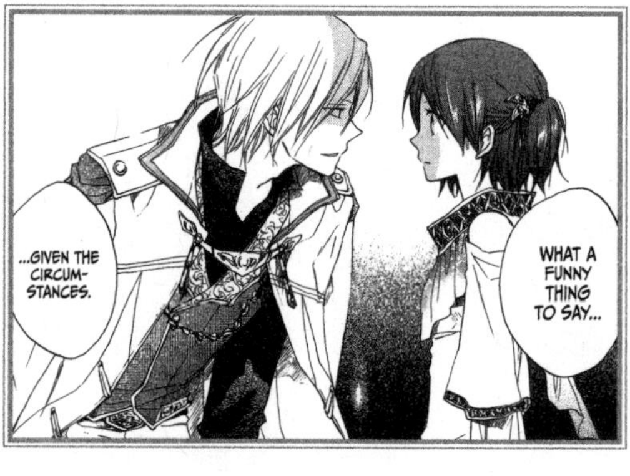
WHAT A FUNNY THING TO SAY...
...GIVEN THE CIRCUMSTANCES.

Snow White with the Red Hair

VOLUME 3
TABLE *of* CONTENTS

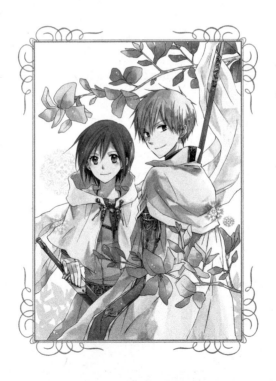

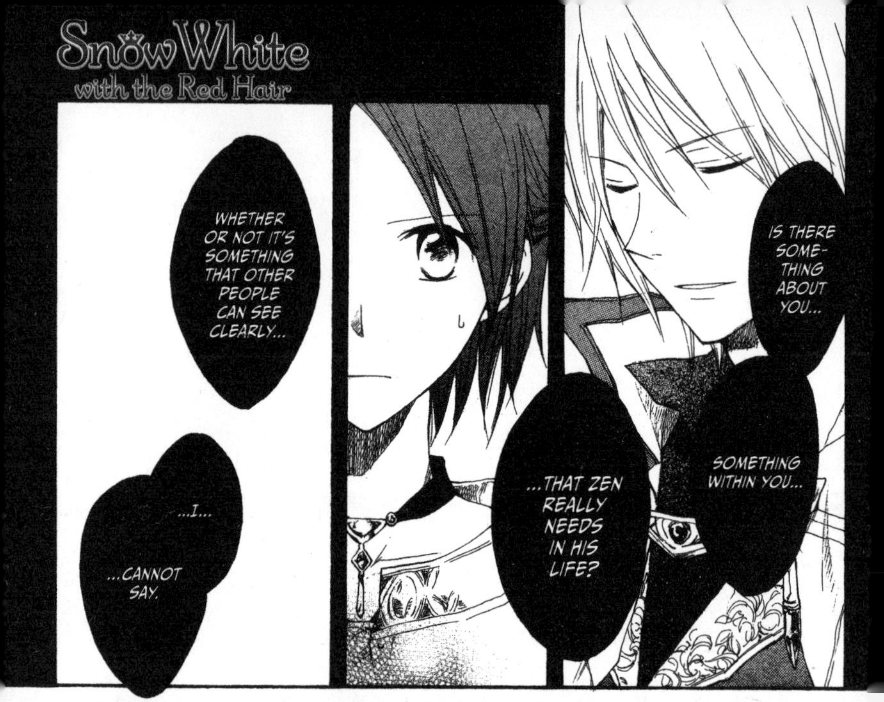
Snow White
with the Red Hair
IS THERE SOMETHING ABOUT YOU...
SOMETHING WITHIN YOU...
...THAT ZEN REALLY NEEDS IN HIS LIFE?
WHETHER OR NOT IT'S SOMETHING THAT OTHER PEOPLE CAN SEE CLEARLY...
...I...
...CANNOT SAY.

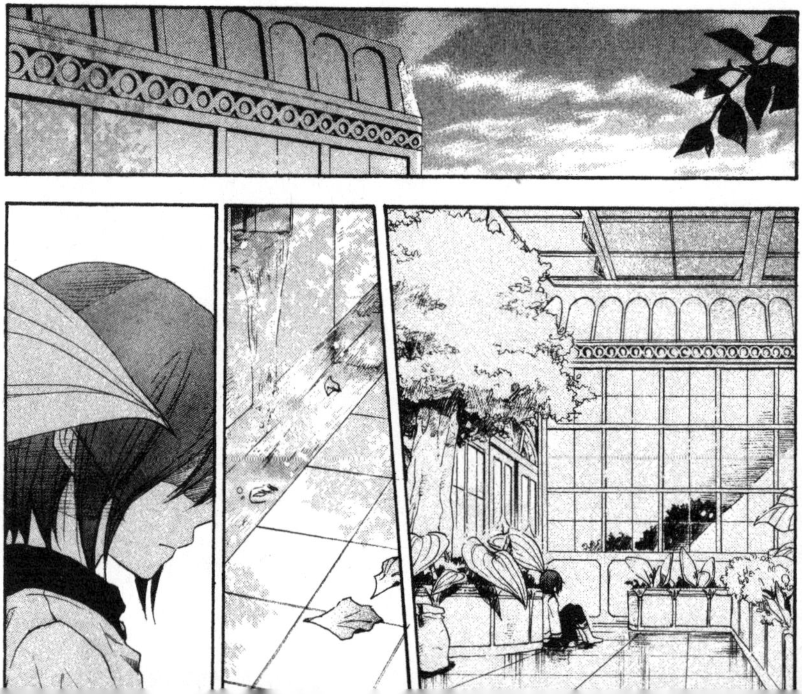

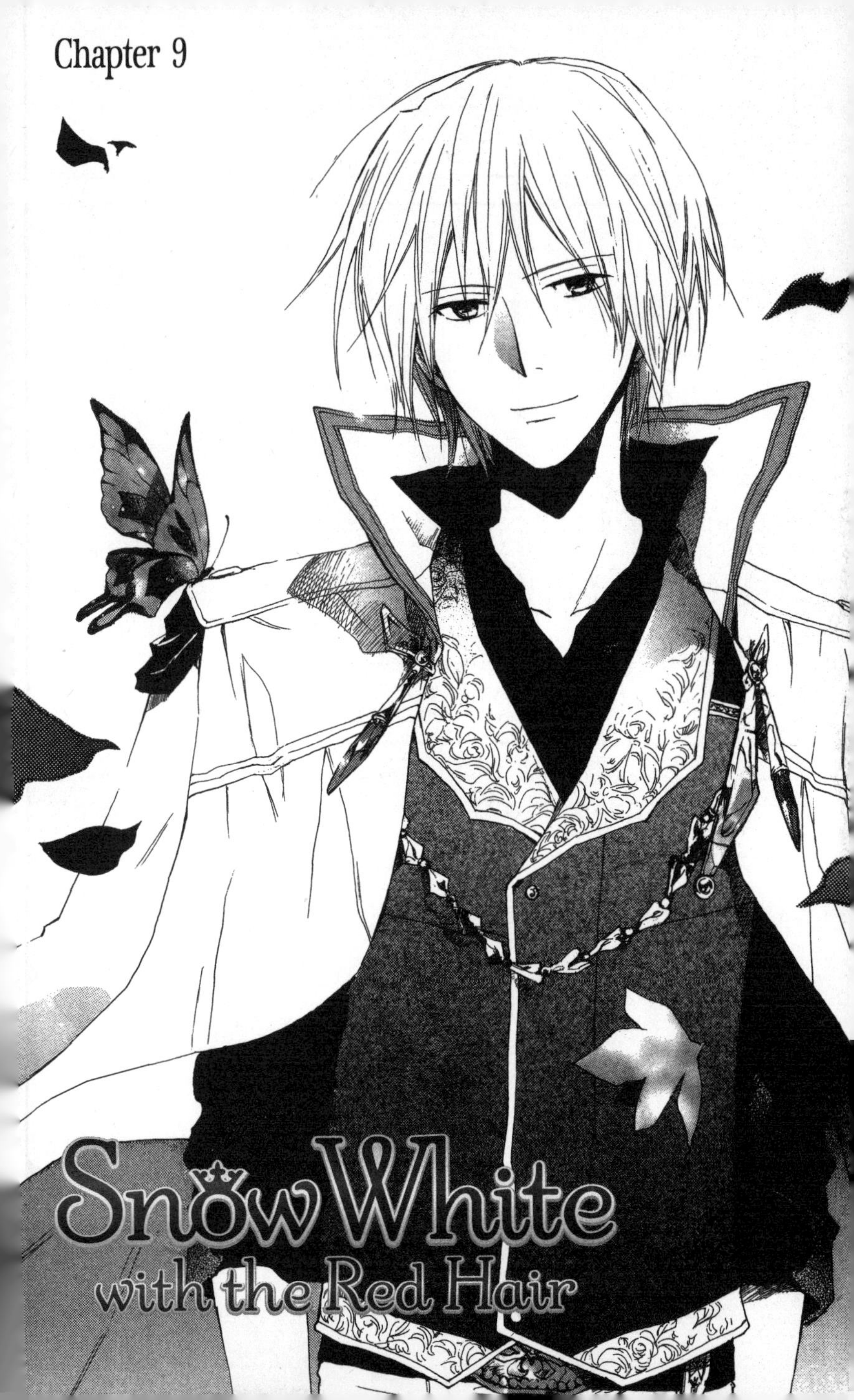
Chapter 9
Snow White
with the Red Hair

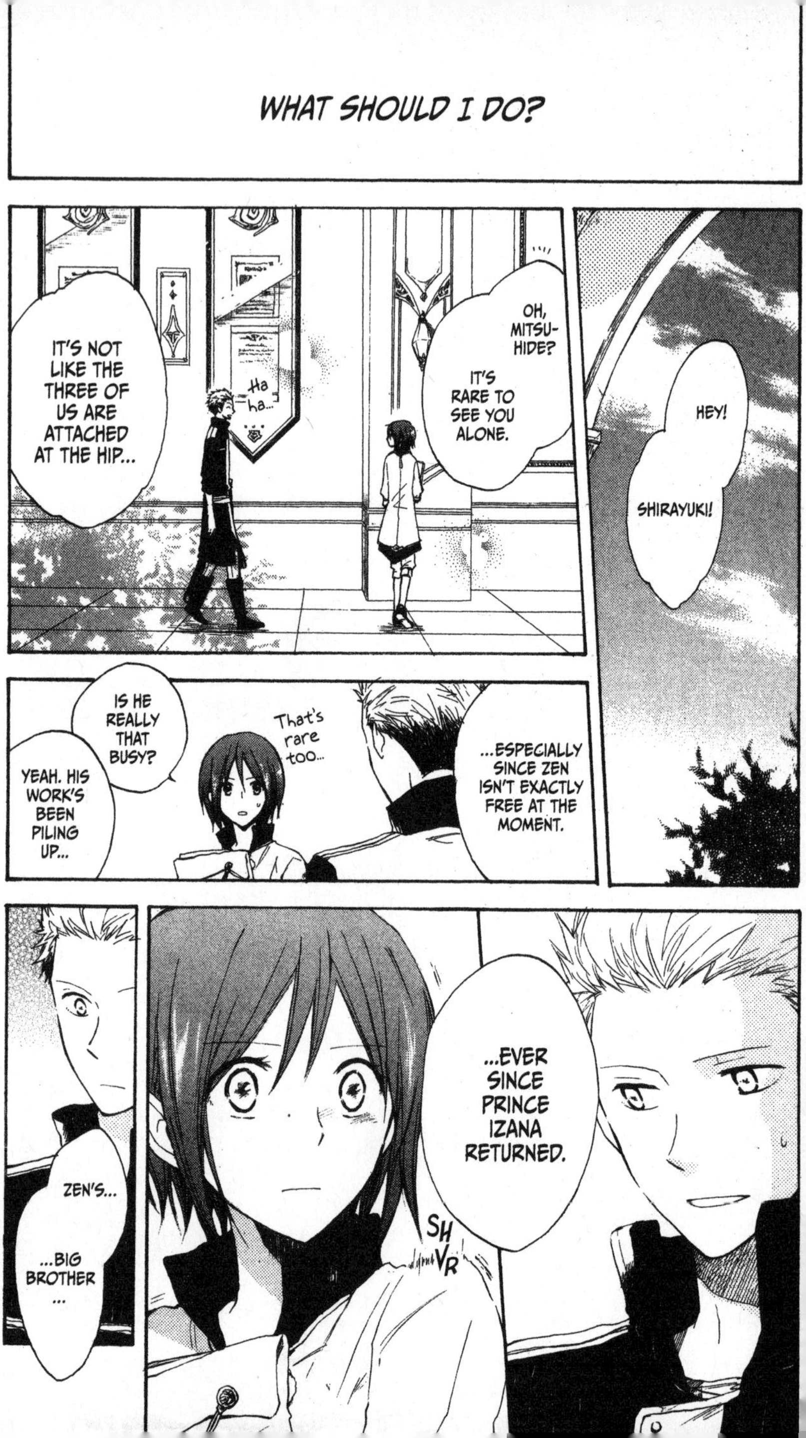
WHAT SHOULD I DO?
HEY!
SHIRAYUKI!
...
OH, MITSUHIDE?
IT'S RARE TO SEE YOU ALONE.
Ha ha...
IT'S NOT LIKE THE THREE OF US ARE ATTACHED AT THE HIP...
...ESPECIALLY SINCE ZEN ISN'T EXACTLY FREE AT THE MOMENT.
That's rare too...
IS HE REALLY THAT BUSY?
YEAH. HIS WORK'S BEEN PILING UP...
...EVER SINCE PRINCE IZANA RETURNED.
SHVR
ZEN'S...
...BIG BROTHER ...

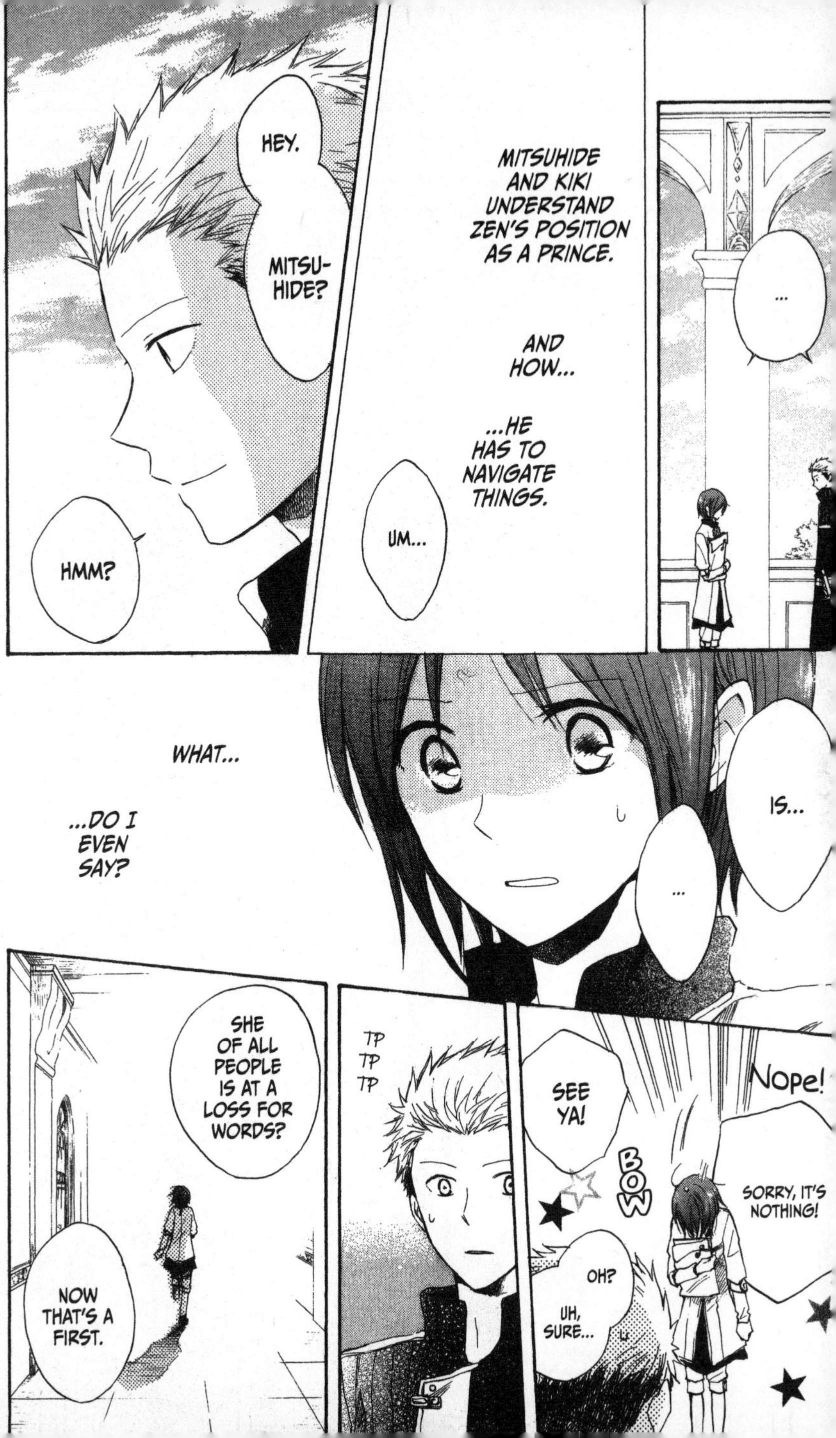
...
MITSUHIDE AND KIKI UNDERSTAND ZEN'S POSITION AS A PRINCE.
AND HOW...
...HE HAS TO NAVIGATE THINGS.
UM...
HEY.
MITSU-HIDE?
HMM?
IS...
...
WHAT...
...DO I EVEN SAY?
Nope!
SORRY, IT'S NOTHING!
BOW
SEE YA!
OH?
UH, SURE...
TP TP TP
SHE OF ALL PEOPLE IS AT A LOSS FOR WORDS?
NOW THAT'S A FIRST.

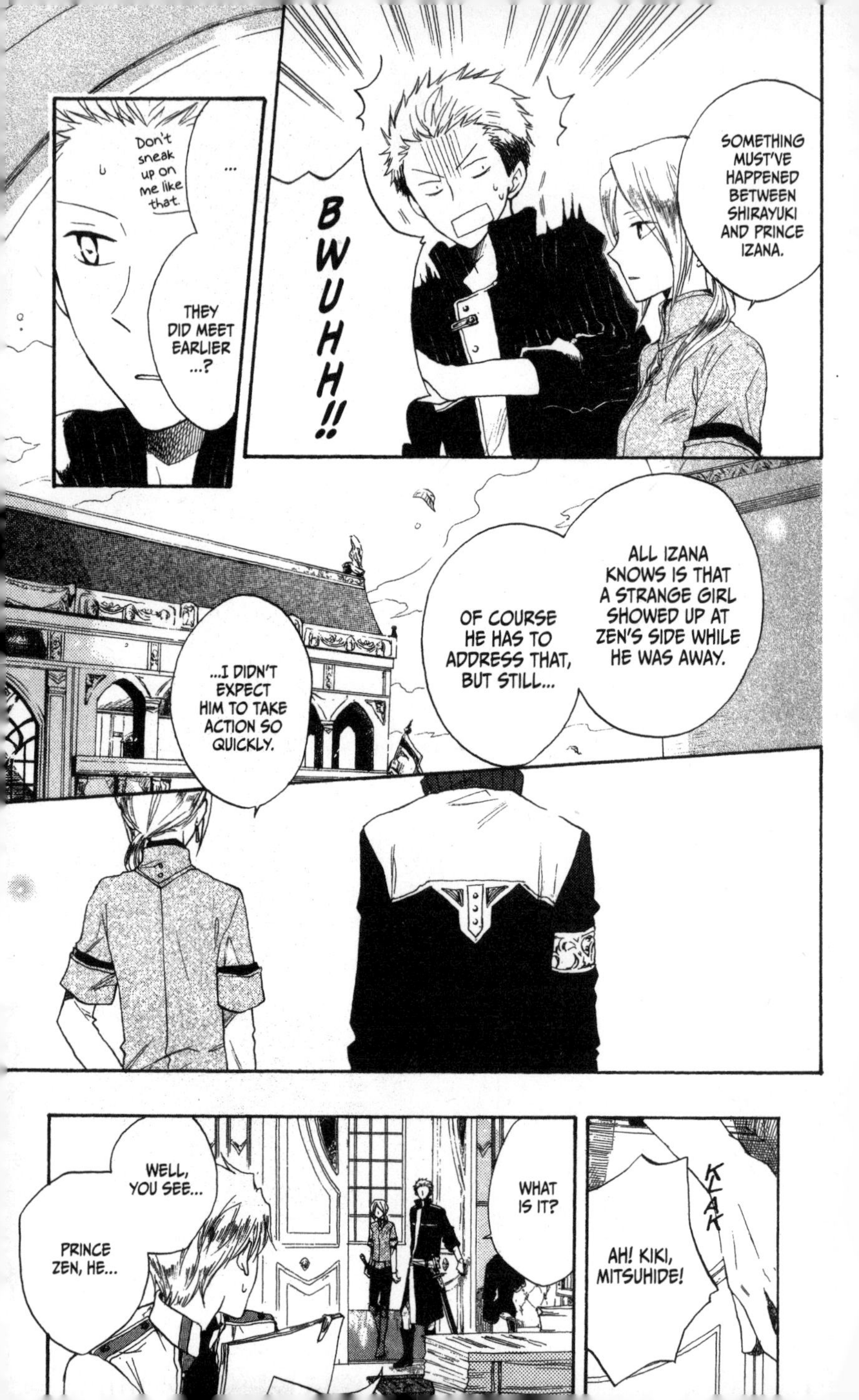
SOMETHING MUST'VE HAPPENED BETWEEN SHIRAYUKI AND PRINCE IZANA.
BWUHH!!
Don't sneak up on me like that.
...
THEY DID MEET EARLIER ...?
ALL IZANA KNOWS IS THAT A STRANGE GIRL SHOWED UP AT ZEN'S SIDE WHILE HE WAS AWAY.
OF COURSE HE HAS TO ADDRESS THAT, BUT STILL...
...I DIDN'T EXPECT HIM TO TAKE ACTION SO QUICKLY.
KLAK
AH! KIKI, MITSUHIDE!
WHAT IS IT?
WELL, YOU SEE...
PRINCE ZEN, HE...

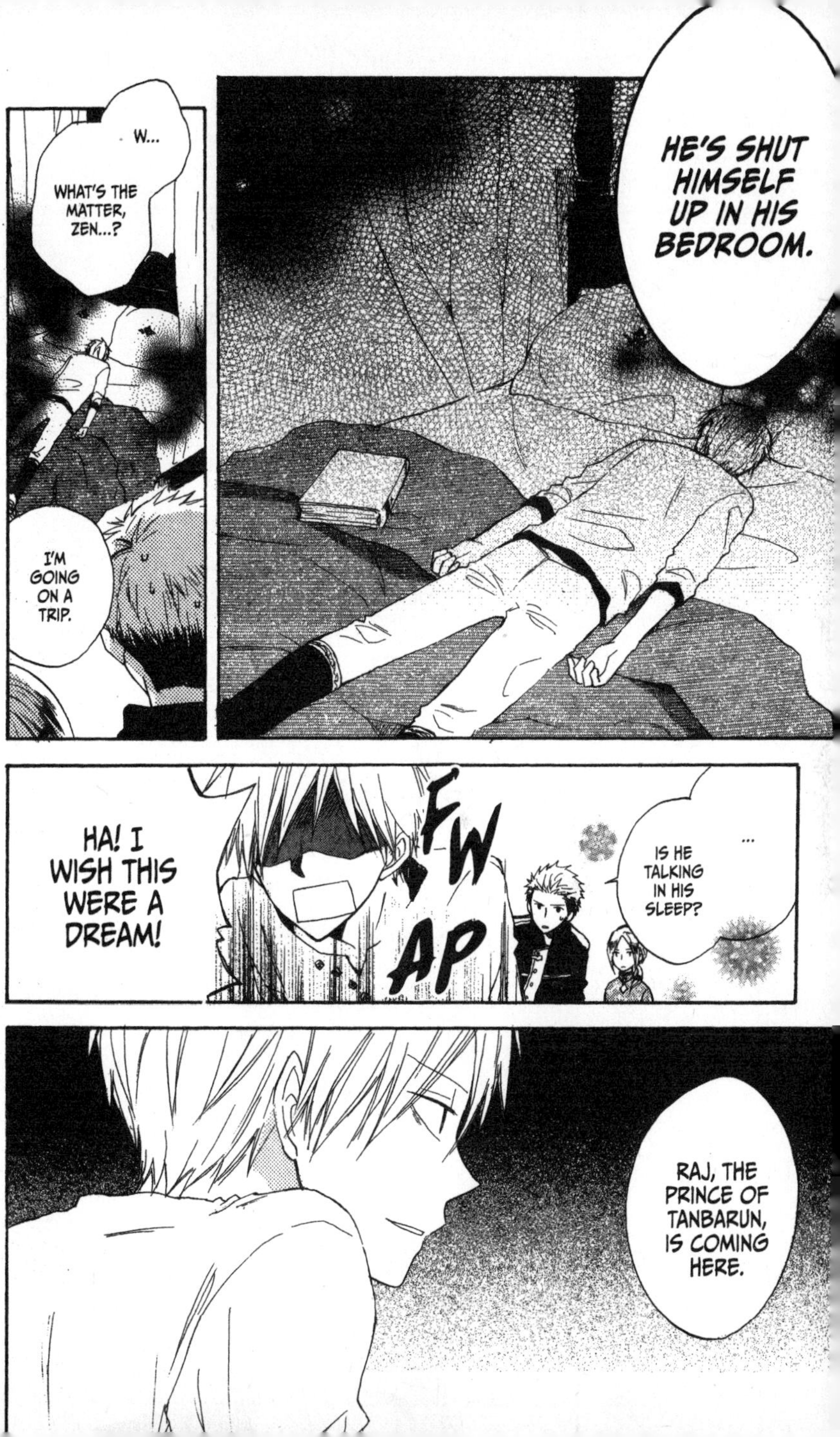
HE'S SHUT HIMSELF UP IN HIS BEDROOM.
W...
WHAT'S THE MATTER, ZEN...?
I'M GOING ON A TRIP.
...
IS HE TALKING IN HIS SLEEP?
FWAP
HA! I WISH THIS WERE A DREAM!
RAJ, THE PRINCE OF TANBARUN, IS COMING HERE.

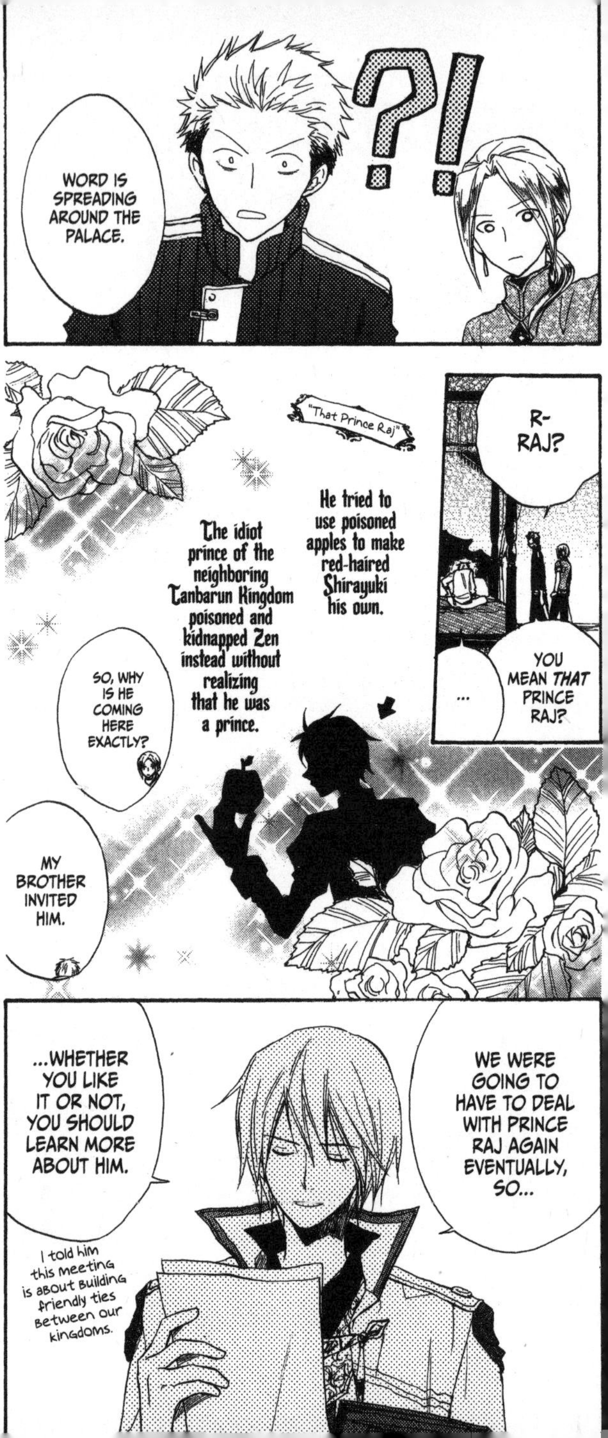
?!
WORD IS SPREADING AROUND THE PALACE.
R- RAJ?
YOU MEAN *THAT* PRINCE RAJ?
...
"That Prince Raj"
He tried to use poisoned apples to make red-haired Shirayuki his own.
The idiot prince of the neighboring Tanbarun Kingdom poisoned and kidnapped Zen instead without realizing that he was a prince.
SO, WHY IS HE COMING HERE EXACTLY?
MY BROTHER INVITED HIM.
WE WERE GOING TO HAVE TO DEAL WITH PRINCE RAJ AGAIN EVENTUALLY, SO...
...WHETHER YOU LIKE IT OR NOT, YOU SHOULD LEARN MORE ABOUT HIM.
I told him this meeting is about building friendly ties between our kingdoms.

GREETINGS

Hello. I'm Sorata Akiduki. This volume of *Snow White with the Red Hair* is purely *Snow White with the Red Hair.*

100% Snow White with the Red Hair

Volumes 1 and 2 included past one-shots of mine, which were honestly a little embarrassing. But now that those are done, it's a little melancholic... like something's missing.

I'm not sure how to process this...

Anyhow, I hope you enjoy volume 3.

—Sora

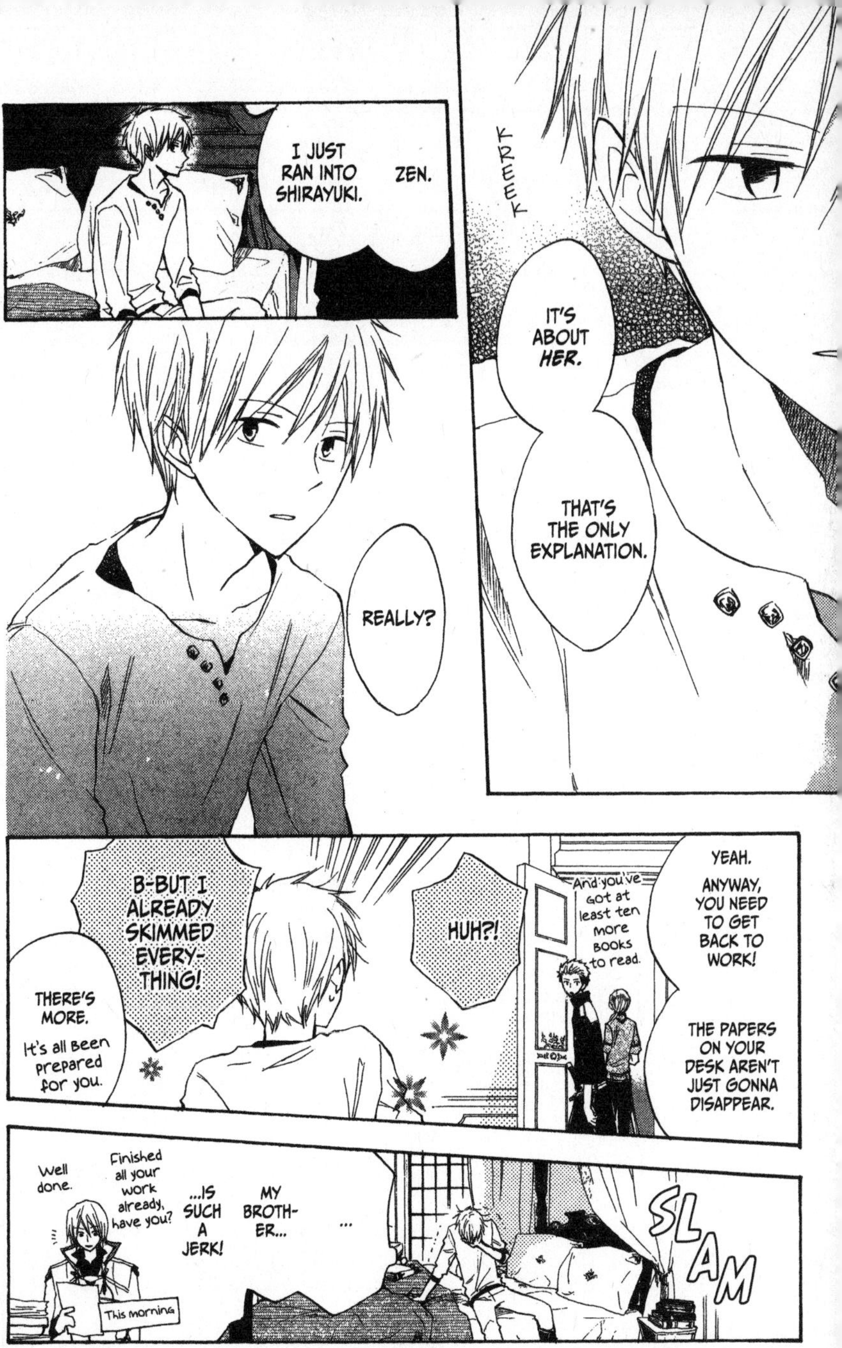
KREEK
IT'S ABOUT HER.
THAT'S THE ONLY EXPLANATION.
ZEN.
I JUST RAN INTO SHIRAYUKI.
REALLY?
YEAH. ANYWAY, YOU NEED TO GET BACK TO WORK!
THE PAPERS ON YOUR DESK AREN'T JUST GONNA DISAPPEAR.
And you've got at least ten more books to read.
HUH?!
B-BUT I ALREADY SKIMMED EVERYTHING!
THERE'S MORE.
It's all been prepared for you.
SLAM
...
MY BROTHER...
...IS SUCH A JERK!
Finished all your work already, have you?
Well done.
This morning

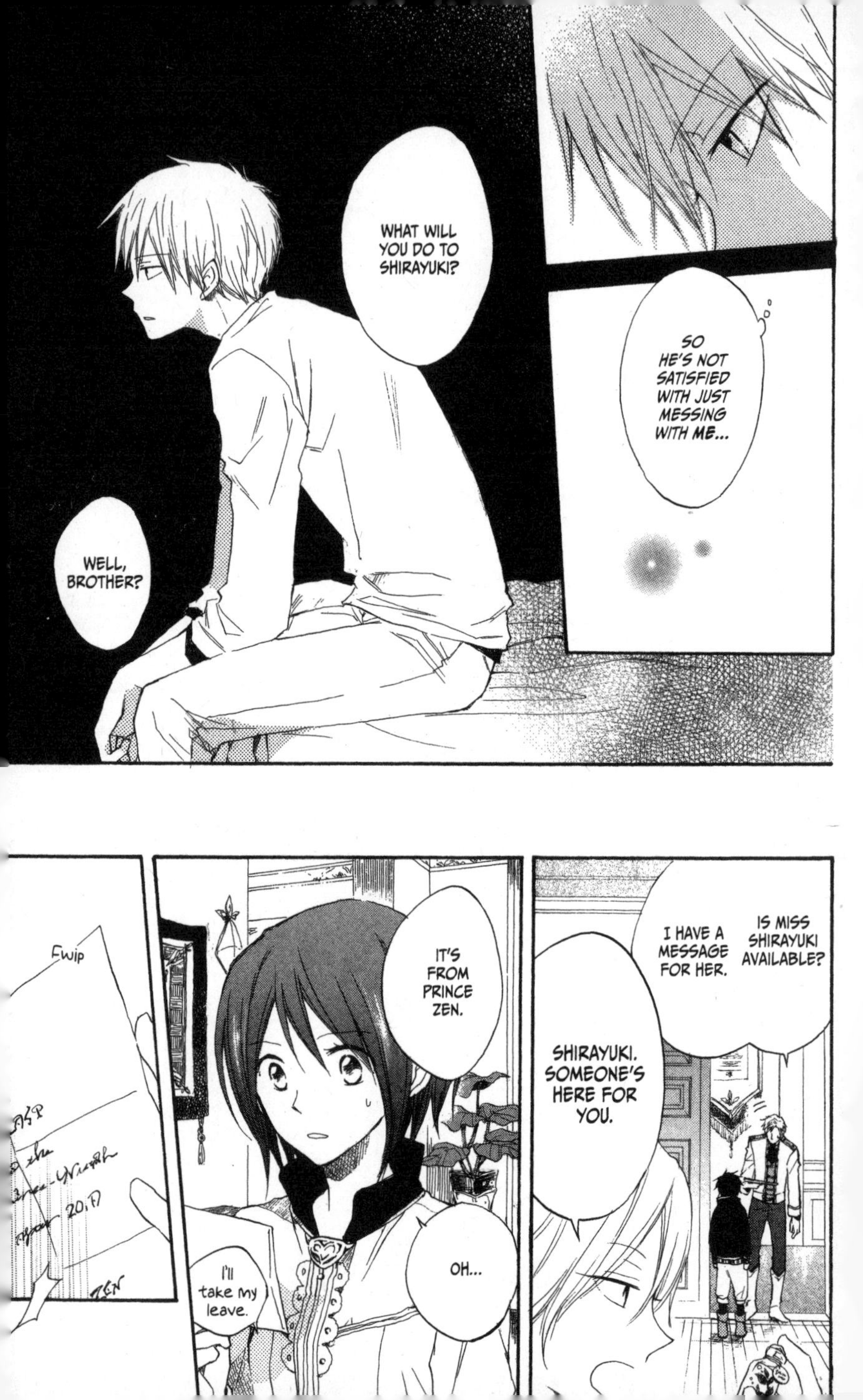
SO HE'S NOT SATISFIED WITH JUST MESSING WITH ME...
WHAT WILL YOU DO TO SHIRAYUKI?
WELL, BROTHER?
IS MISS SHIRAYUKI AVAILABLE?
I HAVE A MESSAGE FOR HER.
SHIRAYUKI. SOMEONE'S HERE FOR YOU.
IT'S FROM PRINCE ZEN.
OH...
I'll take my leave.
Fwip
ZEN

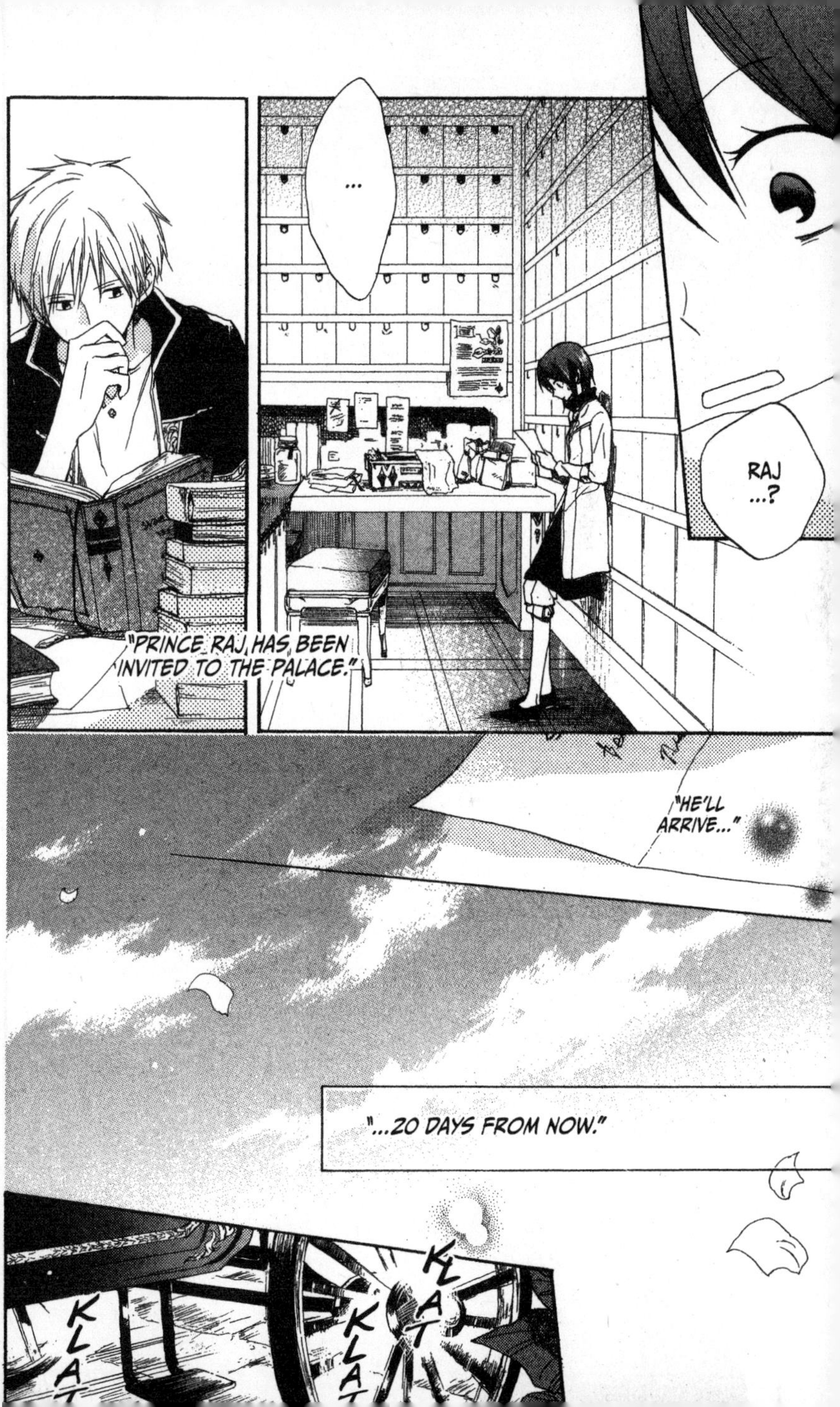
RAJ ...?
...
"PRINCE RAJ HAS BEEN INVITED TO THE PALACE."
"HE'LL ARRIVE..."
"...20 DAYS FROM NOW."
KLAT
KLAT
KLAT

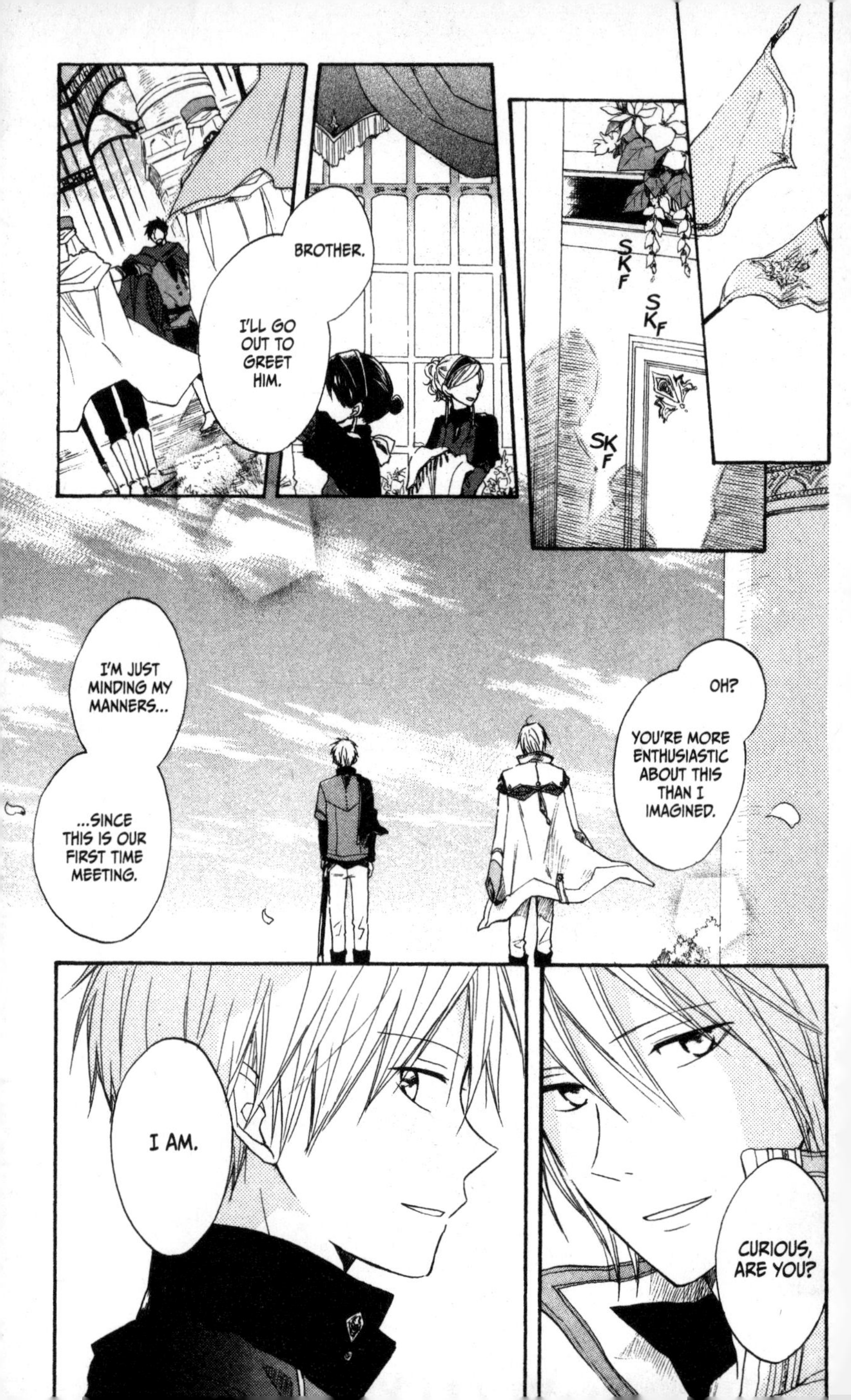
SKF
SKF
SKF
BROTHER.
I'LL GO OUT TO GREET HIM.
OH?
YOU'RE MORE ENTHUSIASTIC ABOUT THIS THAN I IMAGINED.
I'M JUST MINDING MY MANNERS...
...SINCE THIS IS OUR FIRST TIME MEETING.
CURIOUS, ARE YOU?
I AM.

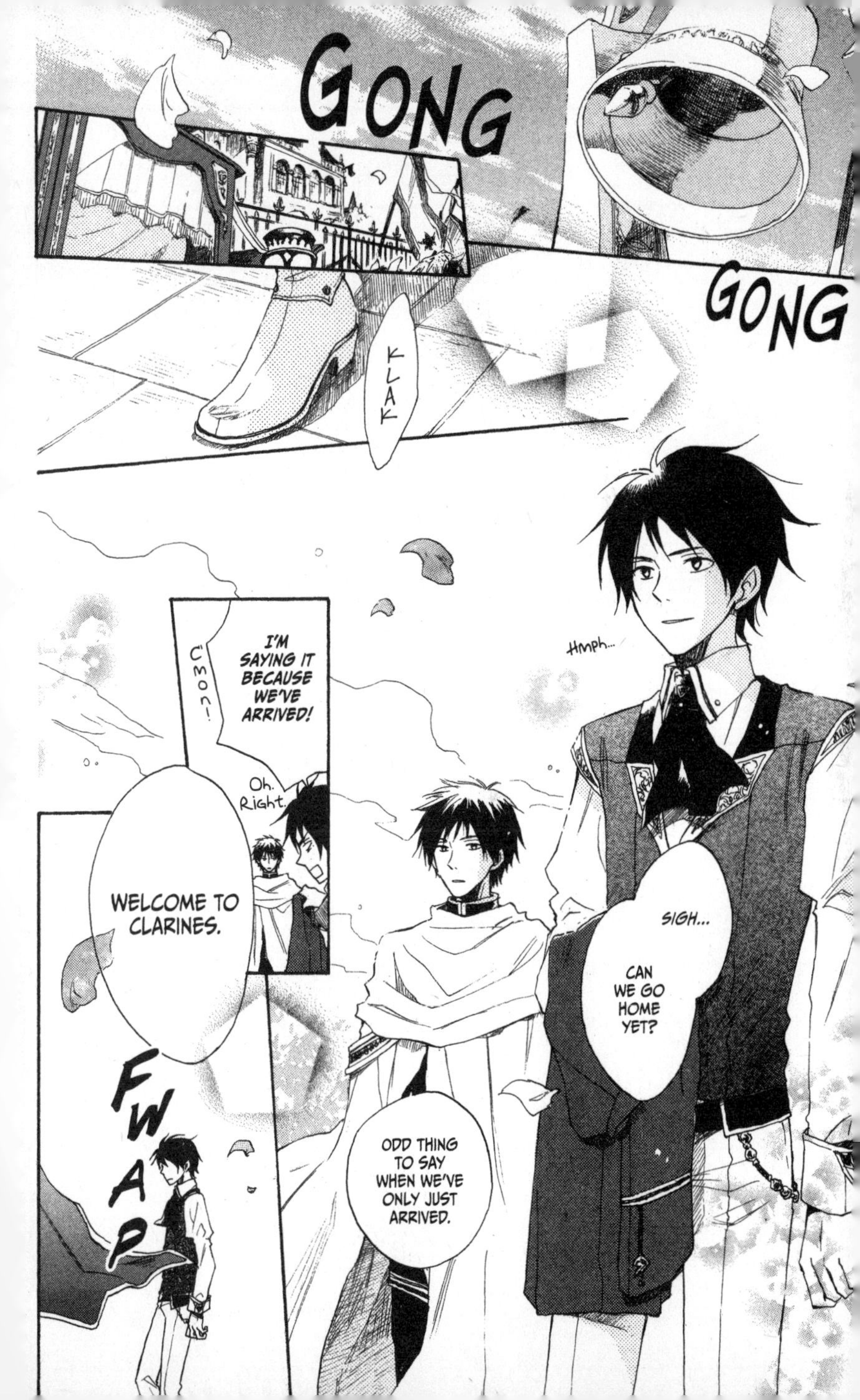
GONG
GONG
KLAK
Hmph...
SIGH...
CAN WE GO HOME YET?
ODD THING TO SAY WHEN WE'VE ONLY JUST ARRIVED.
I'M SAYING IT BECAUSE WE'VE ARRIVED!
C'mon!
Oh. Right.
WELCOME TO CLARINES.
FWAP

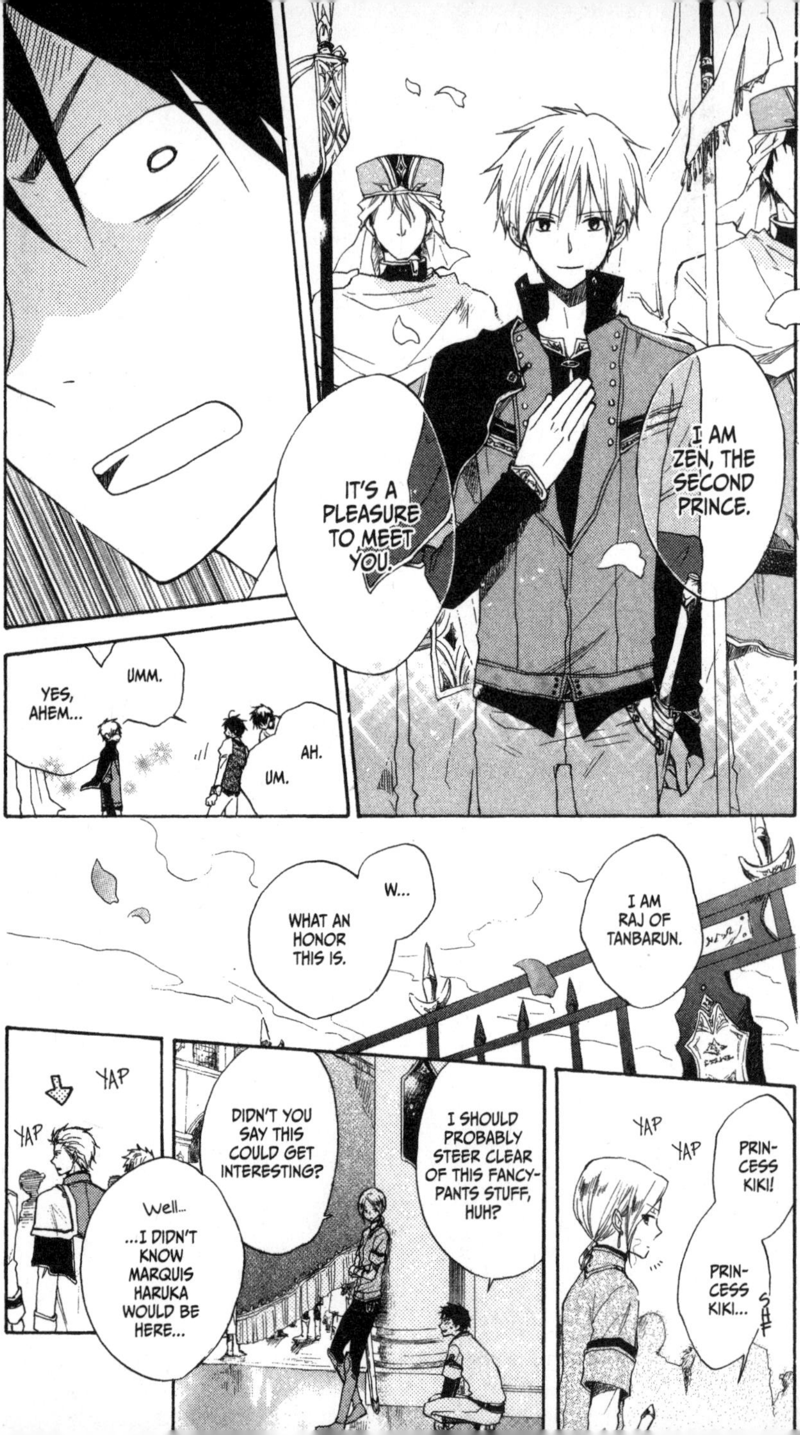
I AM ZEN, THE SECOND PRINCE.
IT'S A PLEASURE TO MEET YOU.
UMM.
YES, AHEM...
AH.
UM.
I AM RAJ OF TANBARUN.
W...
WHAT AN HONOR THIS IS.
YAP
YAP
PRIN-CESS KIKI!
PRIN-CESS KIKI...
SHF
I SHOULD PROBABLY STEER CLEAR OF THIS FANCY-PANTS STUFF, HUH?
DIDN'T YOU SAY THIS COULD GET INTERESTING?
YAP
YAP
Well...
...I DIDN'T KNOW MARQUIS HARUKA WOULD BE HERE...

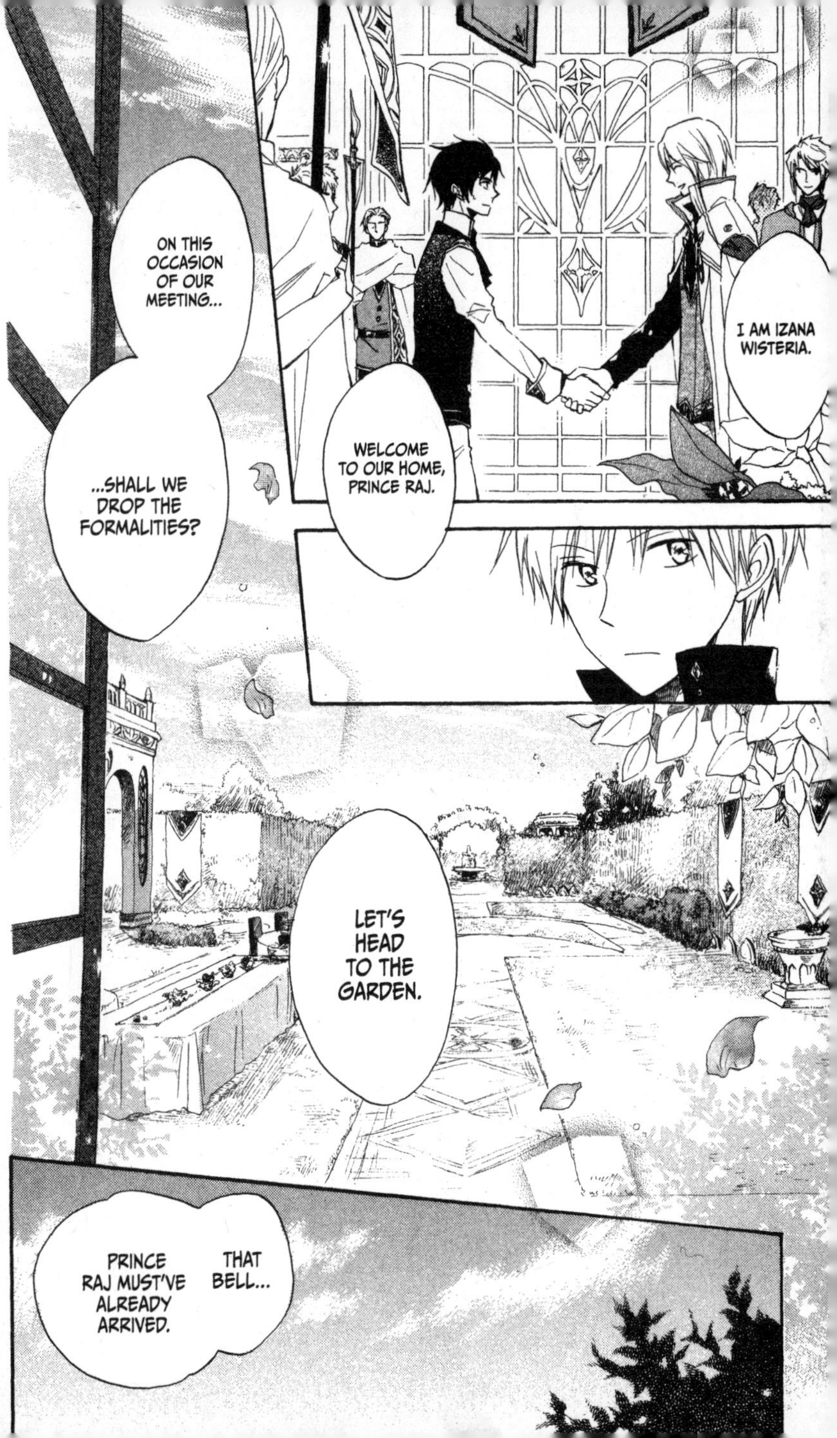
I AM IZANA WISTERIA.
WELCOME TO OUR HOME, PRINCE RAJ.
ON THIS OCCASION OF OUR MEETING...
...SHALL WE DROP THE FORMALITIES?
LET'S HEAD TO THE GARDEN.
THAT BELL...
PRINCE RAJ MUST'VE ALREADY ARRIVED.

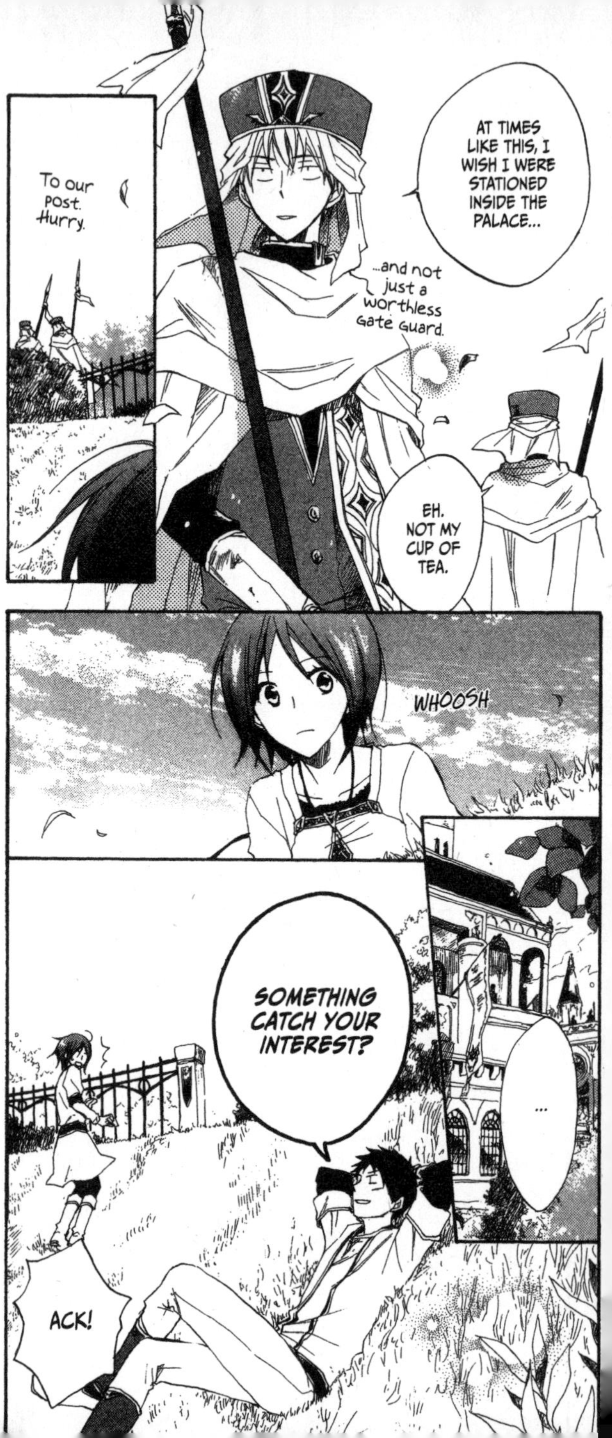
AT TIMES LIKE THIS, I WISH I WERE STATIONED INSIDE THE PALACE...
...and not just a worthless Gate Guard.
EH. NOT MY CUP OF TEA.
To our post. Hurry.
WHOOSH
...
SOMETHING CATCH YOUR INTEREST?
ACK!

I bought a magazine on riding horses recently. I want to master horses—not riding them, but drawing them.

In the magazine there was an intriguing article that featured the 10 best hairstyles for equestrians.

There were all sorts of lovely hairstyles with hair tied up in buns, etc. I'm going to reference all of that. For drawing, I mean.

There was also a style called "the beloved ponytail," and I was thinking, "Beloved by whom?" The horse? Is that necessary?

I was telling my sister about this and she thought I meant hairstyles for the horses.

That sure would be something...

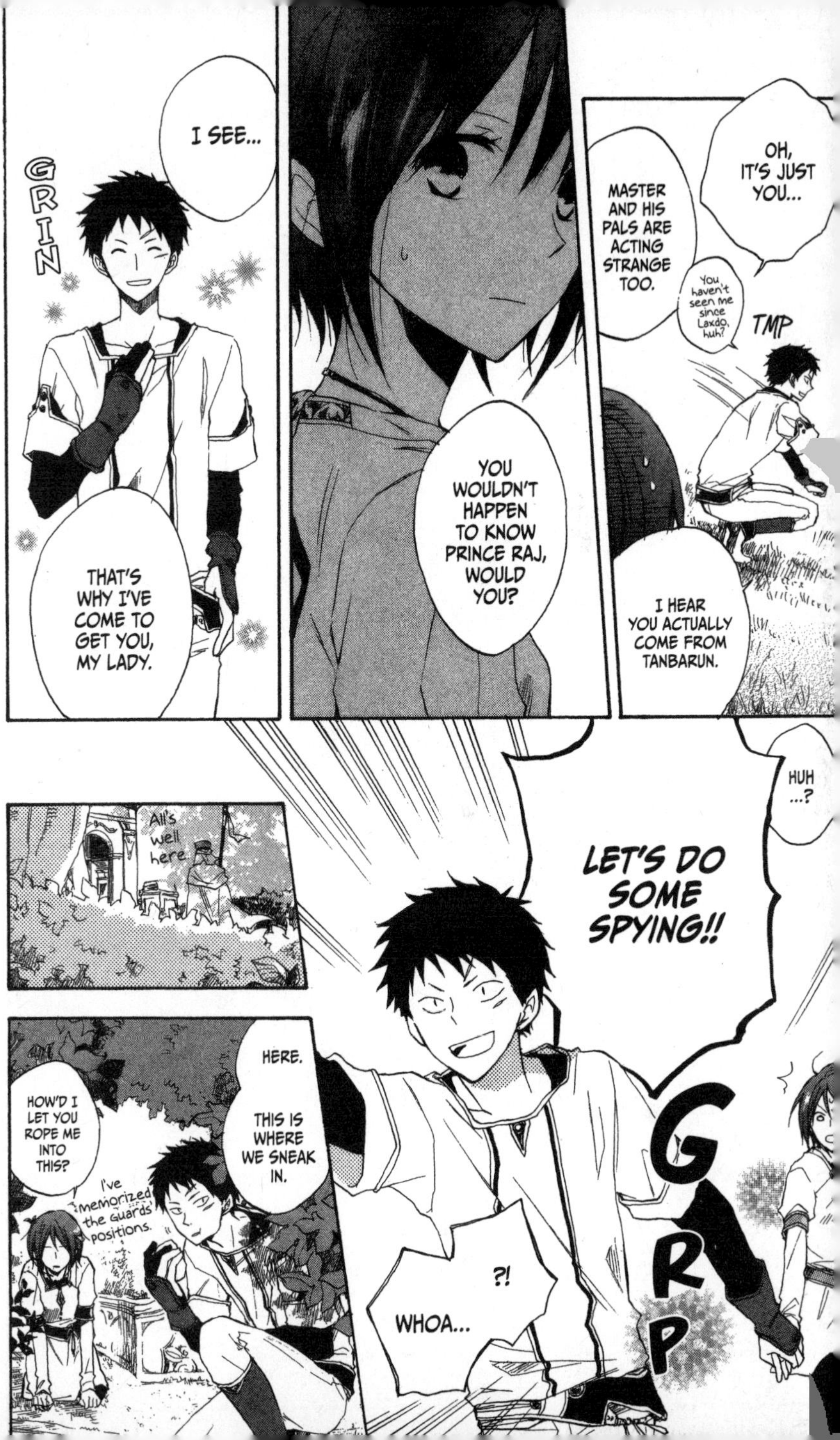

OH, IT'S JUST YOU...
MASTER AND HIS PALS ARE ACTING STRANGE TOO.
You haven't seen me since Laxdo, huh?
TMP
I HEAR YOU ACTUALLY COME FROM TANBARUN.
YOU WOULDN'T HAPPEN TO KNOW PRINCE RAJ, WOULD YOU?
I SEE...
GRIN
THAT'S WHY I'VE COME TO GET YOU, MY LADY.
HUH ...?
LET'S DO SOME SPYING!!
GRP
?!
WHOA...
All's well here.
HERE.
THIS IS WHERE WE SNEAK IN.
HOW'D I LET YOU ROPE ME INTO THIS?
I've memorized the Guards' positions.

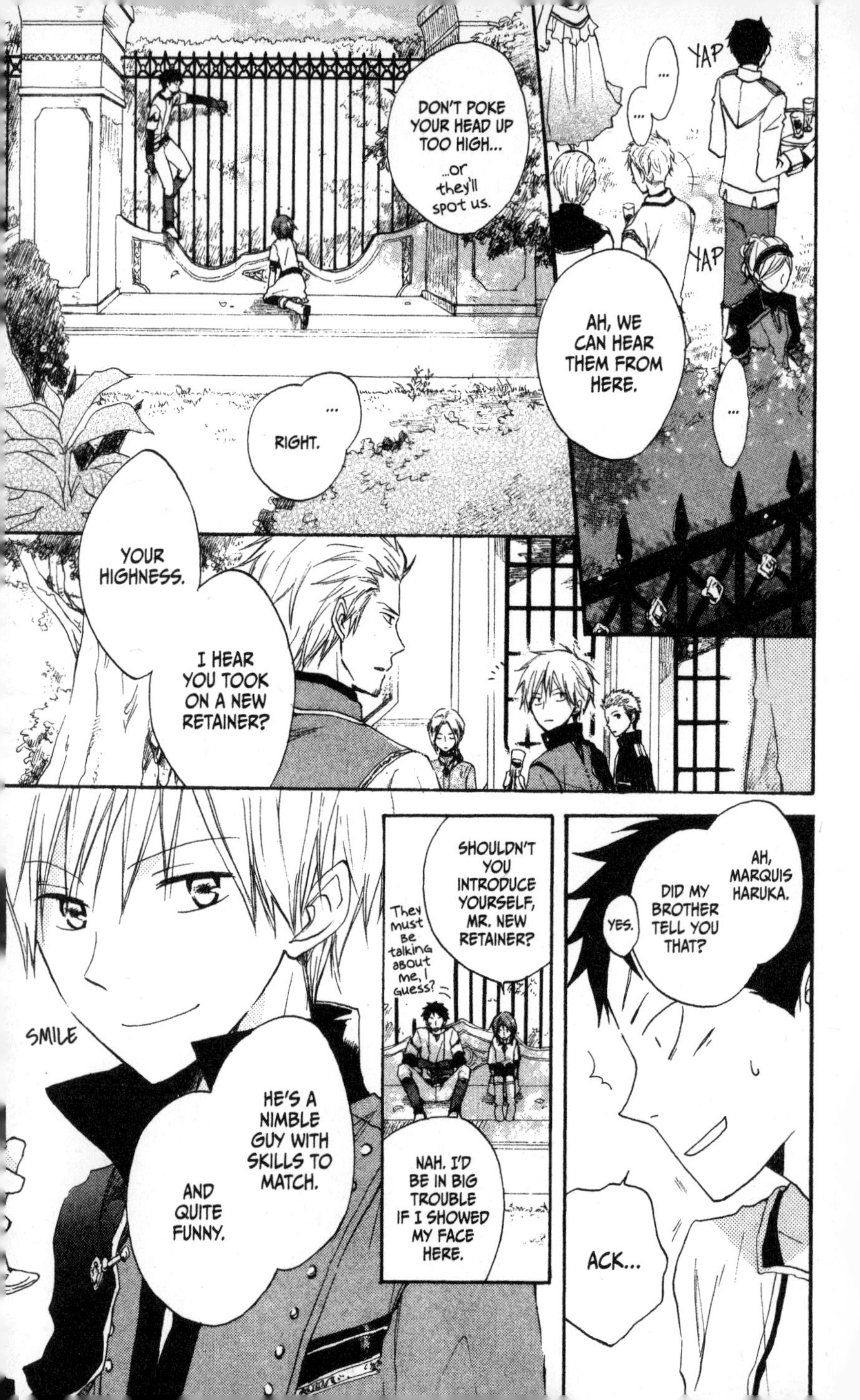
YAP
...
...
YAP
AH, WE CAN HEAR THEM FROM HERE.
...
DON'T POKE YOUR HEAD UP TOO HIGH...
...or they'll spot us.
... RIGHT.
YOUR HIGHNESS.
I HEAR YOU TOOK ON A NEW RETAINER?
AH, MARQUIS HARUKA.
DID MY BROTHER TELL YOU THAT?
YES.
ACK...
SHOULDN'T YOU INTRODUCE YOURSELF, MR. NEW RETAINER?
They must be talking about me, I guess?
NAH. I'D BE IN BIG TROUBLE IF I SHOWED MY FACE HERE.
HE'S A NIMBLE GUY WITH SKILLS TO MATCH.
AND QUITE FUNNY.
SMILE

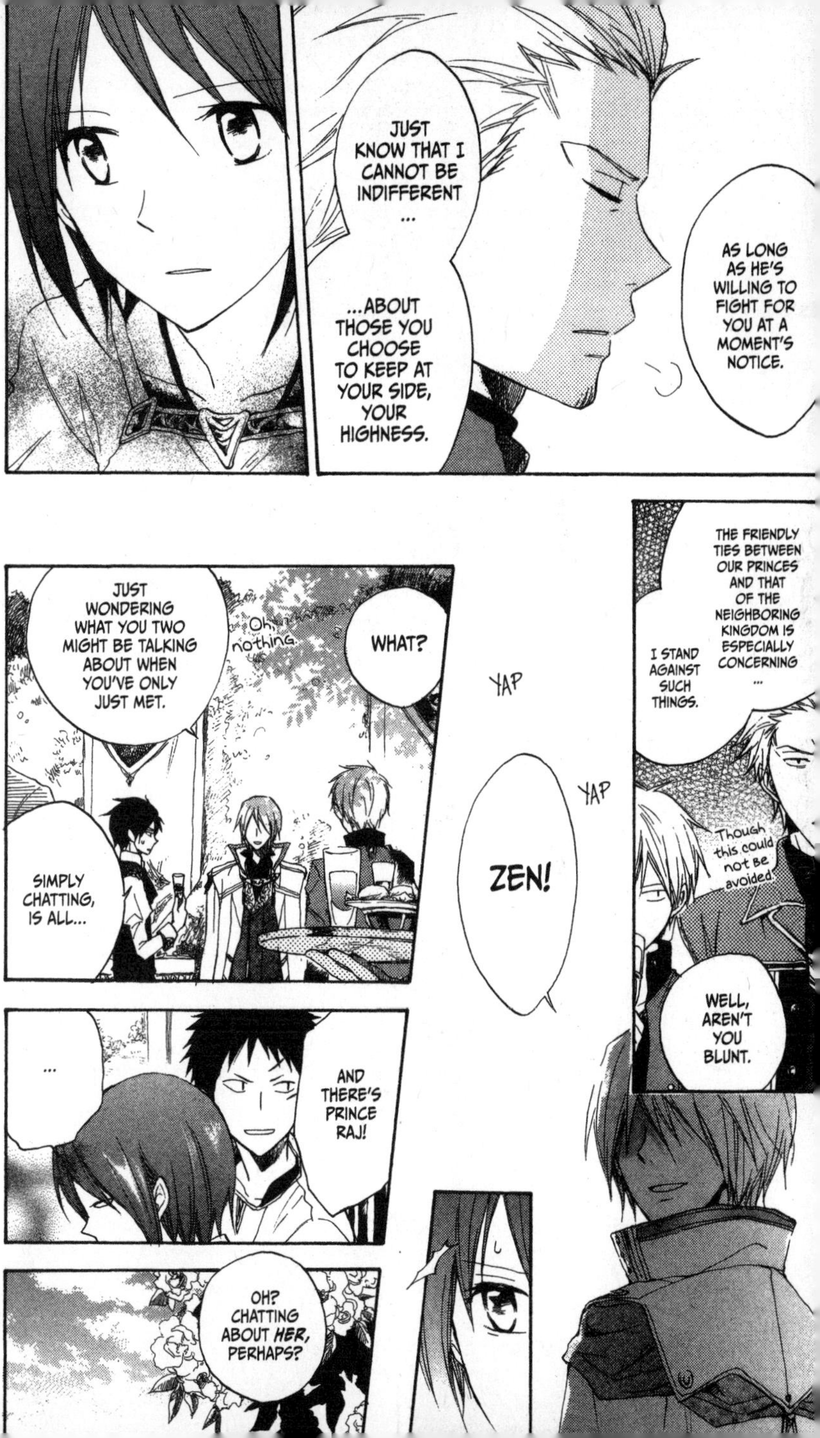
AS LONG AS HE'S WILLING TO FIGHT FOR YOU AT A MOMENT'S NOTICE.
JUST KNOW THAT I CANNOT BE INDIFFERENT ...
...ABOUT THOSE YOU CHOOSE TO KEEP AT YOUR SIDE, YOUR HIGHNESS.
THE FRIENDLY TIES BETWEEN OUR PRINCES AND THAT OF THE NEIGHBORING KINGDOM IS ESPECIALLY CONCERNING ...
I STAND AGAINST SUCH THINGS.
Though this could not be avoided.
WELL, AREN'T YOU BLUNT.
YAP
YAP
ZEN!
WHAT?
Oh, nothing.
JUST WONDERING WHAT YOU TWO MIGHT BE TALKING ABOUT WHEN YOU'VE ONLY JUST MET.
SIMPLY CHATTING, IS ALL...
AND THERE'S PRINCE RAJ!
...
OH? CHATTING ABOUT *HER*, PERHAPS?

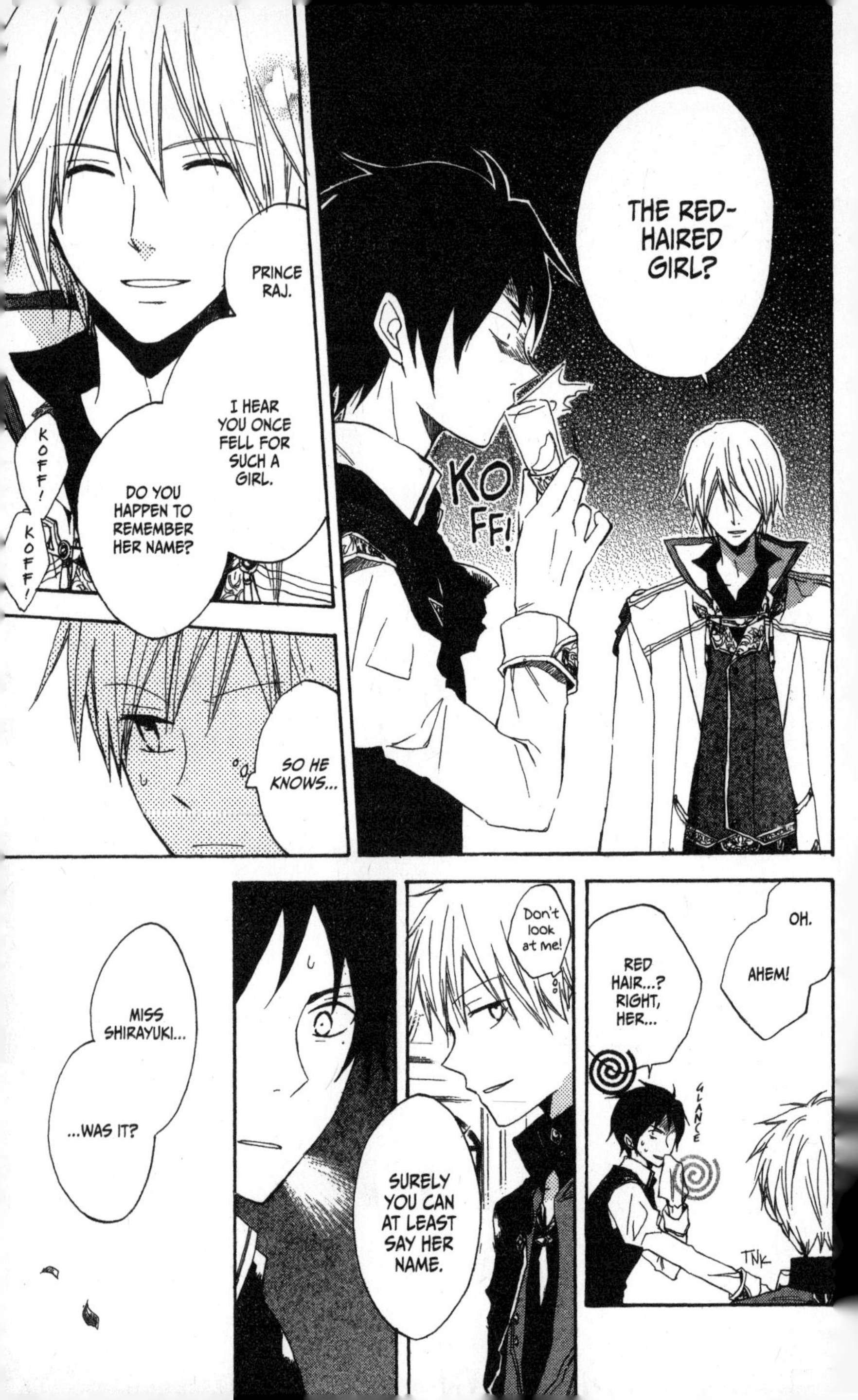
THE RED-HAIRED GIRL?
KOFF!
PRINCE RAJ.
I HEAR YOU ONCE FELL FOR SUCH A GIRL.
DO YOU HAPPEN TO REMEMBER HER NAME?
KOFF! KOFF!
SO HE KNOWS...
OH.
AHEM!
RED HAIR...? RIGHT, HER...
GLANCE
TNK
Don't look at me!
SURELY YOU CAN AT LEAST SAY HER NAME.
MISS SHIRAYUKI...
...WAS IT?

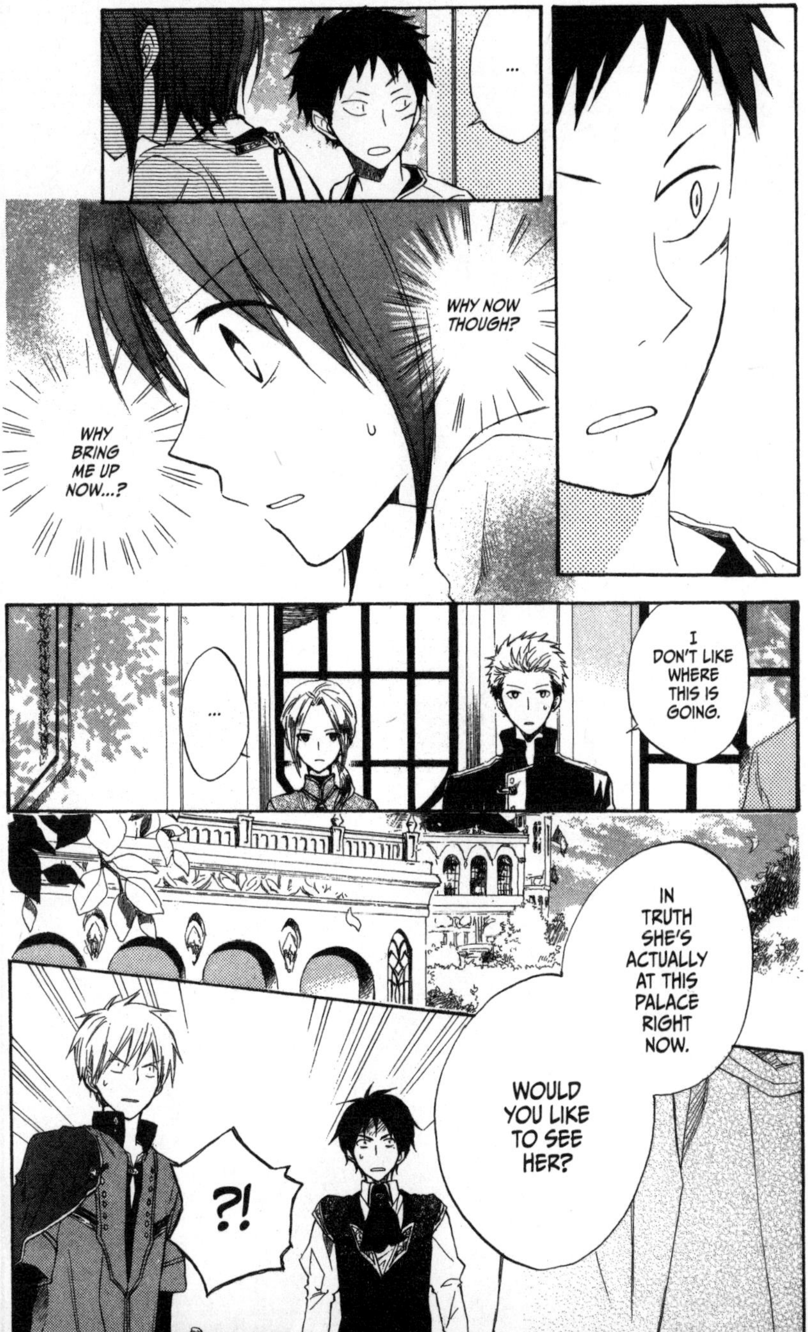
...
WHY NOW THOUGH?
WHY BRING ME UP NOW...?
I DON'T LIKE WHERE THIS IS GOING.
...
IN TRUTH SHE'S ACTUALLY AT THIS PALACE RIGHT NOW.
WOULD YOU LIKE TO SEE HER?
?!

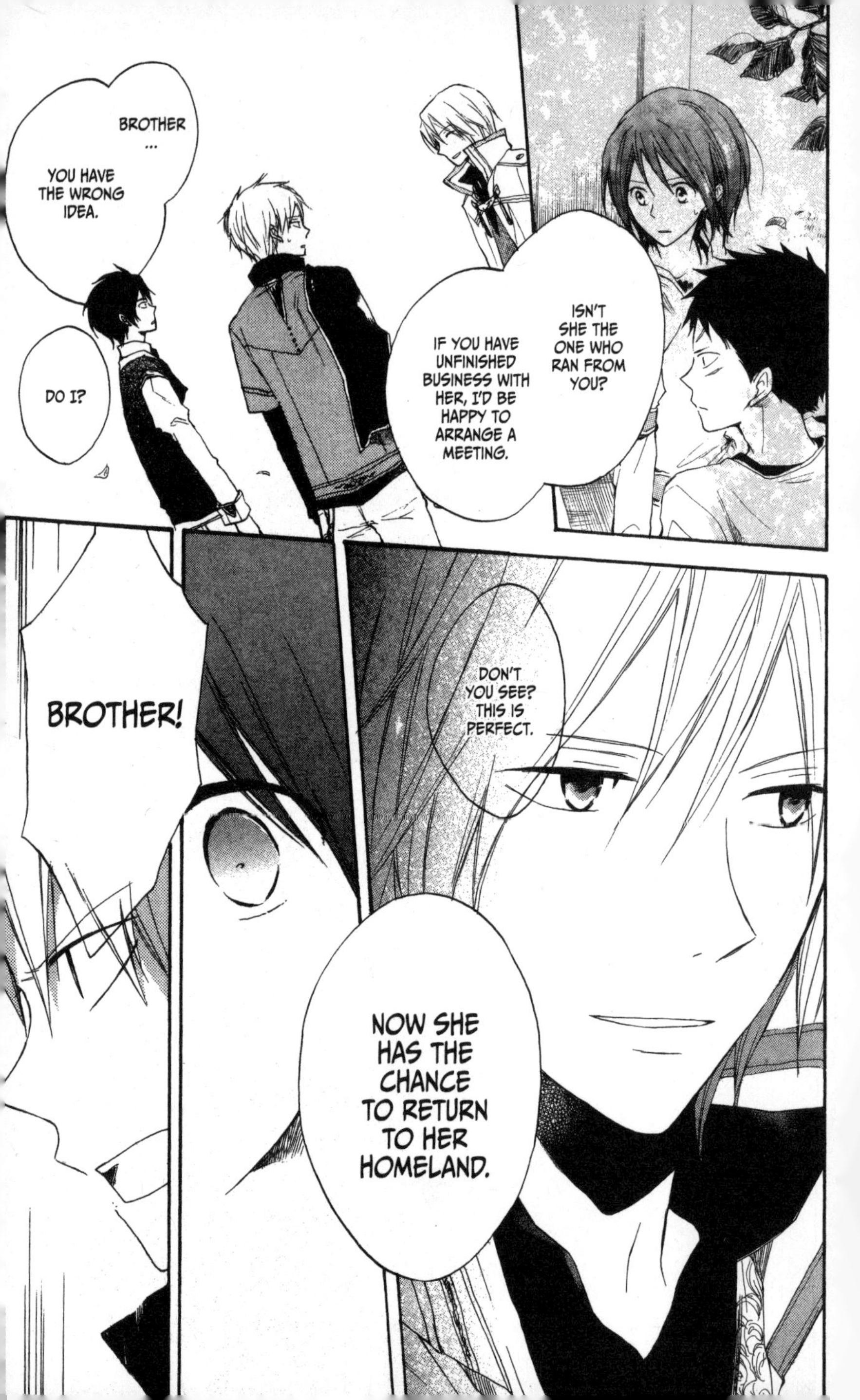
ISN'T SHE THE ONE WHO RAN FROM YOU?
IF YOU HAVE UNFINISHED BUSINESS WITH HER, I'D BE HAPPY TO ARRANGE A MEETING.
BROTHER ... YOU HAVE THE WRONG IDEA.
DO I?
DON'T YOU SEE? THIS IS PERFECT.
NOW SHE HAS THE CHANCE TO RETURN TO HER HOMELAND.
BROTHER!

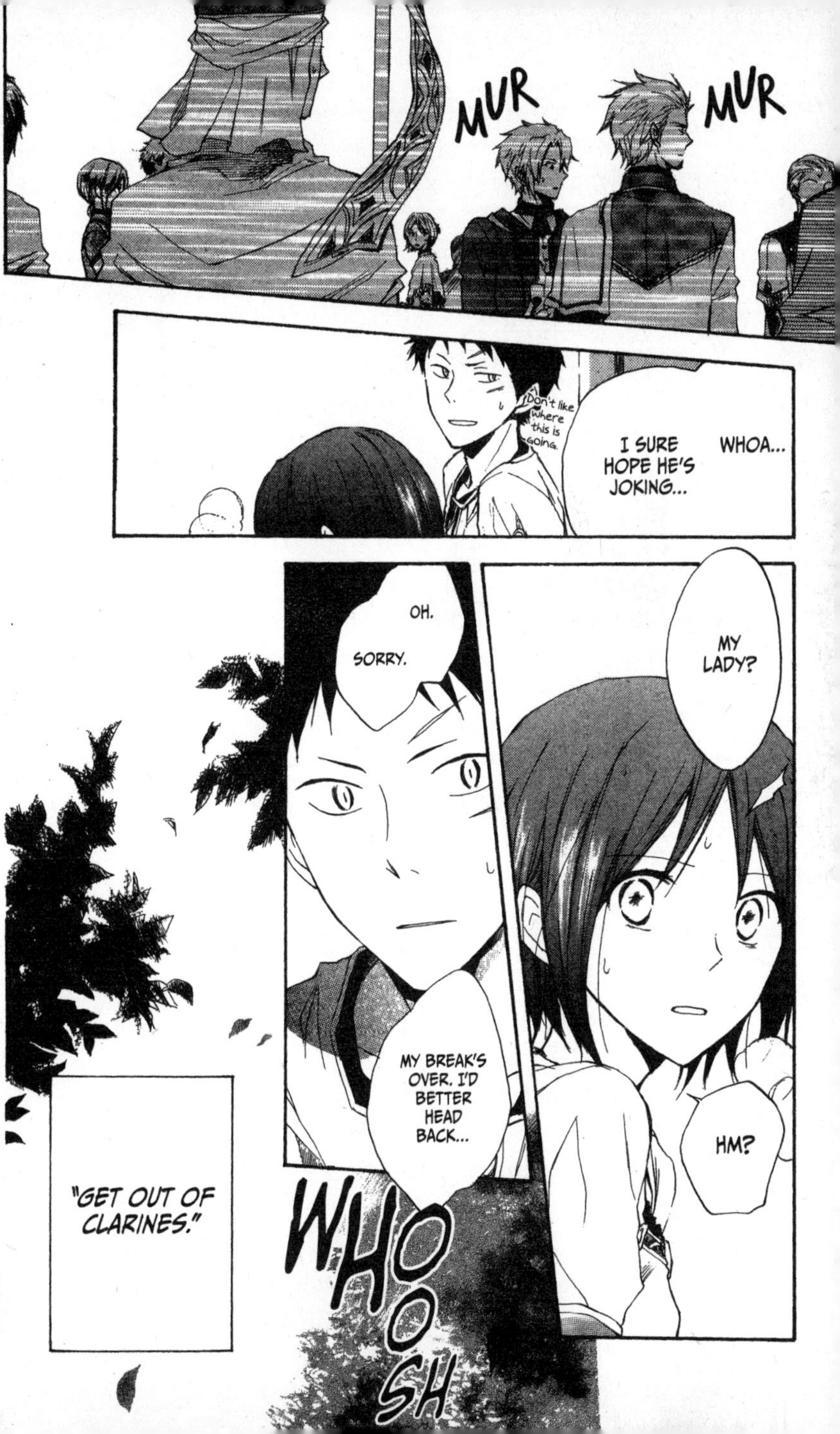
MUR
MUR
WHOA...
I SURE HOPE HE'S JOKING...
Don't like where this is going.
MY LADY?
HM?
OH.
SORRY.
MY BREAK'S OVER. I'D BETTER HEAD BACK...
WHOOSH
"GET OUT OF CLARINES."

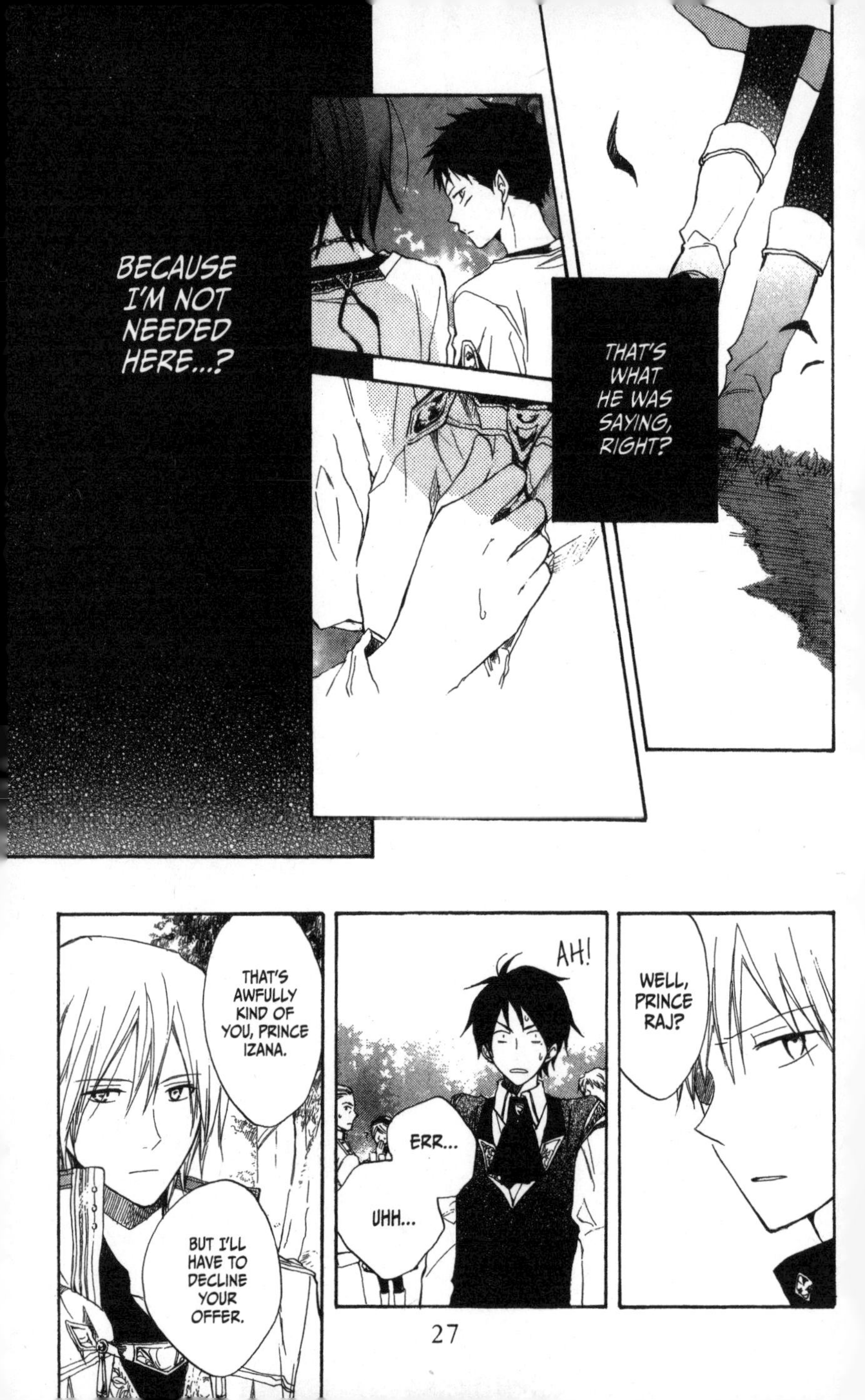
THAT'S WHAT HE WAS SAYING, RIGHT?
BECAUSE I'M NOT NEEDED HERE...?
WELL, PRINCE RAJ?
AH!
ERR...
UHH...
THAT'S AWFULLY KIND OF YOU, PRINCE IZANA.
BUT I'LL HAVE TO DECLINE YOUR OFFER.

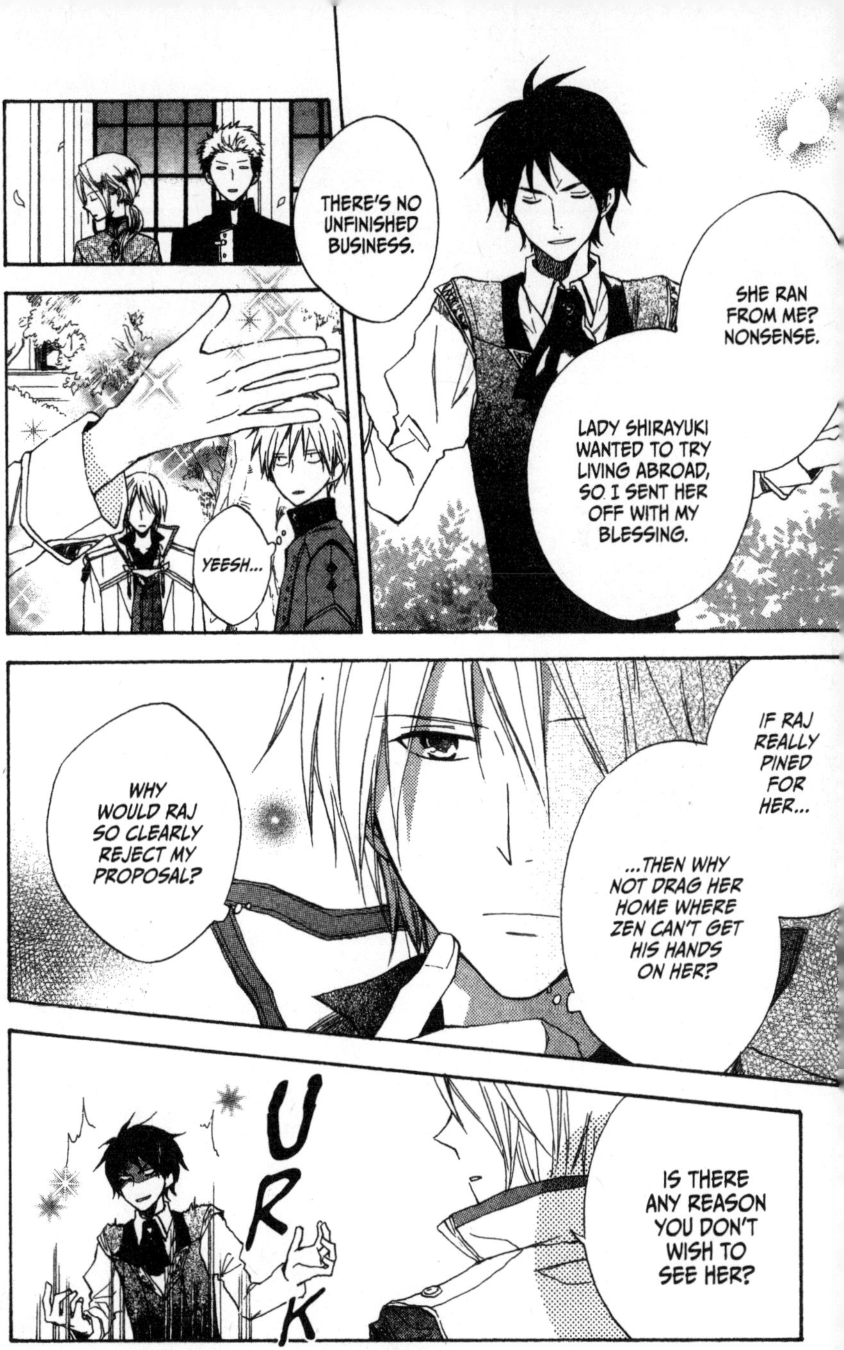
SHE RAN FROM ME? NONSENSE.
LADY SHIRAYUKI WANTED TO TRY LIVING ABROAD, SO I SENT HER OFF WITH MY BLESSING.
THERE'S NO UNFINISHED BUSINESS.
YEESH...
IF RAJ REALLY PINED FOR HER...
...THEN WHY NOT DRAG HER HOME WHERE ZEN CAN'T GET HIS HANDS ON HER?
WHY WOULD RAJ SO CLEARLY REJECT MY PROPOSAL?
IS THERE ANY REASON YOU DON'T WISH TO SEE HER?
URK

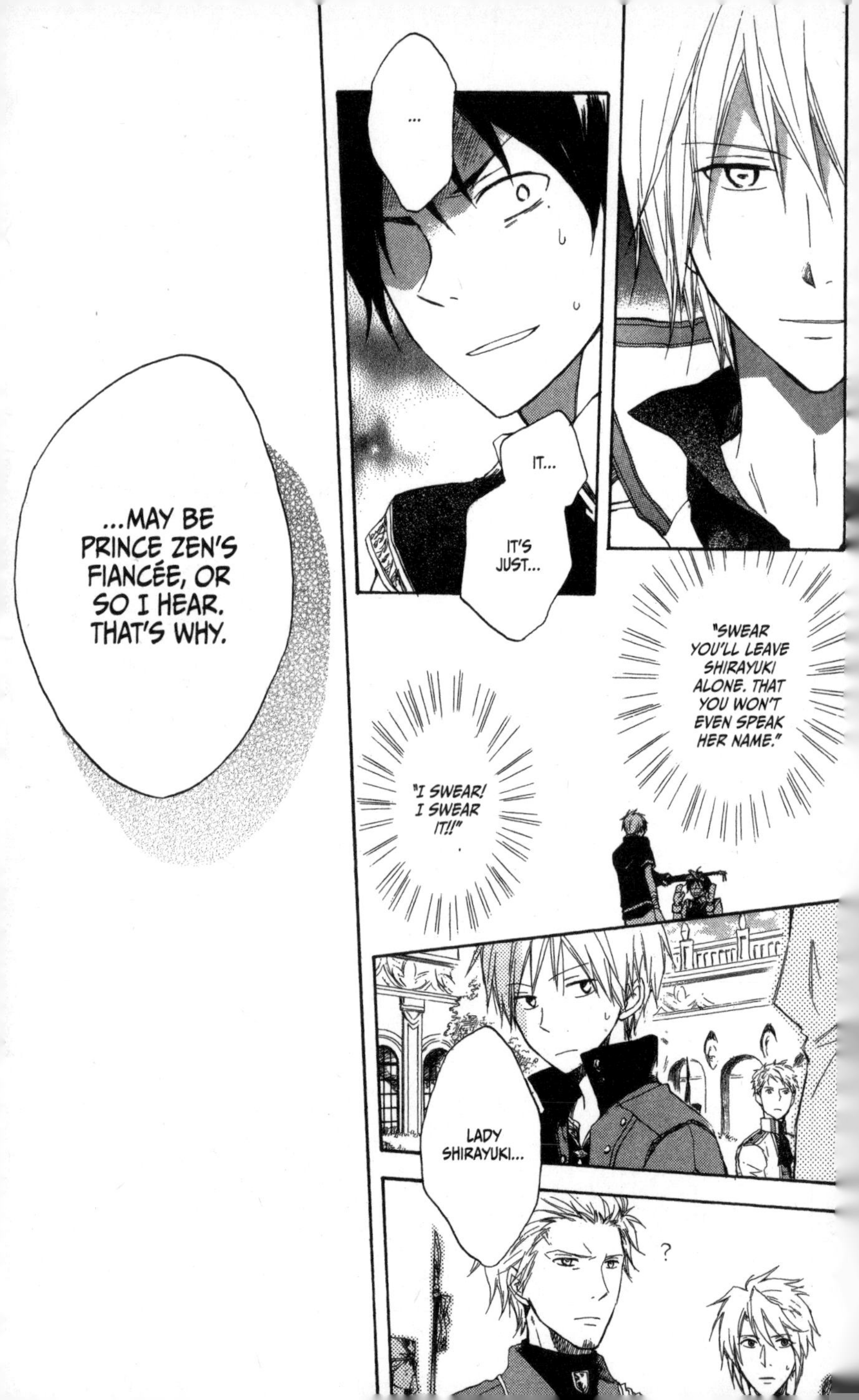
...
IT...
IT'S JUST...
"SWEAR YOU'LL LEAVE SHIRAYUKI ALONE. THAT YOU WON'T EVEN SPEAK HER NAME."
"I SWEAR! I SWEAR IT!!"
LADY SHIRAYUKI...
?
...MAY BE PRINCE ZEN'S FIANCÉE, OR SO I HEAR. THAT'S WHY.

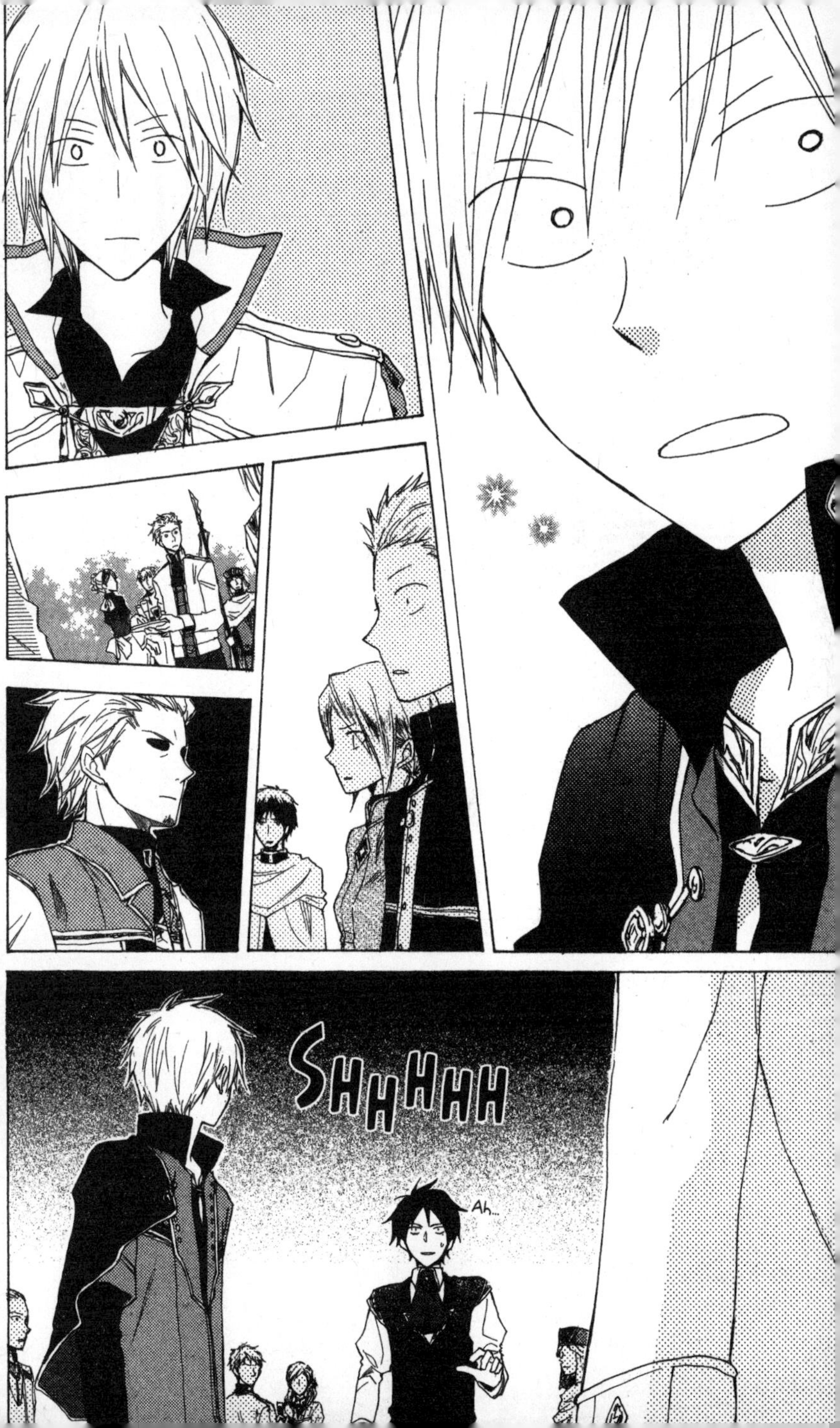
SHHHHH
Ah...

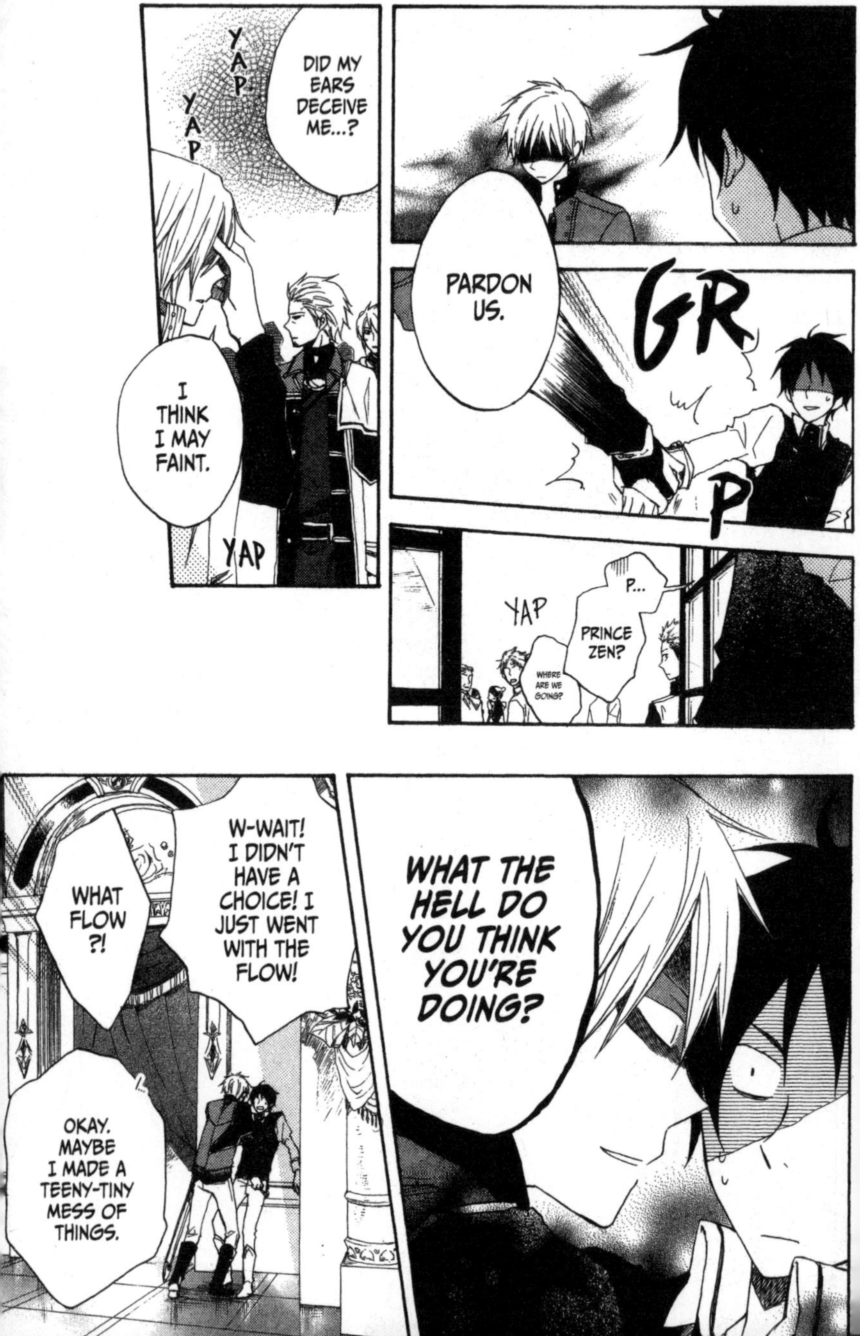
PARDON US.
GRP
P... PRINCE ZEN?
YAP
WHERE ARE WE GOING?
DID MY EARS DECEIVE ME...?
YAP YAP
I THINK I MAY FAINT.
YAP
WHAT THE HELL DO YOU THINK YOU'RE DOING?
W-WAIT! I DIDN'T HAVE A CHOICE! I JUST WENT WITH THE FLOW!
WHAT FLOW?!
OKAY. MAYBE I MADE A TEENY-TINY MESS OF THINGS.

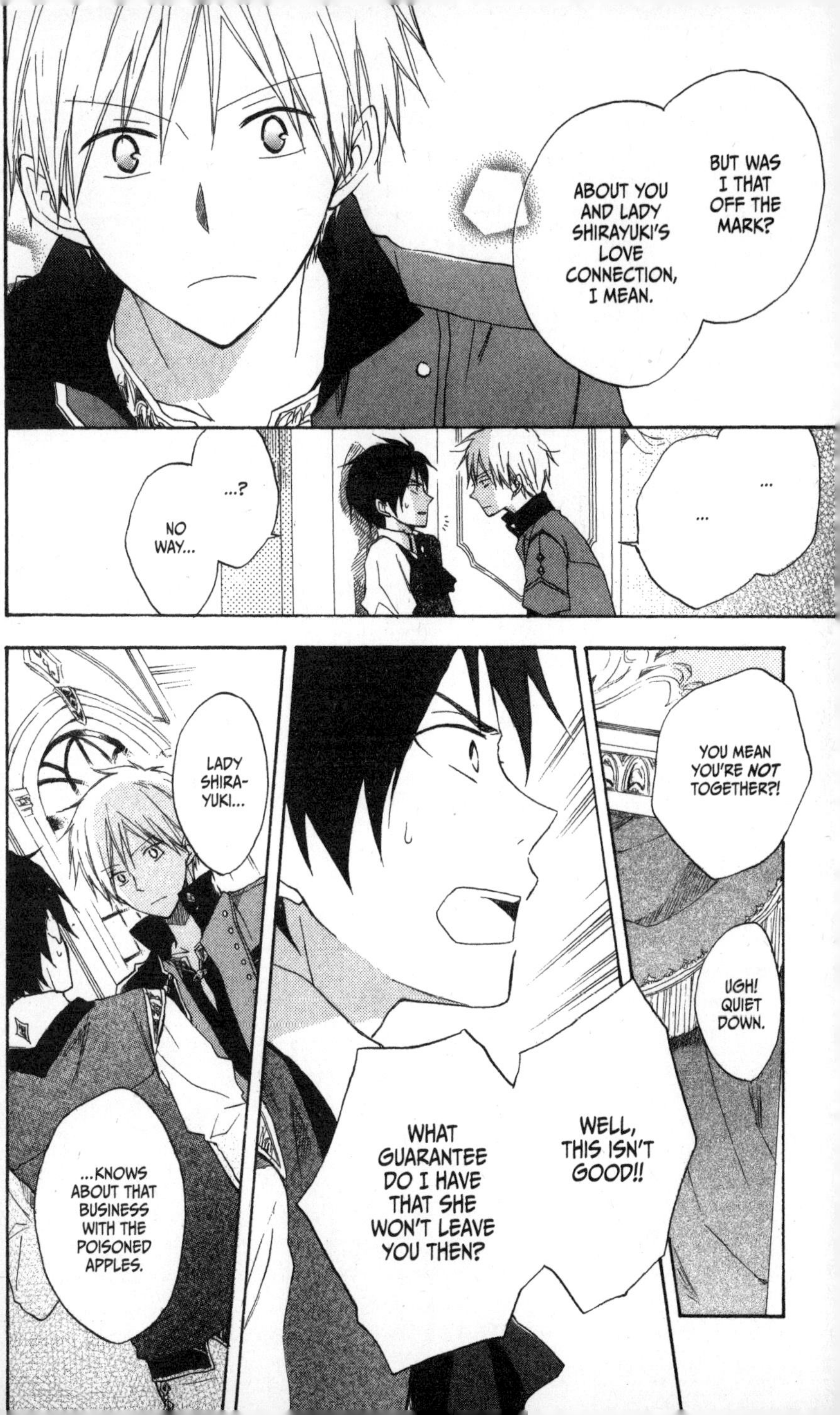
BUT WAS I THAT OFF THE MARK?
ABOUT YOU AND LADY SHIRAYUKI'S LOVE CONNECTION, I MEAN.
... ...
...?
NO WAY...
YOU MEAN YOU'RE *NOT* TOGETHER?!
UGH! QUIET DOWN.
WELL, THIS ISN'T GOOD!!
WHAT GUARANTEE DO I HAVE THAT SHE WON'T LEAVE YOU THEN?
LADY SHIRA-YUKI...
...KNOWS ABOUT THAT BUSINESS WITH THE POISONED APPLES.

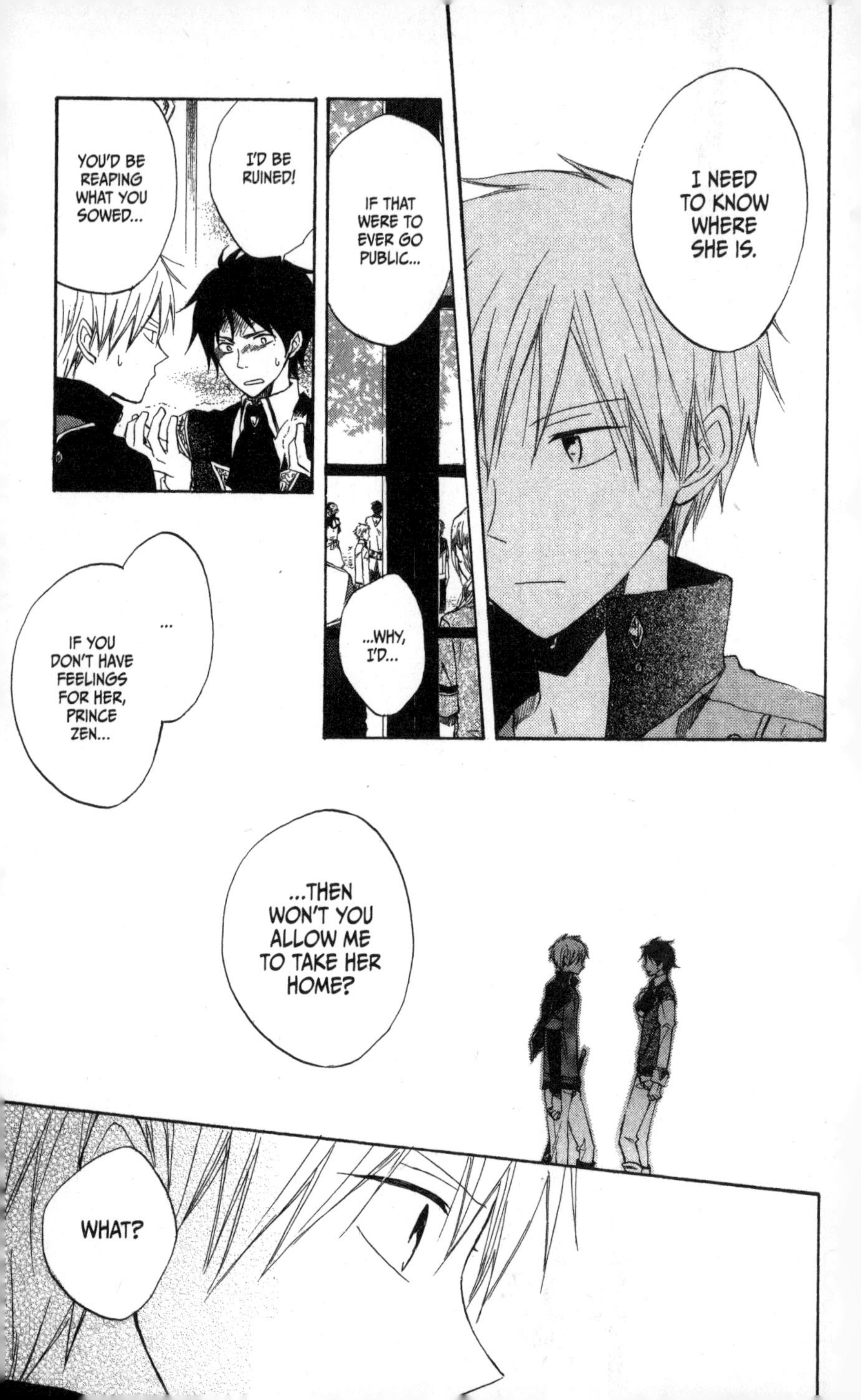
I NEED TO KNOW WHERE SHE IS.
IF THAT WERE TO EVER GO PUBLIC...
...WHY, I'D...
I'D BE RUINED!
YOU'D BE REAPING WHAT YOU SOWED...
...
IF YOU DON'T HAVE FEELINGS FOR HER, PRINCE ZEN...
...THEN WON'T YOU ALLOW ME TO TAKE HER HOME?
WHAT?

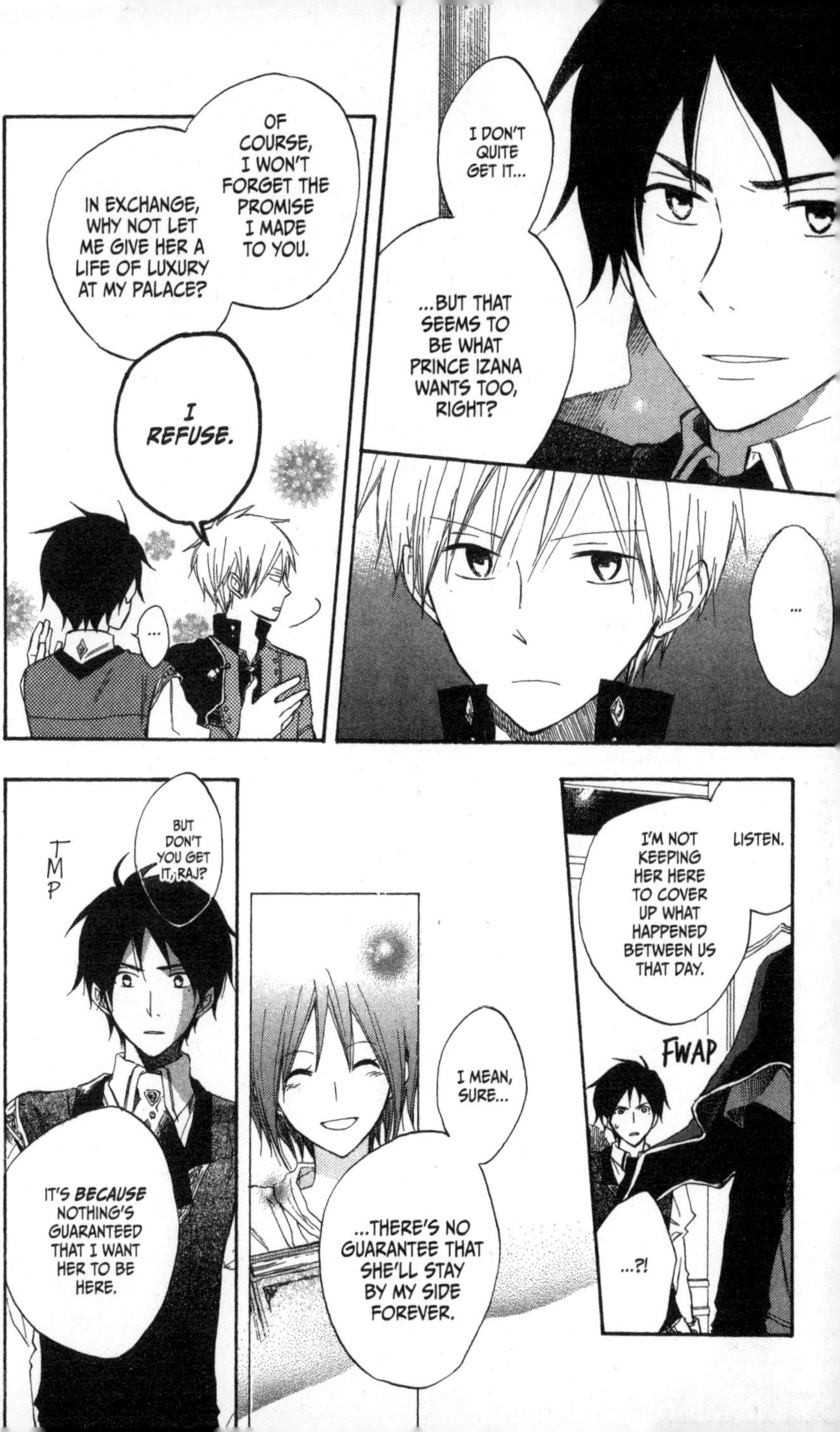
I DON'T QUITE GET IT...
...BUT THAT SEEMS TO BE WHAT PRINCE IZANA WANTS TOO, RIGHT?
...
OF COURSE, I WON'T FORGET THE PROMISE I MADE TO YOU.
IN EXCHANGE, WHY NOT LET ME GIVE HER A LIFE OF LUXURY AT MY PALACE?
I REFUSE.
...
LISTEN.
I'M NOT KEEPING HER HERE TO COVER UP WHAT HAPPENED BETWEEN US THAT DAY.
FWAP
...?!
I MEAN, SURE...
...THERE'S NO GUARANTEE THAT SHE'LL STAY BY MY SIDE FOREVER.
BUT DON'T YOU GET IT, RAJ?
TMP
IT'S BECAUSE NOTHING'S GUARANTEED THAT I WANT HER TO BE HERE.

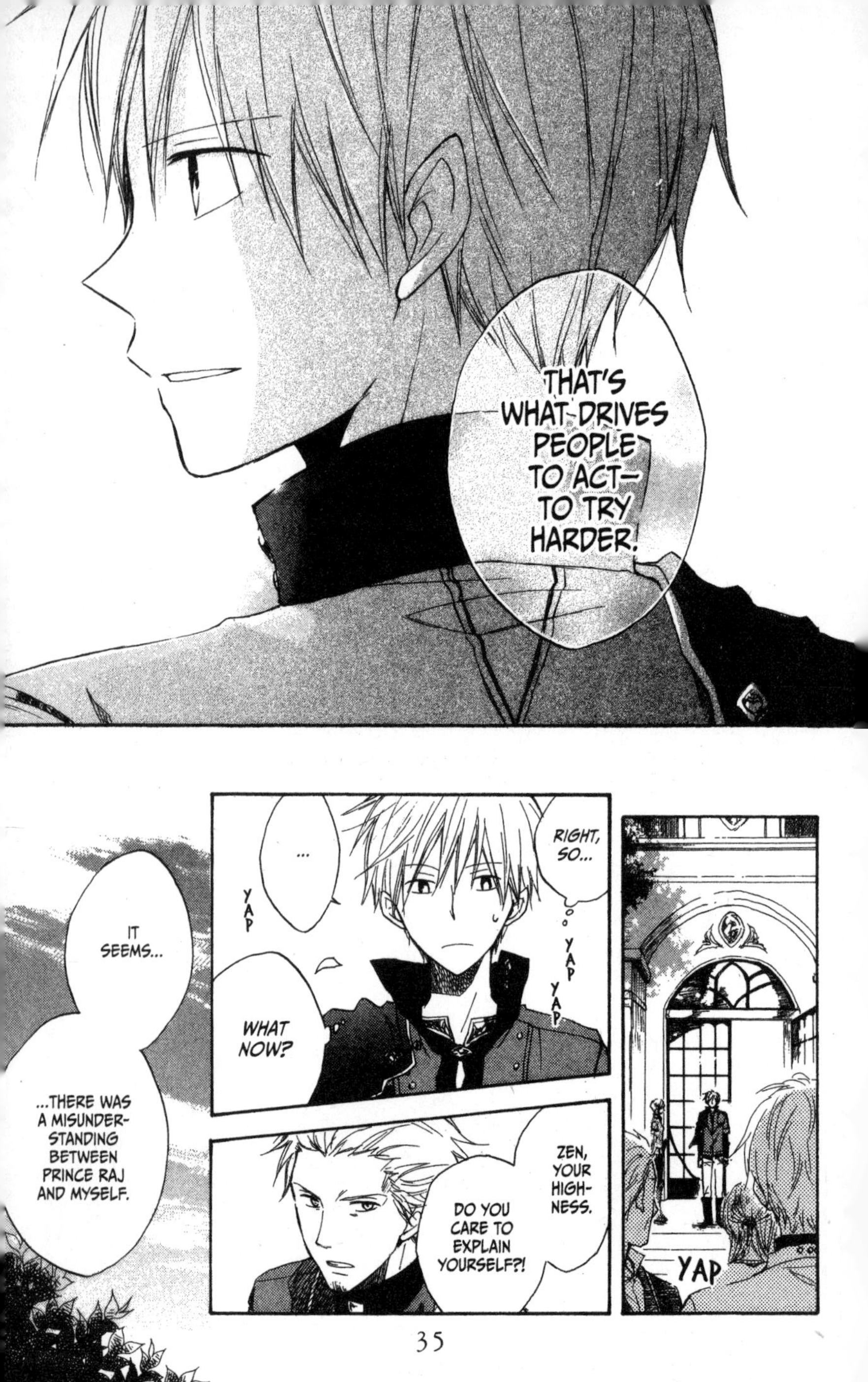
THAT'S WHAT DRIVES PEOPLE TO ACT—TO TRY HARDER!
YAP
RIGHT, SO...
YAP
YAP
...
YAP
WHAT NOW?
ZEN, YOUR HIGHNESS.
DO YOU CARE TO EXPLAIN YOURSELF?!
IT SEEMS...
...THERE WAS A MISUNDERSTANDING BETWEEN PRINCE RAJ AND MYSELF.

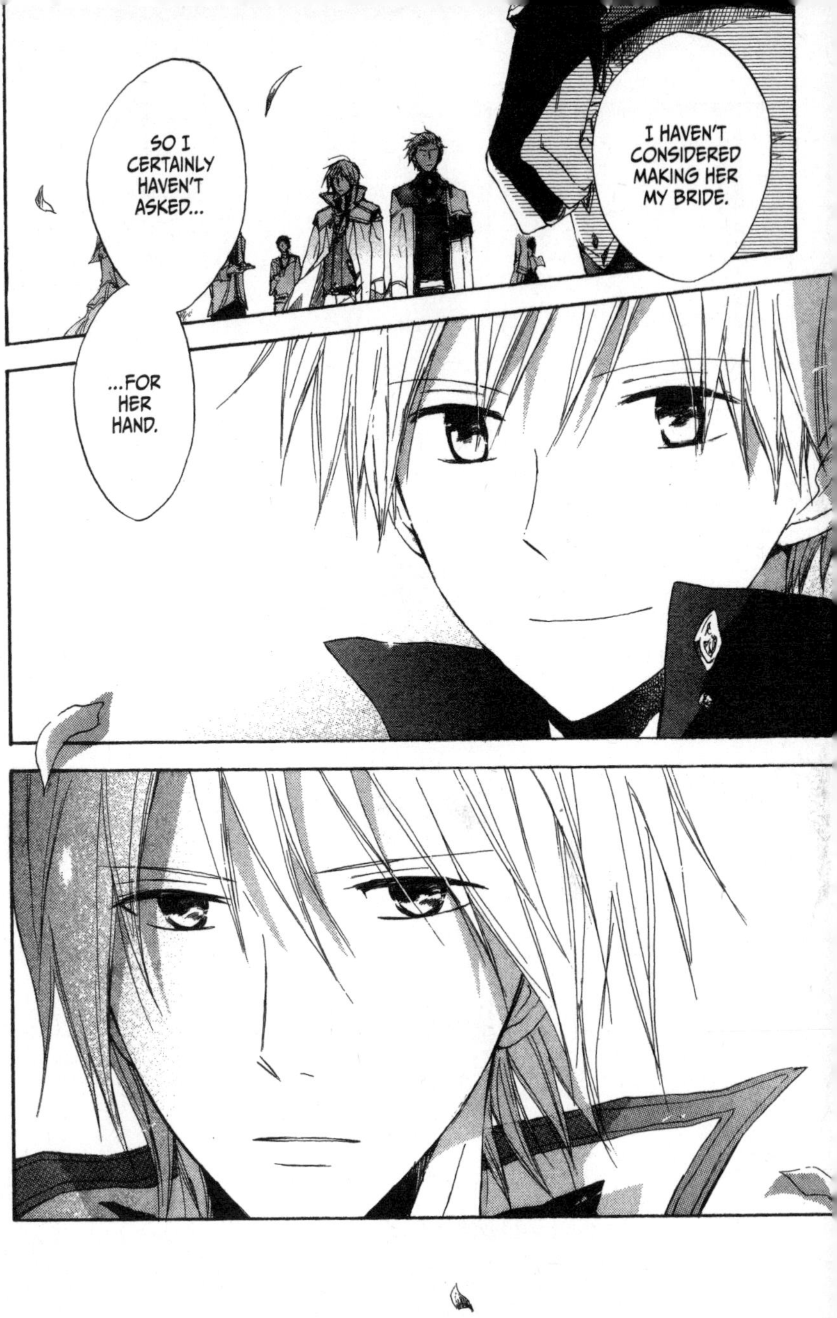
I HAVEN'T CONSIDERED MAKING HER MY BRIDE.
SO I CERTAINLY HAVEN'T ASKED...
...FOR HER HAND.

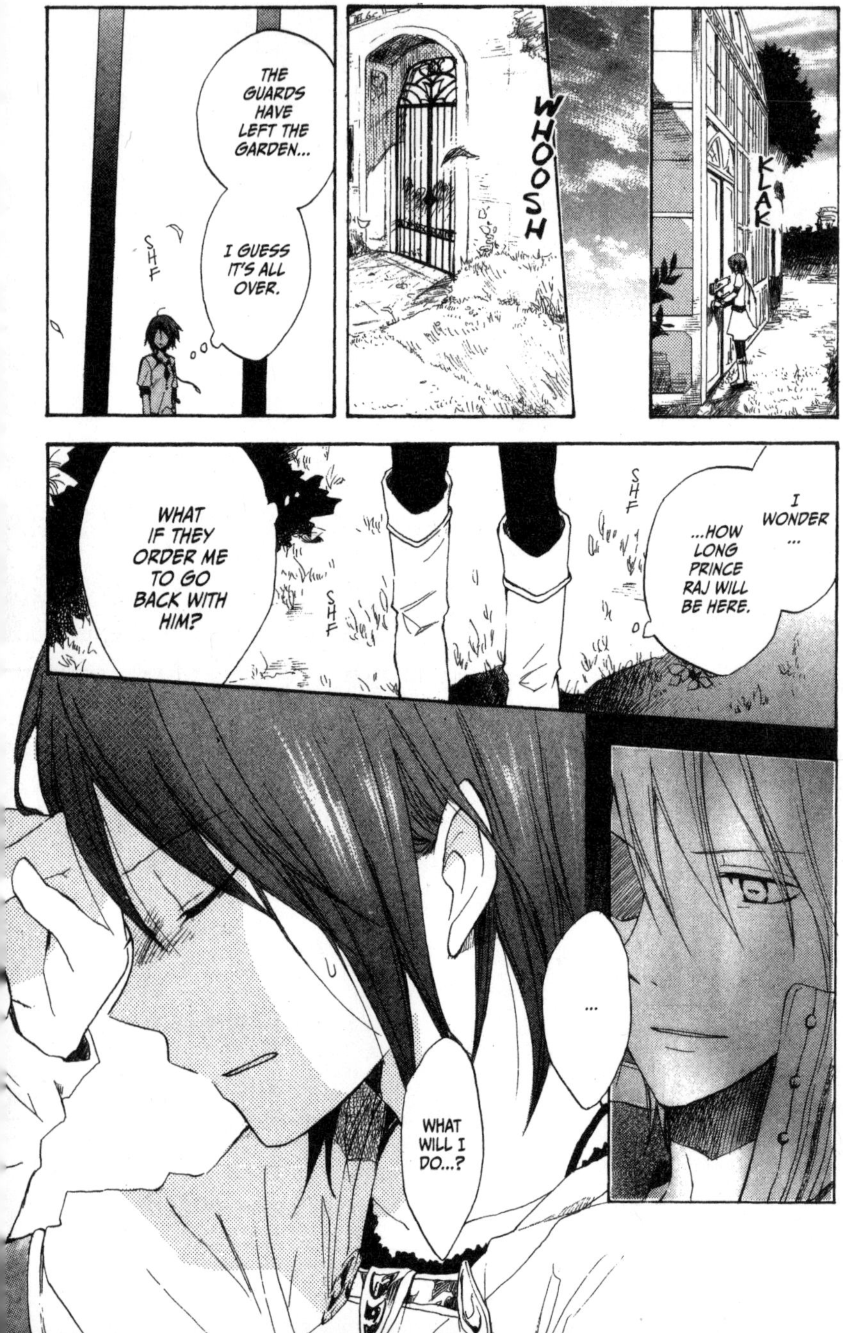
KLAK
WHOOSH
THE GUARDS HAVE LEFT THE GARDEN...
I GUESS IT'S ALL OVER.
SHF
I WONDER...
...HOW LONG PRINCE RAJ WILL BE HERE.
SHF
SHF
WHAT IF THEY ORDER ME TO GO BACK WITH HIM?
...
WHAT WILL I DO...?

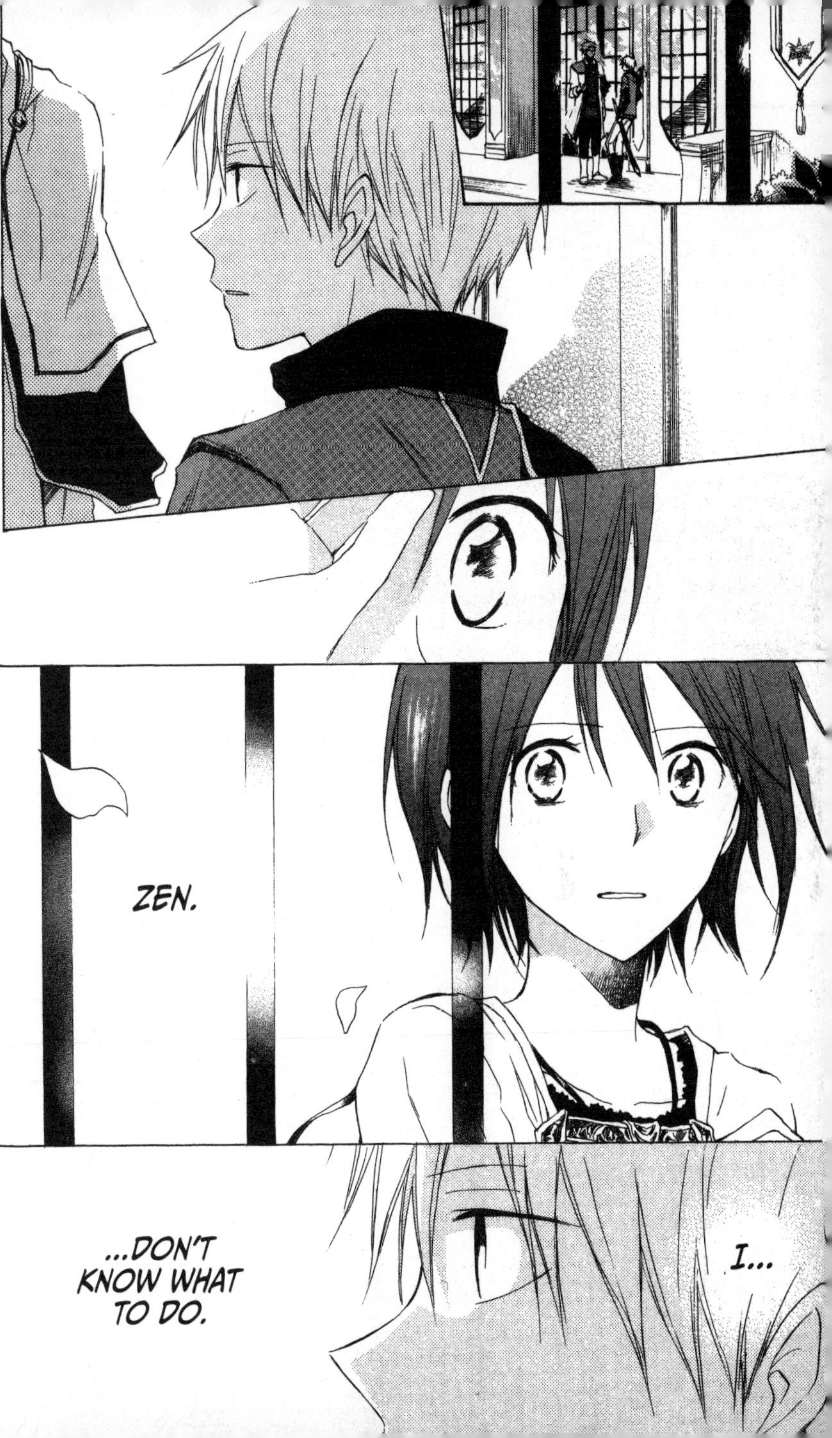
ZEN.
I...
...DON'T KNOW WHAT TO DO.

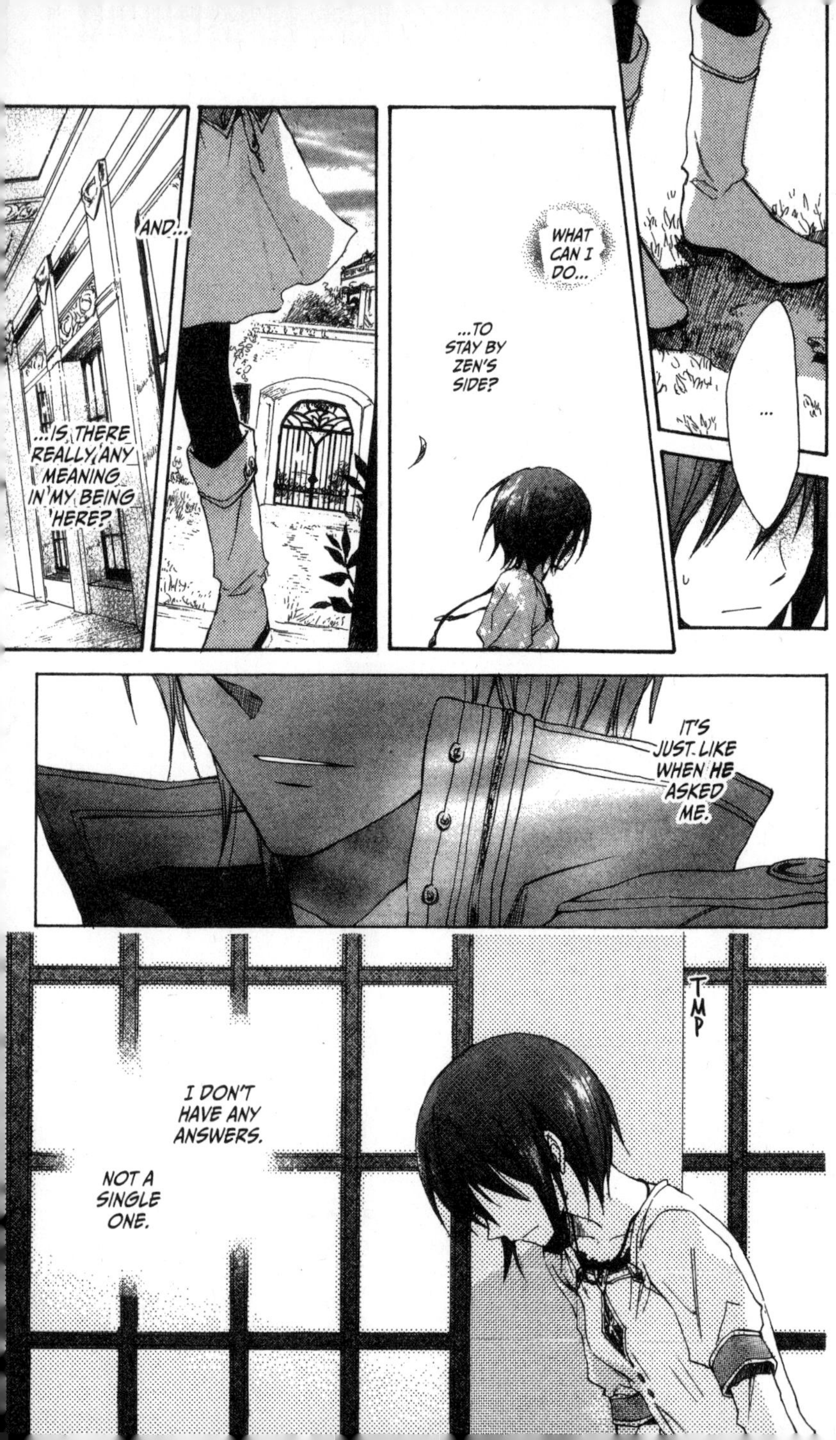
...
WHAT CAN I DO...
...TO STAY BY ZEN'S SIDE?
AND...
...IS THERE REALLY ANY MEANING IN MY BEING HERE?
IT'S JUST LIKE WHEN HE ASKED ME.
TMP
I DON'T HAVE ANY ANSWERS.
NOT A SINGLE ONE.

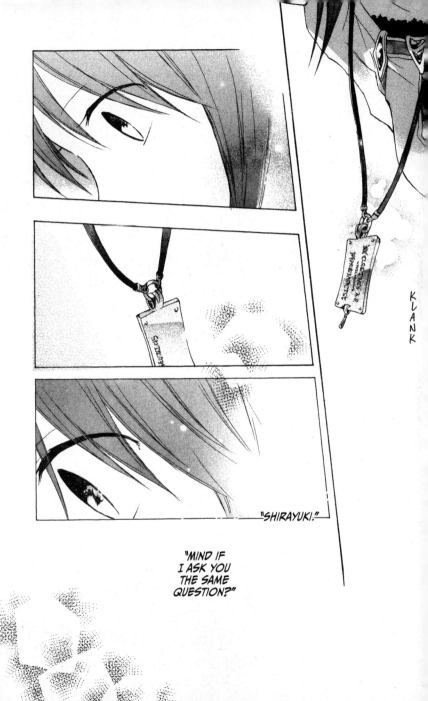

KLANK

"SHIRAYUKI."

"MIND IF
I ASK YOU
THE SAME
QUESTION?"

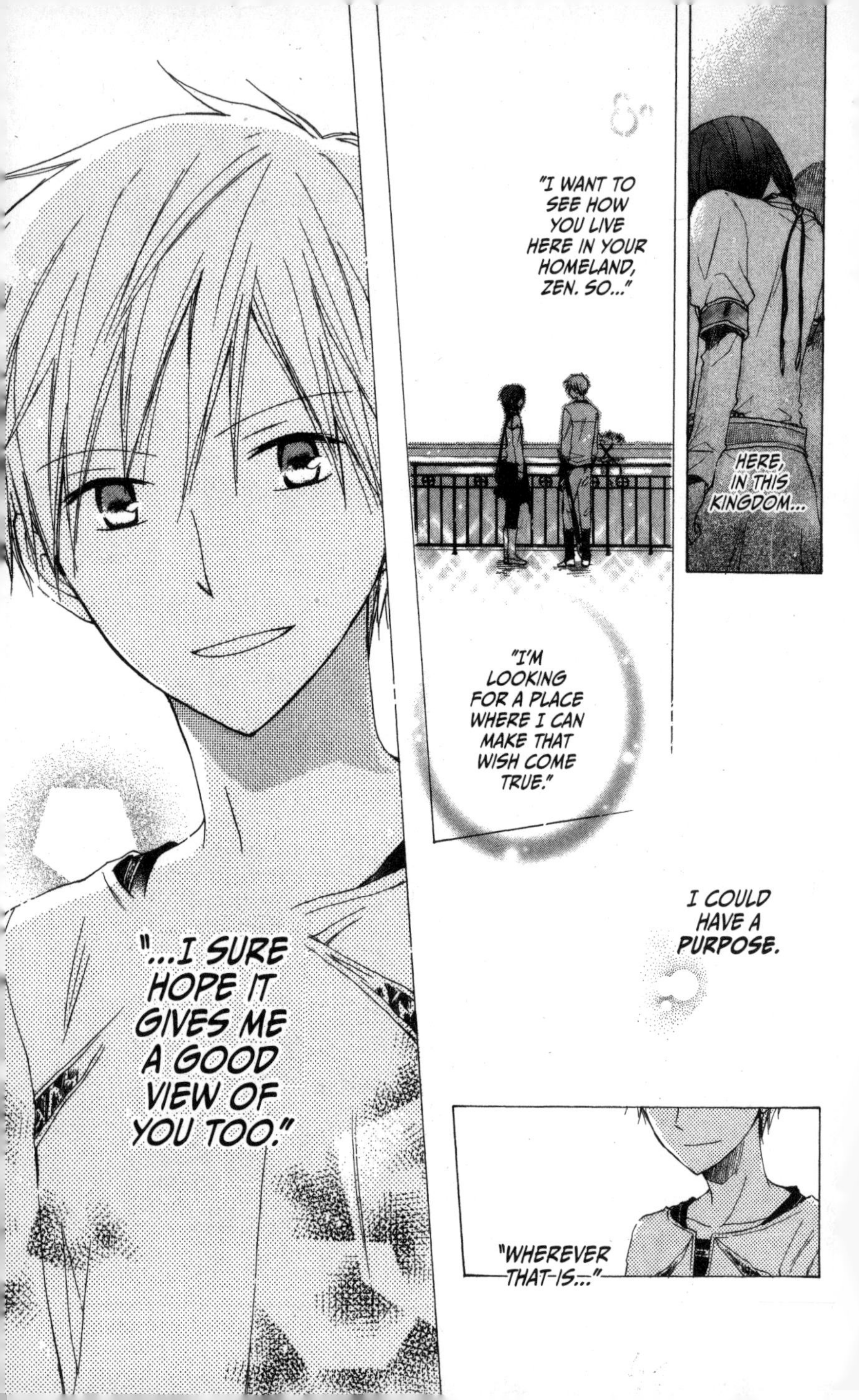
HERE, IN THIS KINGDOM...
"I WANT TO SEE HOW YOU LIVE HERE IN YOUR HOMELAND, ZEN. SO..."
"I'M LOOKING FOR A PLACE WHERE I CAN MAKE THAT WISH COME TRUE."
I COULD HAVE A PURPOSE.
"WHEREVER THAT IS..."
"...I SURE HOPE IT GIVES ME A GOOD VIEW OF YOU TOO."

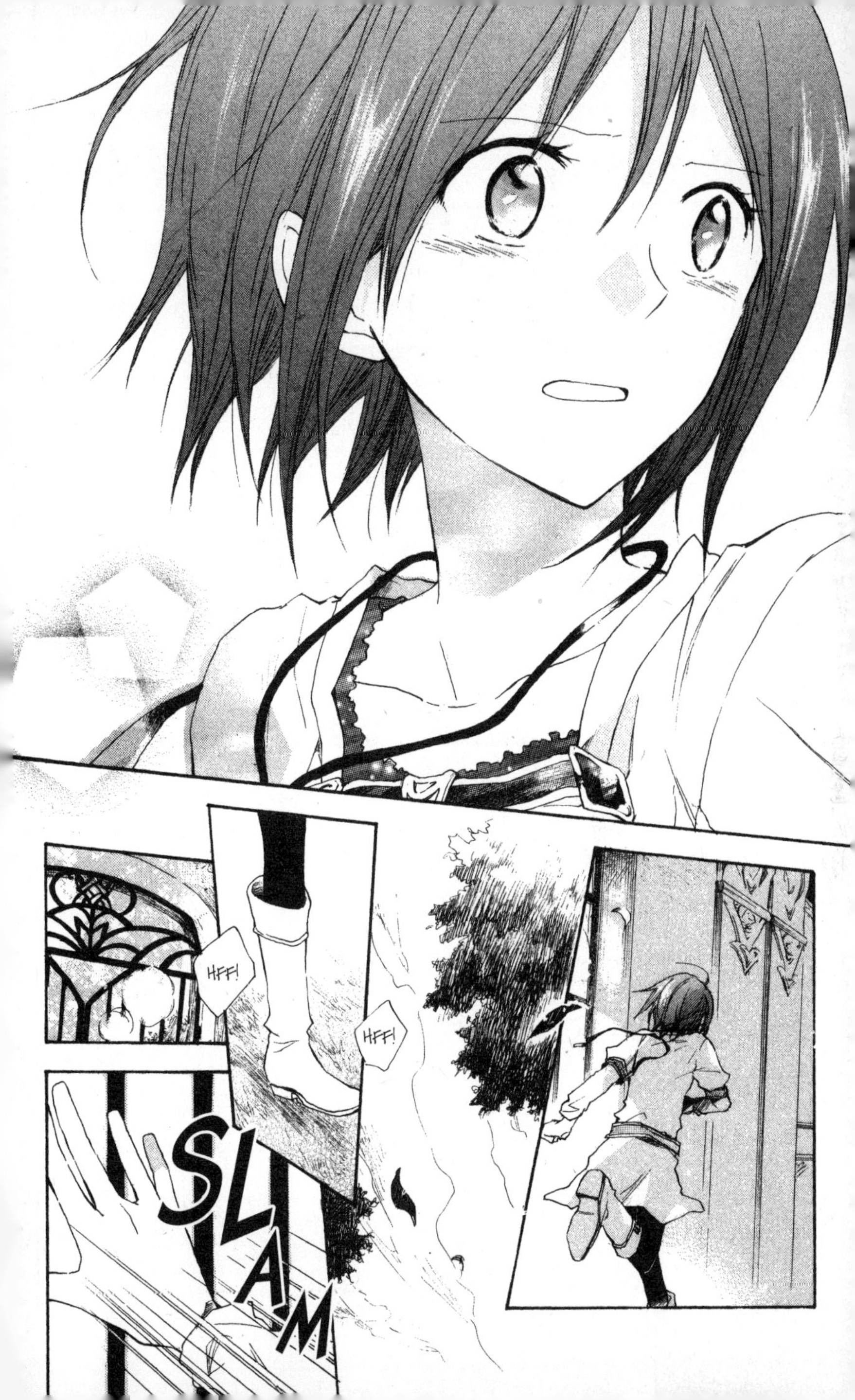
HFF!
HFF!
SLAM

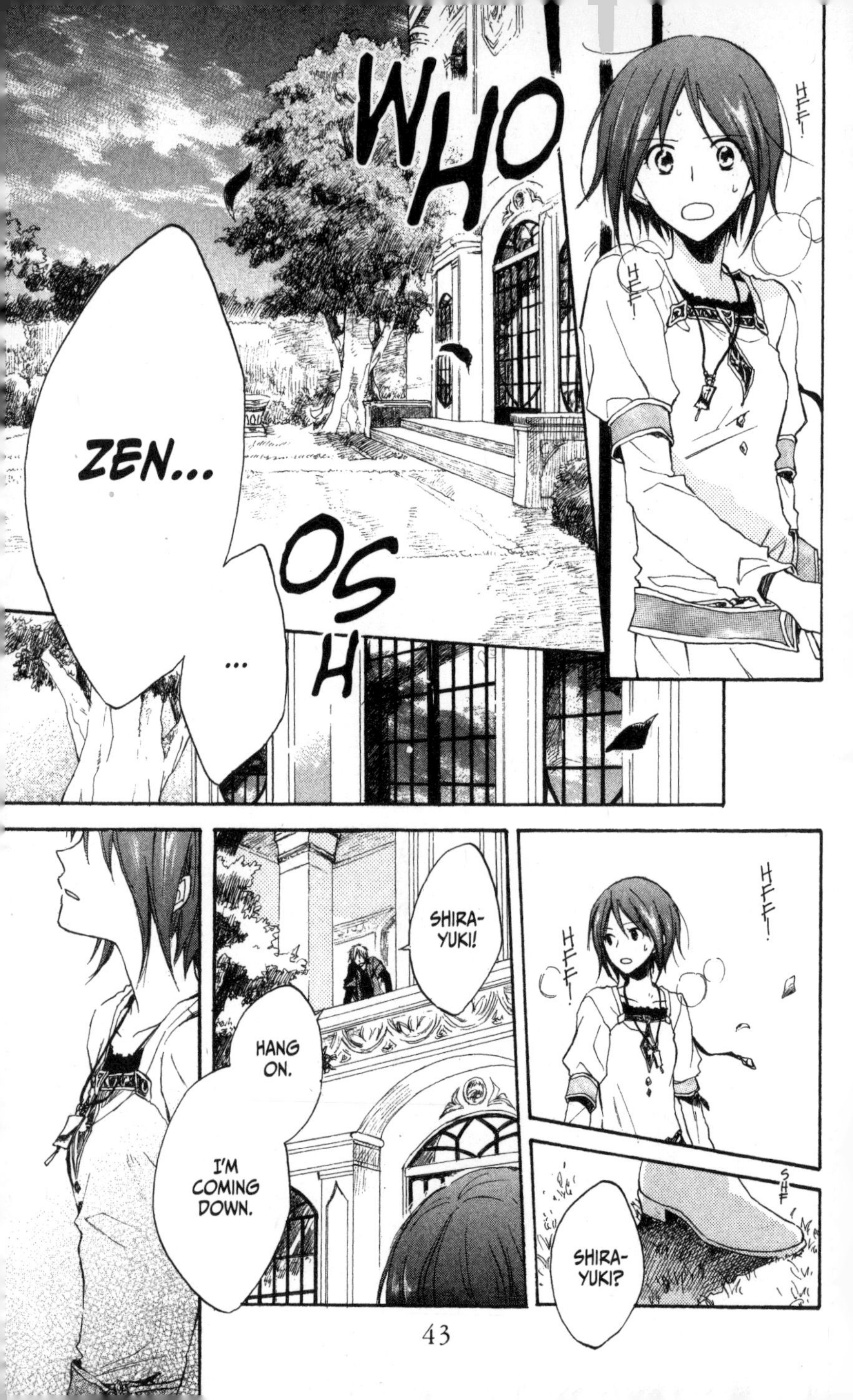
HFF!
HFF!
WHOOSH
ZEN...
...
HFF!
HFF!
SHF
SHIRA-YUKI?
SHIRA-YUKI!
HANG ON.
I'M COMING DOWN.

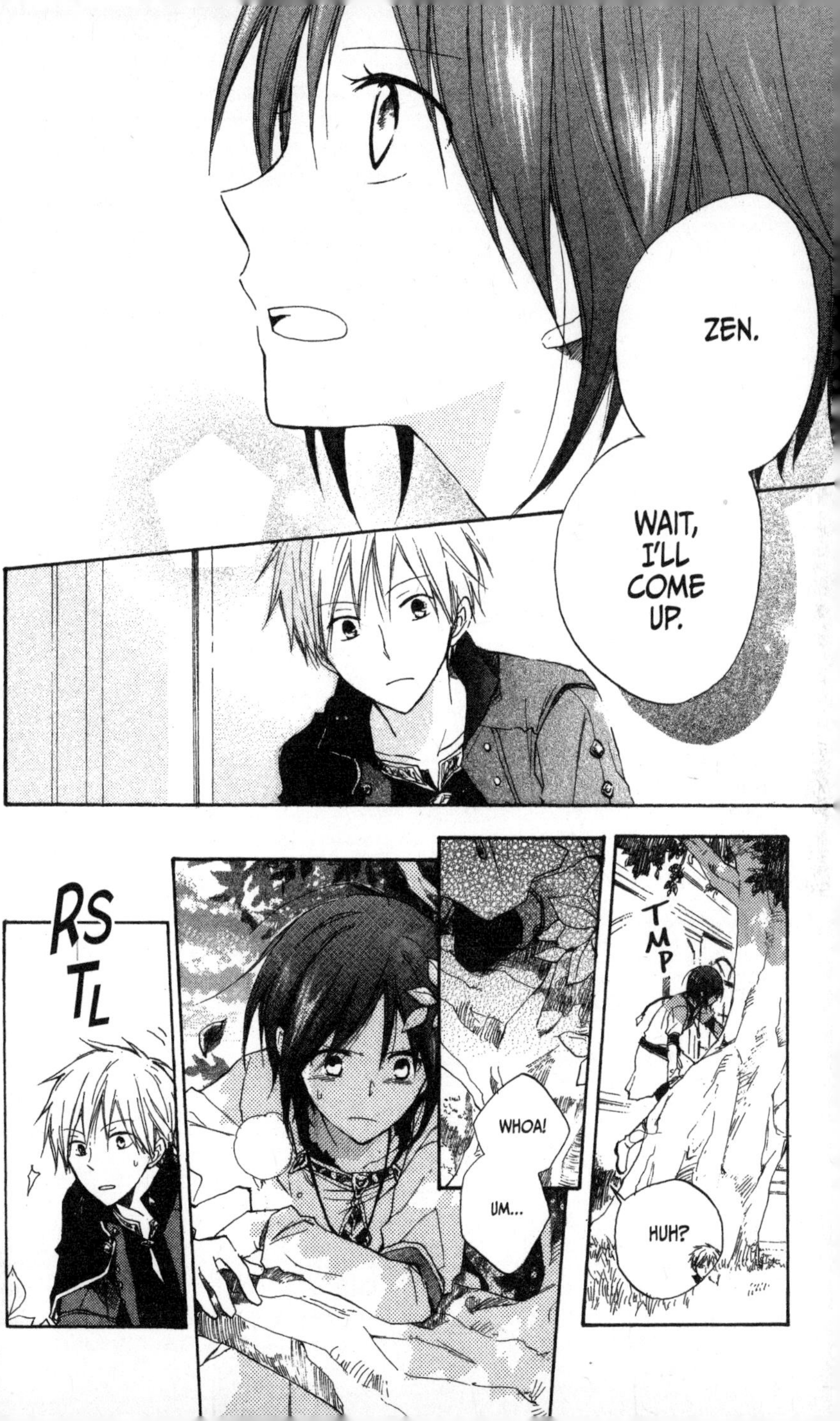
ZEN.
WAIT, I'LL COME UP.
TMP
HUH?
WHOA!
UM...
RSTL

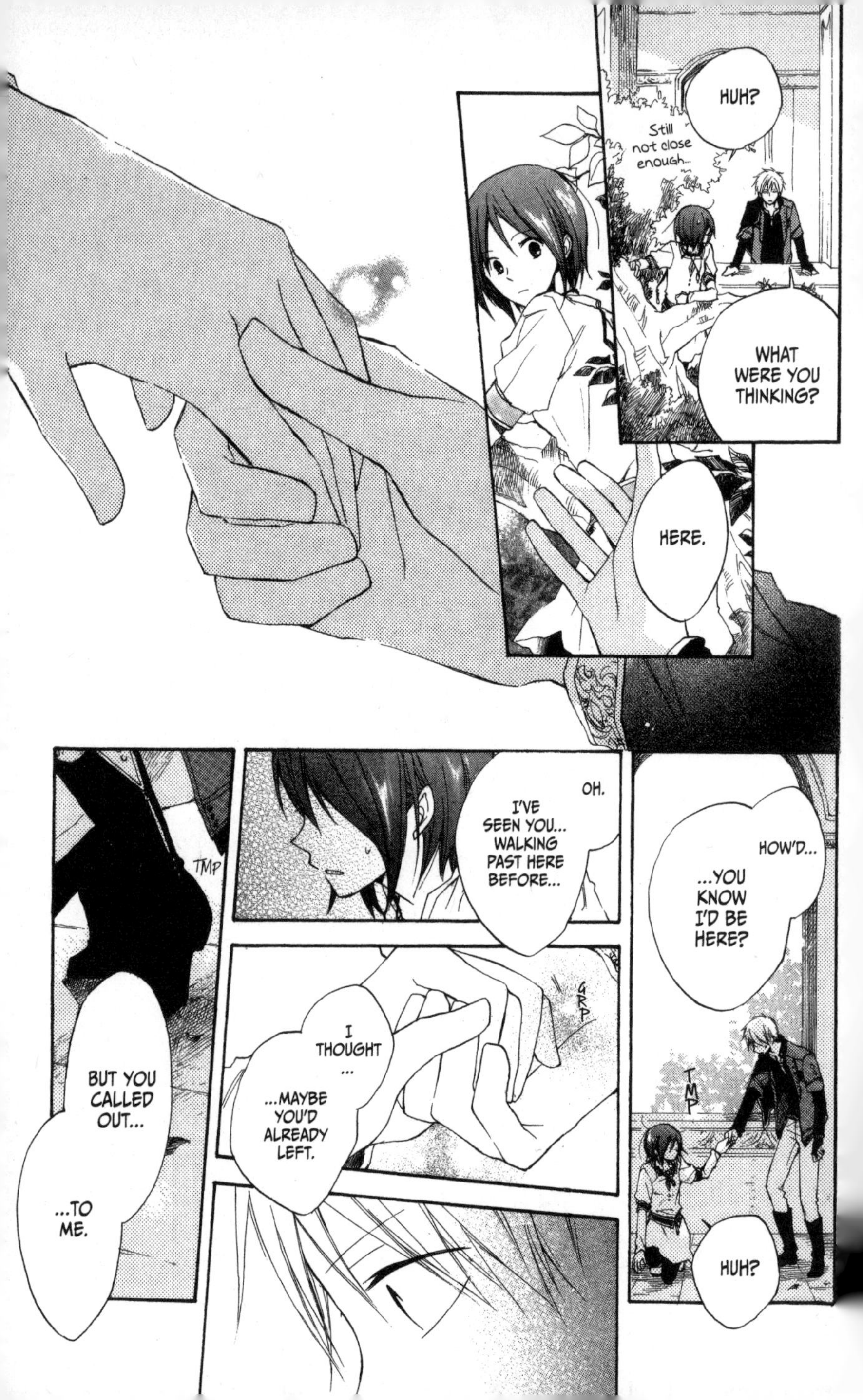
HUH?
Still not close enough...
WHAT WERE YOU THINKING?
HERE.
HOW'D...
...YOU KNOW I'D BE HERE?
TMP
HUH?
OH.
I'VE SEEN YOU... WALKING PAST HERE BEFORE...
GRP
I THOUGHT...
...MAYBE YOU'D ALREADY LEFT.
TMP
BUT YOU CALLED OUT...
...TO ME.

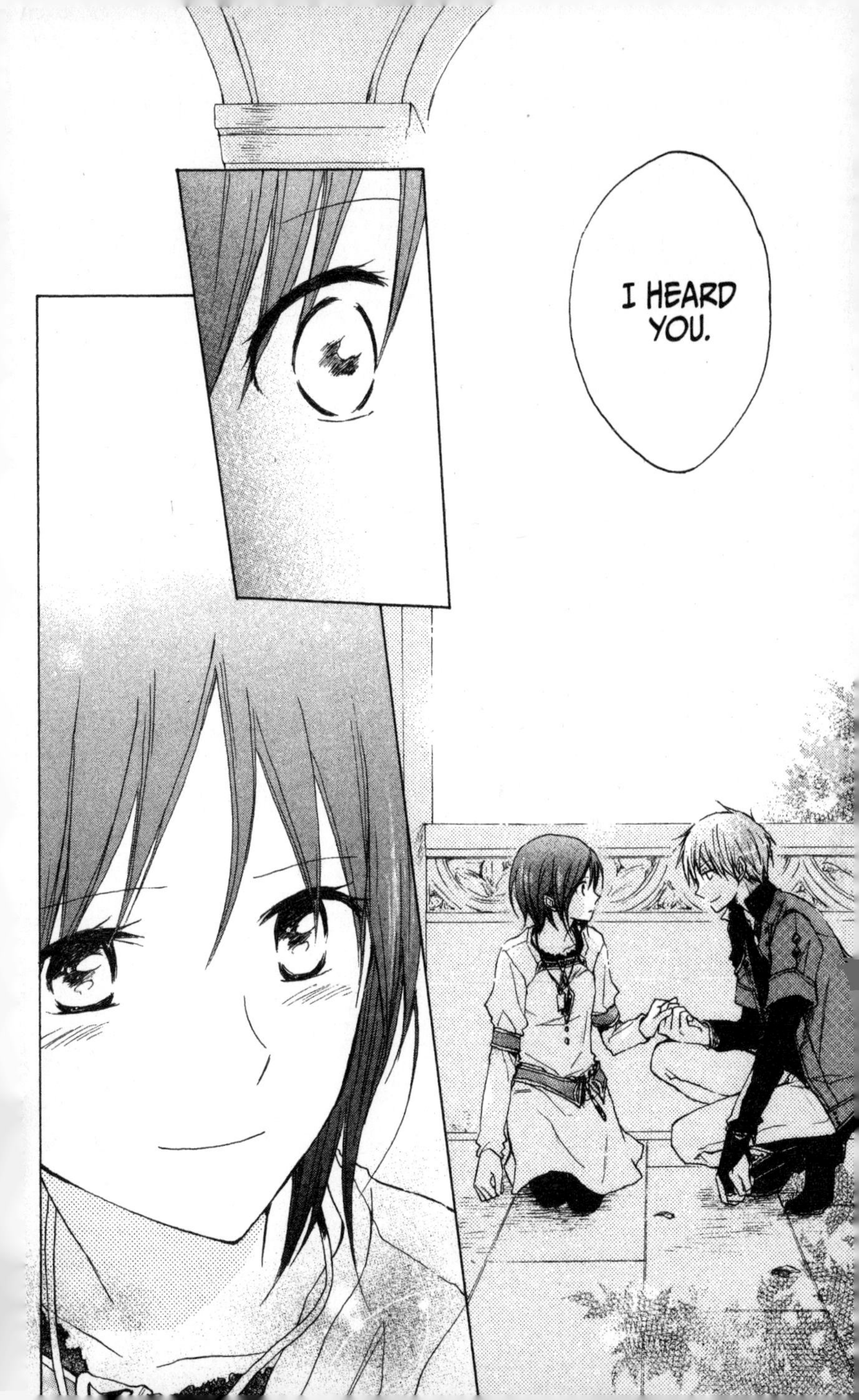
I HEARD YOU.

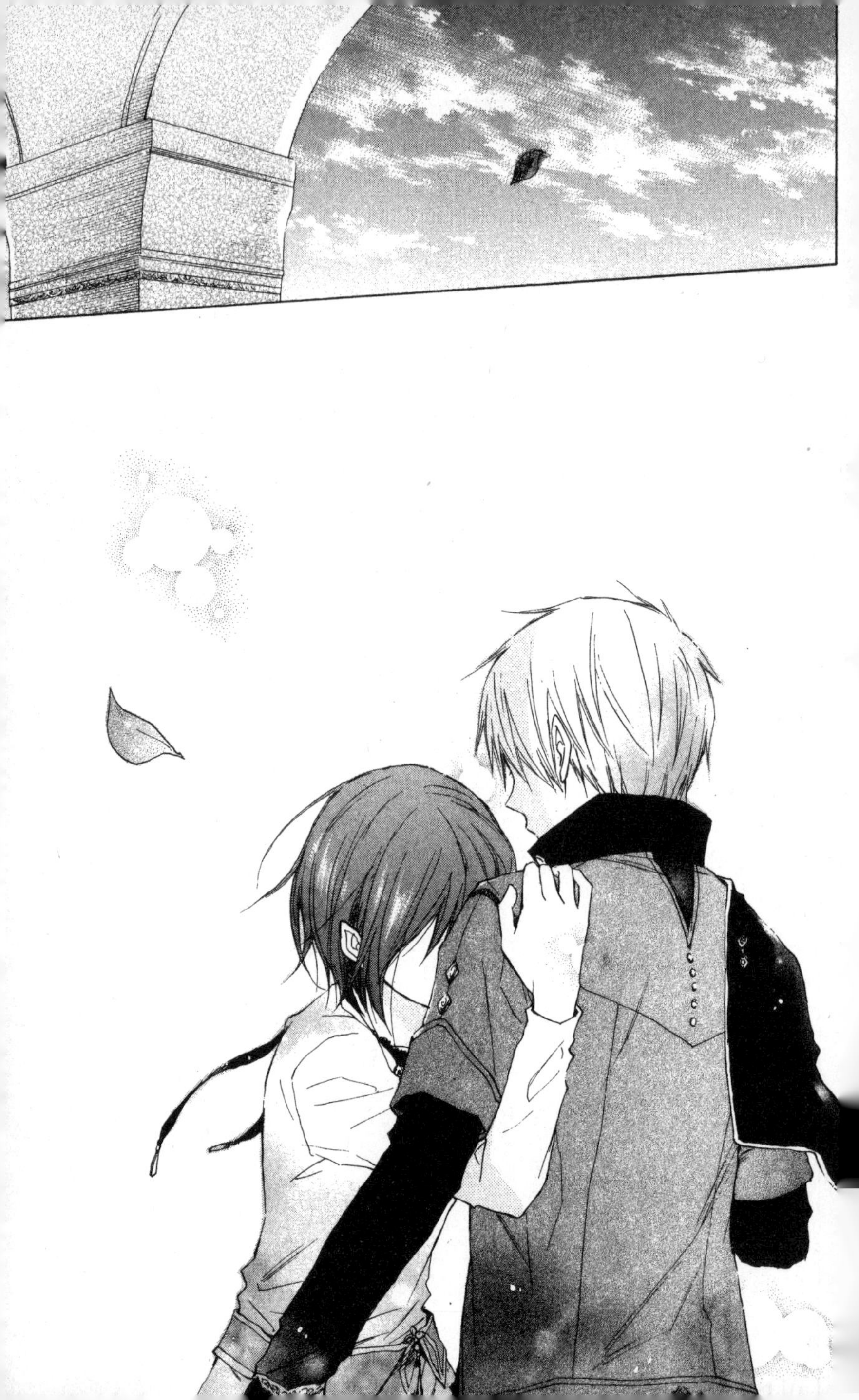

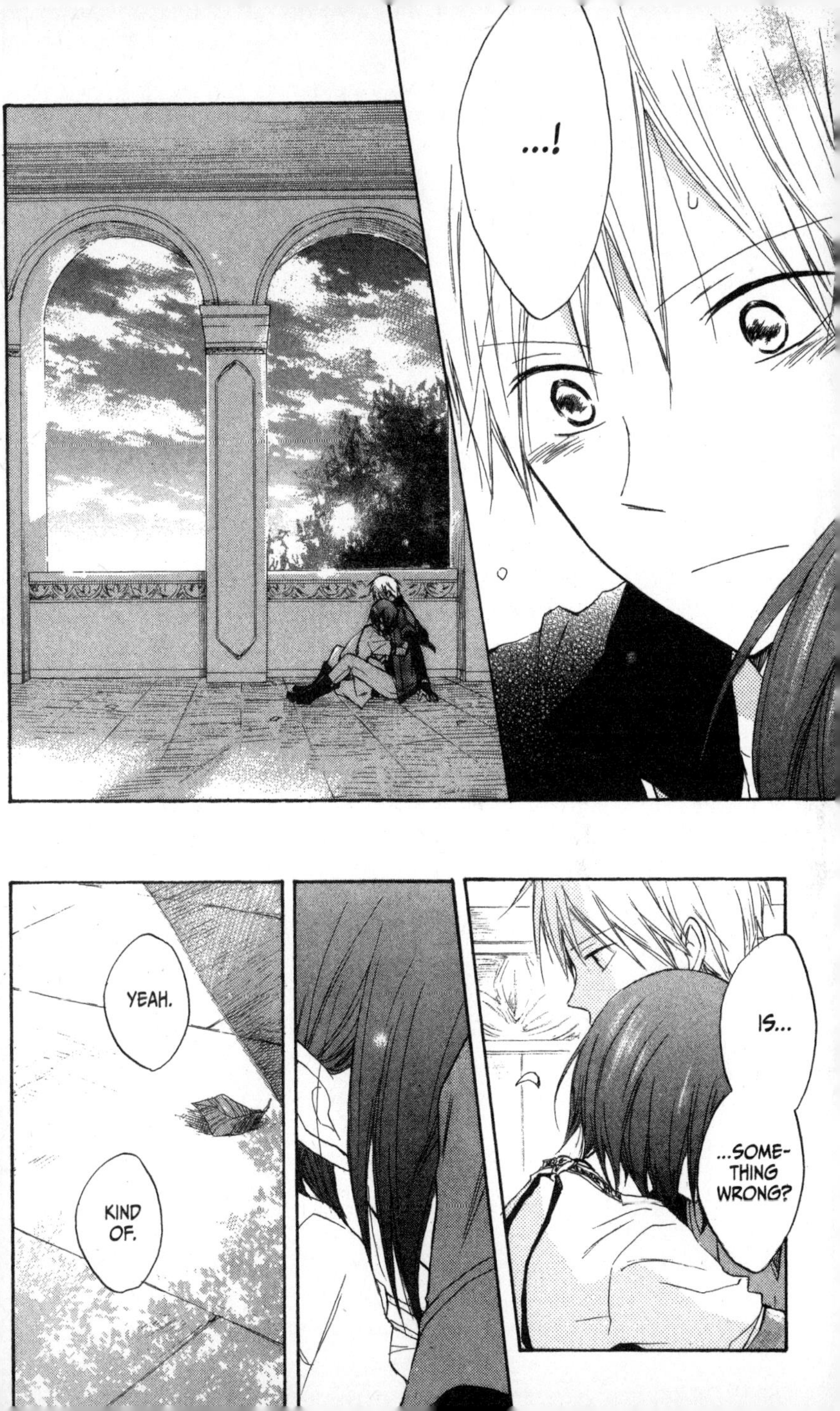
...!
IS...
...SOME-THING WRONG?
YEAH.
KIND OF.

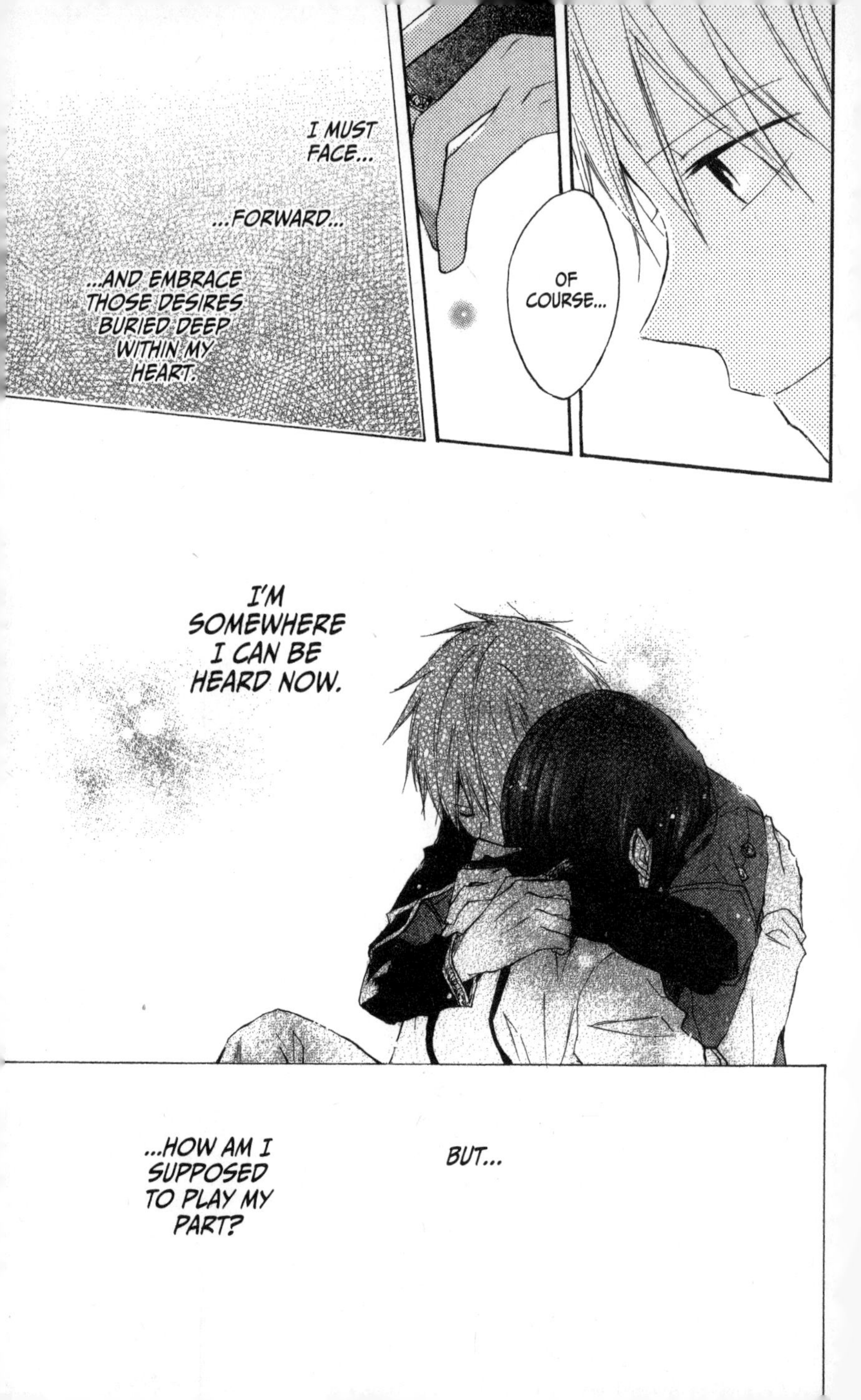
OF COURSE...
I MUST FACE...
...FORWARD...
...AND EMBRACE THOSE DESIRES BURIED DEEP WITHIN MY HEART.
I'M SOMEWHERE I CAN BE HEARD NOW.
BUT...
...HOW AM I SUPPOSED TO PLAY MY PART?

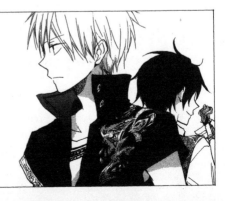

Chapter 9 Preview Image

Chapter 10

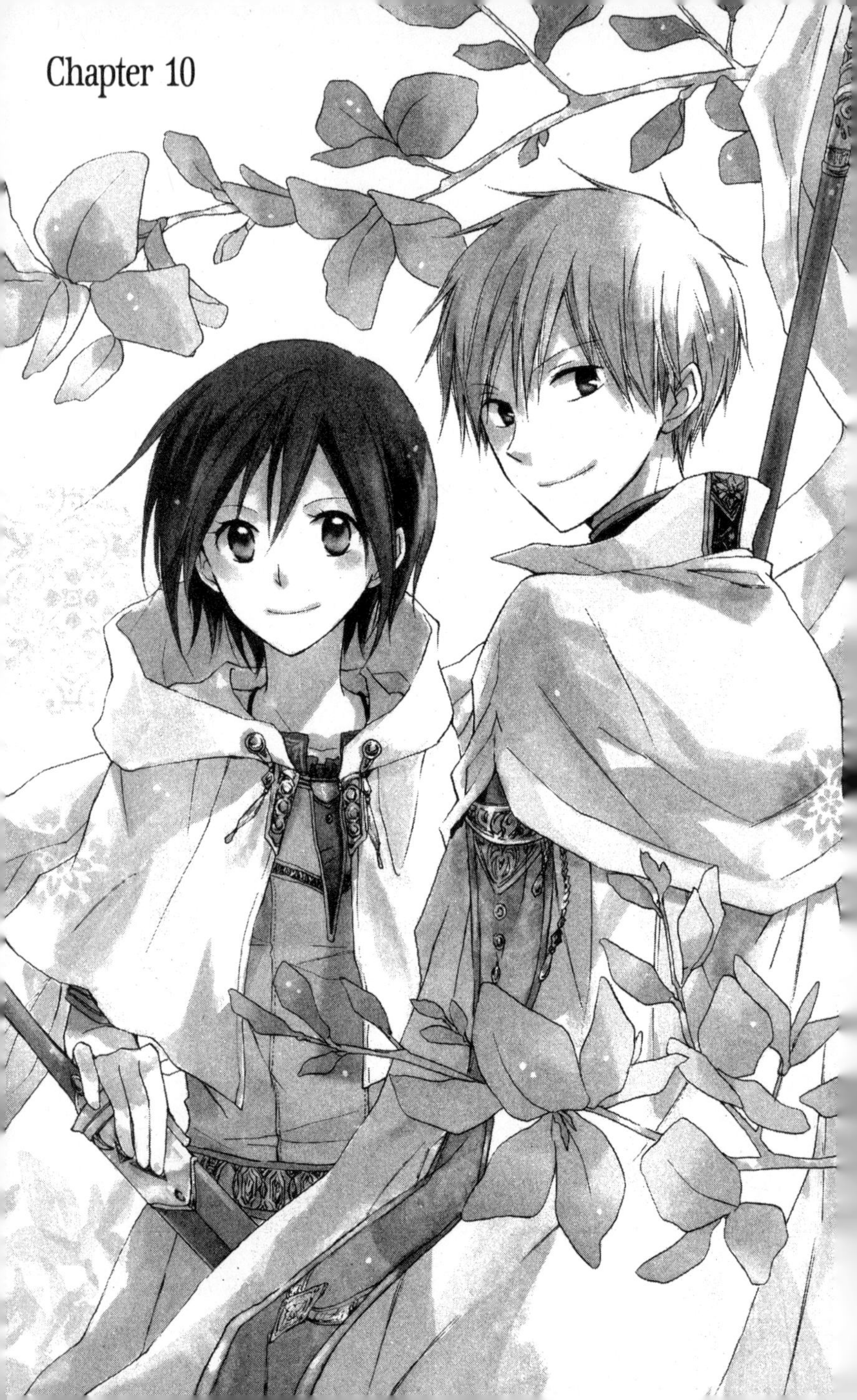

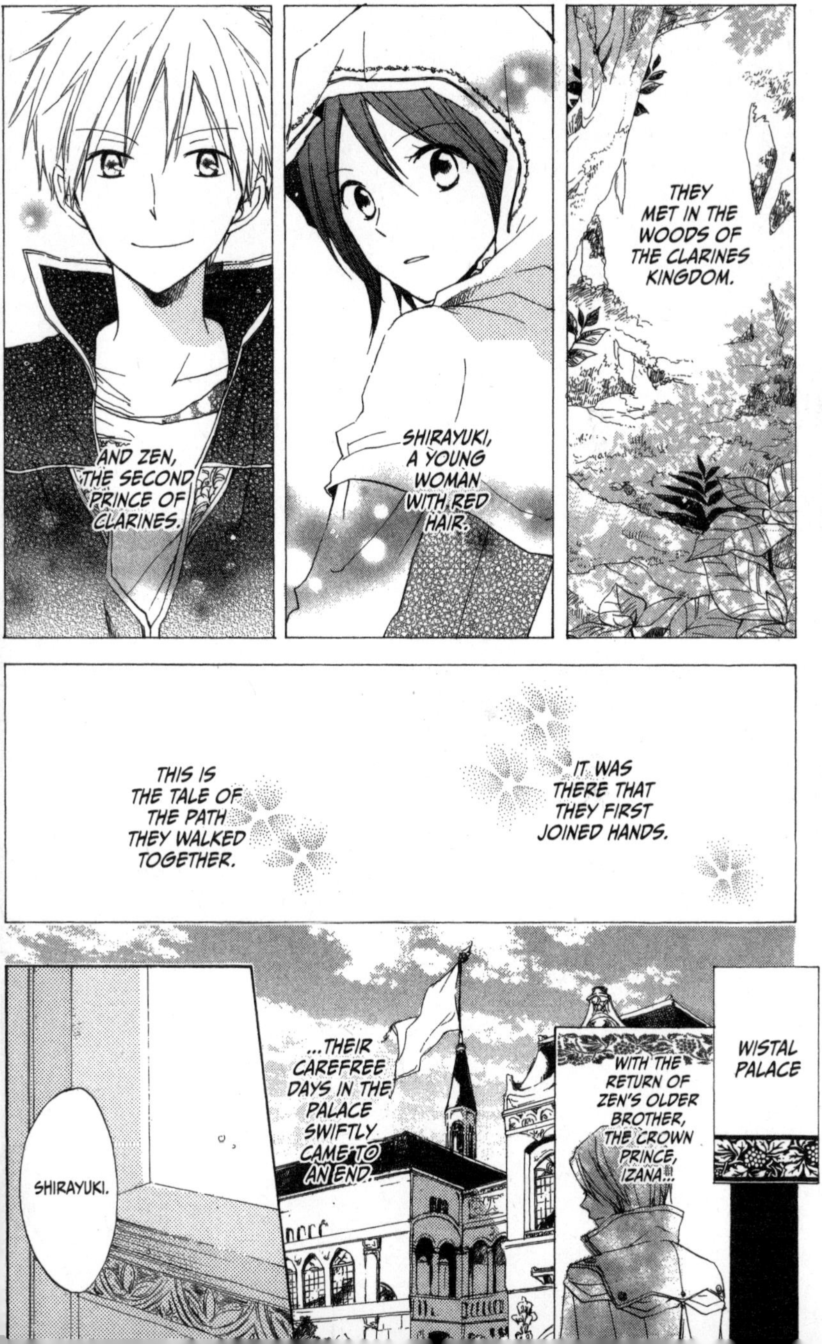
THEY MET IN THE WOODS OF THE CLARINES KINGDOM.
SHIRAYUKI, A YOUNG WOMAN WITH RED HAIR.
AND ZEN, THE SECOND PRINCE OF CLARINES.
IT WAS THERE THAT THEY FIRST JOINED HANDS.
THIS IS THE TALE OF THE PATH THEY WALKED TOGETHER.
WISTAL PALACE
WITH THE RETURN OF ZEN'S OLDER BROTHER, THE CROWN PRINCE, IZANA...
...THEIR CAREFREE DAYS IN THE PALACE SWIFTLY CAME TO AN END.
SHIRAYUKI.

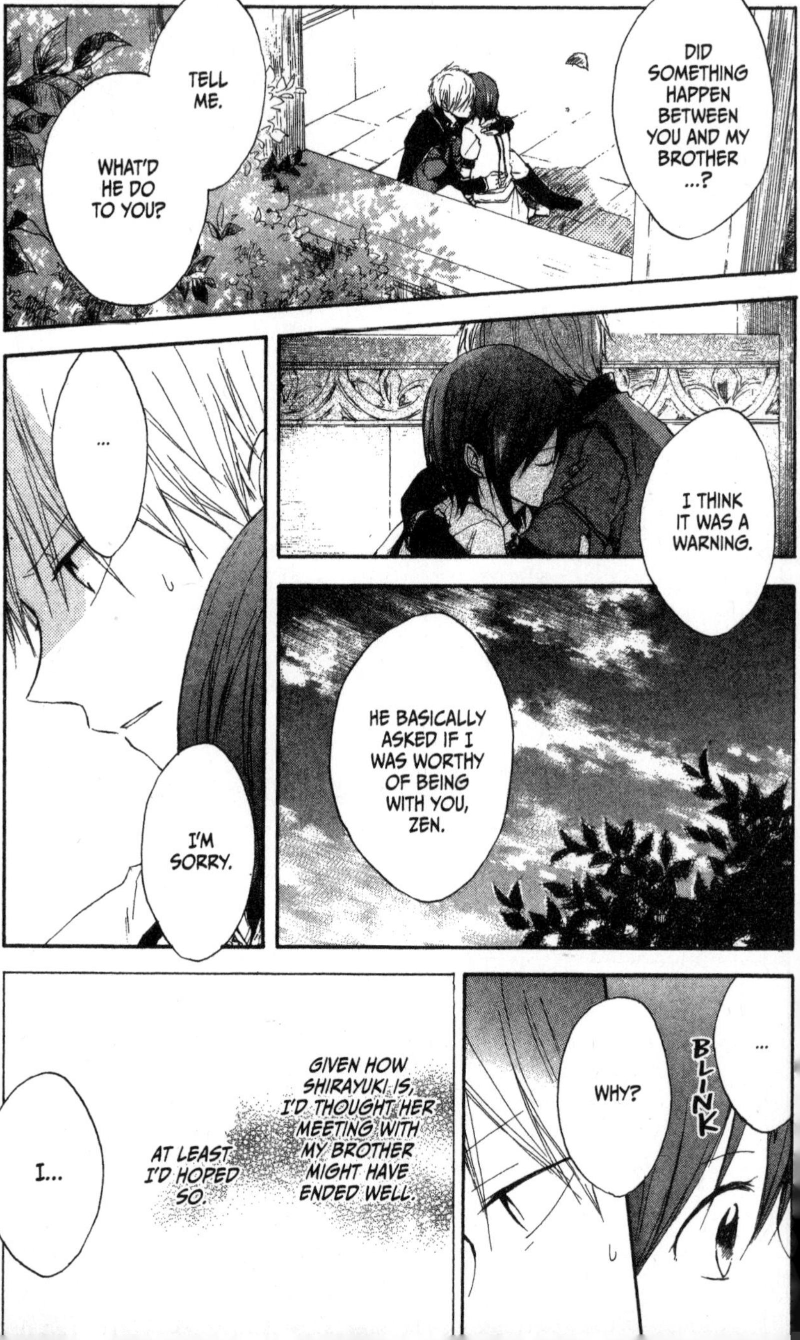
DID SOMETHING HAPPEN BETWEEN YOU AND MY BROTHER ...?
TELL ME.
WHAT'D HE DO TO YOU?
I THINK IT WAS A WARNING.
HE BASICALLY ASKED IF I WAS WORTHY OF BEING WITH YOU, ZEN.
...
I'M SORRY.
...
BLINK
WHY?
GIVEN HOW SHIRAYUKI IS, I'D THOUGHT HER MEETING WITH MY BROTHER MIGHT HAVE ENDED WELL.
AT LEAST I'D HOPED SO.
I...

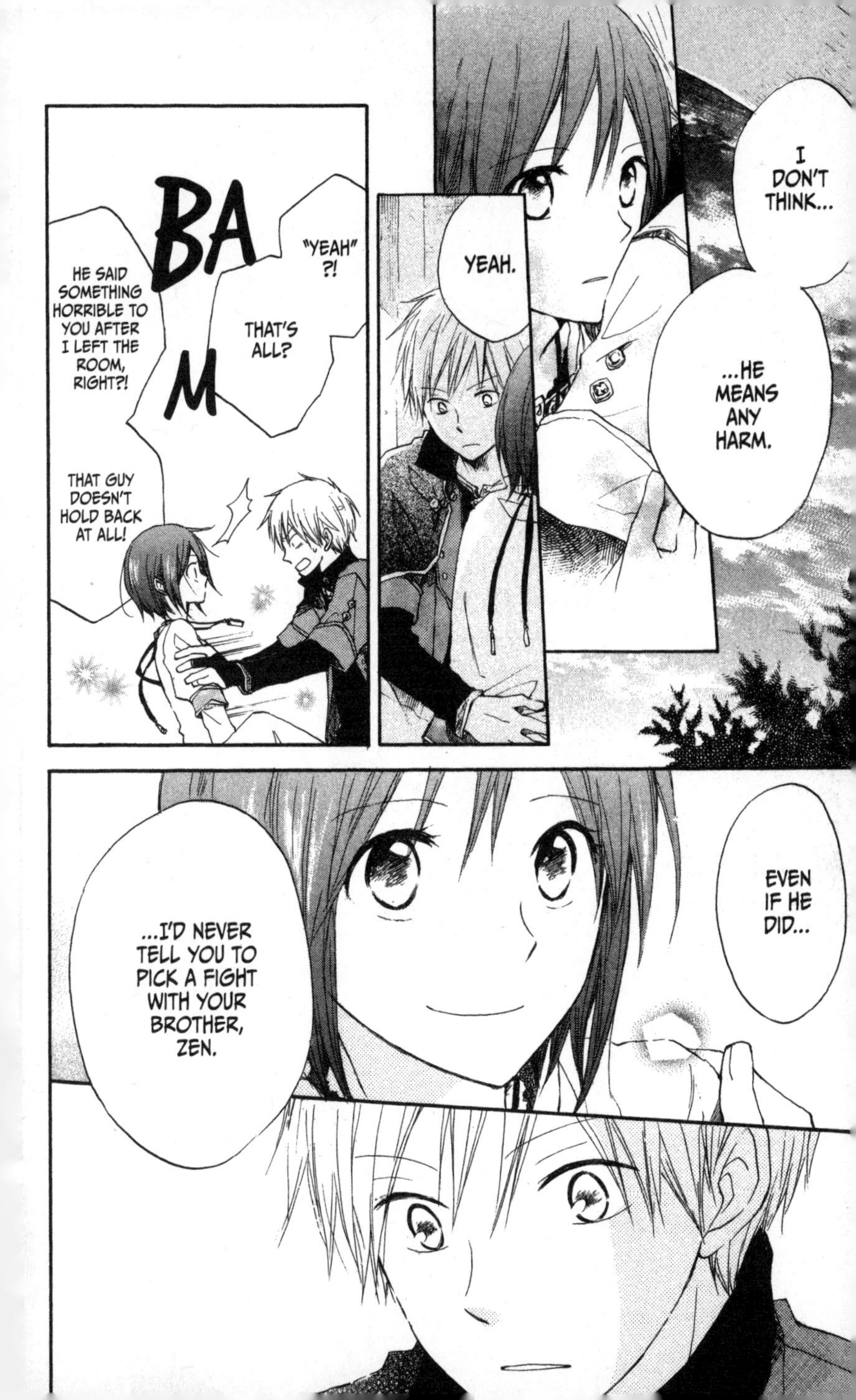
I DON'T THINK...
...HE MEANS ANY HARM.
YEAH.
"YEAH" ?!
THAT'S ALL?
BAM
HE SAID SOMETHING HORRIBLE TO YOU AFTER I LEFT THE ROOM, RIGHT?!
THAT GUY DOESN'T HOLD BACK AT ALL!
EVEN IF HE DID...
...I'D NEVER TELL YOU TO PICK A FIGHT WITH YOUR BROTHER, ZEN.

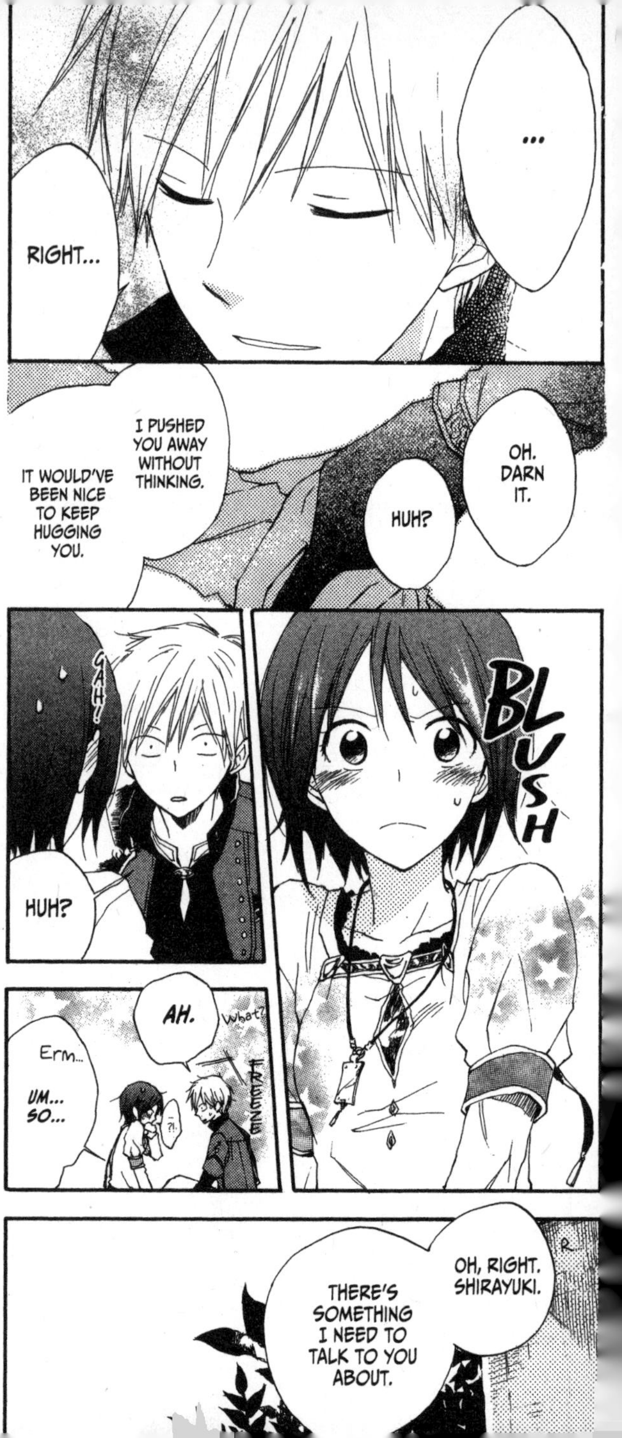
...
RIGHT...
OH. DARN IT.
HUH?
I PUSHED YOU AWAY WITHOUT THINKING.
IT WOULD'VE BEEN NICE TO KEEP HUGGING YOU.
BLUSH
GAH!
HUH?
AH.
What?
FREEZE
Erm...
UM... SO...
...?!
OH, RIGHT. SHIRAYUKI.
THERE'S SOMETHING I NEED TO TALK TO YOU ABOUT.

Chapter 9

Chapter 9 gets the plot rolling. It contains what I call the "Raj Shock."

Raj's tendency to act on a whim actually makes my life as the writer easier. Though none of the other characters give him a warm welcome. Cheer up, idiot prince.

Also, the ink tone I use on Raj's vest is nicknamed "Raj Vest."

Even if that tone is used somewhere that has nothing to do with him, I'll write, "Use Raj Vest here."

The product number is IC Screen S-458.

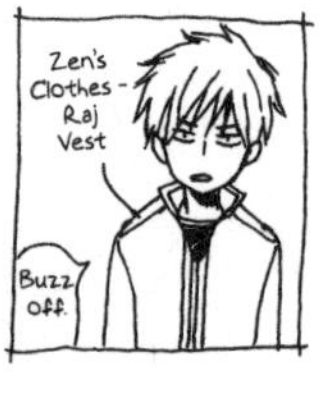
Zen's Clothes - Raj Vest
Buzz off.

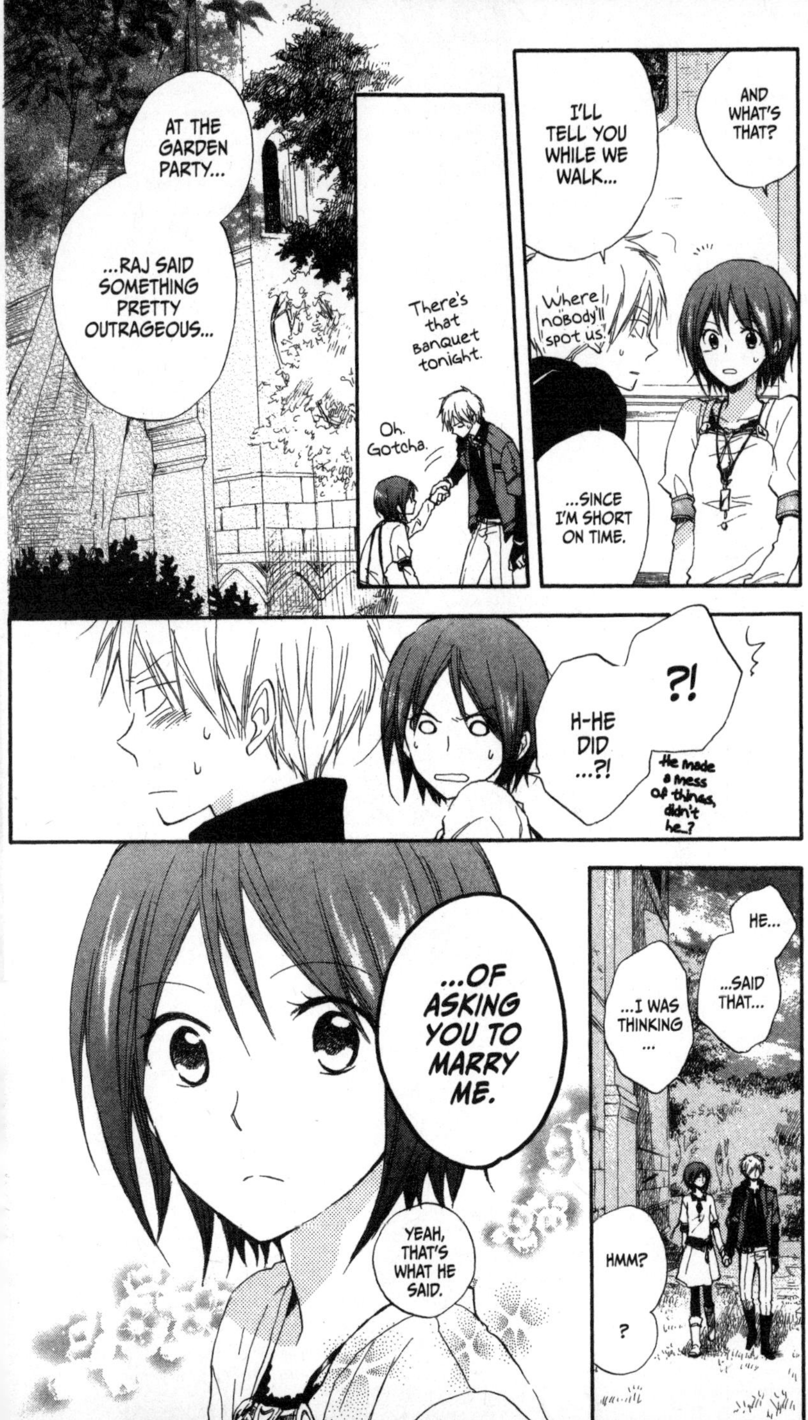
AND WHAT'S THAT?
I'LL TELL YOU WHILE WE WALK...
Where nobody'll spot us.
...SINCE I'M SHORT ON TIME.
There's that banquet tonight.
Oh. Gotcha.
AT THE GARDEN PARTY...
...RAJ SAID SOMETHING PRETTY OUTRAGEOUS...
?!
H-HE DID ...?!
He made a mess of things, didn't he...?
HE...
...SAID THAT...
...I WAS THINKING ...
HMM?
?
...OF ASKING YOU TO MARRY ME.
YEAH, THAT'S WHAT HE SAID.

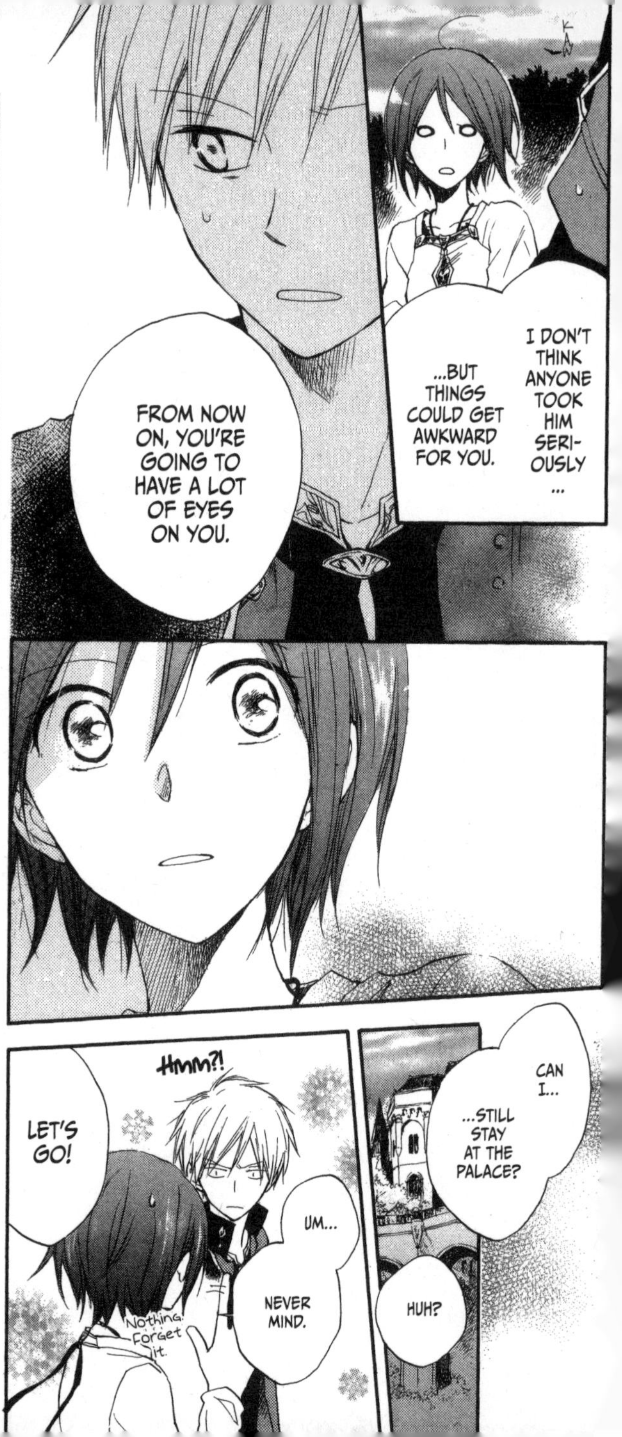
KAN
I DON'T THINK ANYONE TOOK HIM SERIOUSLY...
...BUT THINGS COULD GET AWKWARD FOR YOU.
FROM NOW ON, YOU'RE GOING TO HAVE A LOT OF EYES ON YOU.
CAN I...
...STILL STAY AT THE PALACE?
HUH?
HMM?!
LET'S GO!
UM...
NEVER MIND.
Nothing. Forget it.

Chapter 10

I had my big sister model sword poses for me...

...with a replica of Isami Kondo's Kotetsu blade...

It was super heavy so she wasn't happy about it. But it's just so elegant... Not that the swords used in this manga are Japanese katana anyway, but still...

I actually tend to prioritize the way I think poses should look over what people can actually do, so I kept making these unreasonable requests until she got angry with me.

Sorry, sis. Hope you'll help me out again sometime!

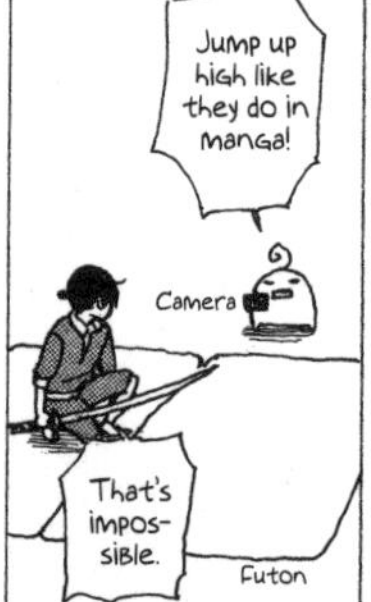
Jump up high like they do in manga!
Camera
That's impos-sible.
Futon

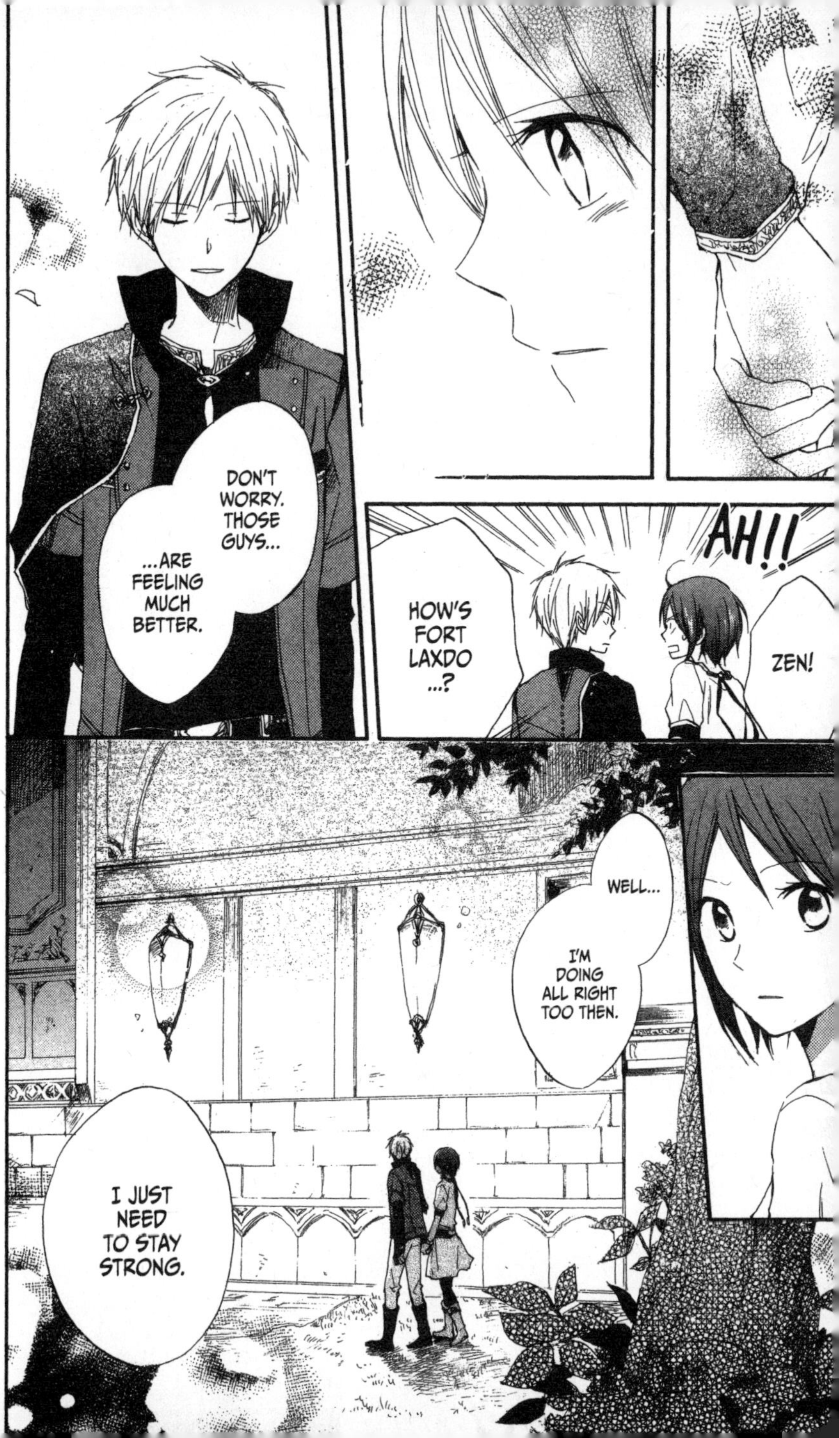
AH!!
ZEN!
HOW'S FORT LAXDO ...?
DON'T WORRY. THOSE GUYS...
...ARE FEELING MUCH BETTER.
WELL...
I'M DOING ALL RIGHT TOO THEN.
I JUST NEED TO STAY STRONG.

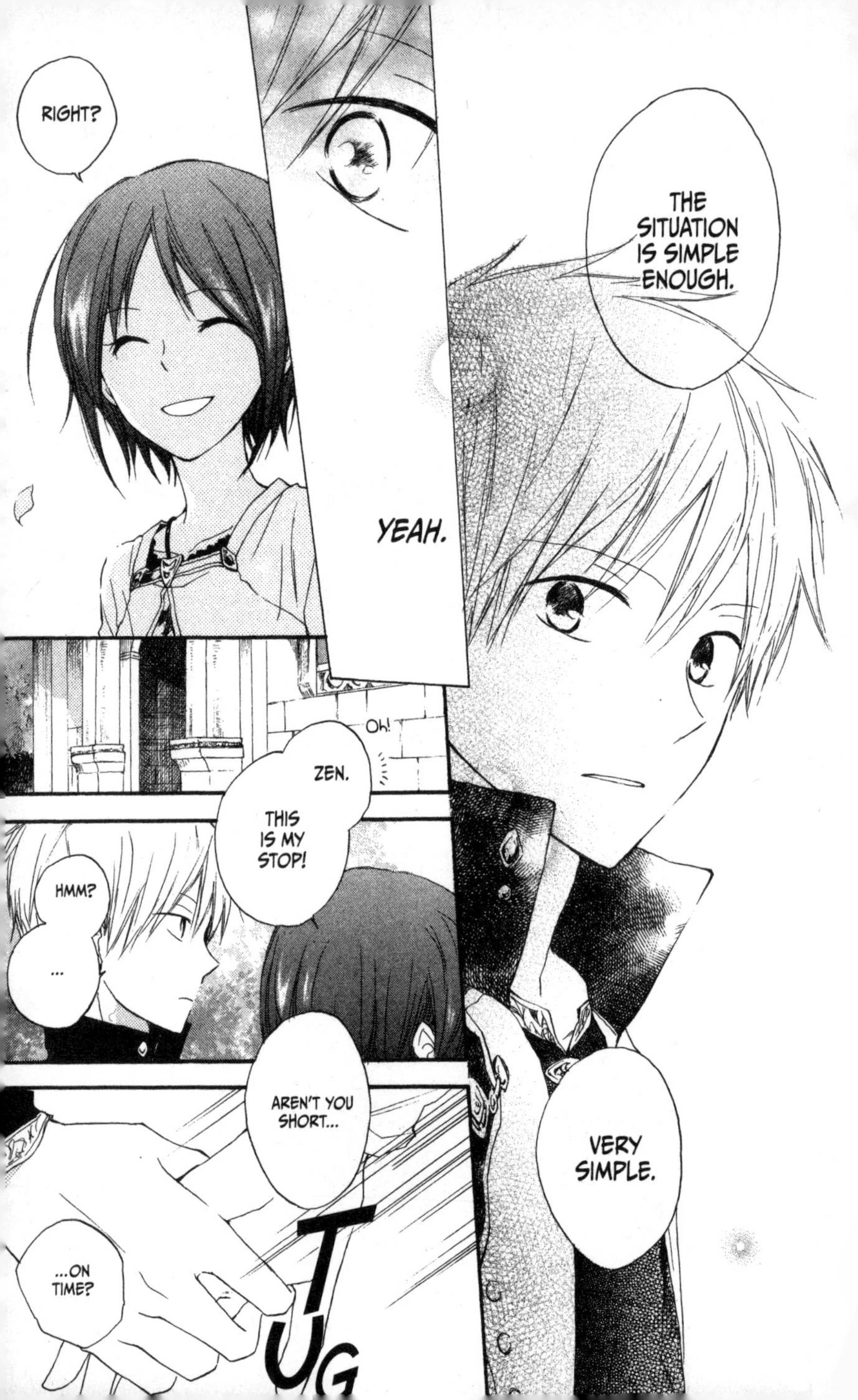
THE SITUATION IS SIMPLE ENOUGH.
VERY SIMPLE.
YEAH.
RIGHT?
OH!
ZEN.
THIS IS MY STOP!
HMM?
...
AREN'T YOU SHORT...
...ON TIME?
TUG

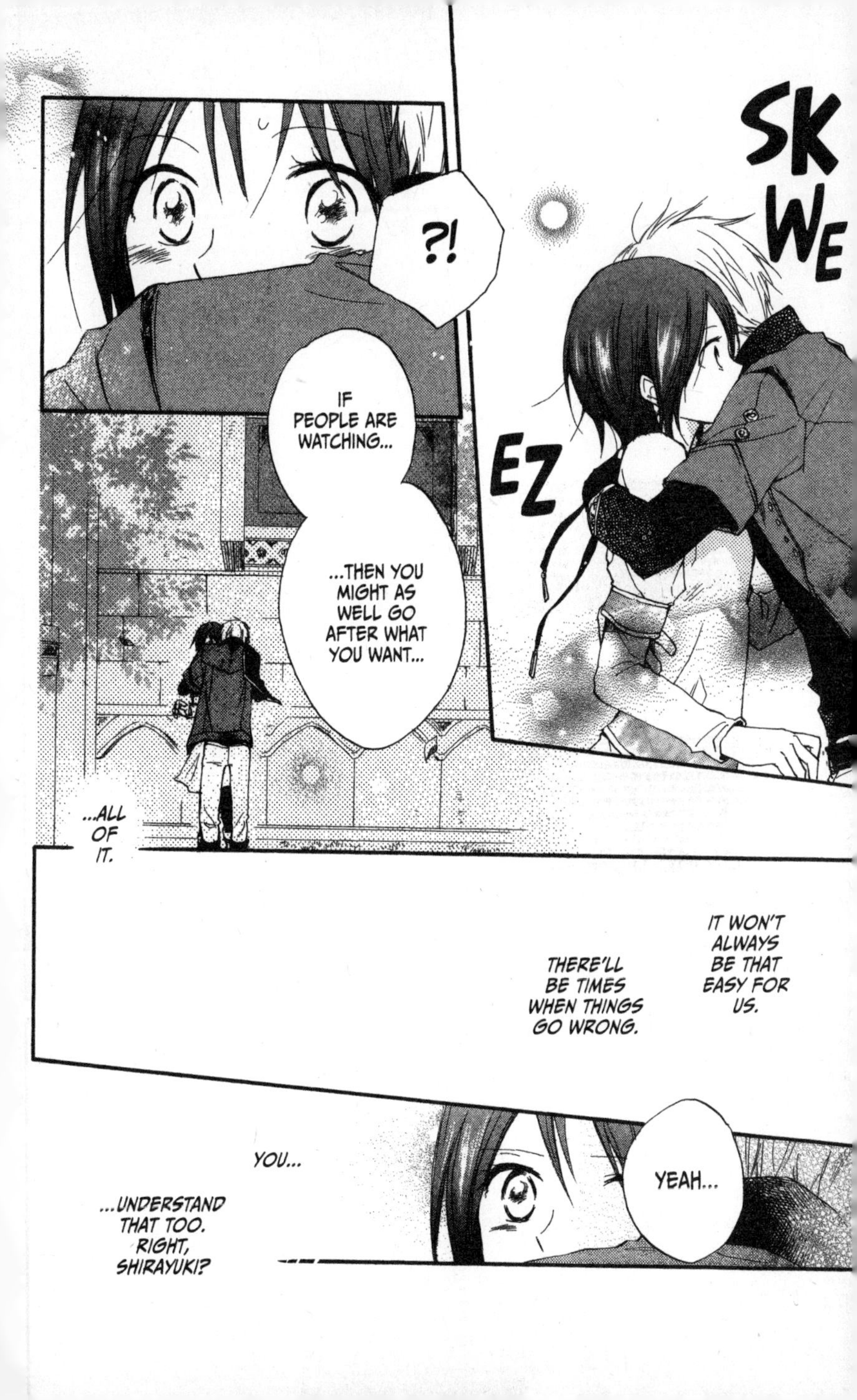
SKWEEZ
?!
IF PEOPLE ARE WATCHING...
...THEN YOU MIGHT AS WELL GO AFTER WHAT YOU WANT...
...ALL OF IT.
IT WON'T ALWAYS BE THAT EASY FOR US.
THERE'LL BE TIMES WHEN THINGS GO WRONG.
YEAH...
YOU...
...UNDERSTAND THAT TOO. RIGHT, SHIRAYUKI?

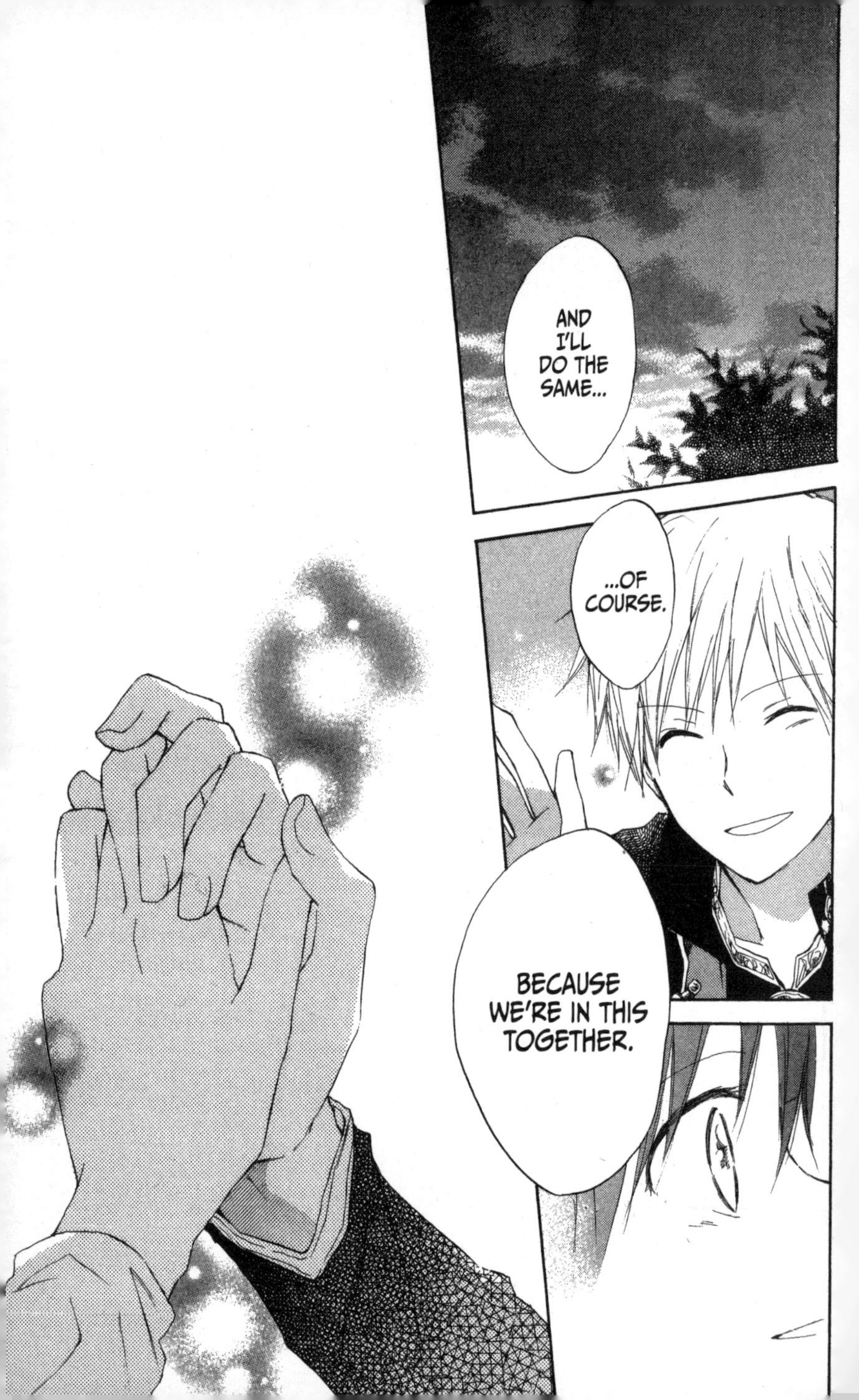
AND I'LL DO THE SAME...
...OF COURSE.
BECAUSE WE'RE IN THIS TOGETHER.

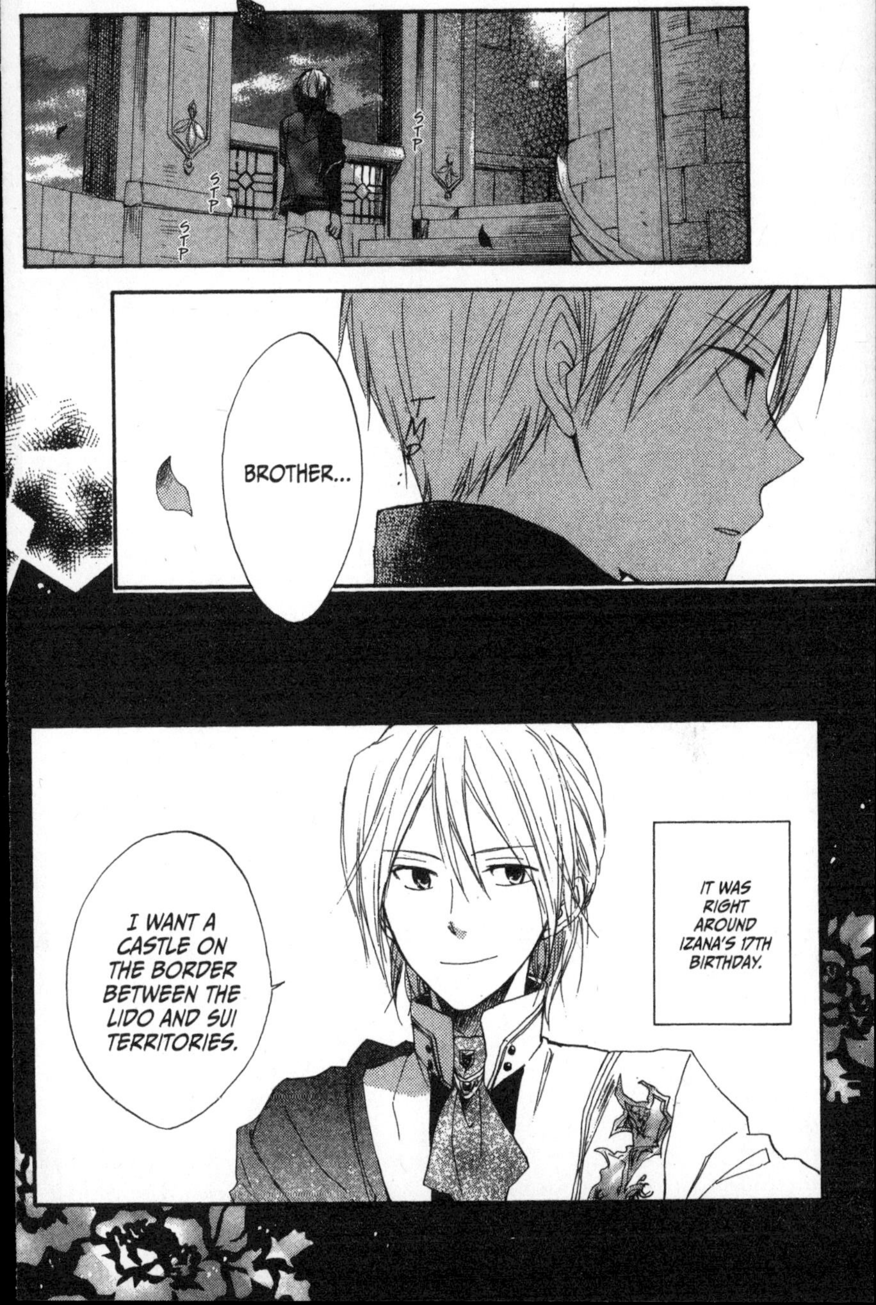
STP
STP
STP
BROTHER...
IT WAS RIGHT AROUND IZANA'S 17TH BIRTHDAY.
I WANT A CASTLE ON THE BORDER BETWEEN THE LIDO AND SUI TERRITORIES.

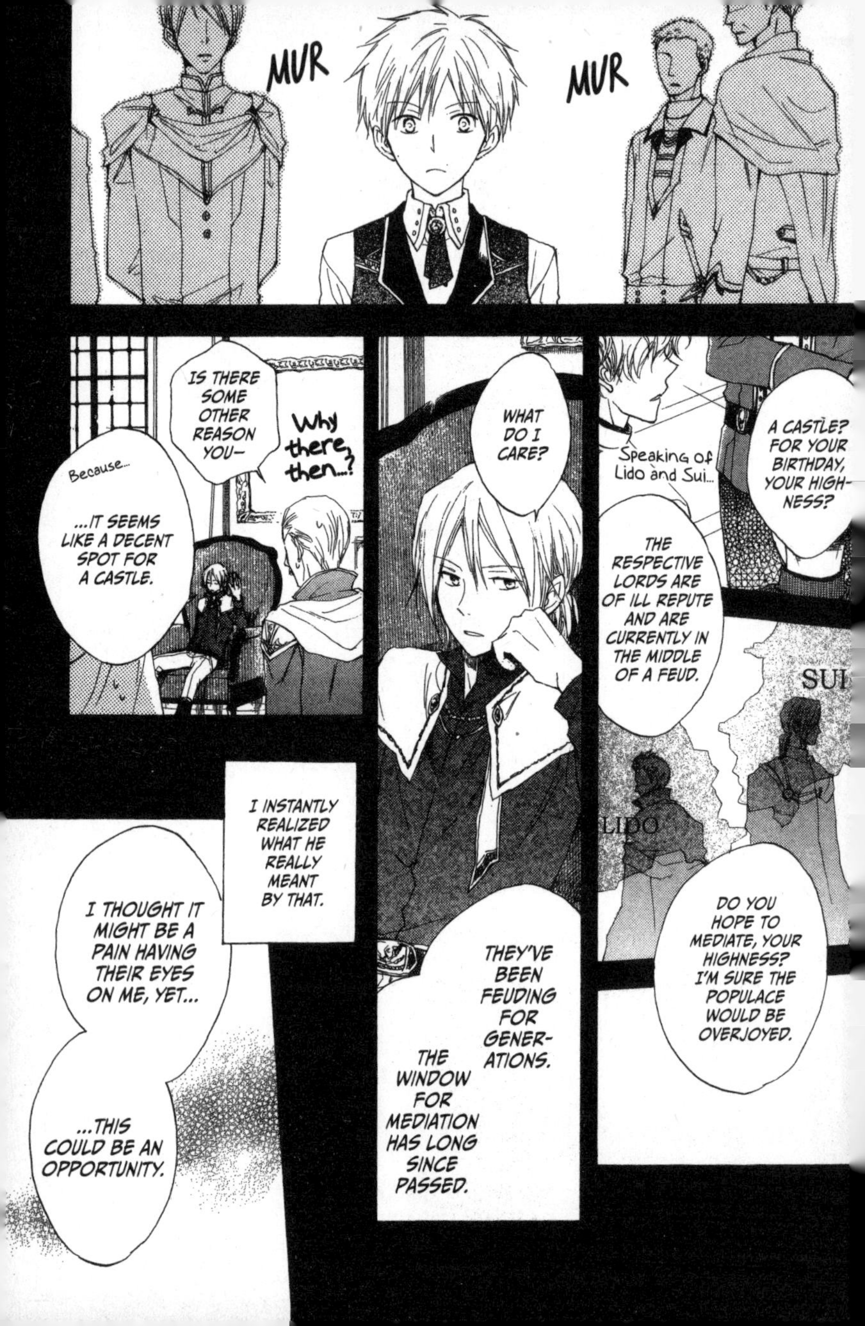
MUR
MUR
A CASTLE? FOR YOUR BIRTHDAY, YOUR HIGHNESS?
Speaking of Lido and Sui...
THE RESPECTIVE LORDS ARE OF ILL REPUTE AND ARE CURRENTLY IN THE MIDDLE OF A FEUD.
SUI
LIDO
DO YOU HOPE TO MEDIATE, YOUR HIGHNESS? I'M SURE THE POPULACE WOULD BE OVERJOYED.
WHAT DO I CARE?
THEY'VE BEEN FEUDING FOR GENER-ATIONS.
THE WINDOW FOR MEDIATION HAS LONG SINCE PASSED.
IS THERE SOME OTHER REASON YOU—
Why there, then...?
Because...
...IT SEEMS LIKE A DECENT SPOT FOR A CASTLE.
I INSTANTLY REALIZED WHAT HE REALLY MEANT BY THAT.
I THOUGHT IT MIGHT BE A PAIN HAVING THEIR EYES ON ME, YET...
...THIS COULD BE AN OPPORTUNITY.

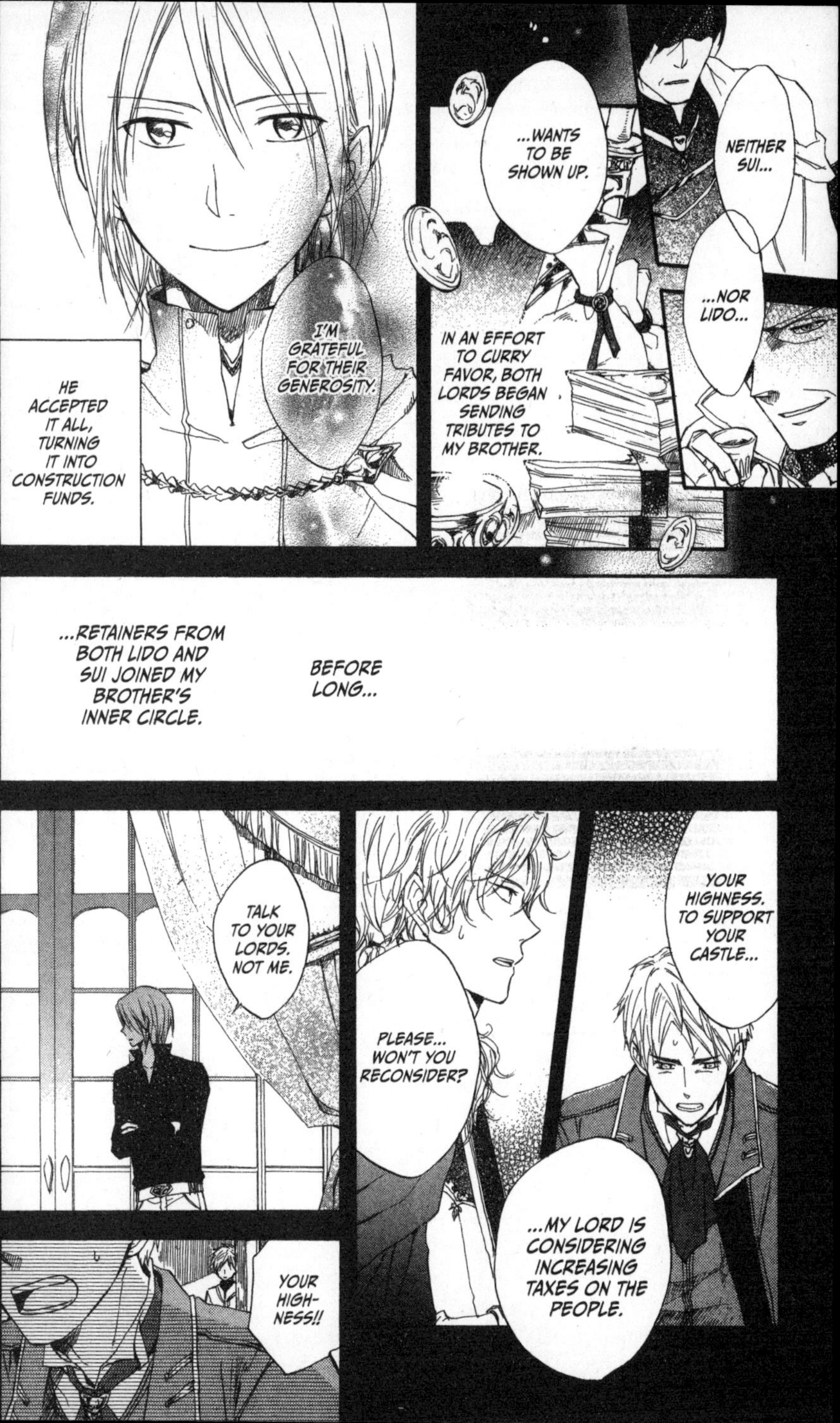
NEITHER SUI...
...NOR LIDO...
...WANTS TO BE SHOWN UP.
IN AN EFFORT TO CURRY FAVOR, BOTH LORDS BEGAN SENDING TRIBUTES TO MY BROTHER.
I'M GRATEFUL FOR THEIR GENEROSITY.
HE ACCEPTED IT ALL, TURNING IT INTO CONSTRUCTION FUNDS.
BEFORE LONG...
...RETAINERS FROM BOTH LIDO AND SUI JOINED MY BROTHER'S INNER CIRCLE.
YOUR HIGHNESS. TO SUPPORT YOUR CASTLE...
...MY LORD IS CONSIDERING INCREASING TAXES ON THE PEOPLE.
PLEASE... WON'T YOU RECONSIDER?
TALK TO YOUR LORDS. NOT ME.
YOUR HIGH-NESS!!

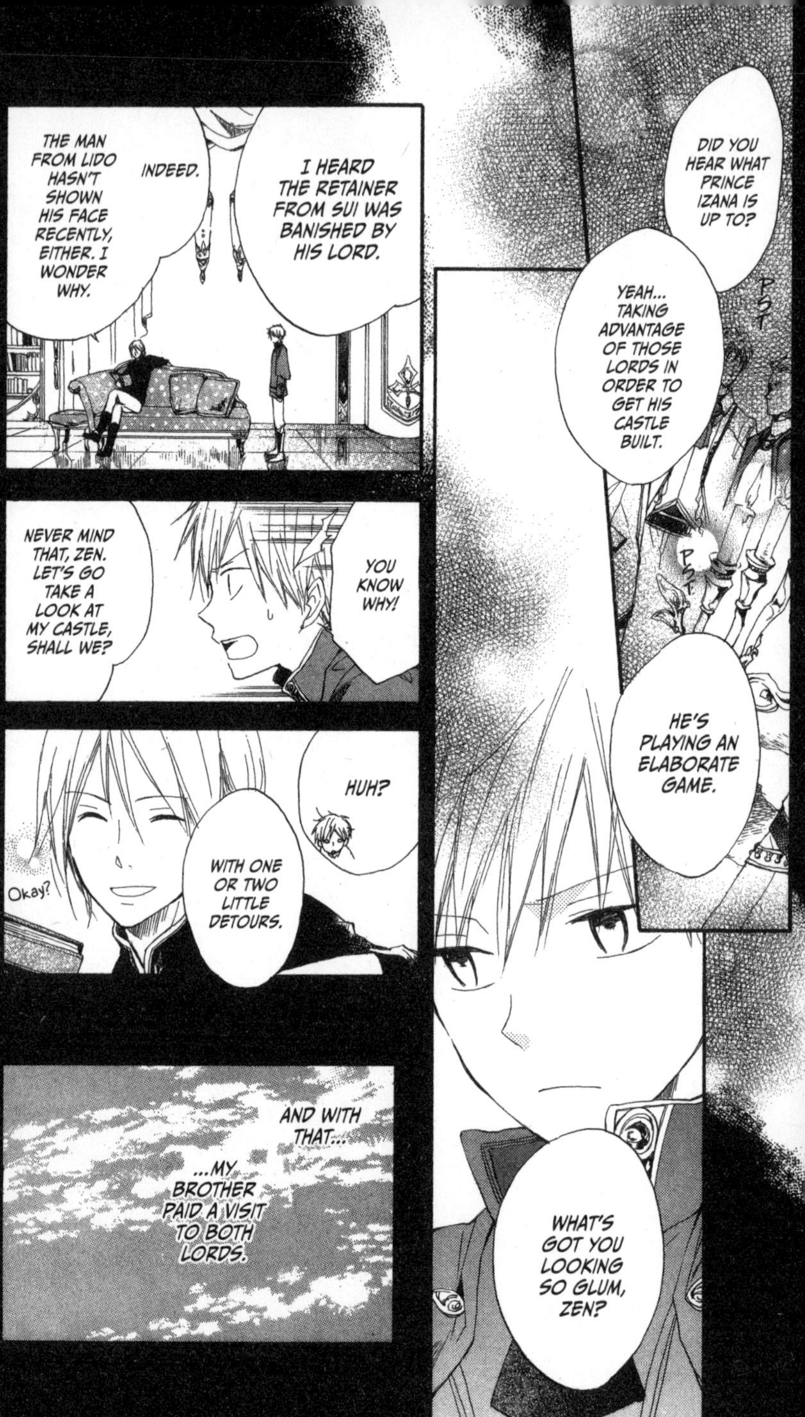
DID YOU HEAR WHAT PRINCE IZANA IS UP TO?
PST
YEAH... TAKING ADVANTAGE OF THOSE LORDS IN ORDER TO GET HIS CASTLE BUILT.
PST
HE'S PLAYING AN ELABORATE GAME.
WHAT'S GOT YOU LOOKING SO GLUM, ZEN?
I HEARD THE RETAINER FROM SUI WAS BANISHED BY HIS LORD.
INDEED.
THE MAN FROM LIDO HASN'T SHOWN HIS FACE RECENTLY, EITHER. I WONDER WHY.
YOU KNOW WHY!
NEVER MIND THAT, ZEN. LET'S GO TAKE A LOOK AT MY CASTLE, SHALL WE?
HUH?
WITH ONE OR TWO LITTLE DETOURS.
Okay?
AND WITH THAT...
...MY BROTHER PAID A VISIT TO BOTH LORDS.

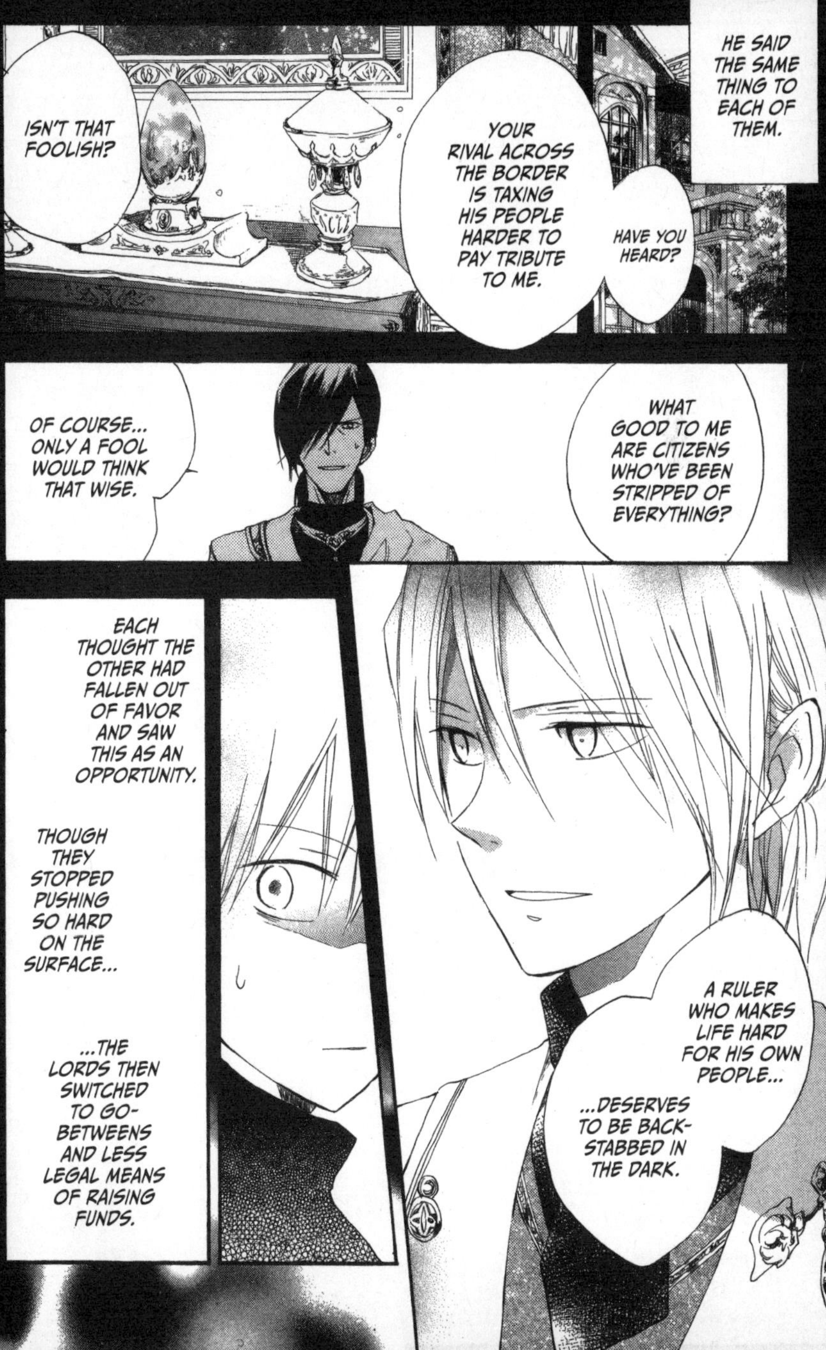
HE SAID THE SAME THING TO EACH OF THEM.
HAVE YOU HEARD?
YOUR RIVAL ACROSS THE BORDER IS TAXING HIS PEOPLE HARDER TO PAY TRIBUTE TO ME.
ISN'T THAT FOOLISH?
WHAT GOOD TO ME ARE CITIZENS WHO'VE BEEN STRIPPED OF EVERYTHING?
OF COURSE... ONLY A FOOL WOULD THINK THAT WISE.
A RULER WHO MAKES LIFE HARD FOR HIS OWN PEOPLE...
...DESERVES TO BE BACK-STABBED IN THE DARK.
EACH THOUGHT THE OTHER HAD FALLEN OUT OF FAVOR AND SAW THIS AS AN OPPORTUNITY.
THOUGH THEY STOPPED PUSHING SO HARD ON THE SURFACE...
...THE LORDS THEN SWITCHED TO GO-BETWEENS AND LESS LEGAL MEANS OF RAISING FUNDS.

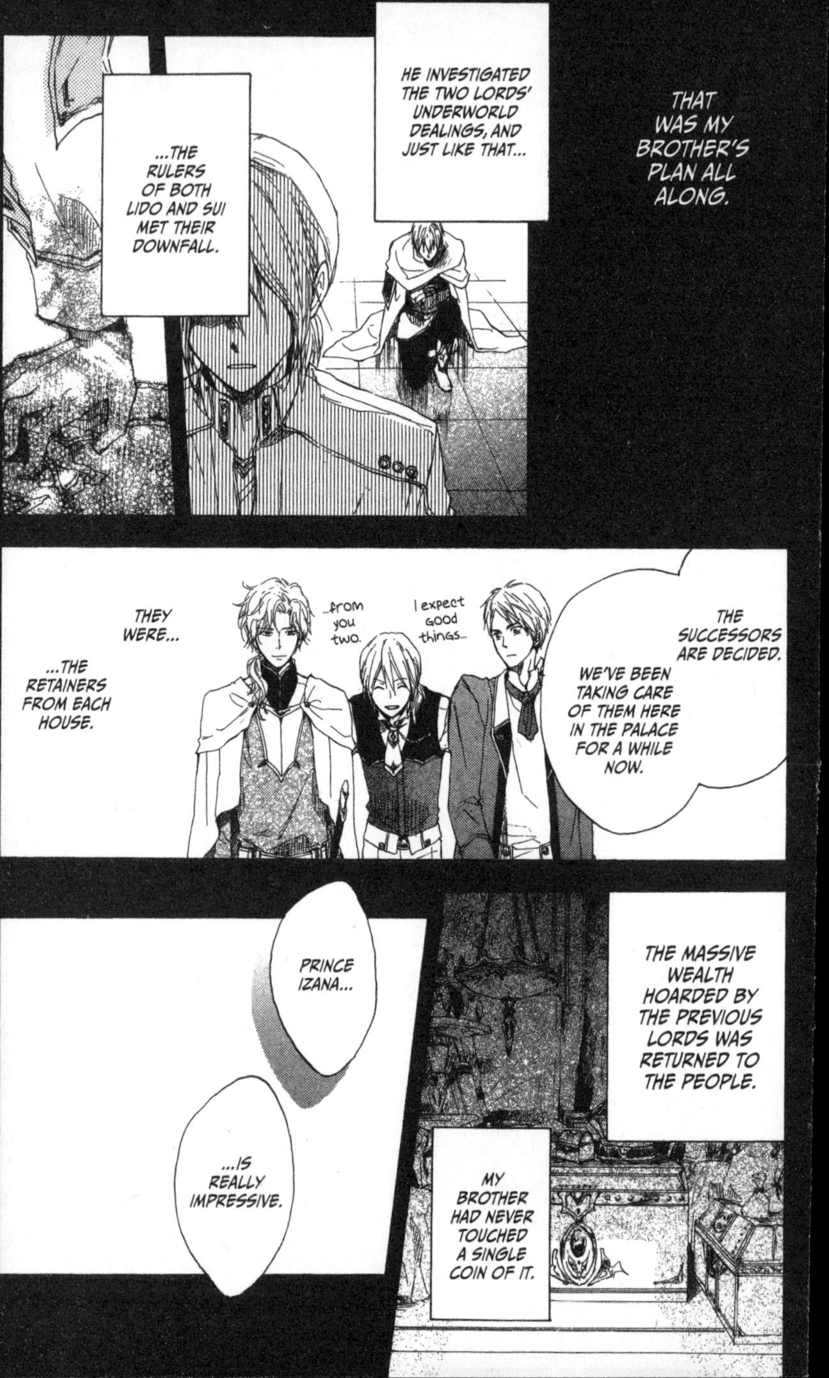
THAT WAS MY BROTHER'S PLAN ALL ALONG.
HE INVESTIGATED THE TWO LORDS' UNDERWORLD DEALINGS, AND JUST LIKE THAT...
...THE RULERS OF BOTH LIDO AND SUI MET THEIR DOWNFALL.
THE SUCCESSORS ARE DECIDED.
WE'VE BEEN TAKING CARE OF THEM HERE IN THE PALACE FOR A WHILE NOW.
I expect good things...
...from you two.
THEY WERE...
...THE RETAINERS FROM EACH HOUSE.
THE MASSIVE WEALTH HOARDED BY THE PREVIOUS LORDS WAS RETURNED TO THE PEOPLE.
MY BROTHER HAD NEVER TOUCHED A SINGLE COIN OF IT.
PRINCE IZANA...
...IS REALLY IMPRESSIVE.

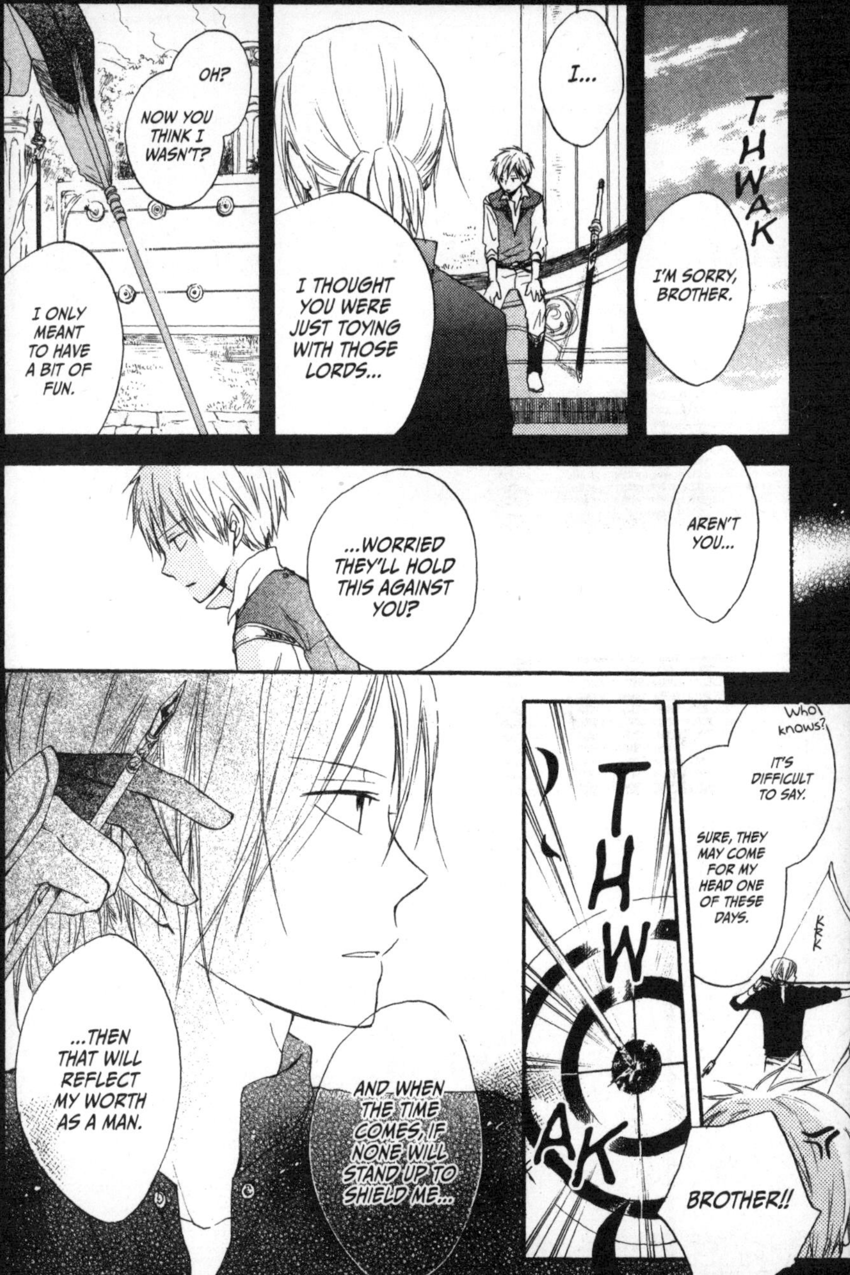
THWAK
I'M SORRY, BROTHER.
I...
I THOUGHT YOU WERE JUST TOYING WITH THOSE LORDS...
OH?
NOW YOU THINK I WASN'T?
I ONLY MEANT TO HAVE A BIT OF FUN.
AREN'T YOU...
...WORRIED THEY'LL HOLD THIS AGAINST YOU?
Who knows?
IT'S DIFFICULT TO SAY.
SURE, THEY MAY COME FOR MY HEAD ONE OF THESE DAYS.
KRK
BROTHER!!
THWAK
AND WHEN THE TIME COMES, IF NONE WILL STAND UP TO SHIELD ME...
...THEN THAT WILL REFLECT MY WORTH AS A MAN.

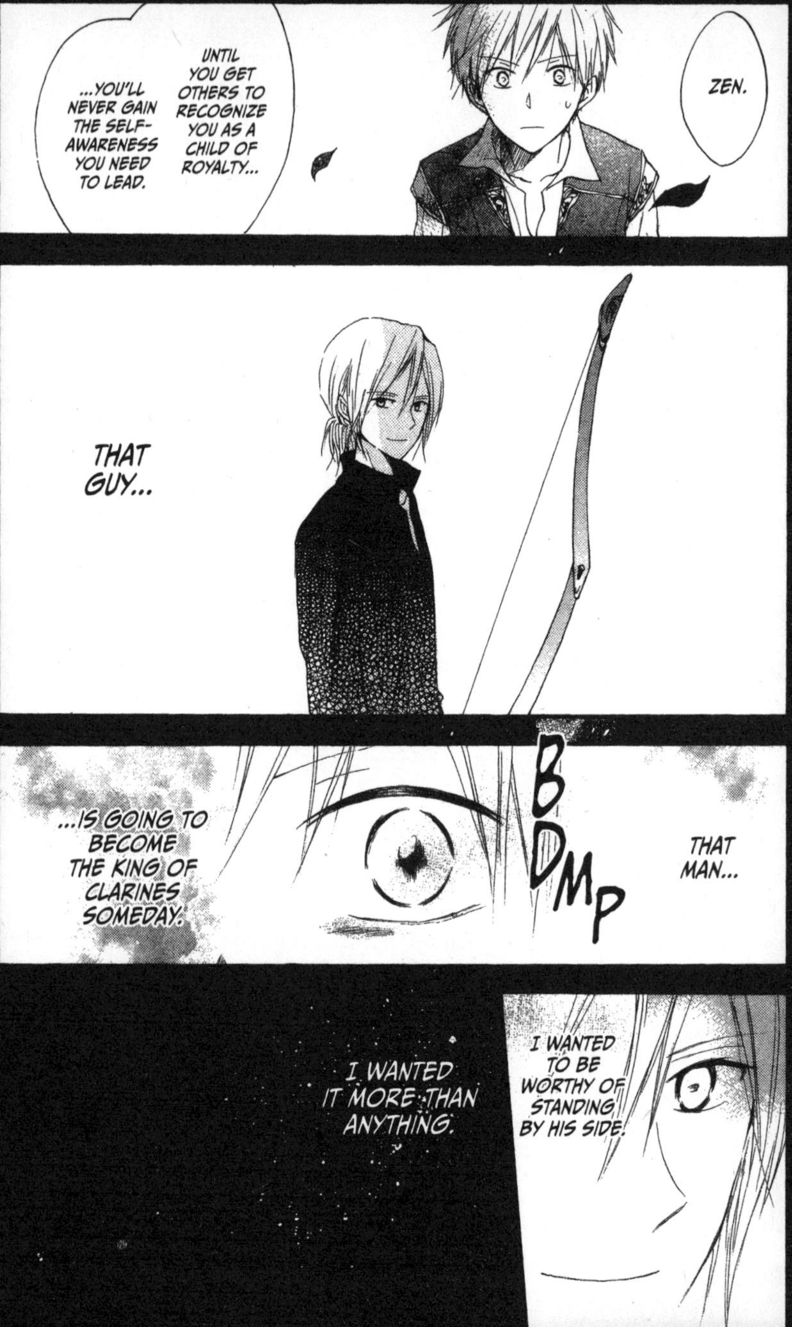
ZEN.
UNTIL YOU GET OTHERS TO RECOGNIZE YOU AS A CHILD OF ROYALTY...
...YOU'LL NEVER GAIN THE SELF-AWARENESS YOU NEED TO LEAD.
THAT GUY...
THAT MAN...
BDMP
...IS GOING TO BECOME THE KING OF CLARINES SOMEDAY.
I WANTED TO BE WORTHY OF STANDING BY HIS SIDE.
I WANTED IT MORE THAN ANYTHING.

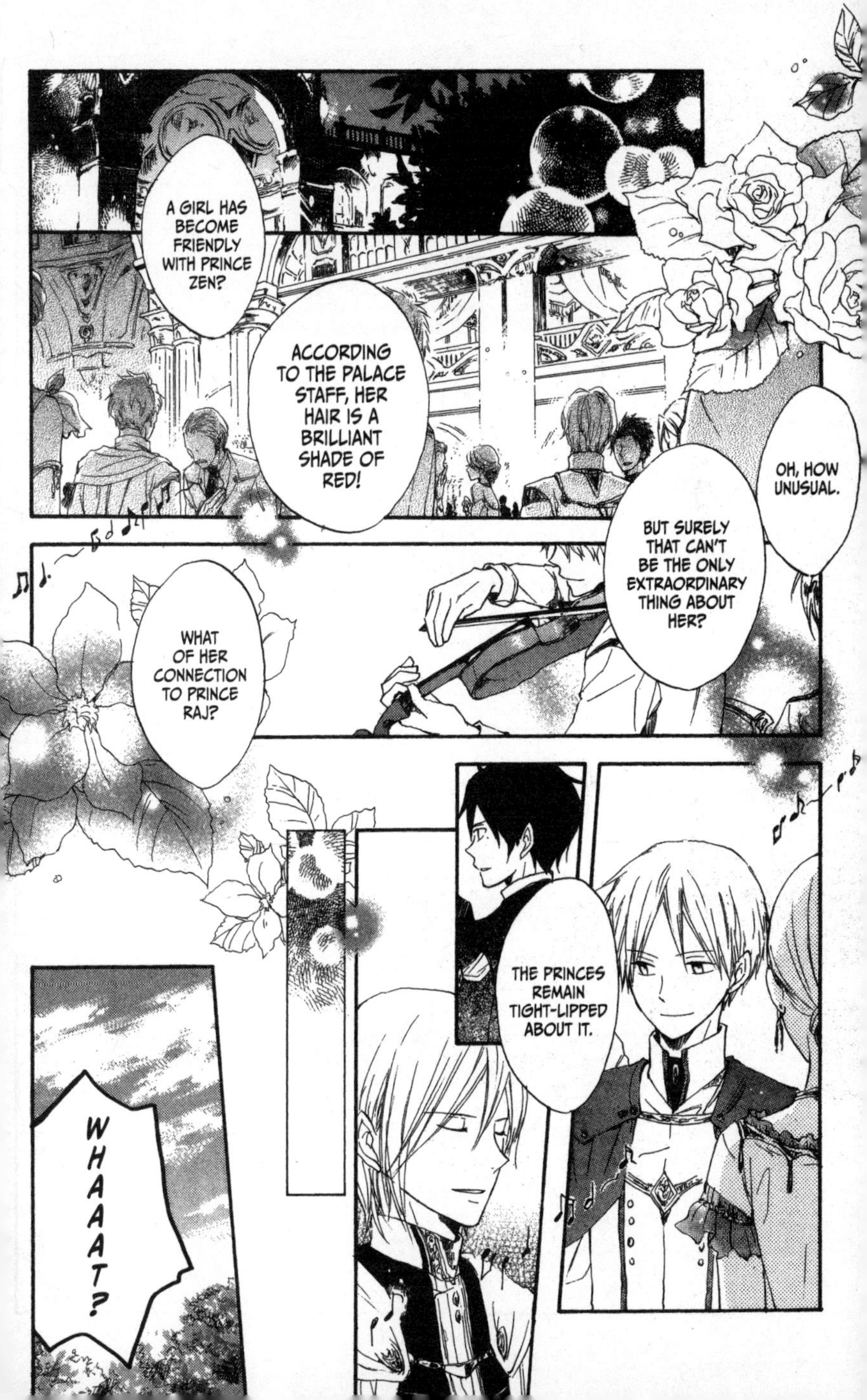
A GIRL HAS BECOME FRIENDLY WITH PRINCE ZEN?
ACCORDING TO THE PALACE STAFF, HER HAIR IS A BRILLIANT SHADE OF RED!
OH, HOW UNUSUAL.
BUT SURELY THAT CAN'T BE THE ONLY EXTRAORDINARY THING ABOUT HER?
WHAT OF HER CONNECTION TO PRINCE RAJ?
THE PRINCES REMAIN TIGHT-LIPPED ABOUT IT.
WHAAAAT?

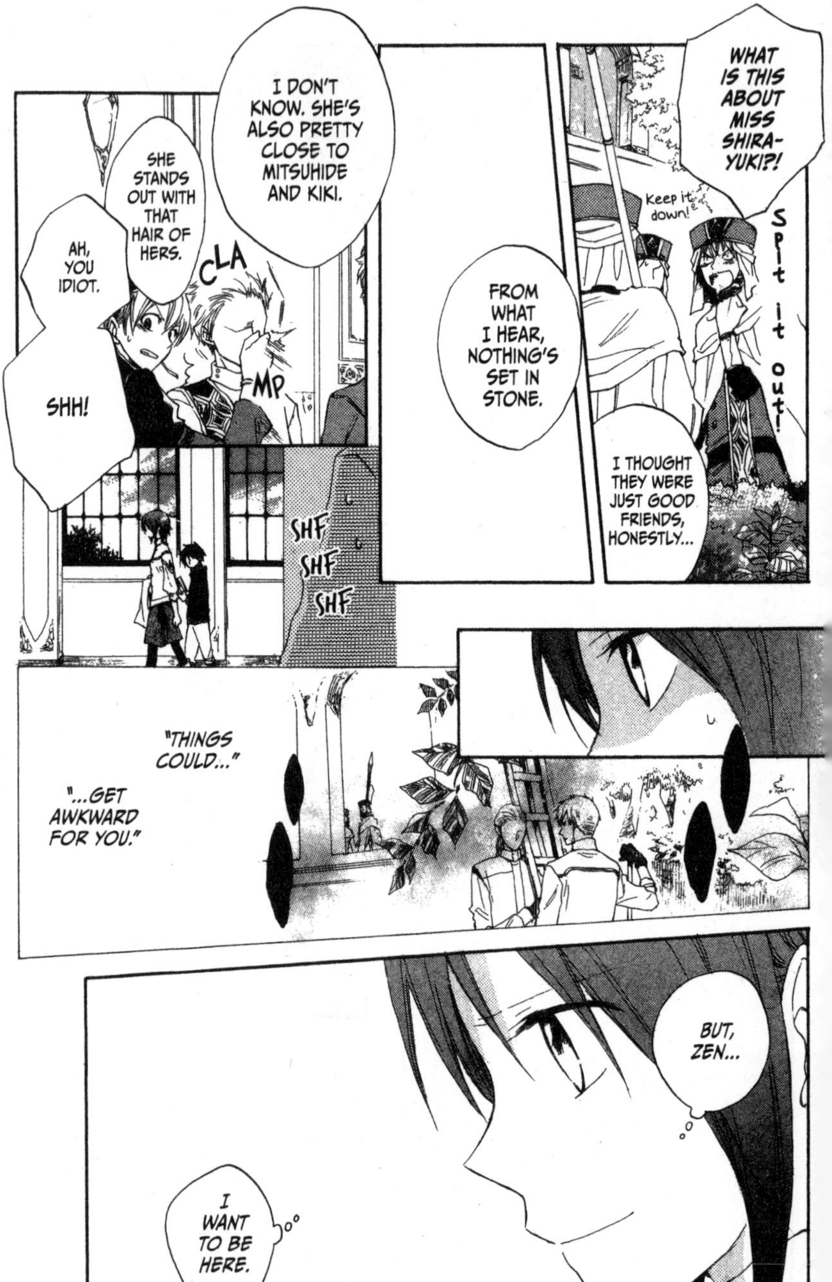
WHAT IS THIS ABOUT MISS SHIRAYUKI?!
Keep it down!
Spit it out!
I THOUGHT THEY WERE JUST GOOD FRIENDS, HONESTLY...
FROM WHAT I HEAR, NOTHING'S SET IN STONE.
I DON'T KNOW. SHE'S ALSO PRETTY CLOSE TO MITSUHIDE AND KIKI.
SHE STANDS OUT WITH THAT HAIR OF HERS.
AH, YOU IDIOT.
CLAMP
SHH!
SHF
SHF
SHF
"THINGS COULD..."
"...GET AWKWARD FOR YOU."
BUT, ZEN...
I WANT TO BE HERE.

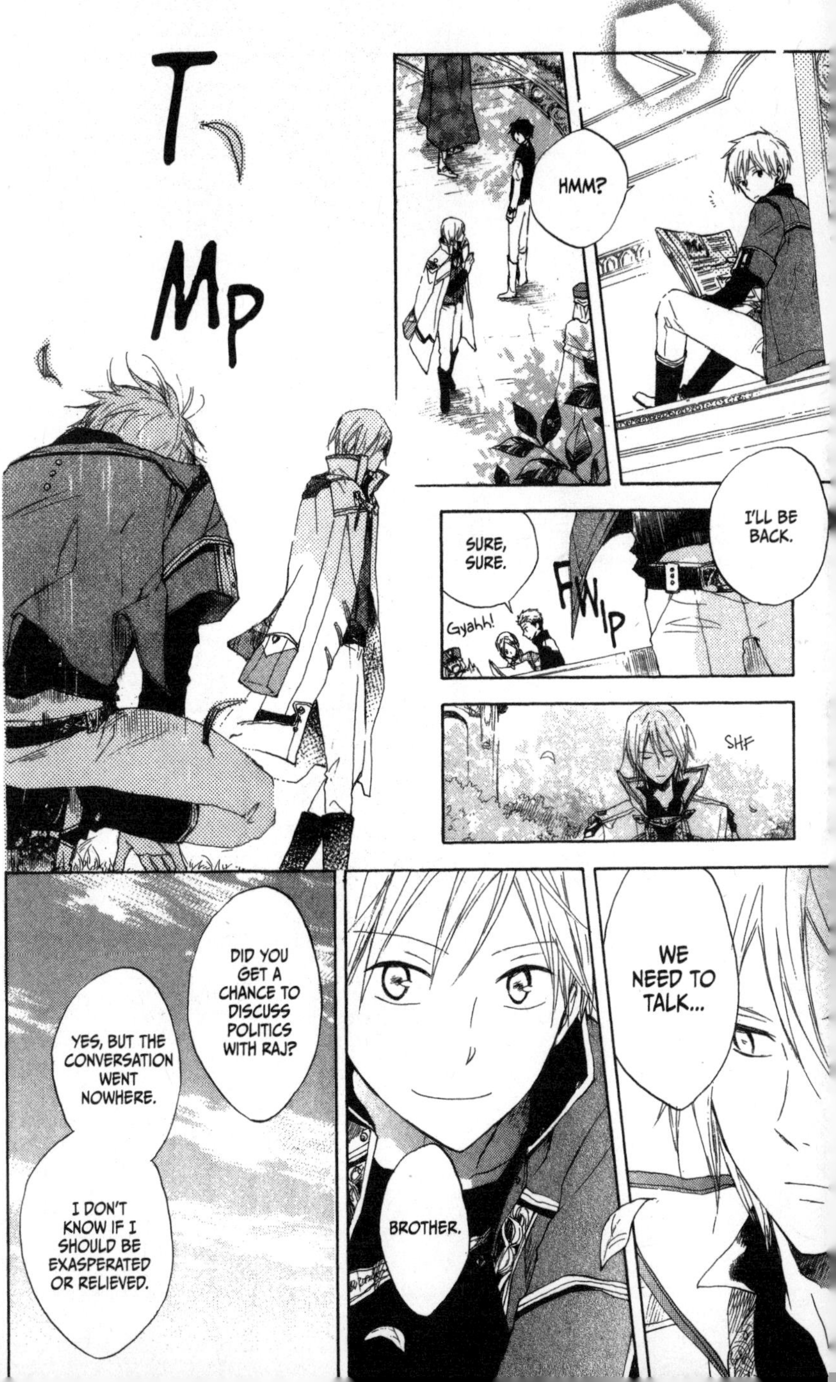
HMM?
I'LL BE BACK.
FWIP
SURE, SURE.
Gyahh!
SHF
TMP
WE NEED TO TALK...
BROTHER.
DID YOU GET A CHANCE TO DISCUSS POLITICS WITH RAJ?
YES, BUT THE CONVERSATION WENT NOWHERE.
I DON'T KNOW IF I SHOULD BE EXASPERATED OR RELIEVED.

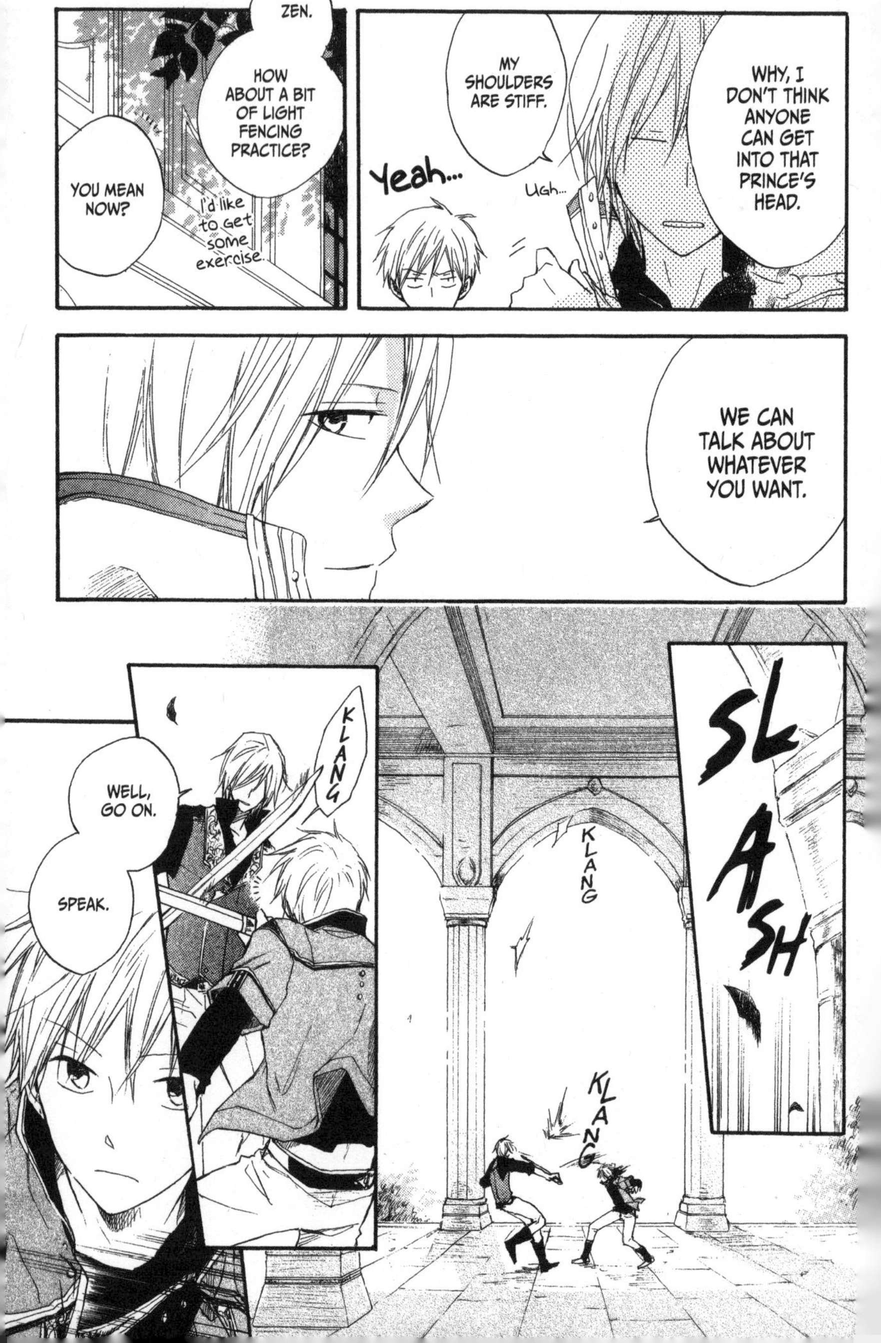
WHY, I DON'T THINK ANYONE CAN GET INTO THAT PRINCE'S HEAD.
Ugh...
MY SHOULDERS ARE STIFF.
Yeah...
ZEN.
HOW ABOUT A BIT OF LIGHT FENCING PRACTICE?
I'd like to get some exercise.
YOU MEAN NOW?
WE CAN TALK ABOUT WHATEVER YOU WANT.
SLASH
KLANG
KLANG
KLANG
WELL, GO ON.
SPEAK.

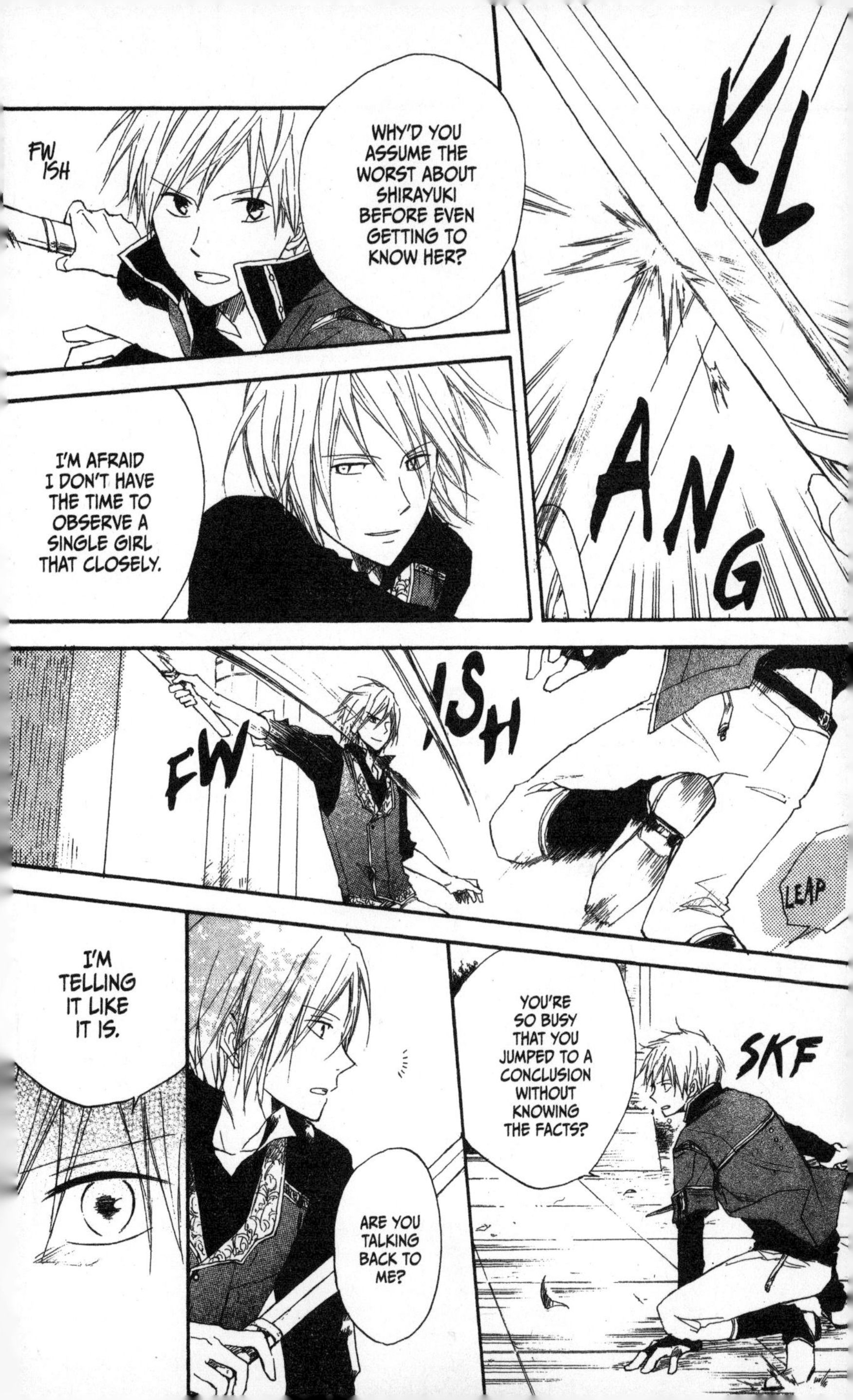
KLANG
WHY'D YOU ASSUME THE WORST ABOUT SHIRAYUKI BEFORE EVEN GETTING TO KNOW HER?
FWISH
I'M AFRAID I DON'T HAVE THE TIME TO OBSERVE A SINGLE GIRL THAT CLOSELY.
FWISH
LEAP
SKF
YOU'RE SO BUSY THAT YOU JUMPED TO A CONCLUSION WITHOUT KNOWING THE FACTS?
ARE YOU TALKING BACK TO ME?
I'M TELLING IT LIKE IT IS.

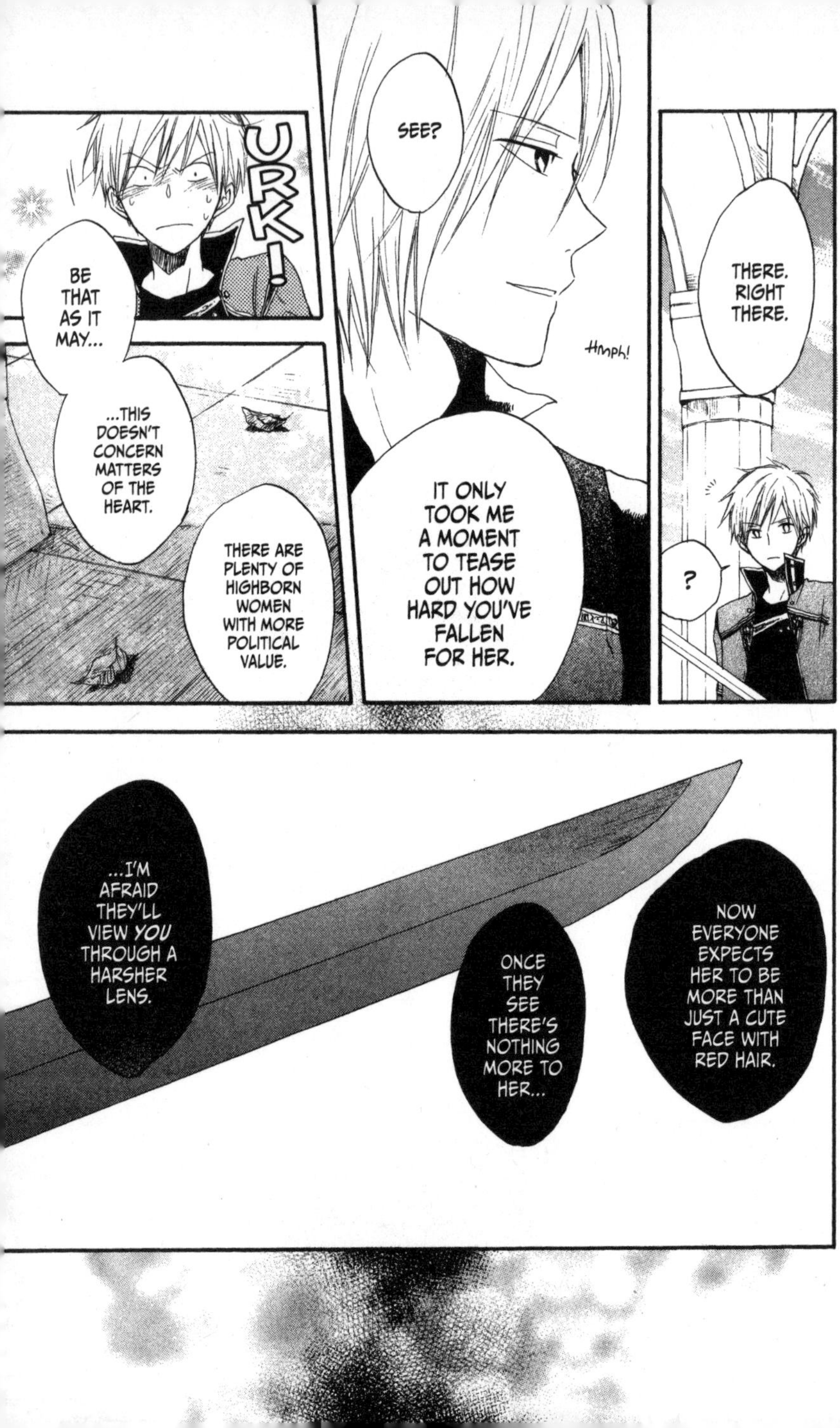
THERE. RIGHT THERE.
?
SEE?
Hmph!
IT ONLY TOOK ME A MOMENT TO TEASE OUT HOW HARD YOU'VE FALLEN FOR HER.
URK!
BE THAT AS IT MAY...
...THIS DOESN'T CONCERN MATTERS OF THE HEART.
THERE ARE PLENTY OF HIGHBORN WOMEN WITH MORE POLITICAL VALUE.
NOW EVERYONE EXPECTS HER TO BE MORE THAN JUST A CUTE FACE WITH RED HAIR.
ONCE THEY SEE THERE'S NOTHING MORE TO HER...
...I'M AFRAID THEY'LL VIEW *YOU* THROUGH A HARSHER LENS.

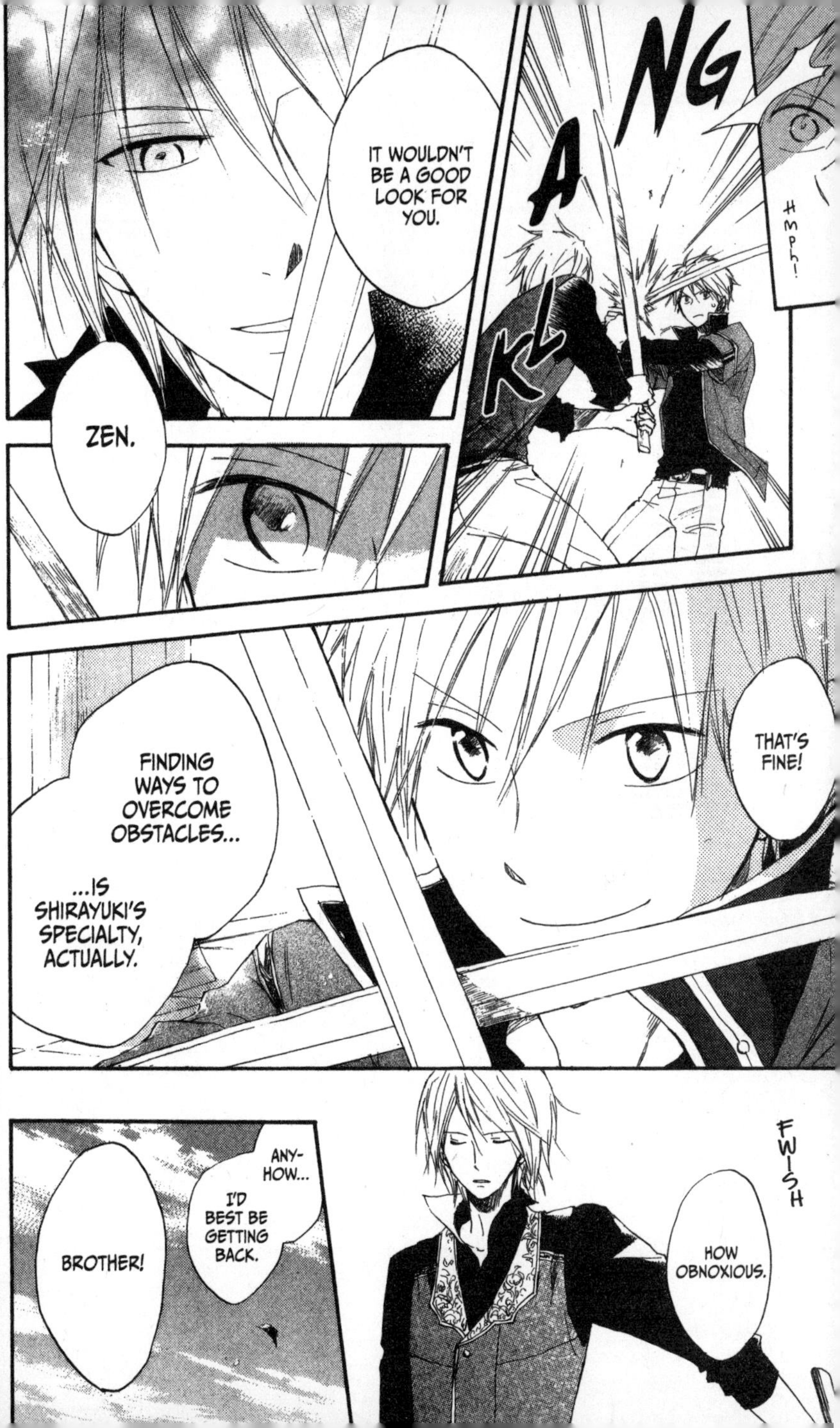
KLANG
Hmph!
IT WOULDN'T BE A GOOD LOOK FOR YOU.
ZEN.
THAT'S FINE!
FINDING WAYS TO OVERCOME OBSTACLES...
...IS SHIRAYUKI'S SPECIALTY, ACTUALLY.
FWISH
HOW OBNOXIOUS.
ANY-HOW...
I'D BEST BE GETTING BACK.
BROTHER!

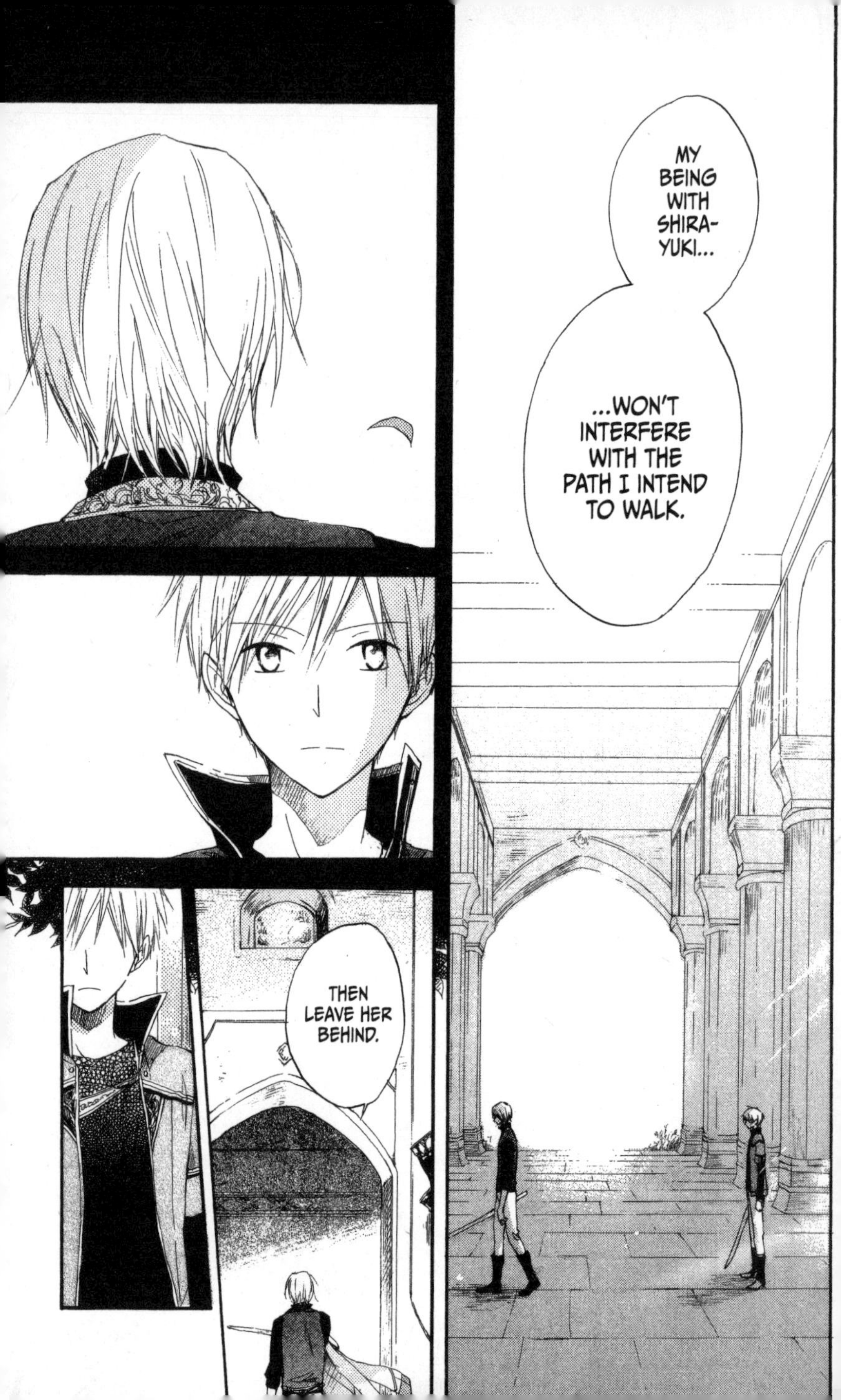
MY BEING WITH SHIRA-YUKI...
...WON'T INTERFERE WITH THE PATH I INTEND TO WALK.
THEN LEAVE HER BEHIND.

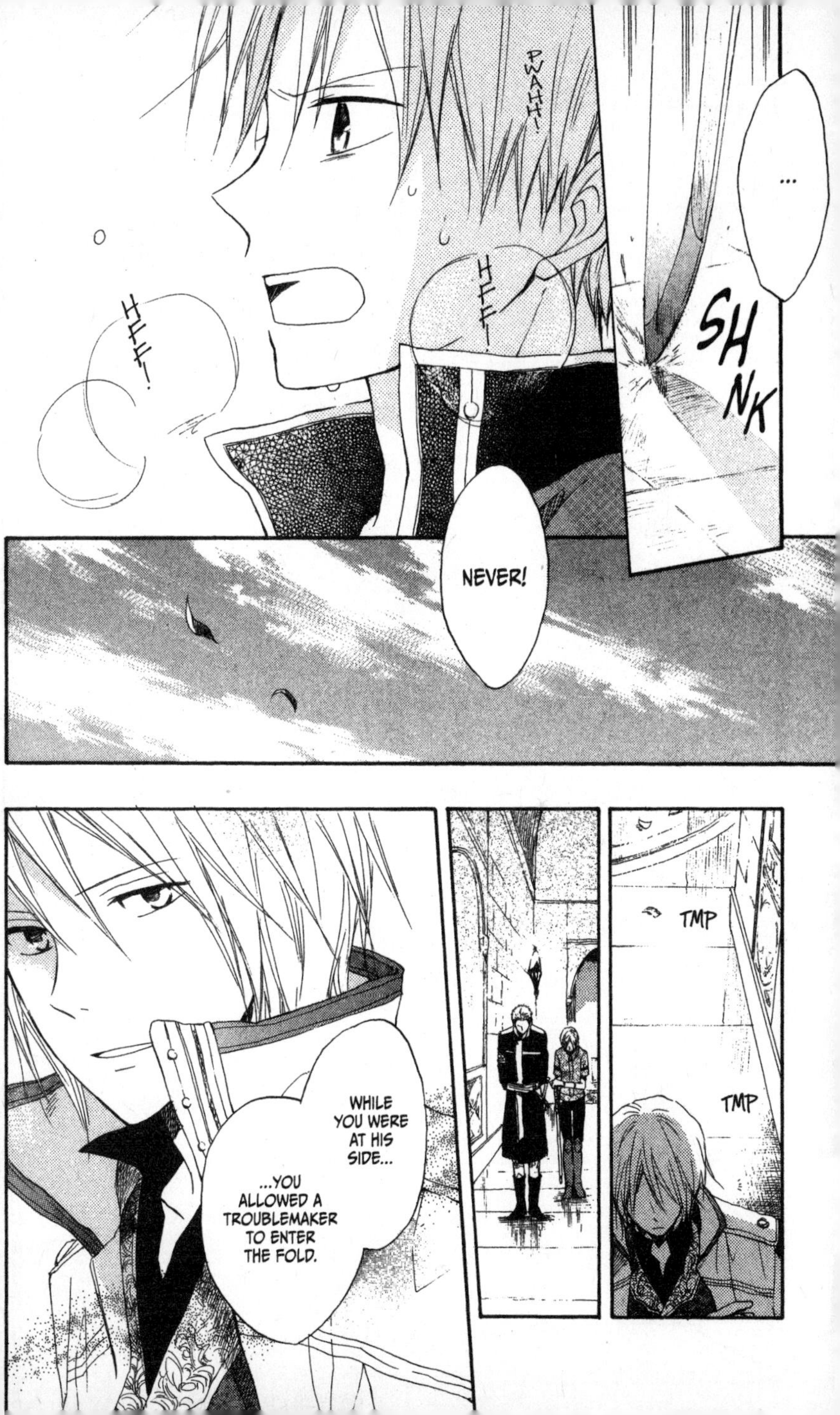
...
SHNK
PWAHH!
HFF!
HFF!
NEVER!
TMP
TMP
WHILE YOU WERE AT HIS SIDE...
...YOU ALLOWED A TROUBLEMAKER TO ENTER THE FOLD.

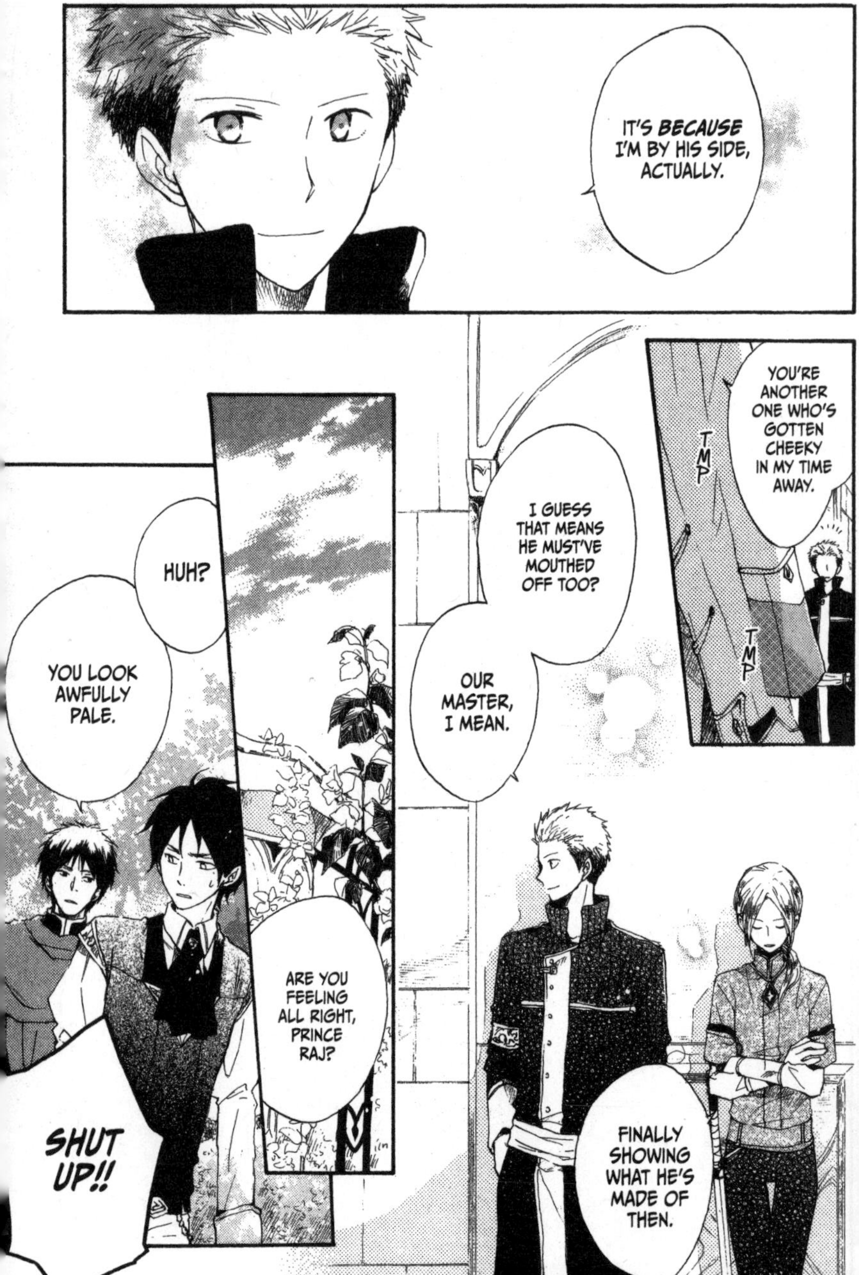
IT'S BECAUSE I'M BY HIS SIDE, ACTUALLY.
YOU'RE ANOTHER ONE WHO'S GOTTEN CHEEKY IN MY TIME AWAY.
TMP
TMP
I GUESS THAT MEANS HE MUST'VE MOUTHED OFF TOO?
OUR MASTER, I MEAN.
FINALLY SHOWING WHAT HE'S MADE OF THEN.
HUH?
YOU LOOK AWFULLY PALE.
ARE YOU FEELING ALL RIGHT, PRINCE RAJ?
SHUT UP!!

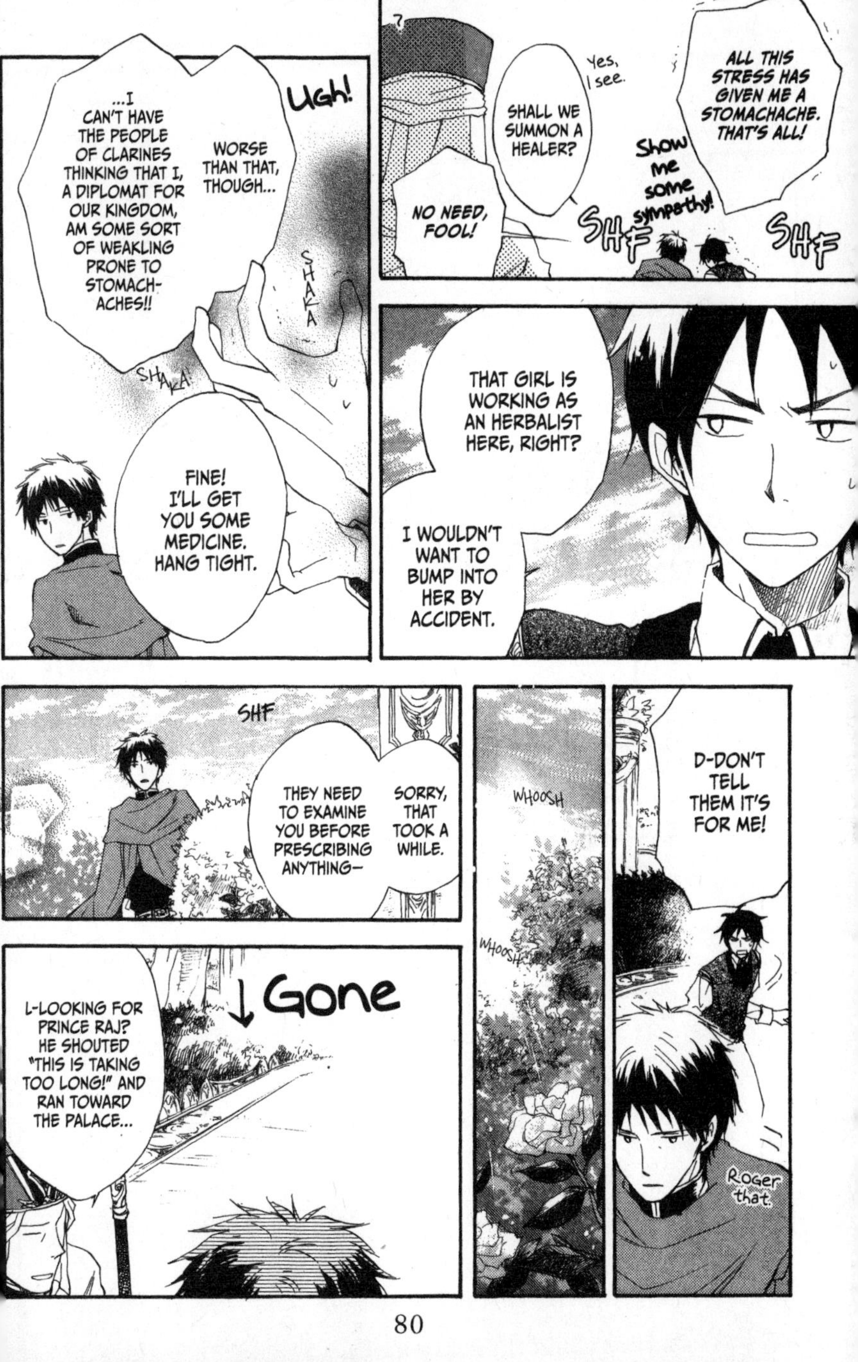
ALL THIS STRESS HAS GIVEN ME A STOMACHACHE. THAT'S ALL!
Show me some sympathy!
SHF
Yes, I see.
SHALL WE SUMMON A HEALER?
SHF
NO NEED, FOOL!
THAT GIRL IS WORKING AS AN HERBALIST HERE, RIGHT?
I WOULDN'T WANT TO BUMP INTO HER BY ACCIDENT.
Ugh!
...I CAN'T HAVE THE PEOPLE OF CLARINES THINKING THAT I, A DIPLOMAT FOR OUR KINGDOM, AM SOME SORT OF WEAKLING PRONE TO STOMACHACHES!!
WORSE THAN THAT, THOUGH...
SHAKA
SHAKA
FINE! I'LL GET YOU SOME MEDICINE. HANG TIGHT.
D-DON'T TELL THEM IT'S FOR ME!
Roger that.
WHOOSH
WHOOSH
SHF
SORRY, THAT TOOK A WHILE.
THEY NEED TO EXAMINE YOU BEFORE PRESCRIBING ANYTHING—
↓Gone
L-LOOKING FOR PRINCE RAJ? HE SHOUTED "THIS IS TAKING TOO LONG!" AND RAN TOWARD THE PALACE...

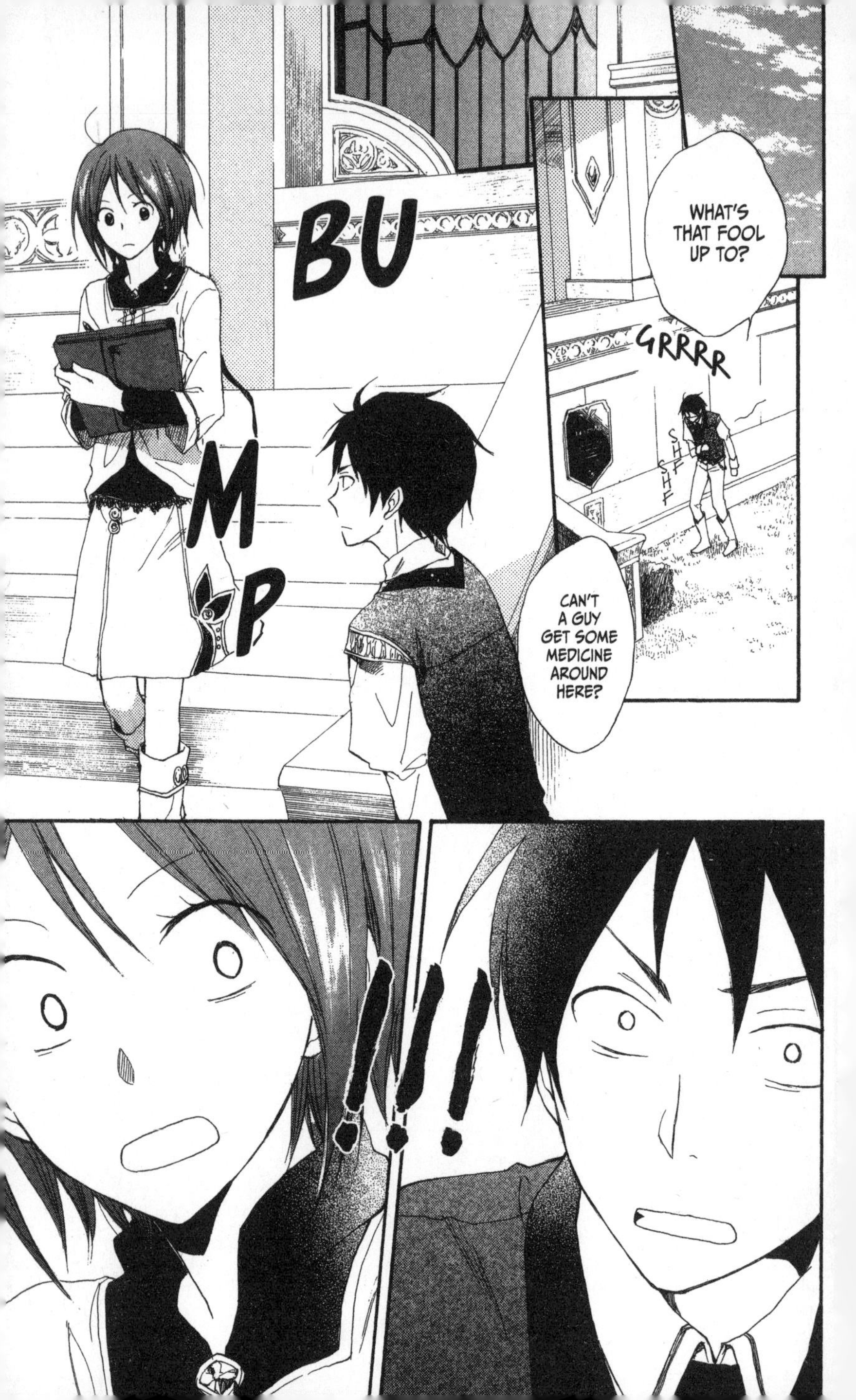
WHAT'S THAT FOOL UP TO?
GRRRR
SHF SHF
CAN'T A GUY GET SOME MEDICINE AROUND HERE?
BUMP
!!!

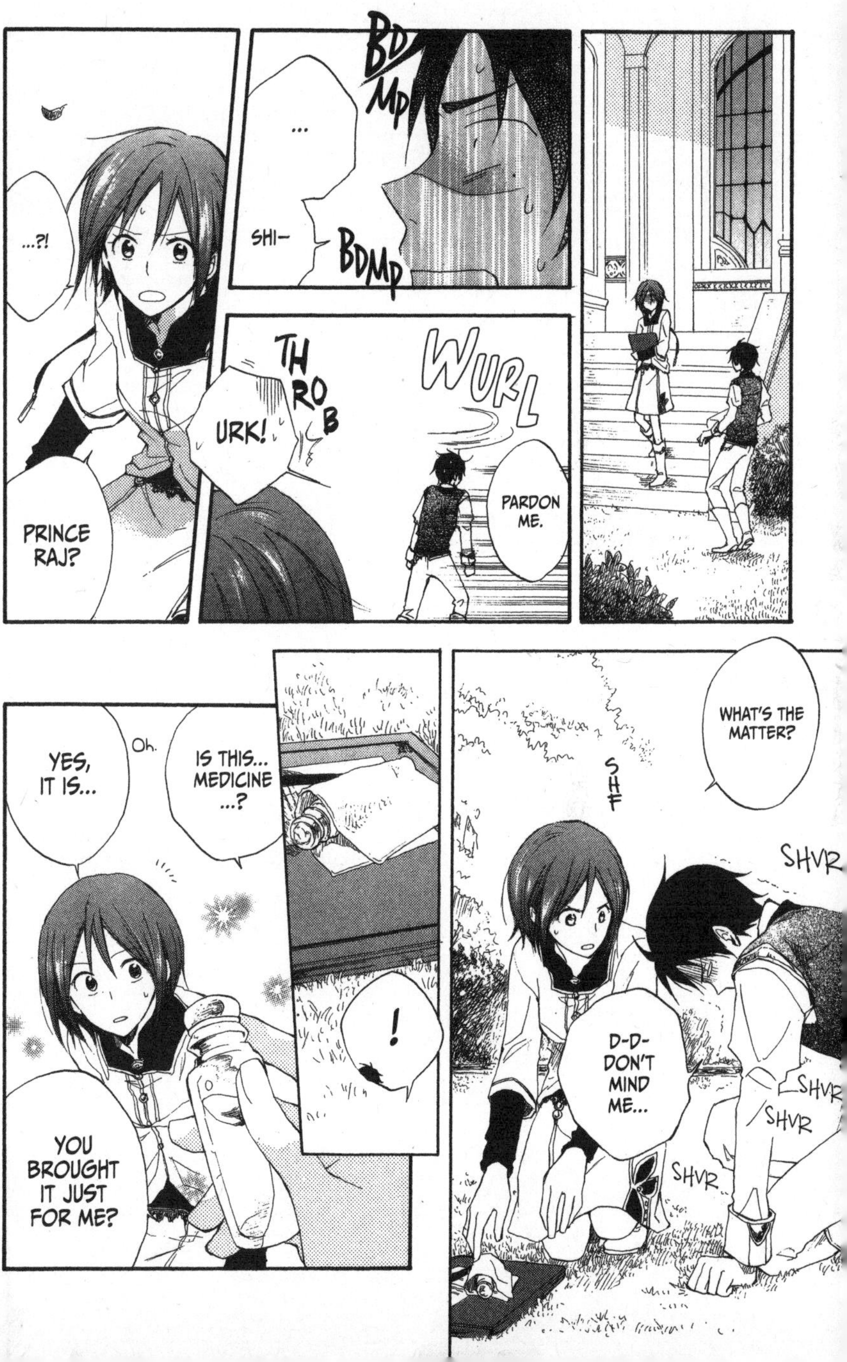
BDMP
...
SHI—
BDMP
WURL
PARDON ME.
THROB
URK!
...?!
PRINCE RAJ?
WHAT'S THE MATTER?
SHF
SHVR
D-D-DON'T MIND ME...
SHVR
SHVR
SHVR
!
IS THIS... MEDICINE ...?
Oh.
YES, IT IS...
YOU BROUGHT IT JUST FOR ME?

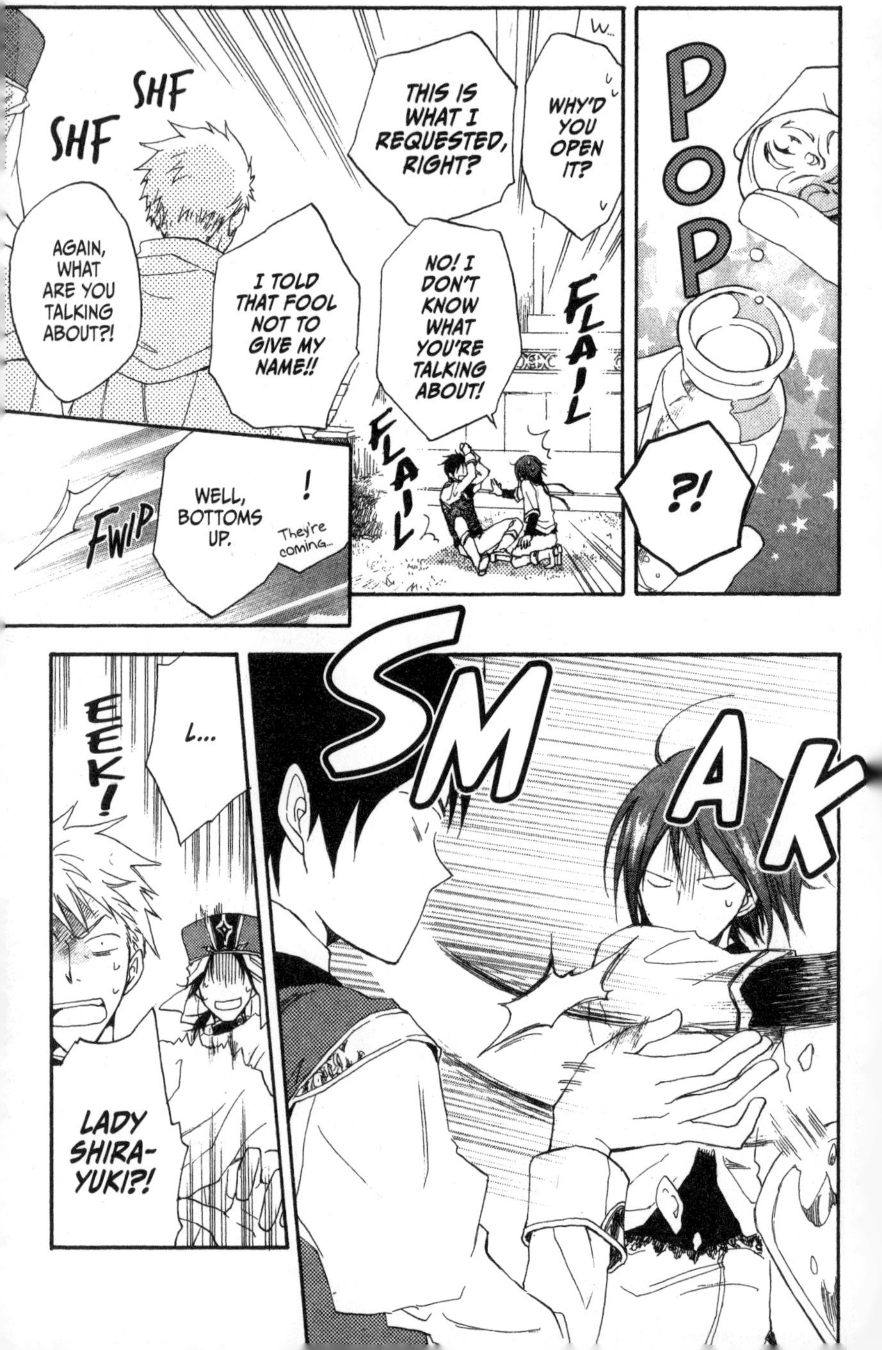
POP
?!
W...
WHY'D YOU OPEN IT?
THIS IS WHAT I REQUESTED, RIGHT?
NO! I DON'T KNOW WHAT YOU'RE TALKING ABOUT!
FLAIL
FLAIL
SHF
SHF
I TOLD THAT FOOL NOT TO GIVE MY NAME!!
AGAIN, WHAT ARE YOU TALKING ABOUT?!
!
They're coming...
WELL, BOTTOMS UP.
FWIP
SMAK
L...
EEK!
LADY SHIRA-YUKI?!

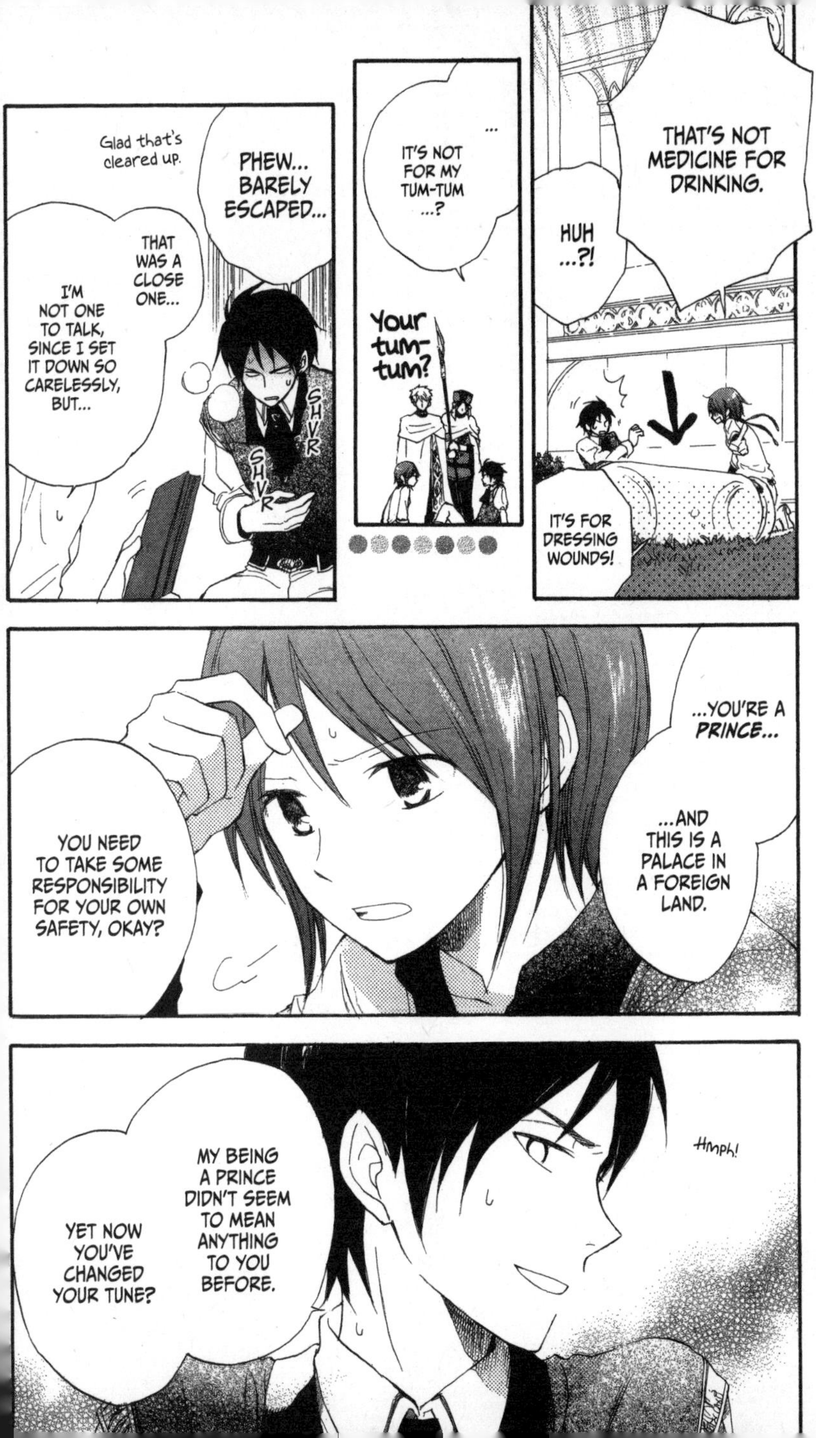
THAT'S NOT MEDICINE FOR DRINKING.
HUH ...?!
IT'S FOR DRESSING WOUNDS!
...
IT'S NOT FOR MY TUM-TUM ...?
Your tum-tum?
PHEW... BARELY ESCAPED...
Glad that's cleared up.
THAT WAS A CLOSE ONE...
I'M NOT ONE TO TALK, SINCE I SET IT DOWN SO CARELESSLY, BUT...
SHVR
SHVR
...YOU'RE A *PRINCE*...
...AND THIS IS A PALACE IN A FOREIGN LAND.
YOU NEED TO TAKE SOME RESPONSIBILITY FOR YOUR OWN SAFETY, OKAY?
Hmph!
MY BEING A PRINCE DIDN'T SEEM TO MEAN ANYTHING TO YOU BEFORE.
YET NOW YOU'VE CHANGED YOUR TUNE?

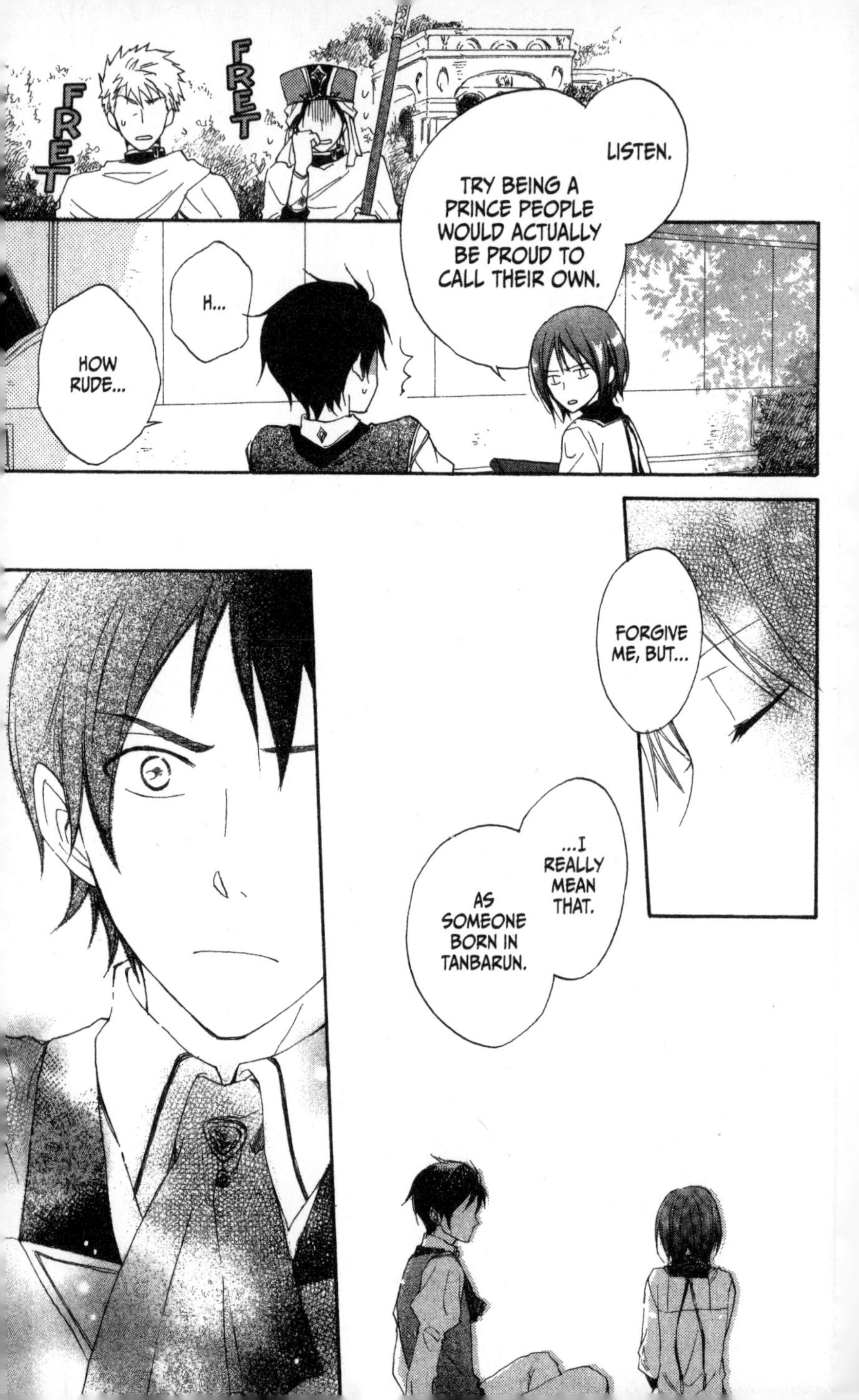
FRET
FRET
LISTEN. TRY BEING A PRINCE PEOPLE WOULD ACTUALLY BE PROUD TO CALL THEIR OWN.
H...
HOW RUDE...
FORGIVE ME, BUT...
...I REALLY MEAN THAT.
AS SOMEONE BORN IN TANBARUN.

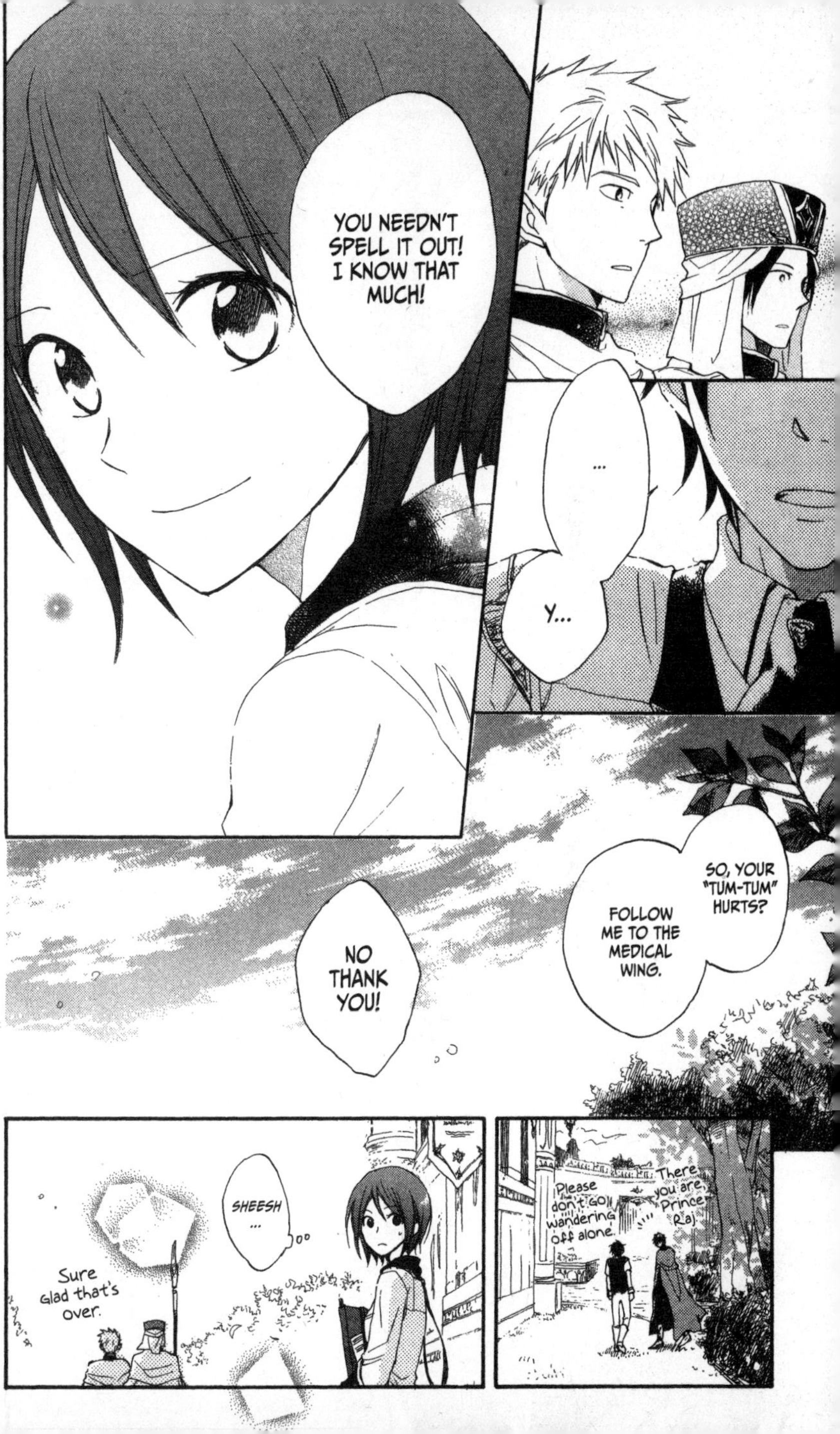
...
Y...
YOU NEEDN'T SPELL IT OUT! I KNOW THAT MUCH!
SO, YOUR "TUM-TUM" HURTS?
FOLLOW ME TO THE MEDICAL WING.
NO THANK YOU!
There you are, Prince Raj.
Please don't go wandering off alone.
SHEESH...
Sure glad that's over.

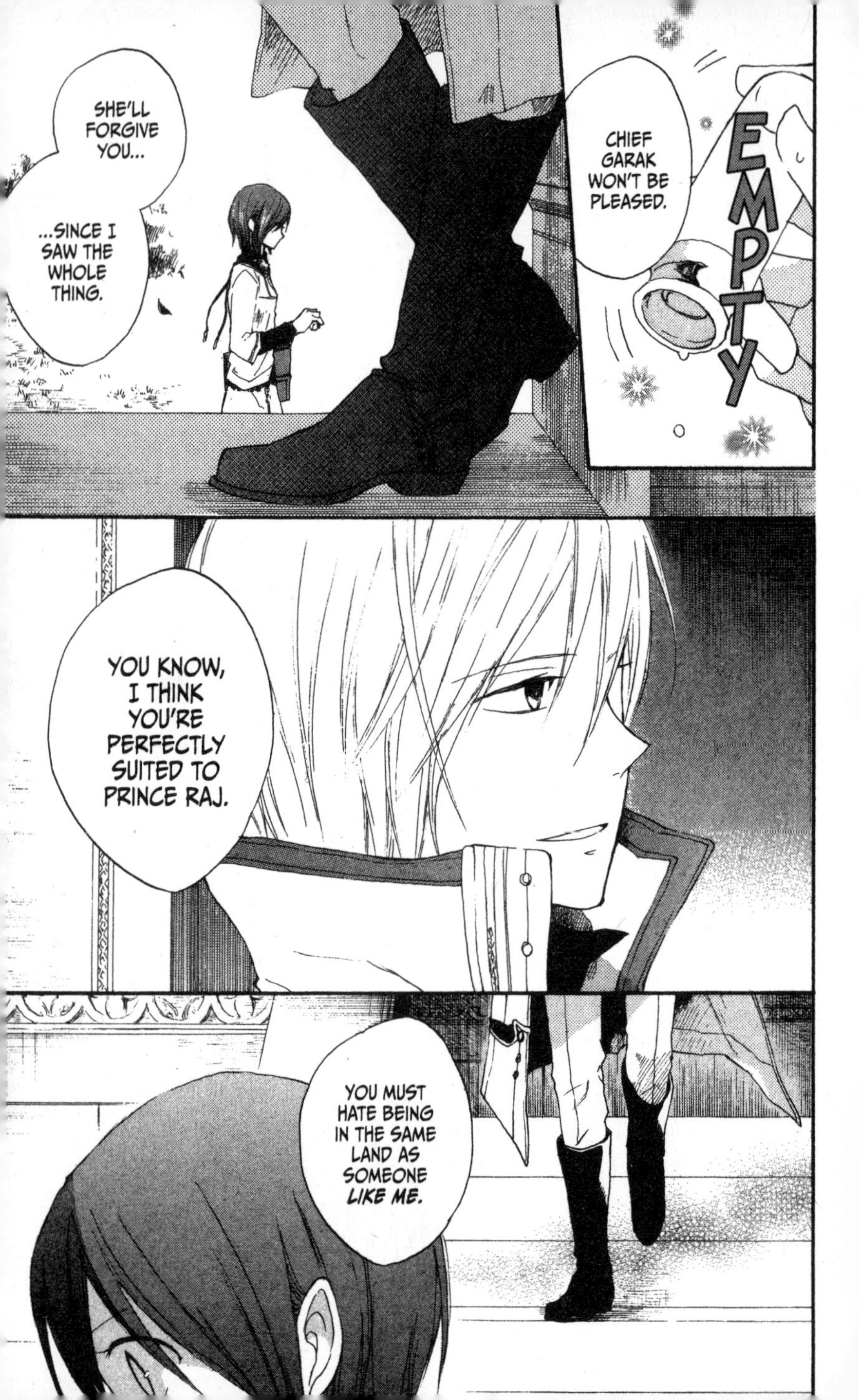
CHIEF GARAK WON'T BE PLEASED.
EMPTY
SHE'LL FORGIVE YOU...
...SINCE I SAW THE WHOLE THING.
YOU KNOW, I THINK YOU'RE PERFECTLY SUITED TO PRINCE RAJ.
YOU MUST HATE BEING IN THE SAME LAND AS SOMEONE *LIKE ME.*

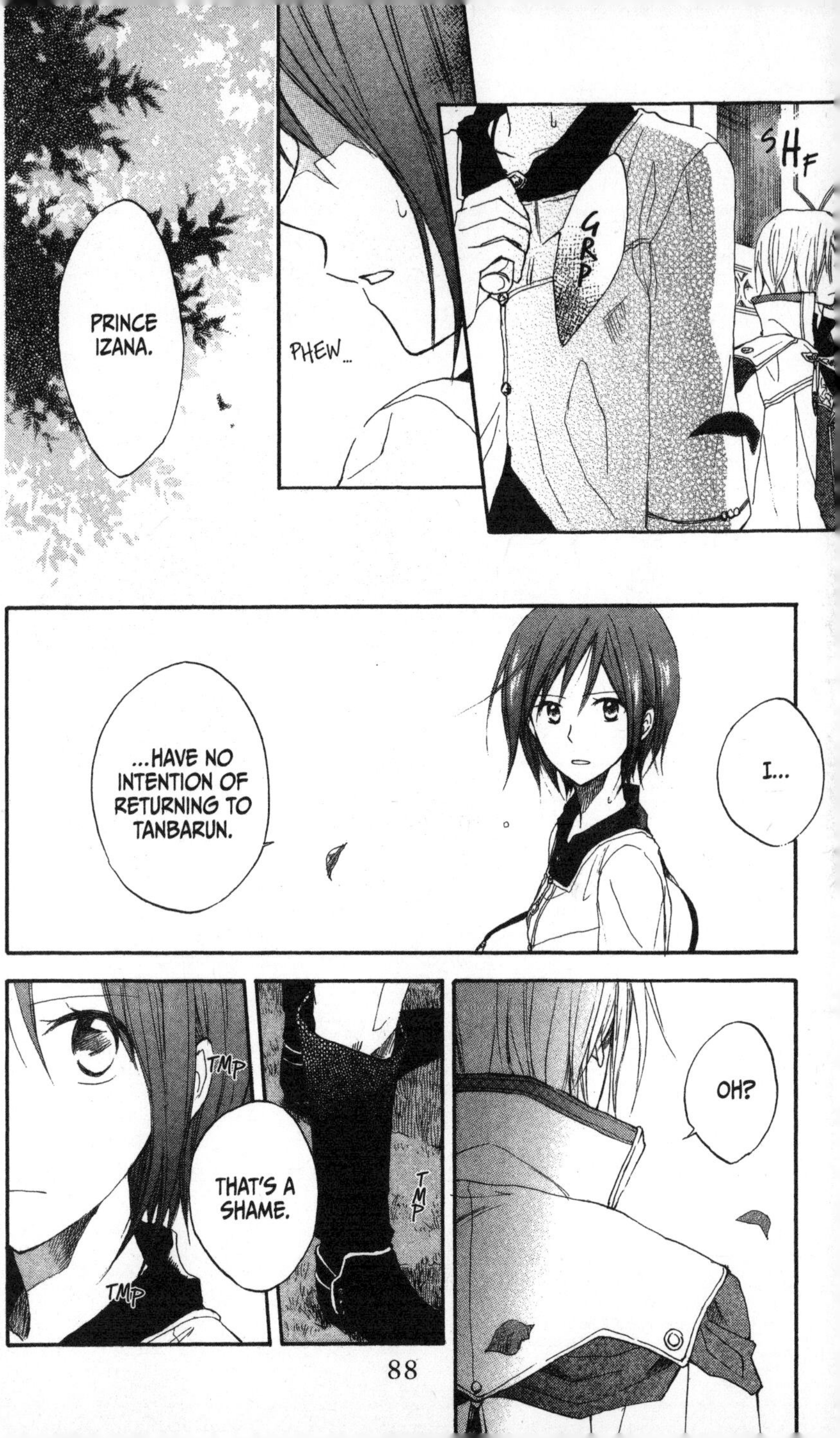
SHF
GRP
PHEW...
PRINCE IZANA.
I...
...HAVE NO INTENTION OF RETURNING TO TANBARUN.
OH?
TMP
TMP
THAT'S A SHAME.
TMP

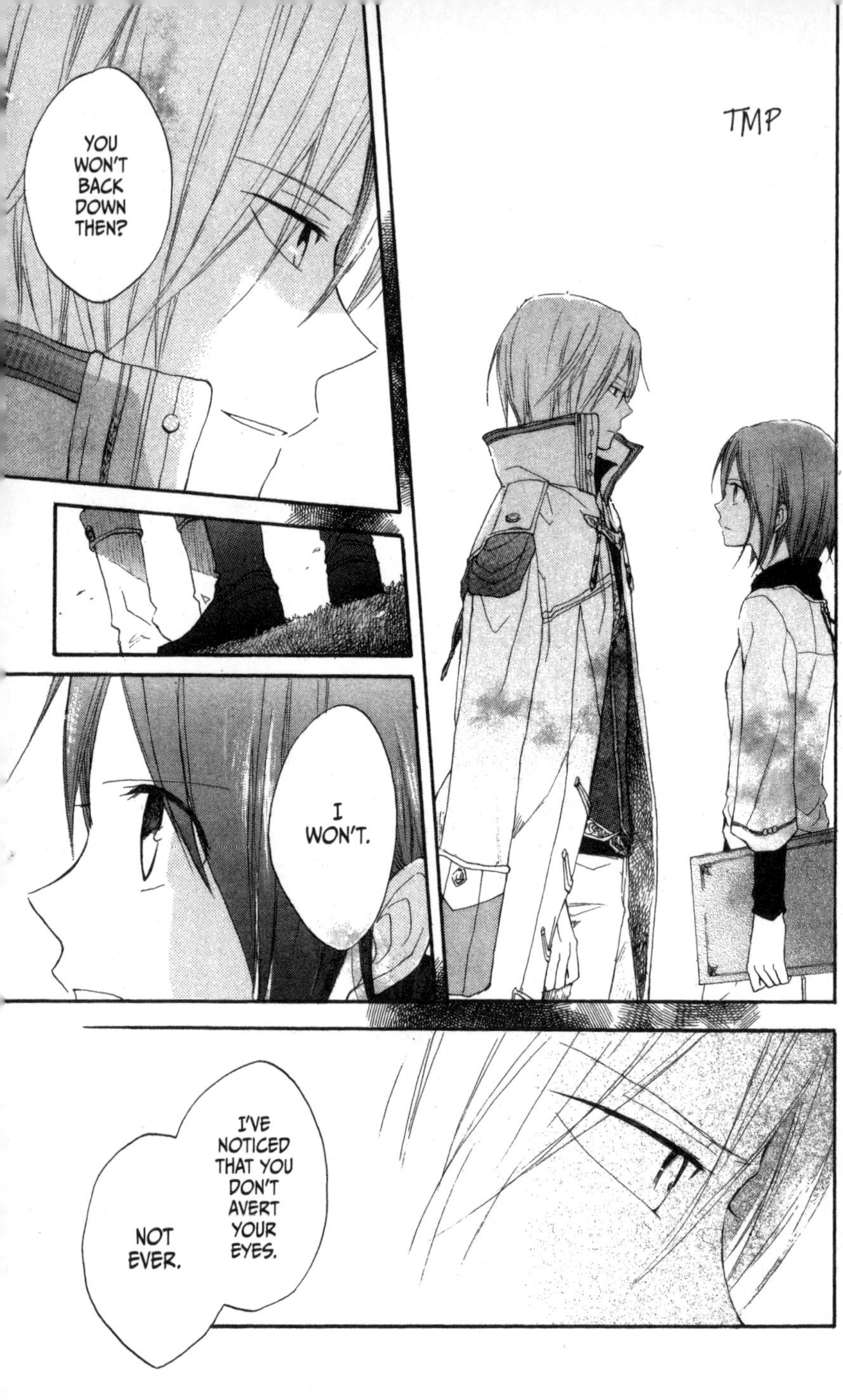
TMP
YOU WON'T BACK DOWN THEN?
I WON'T.
I'VE NOTICED THAT YOU DON'T AVERT YOUR EYES.
NOT EVER.

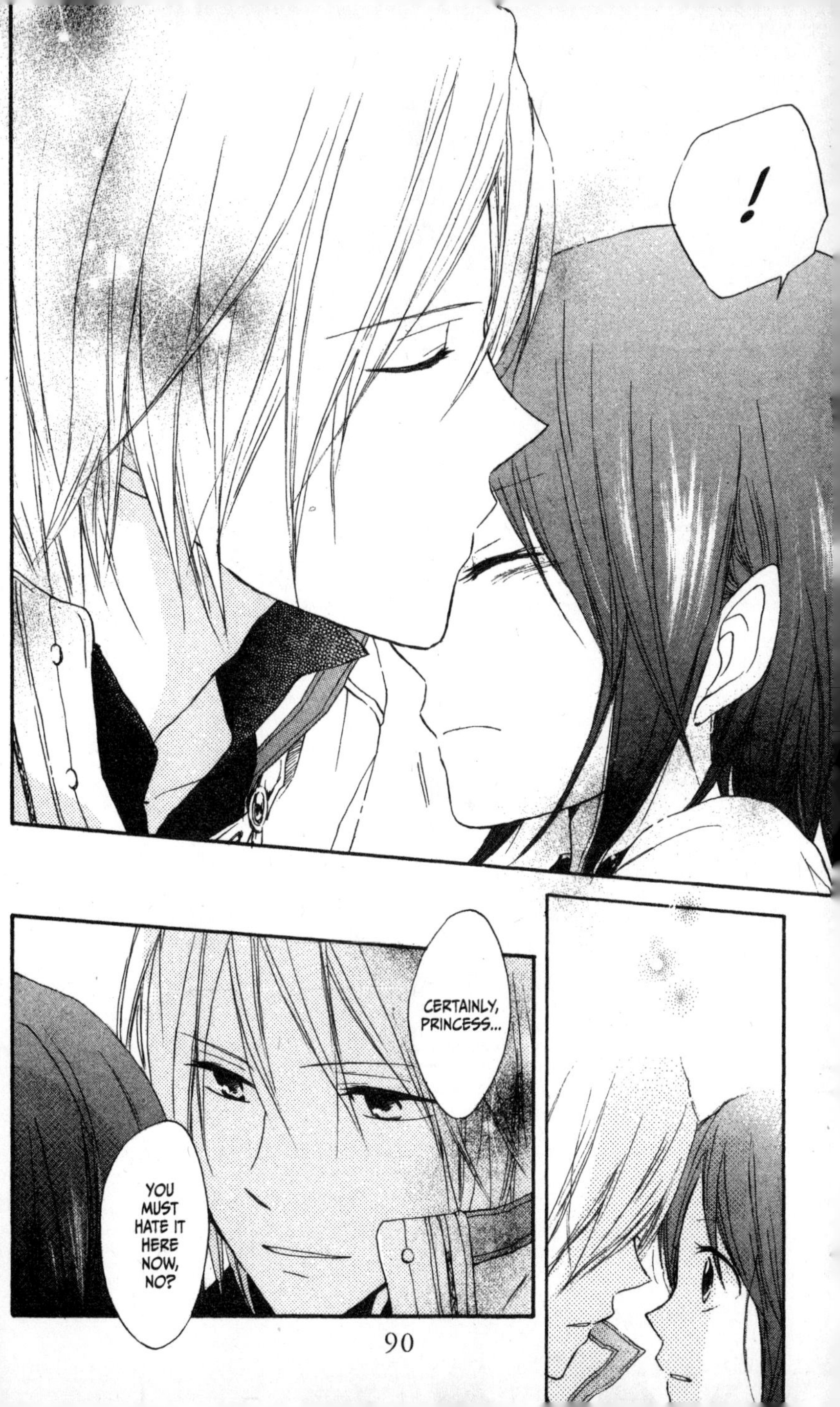
!
CERTAINLY, PRINCESS...
YOU MUST HATE IT HERE NOW, NO?

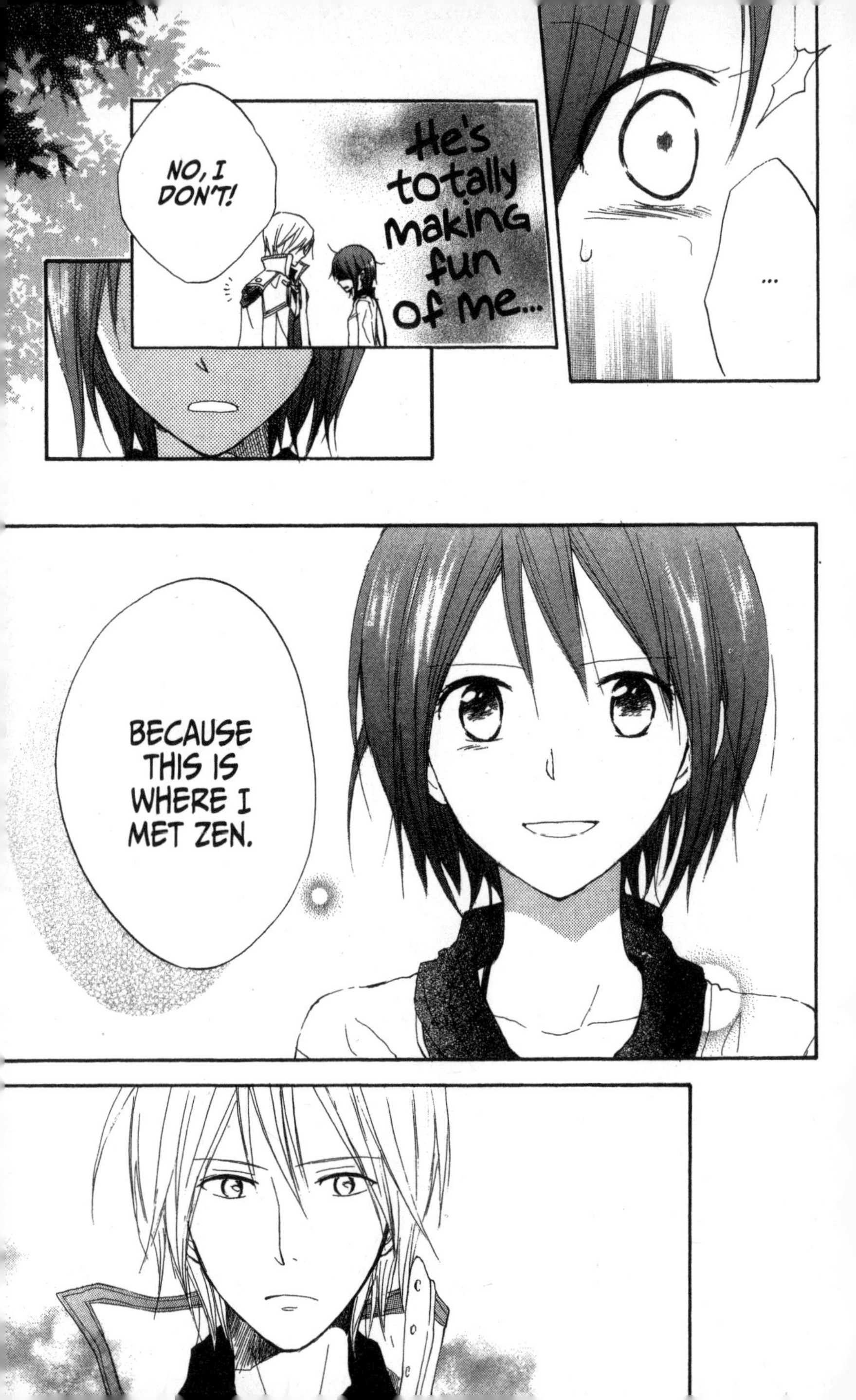
...
He's totally making fun of me...
NO, I DON'T!
BECAUSE THIS IS WHERE I MET ZEN.

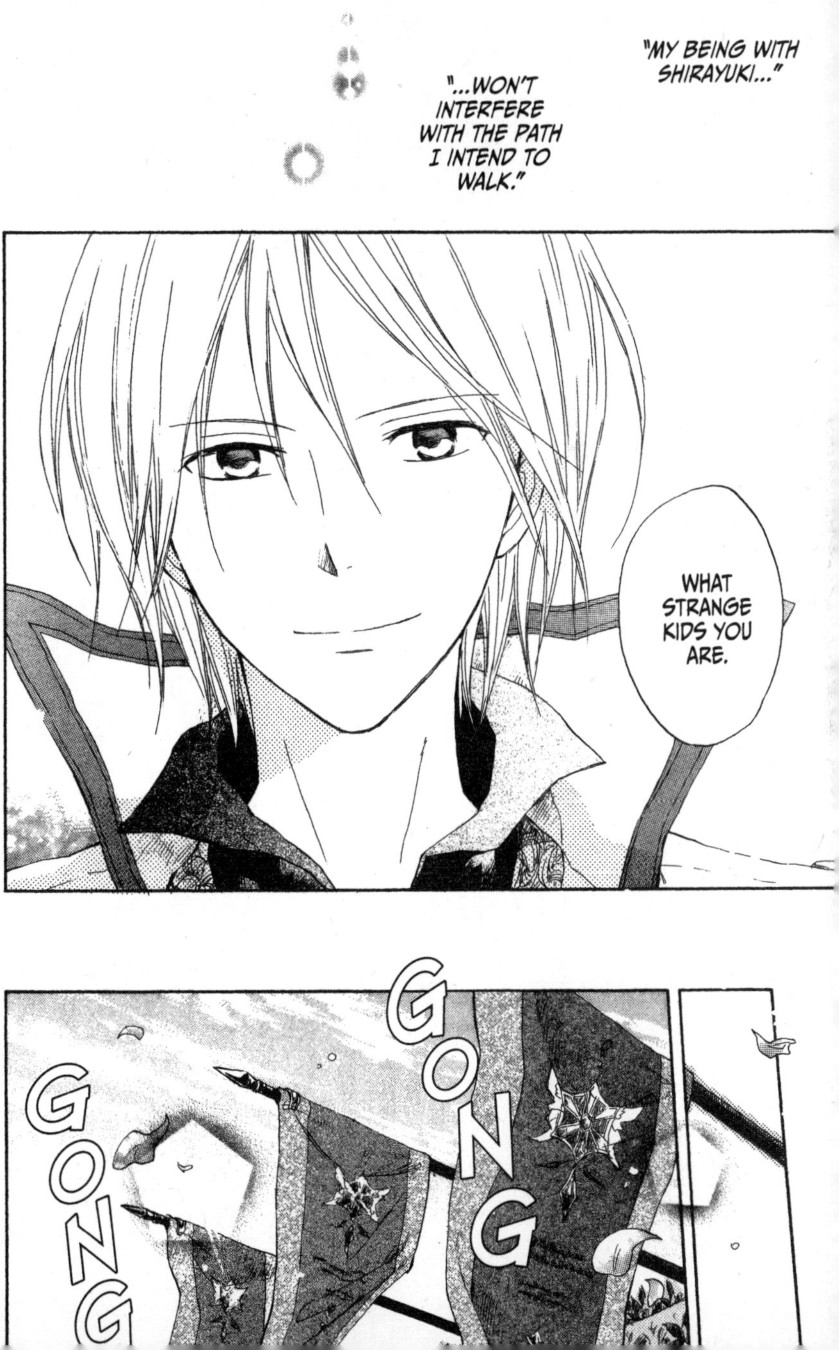
"MY BEING WITH SHIRAYUKI..."
"...WON'T INTERFERE WITH THE PATH I INTEND TO WALK."
WHAT STRANGE KIDS YOU ARE.
GONG
GONG

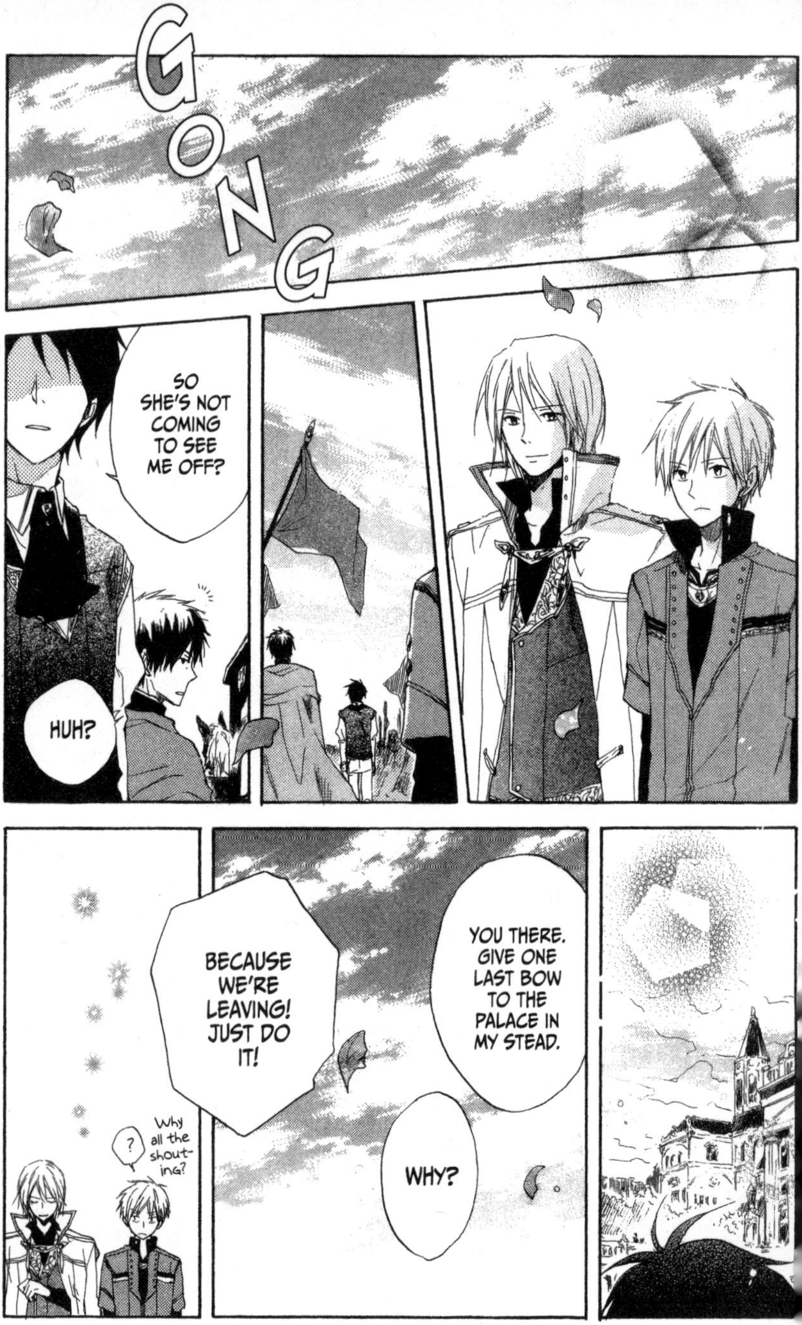
GONG
SO SHE'S NOT COMING TO SEE ME OFF?
HUH?
YOU THERE. GIVE ONE LAST BOW TO THE PALACE IN MY STEAD.
WHY?
BECAUSE WE'RE LEAVING! JUST DO IT!
?
Why all the shout-ing?

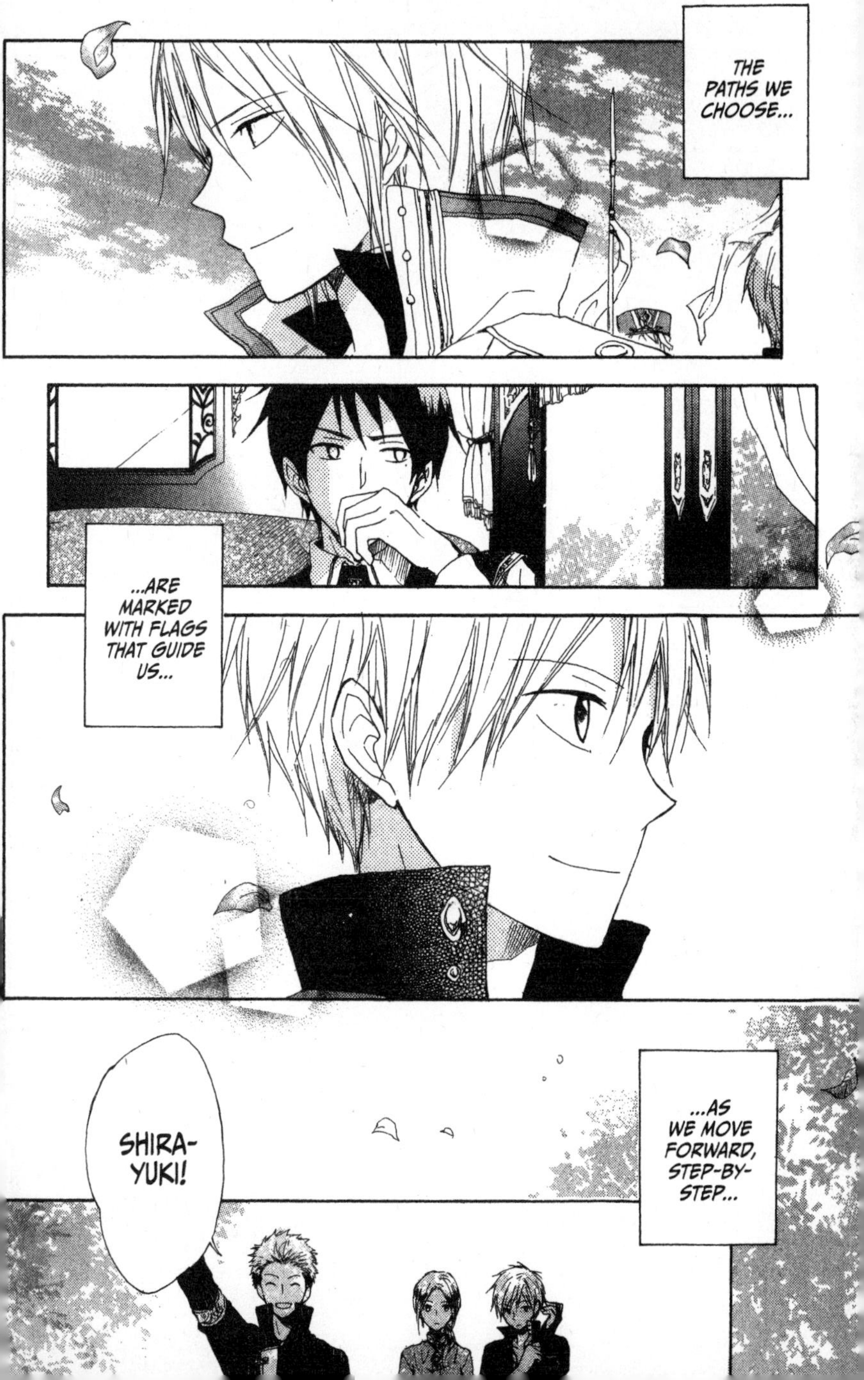
THE PATHS WE CHOOSE...
...ARE MARKED WITH FLAGS THAT GUIDE US...
...AS WE MOVE FORWARD, STEP-BY-STEP...
SHIRA-YUKI!

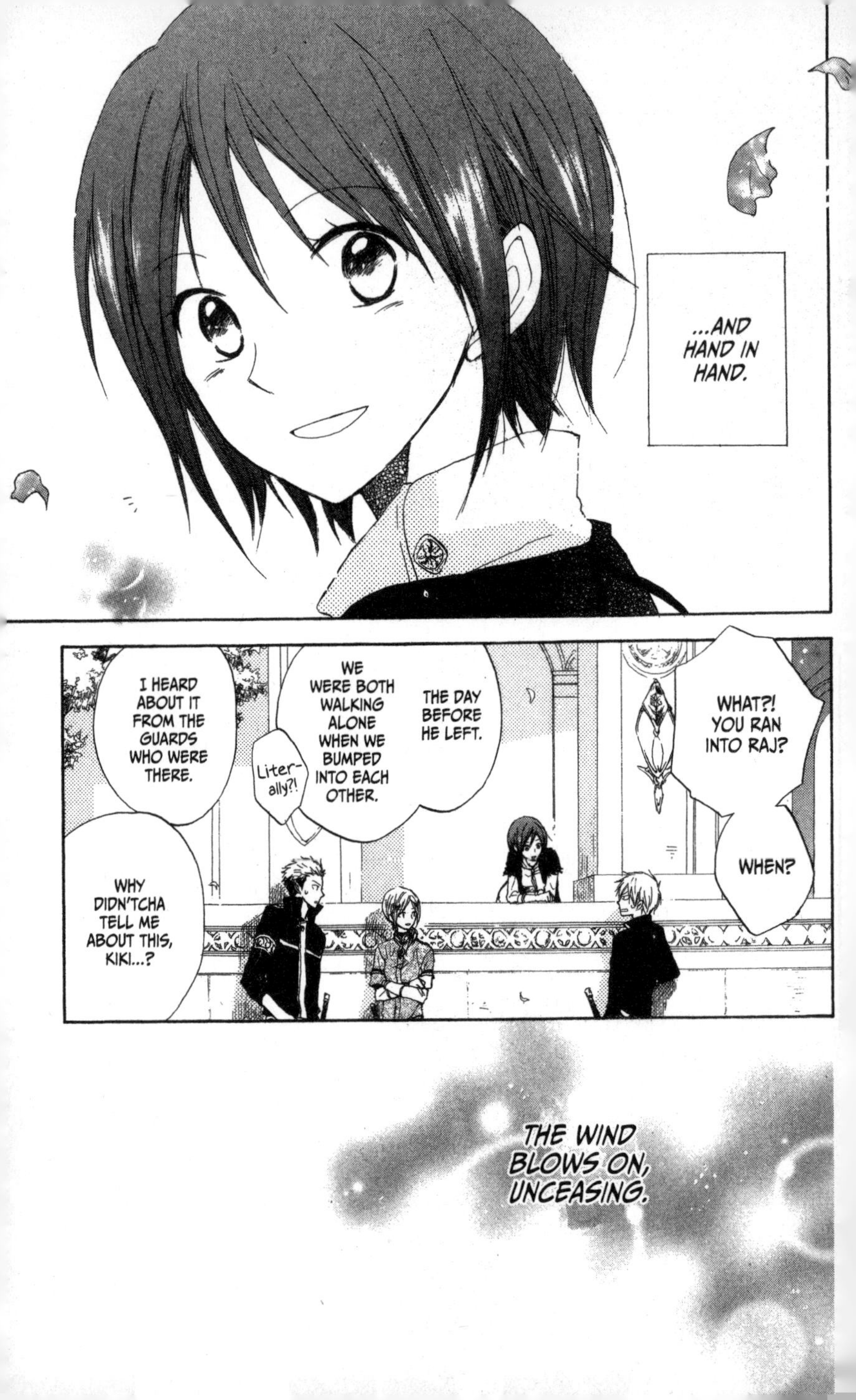
...AND HAND IN HAND.
WHAT?! YOU RAN INTO RAJ?
WHEN?
THE DAY BEFORE HE LEFT.
WE WERE BOTH WALKING ALONE WHEN WE BUMPED INTO EACH OTHER.
Liter-ally?!
I HEARD ABOUT IT FROM THE GUARDS WHO WERE THERE.
WHY DIDN'TCHA TELL ME ABOUT THIS, KIKI...?
THE WIND BLOWS ON, UNCEASING.

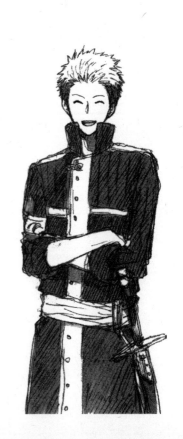

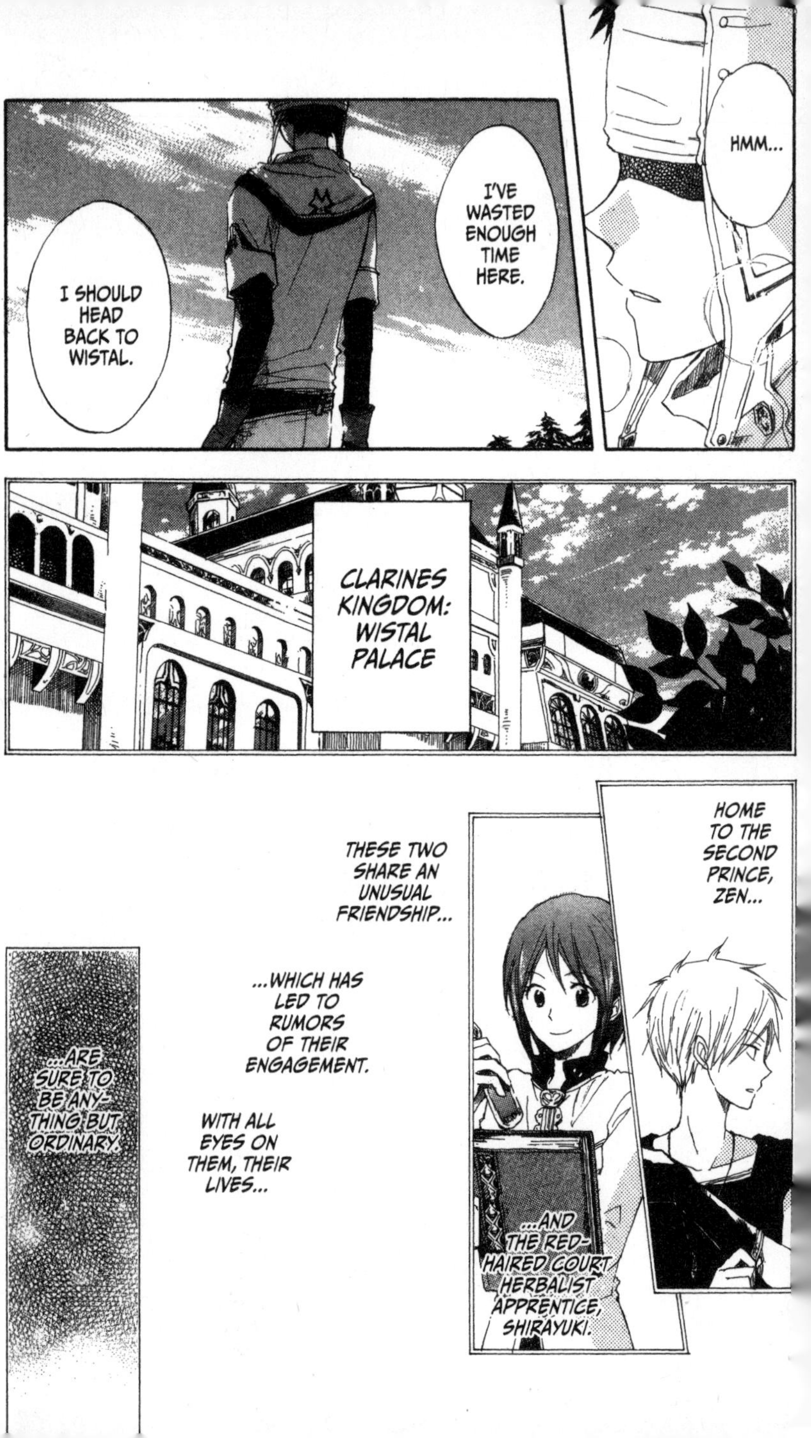
HMM...
I'VE WASTED ENOUGH TIME HERE.
I SHOULD HEAD BACK TO WISTAL.
CLARINES KINGDOM: WISTAL PALACE
HOME TO THE SECOND PRINCE, ZEN...
...AND THE RED-HAIRED COURT HERBALIST APPRENTICE, SHIRAYUKI.
THESE TWO SHARE AN UNUSUAL FRIENDSHIP...
...WHICH HAS LED TO RUMORS OF THEIR ENGAGEMENT.
WITH ALL EYES ON THEM, THEIR LIVES...
...ARE SURE TO BE ANYTHING BUT ORDINARY.

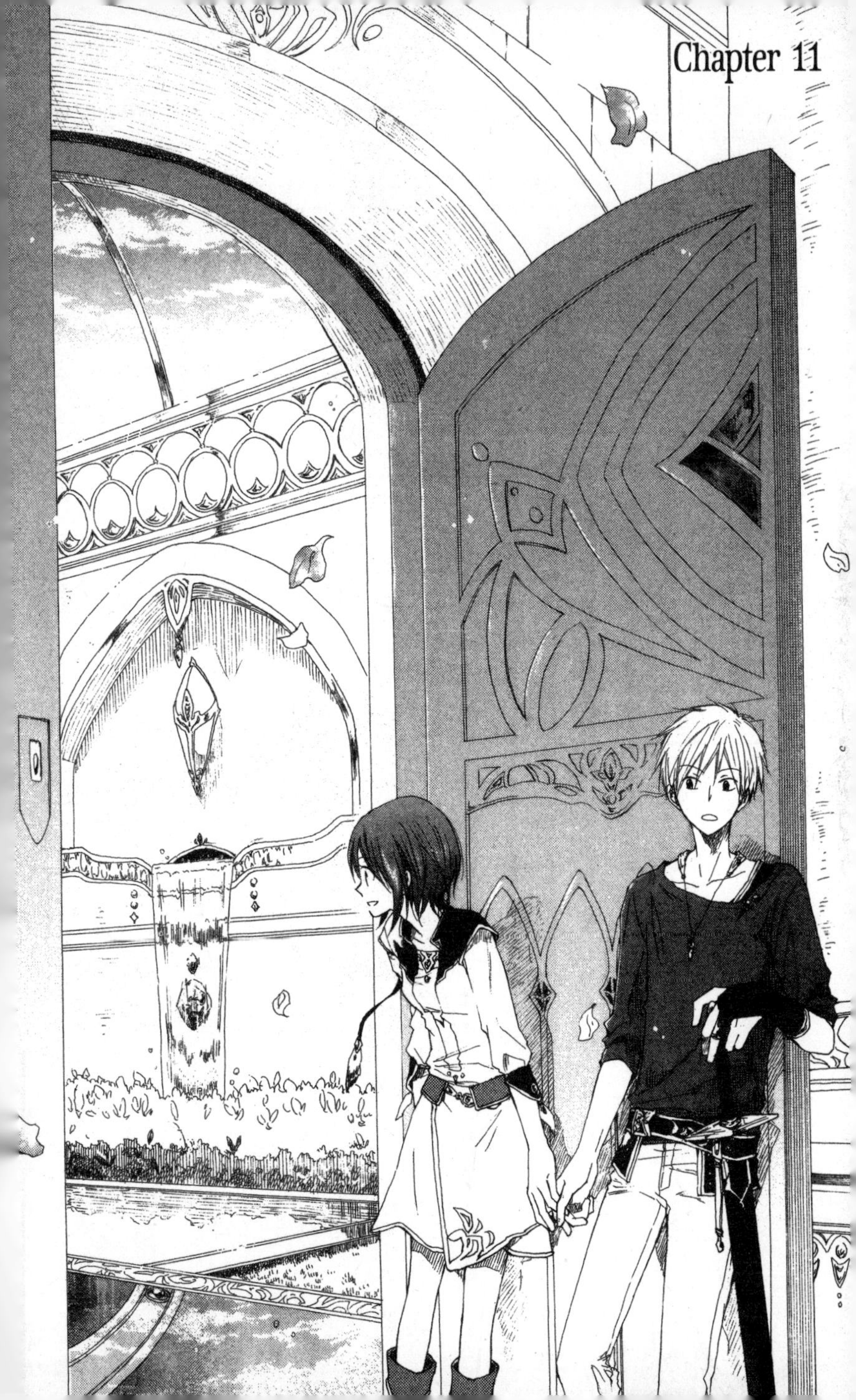
Chapter 11

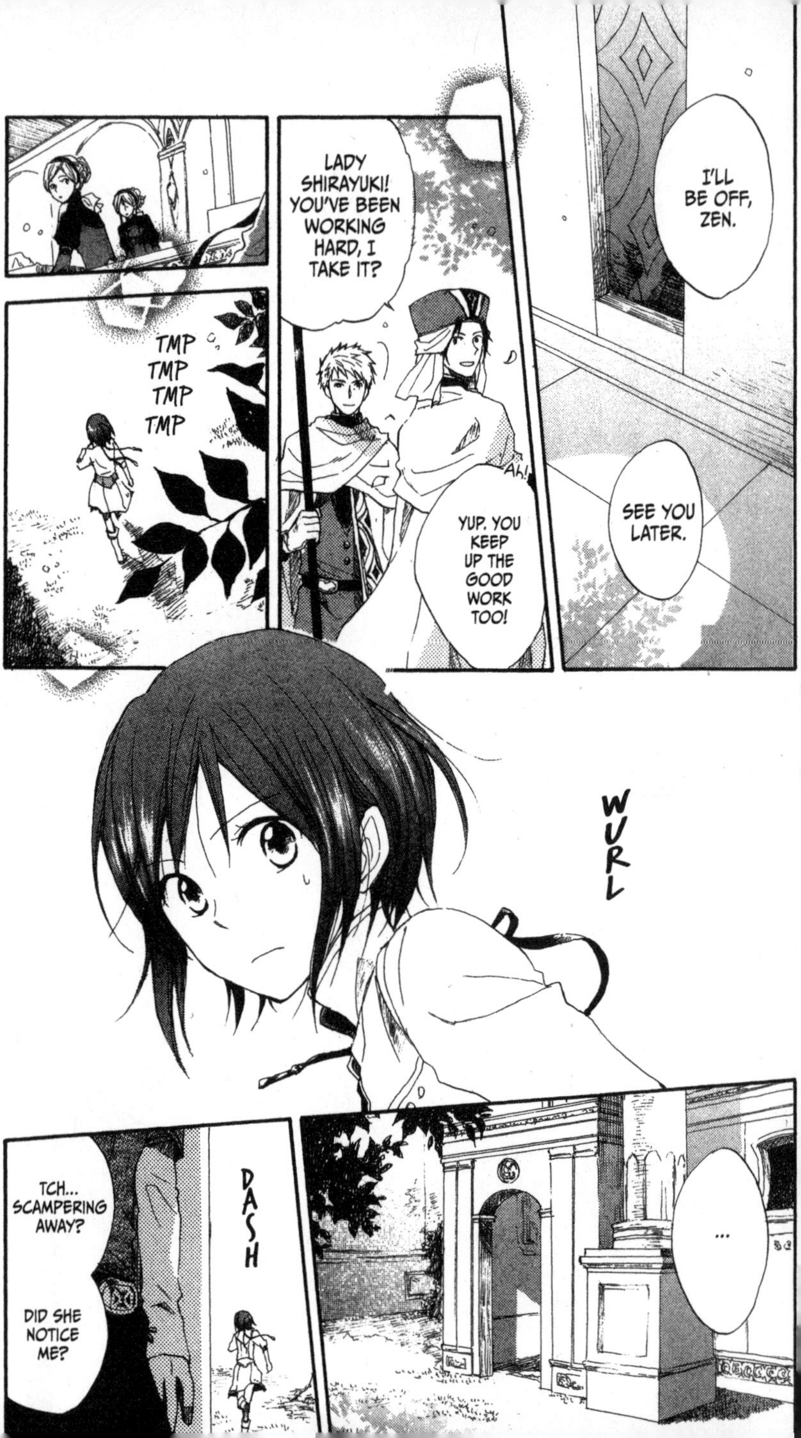
I'LL BE OFF, ZEN.
SEE YOU LATER.
LADY SHIRAYUKI! YOU'VE BEEN WORKING HARD, I TAKE IT?
Ah!
YUP. YOU KEEP UP THE GOOD WORK TOO!
TMP
TMP
TMP
TMP
WURL
...
DASH
TCH... SCAMPERING AWAY?
DID SHE NOTICE ME?

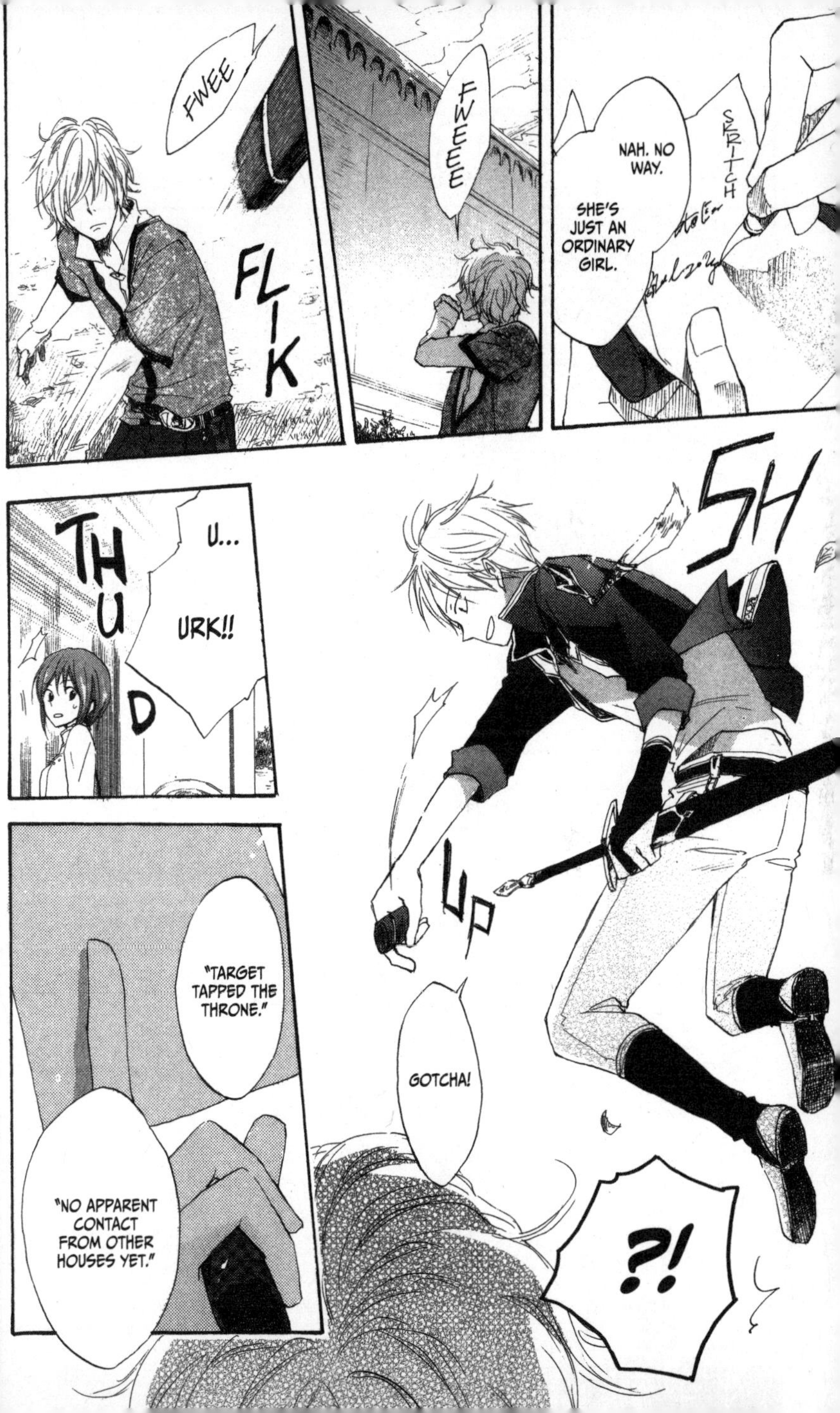
SKRITCH
NAH. NO WAY.
SHE'S JUST AN ORDINARY GIRL.
FWEEE
FWEE
FLIK
SH
UP
GOTCHA!
?!
THUD
U...
URK!!
"TARGET TAPPED THE THRONE."
"NO APPARENT CONTACT FROM OTHER HOUSES YET."

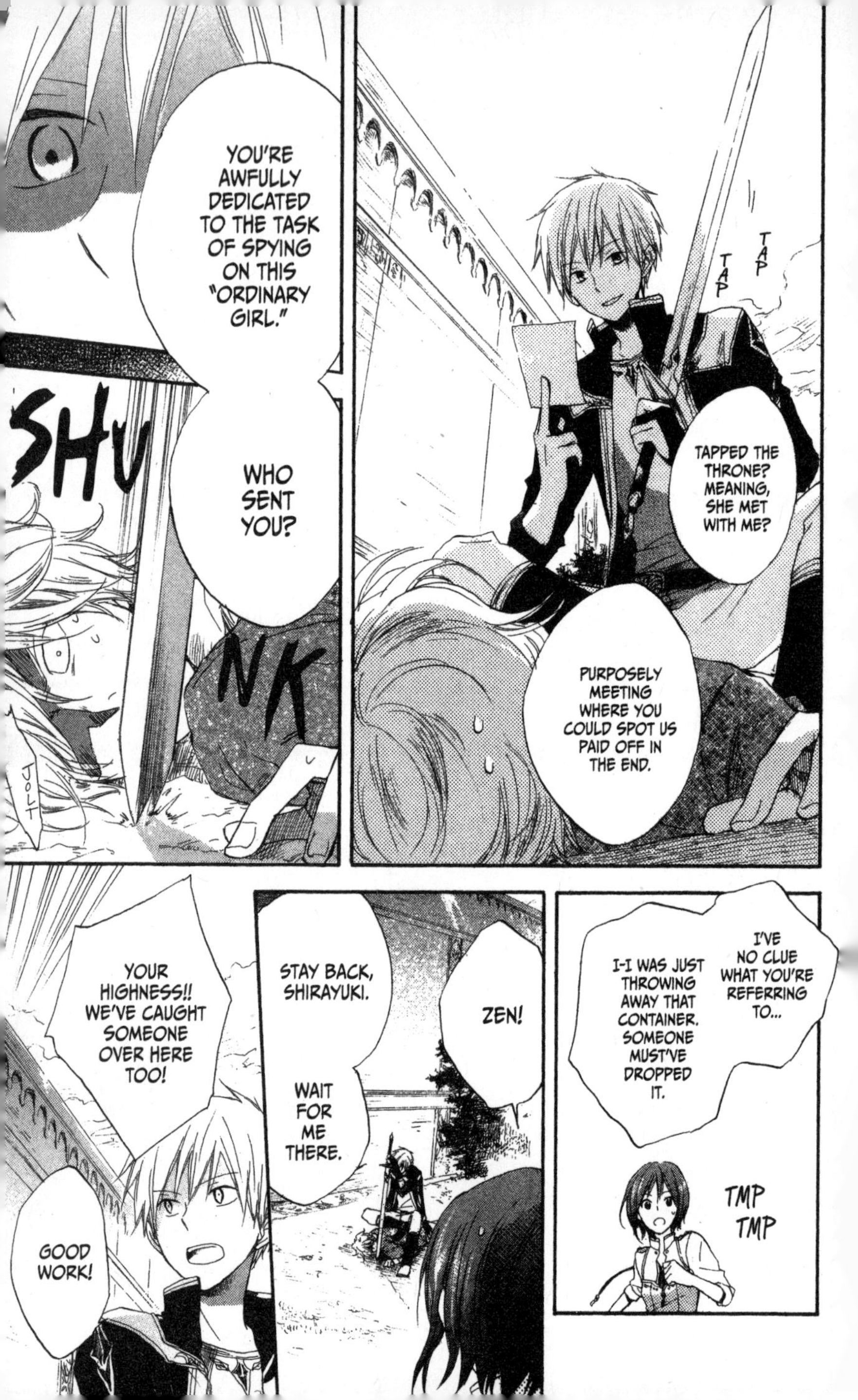
TAP TAP
TAPPED THE THRONE? MEANING, SHE MET WITH ME?
PURPOSELY MEETING WHERE YOU COULD SPOT US PAID OFF IN THE END.
YOU'RE AWFULLY DEDICATED TO THE TASK OF SPYING ON THIS "ORDINARY GIRL."
WHO SENT YOU?
SHUNK
JOLT
I'VE NO CLUE WHAT YOU'RE REFERRING TO...
I-I WAS JUST THROWING AWAY THAT CONTAINER. SOMEONE MUST'VE DROPPED IT.
TMP TMP
ZEN!
STAY BACK, SHIRAYUKI.
WAIT FOR ME THERE.
YOUR HIGHNESS!! WE'VE CAUGHT SOMEONE OVER HERE TOO!
GOOD WORK!

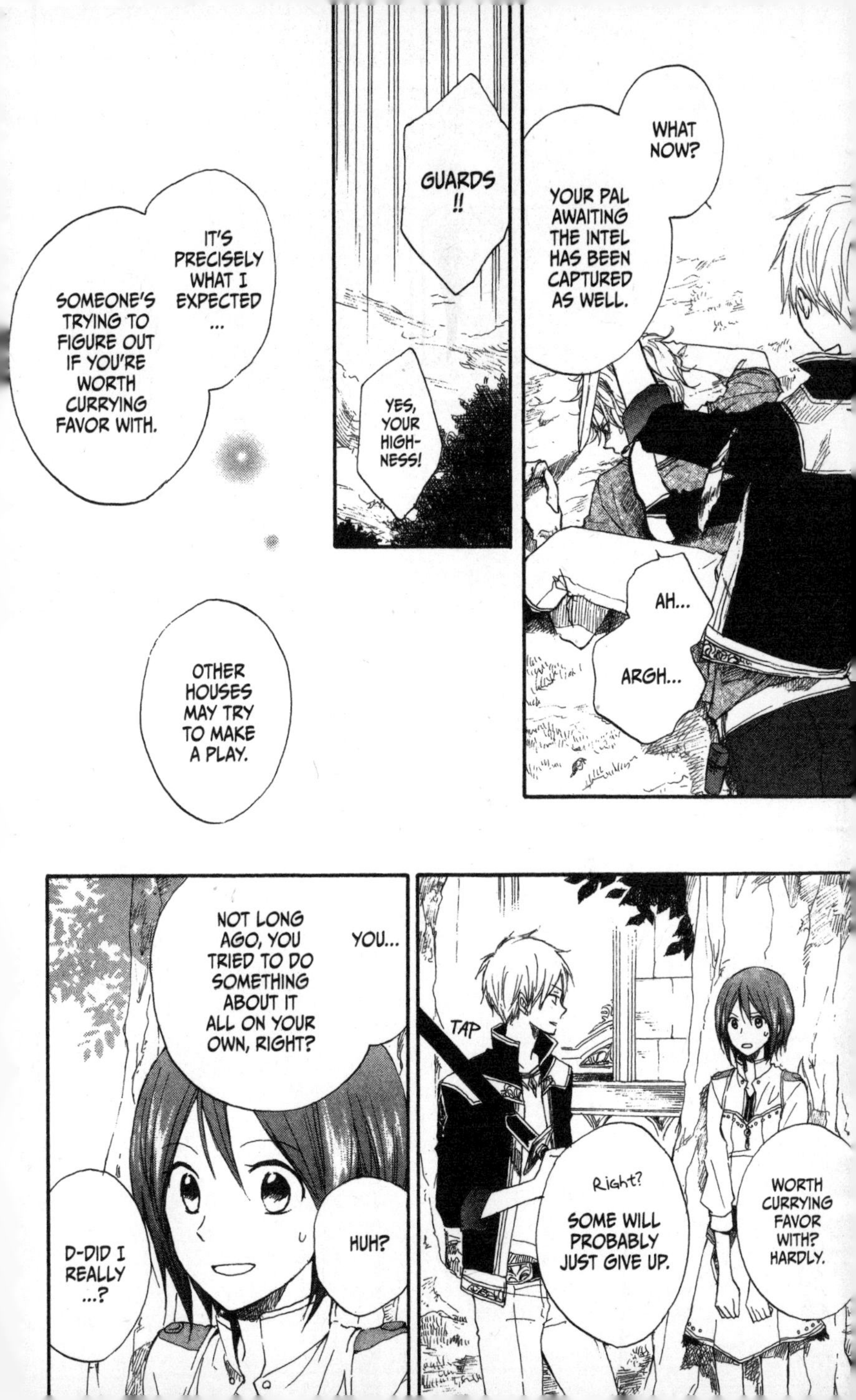
WHAT NOW?
YOUR PAL AWAITING THE INTEL HAS BEEN CAPTURED AS WELL.
AH...
ARGH...
GUARDS !!
YES, YOUR HIGH-NESS!
IT'S PRECISELY WHAT I EXPECTED ...
SOMEONE'S TRYING TO FIGURE OUT IF YOU'RE WORTH CURRYING FAVOR WITH.
OTHER HOUSES MAY TRY TO MAKE A PLAY.
WORTH CURRYING FAVOR WITH? HARDLY.
Right?
SOME WILL PROBABLY JUST GIVE UP.
TAP
YOU...
NOT LONG AGO, YOU TRIED TO DO SOMETHING ABOUT IT ALL ON YOUR OWN, RIGHT?
HUH?
D-DID I REALLY ...?

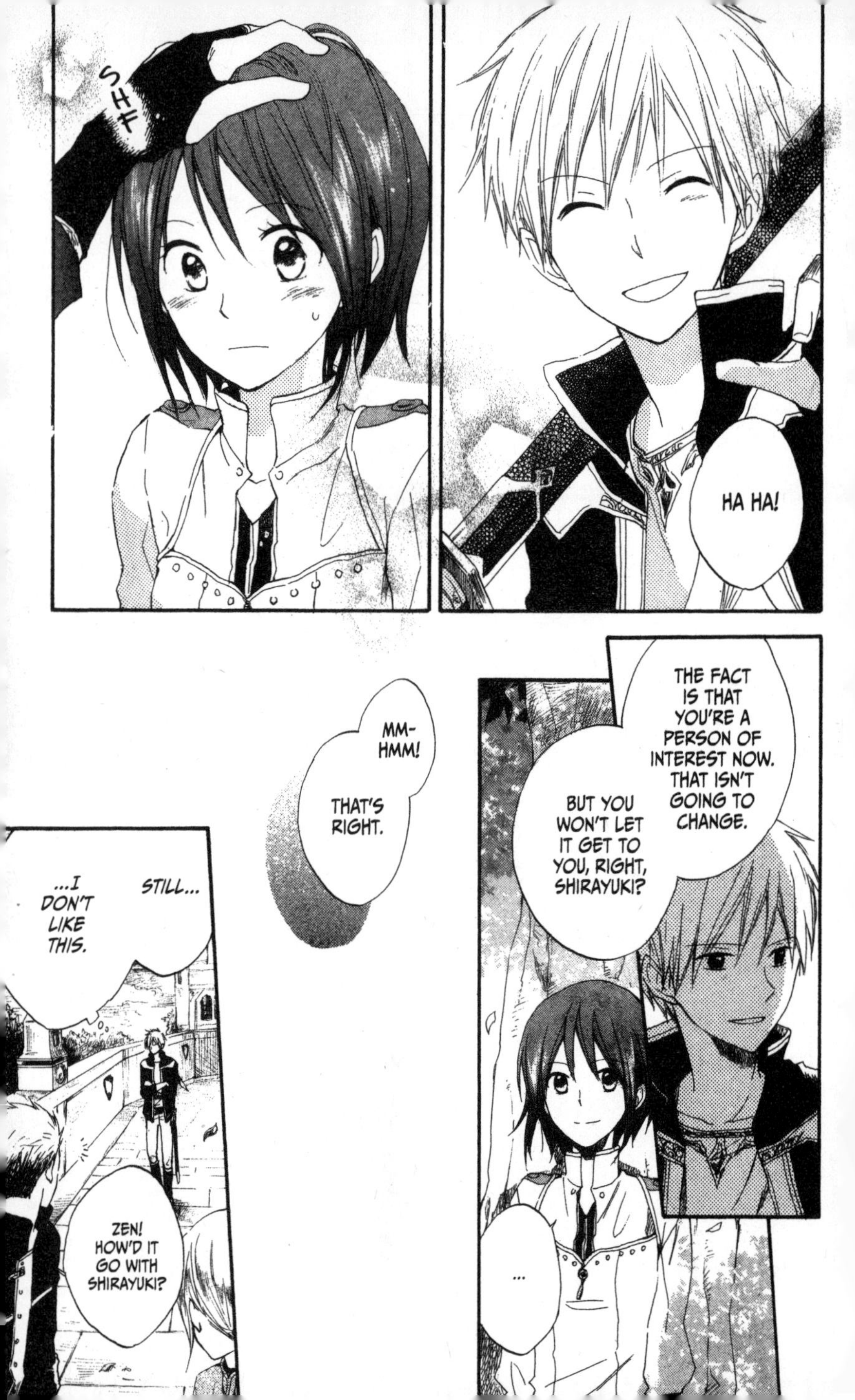
HA HA!
SHF
THE FACT IS THAT YOU'RE A PERSON OF INTEREST NOW. THAT ISN'T GOING TO CHANGE.
BUT YOU WON'T LET IT GET TO YOU, RIGHT, SHIRAYUKI?
...
MM-HMM!
THAT'S RIGHT.
STILL...
...I DON'T LIKE THIS.
ZEN! HOW'D IT GO WITH SHIRAYUKI?

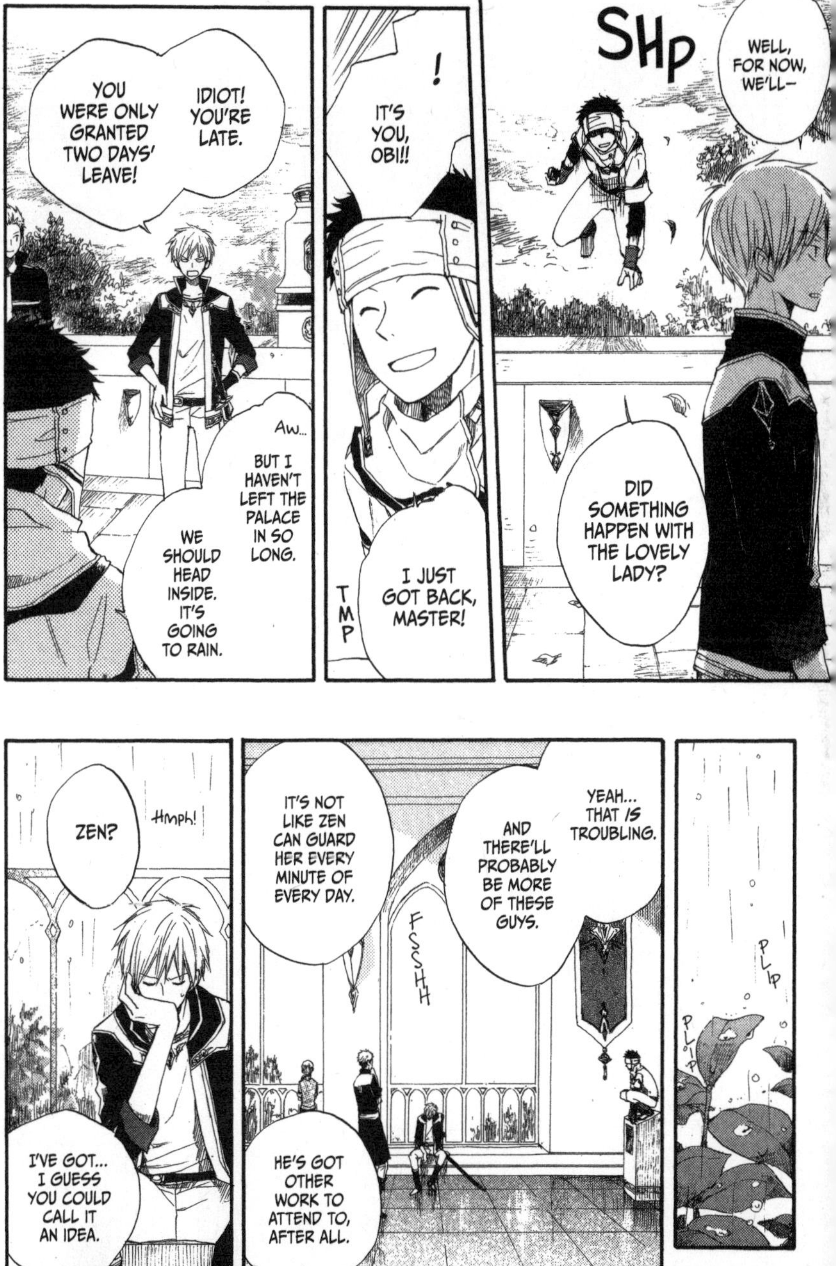
SHp
WELL, FOR NOW, WE'LL—
DID SOMETHING HAPPEN WITH THE LOVELY LADY?
!
IT'S YOU, OBI!!
TMP
I JUST GOT BACK, MASTER!
IDIOT! YOU'RE LATE.
YOU WERE ONLY GRANTED TWO DAYS' LEAVE!
Aw... BUT I HAVEN'T LEFT THE PALACE IN SO LONG.
WE SHOULD HEAD INSIDE. IT'S GOING TO RAIN.
PLIP
PLIP
YEAH... THAT *IS* TROUBLING.
AND THERE'LL PROBABLY BE MORE OF THESE GUYS.
IT'S NOT LIKE ZEN CAN GUARD HER EVERY MINUTE OF EVERY DAY.
FSSHH
HE'S GOT OTHER WORK TO ATTEND TO, AFTER ALL.
Hmph!
ZEN?
I'VE GOT... I GUESS YOU COULD CALL IT AN IDEA.

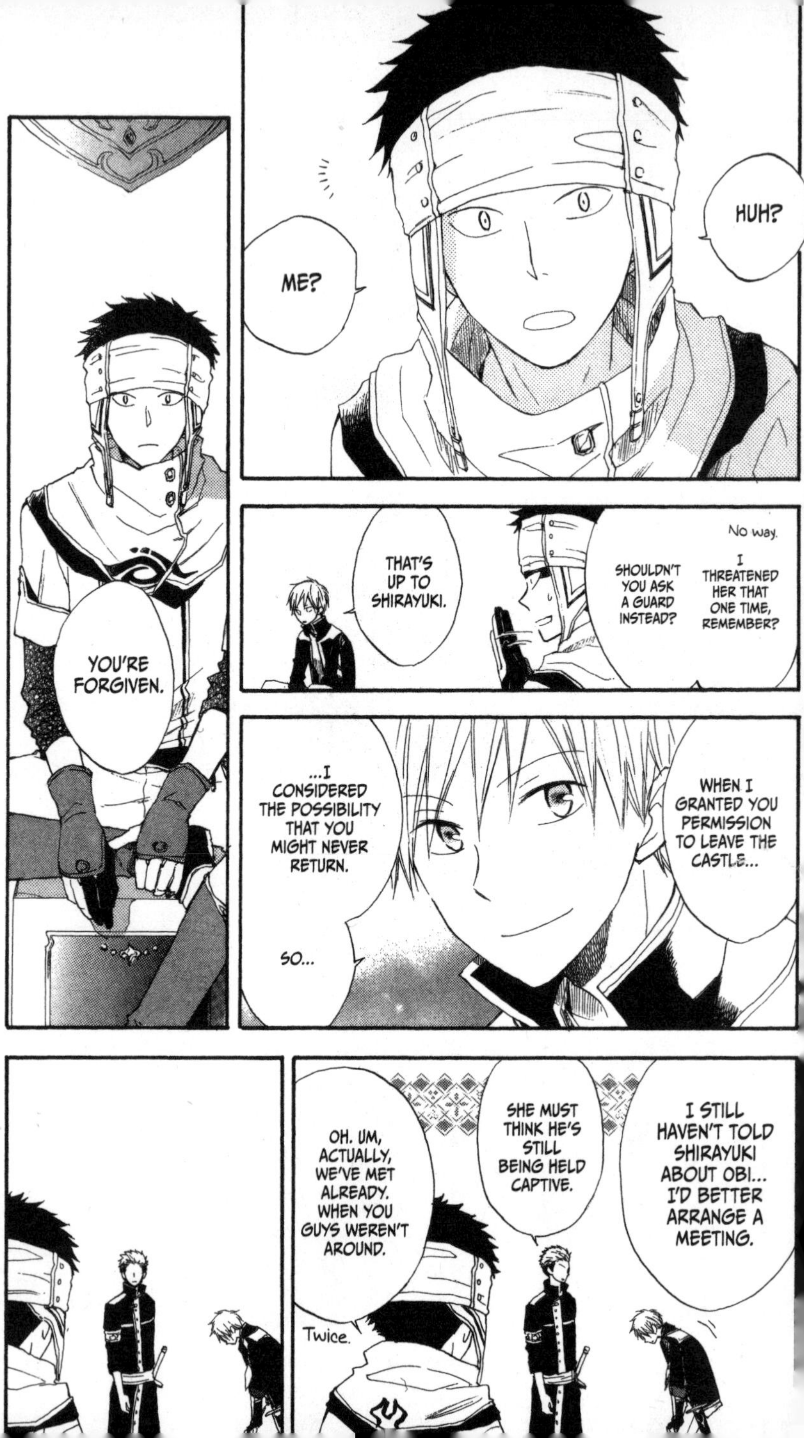
HUH?
ME?
No way.
I THREATENED HER THAT ONE TIME, REMEMBER?
SHOULDN'T YOU ASK A GUARD INSTEAD?
THAT'S UP TO SHIRAYUKI.
WHEN I GRANTED YOU PERMISSION TO LEAVE THE CASTLE...
...I CONSIDERED THE POSSIBILITY THAT YOU MIGHT NEVER RETURN.
SO...
YOU'RE FORGIVEN.
I STILL HAVEN'T TOLD SHIRAYUKI ABOUT OBI... I'D BETTER ARRANGE A MEETING.
SHE MUST THINK HE'S STILL BEING HELD CAPTIVE.
OH. UM, ACTUALLY, WE'VE MET ALREADY. WHEN YOU GUYS WEREN'T AROUND.
Twice.

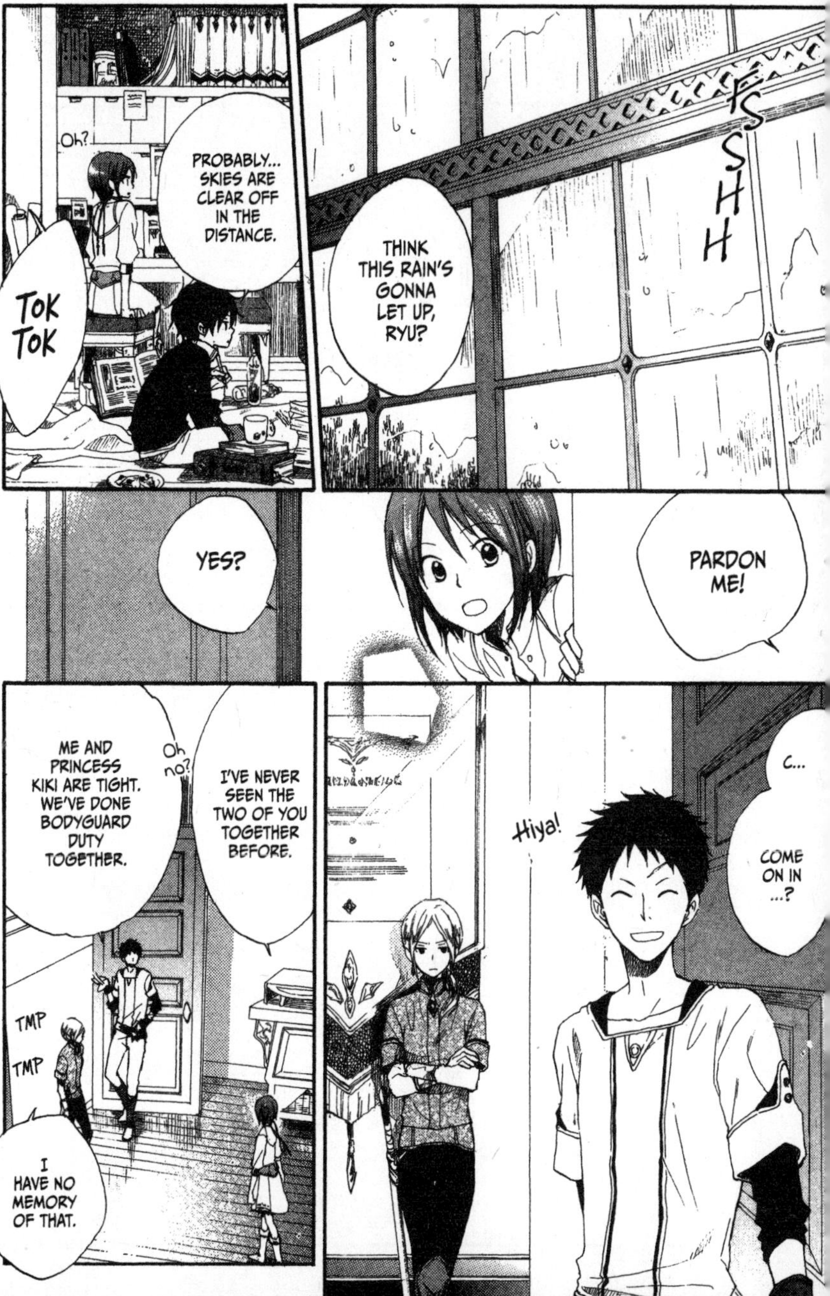
FSSHH
THINK THIS RAIN'S GONNA LET UP, RYU?
PROBABLY... SKIES ARE CLEAR OFF IN THE DISTANCE.
Oh?
TOK TOK
PARDON ME!
YES?
C...
Hiya!
COME ON IN ...?
I'VE NEVER SEEN THE TWO OF YOU TOGETHER BEFORE.
Oh no?
ME AND PRINCESS KIKI ARE TIGHT. WE'VE DONE BODYGUARD DUTY TOGETHER.
TMP TMP
I HAVE NO MEMORY OF THAT.

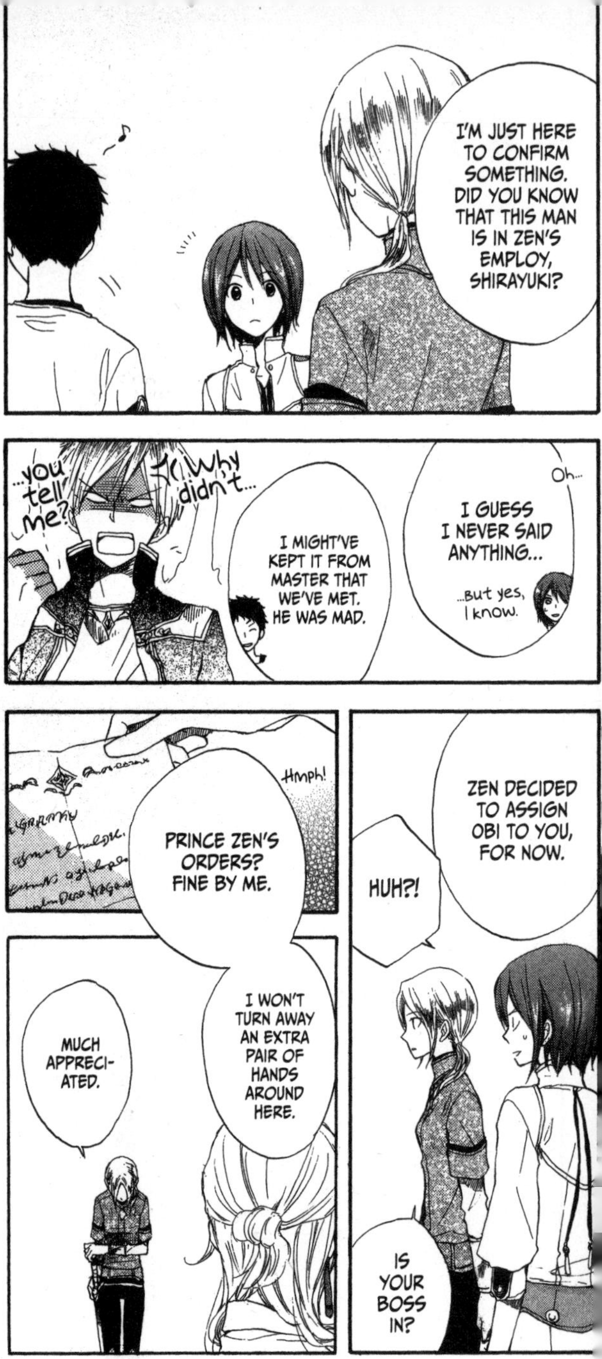
I'M JUST HERE TO CONFIRM SOMETHING. DID YOU KNOW THAT THIS MAN IS IN ZEN'S EMPLOY, SHIRAYUKI?
Oh...
I GUESS I NEVER SAID ANYTHING...
...But yes, I know.
I MIGHT'VE KEPT IT FROM MASTER THAT WE'VE MET. HE WAS MAD.
Why didn't...
...you tell me?
ZEN DECIDED TO ASSIGN OBI TO YOU, FOR NOW.
HUH?!
IS YOUR BOSS IN?
Hmph!
PRINCE ZEN'S ORDERS? FINE BY ME.
I WON'T TURN AWAY AN EXTRA PAIR OF HANDS AROUND HERE.
MUCH APPRECI-ATED.

October 2008

I took a flight alone for the first time.

At the airport, I was momentarily flustered by how quick and efficient the bag checkers were. So speedy.

I ride bullet trains about once or twice a year, and I'm so used to them that when the flight attendant asked, "Would you like something to drink?" I nearly leapt out of my seat in shock.

It wasn't until the trip was over and I was back home that I realized the drinks were free of charge.

So that's how it is, huh?

The flight home was on a small propeller plane. I had to ride a bus out onto the tarmac right up to the plane.

I felt so presidential!

It was fun. Seeing the clouds from up there was amazing.

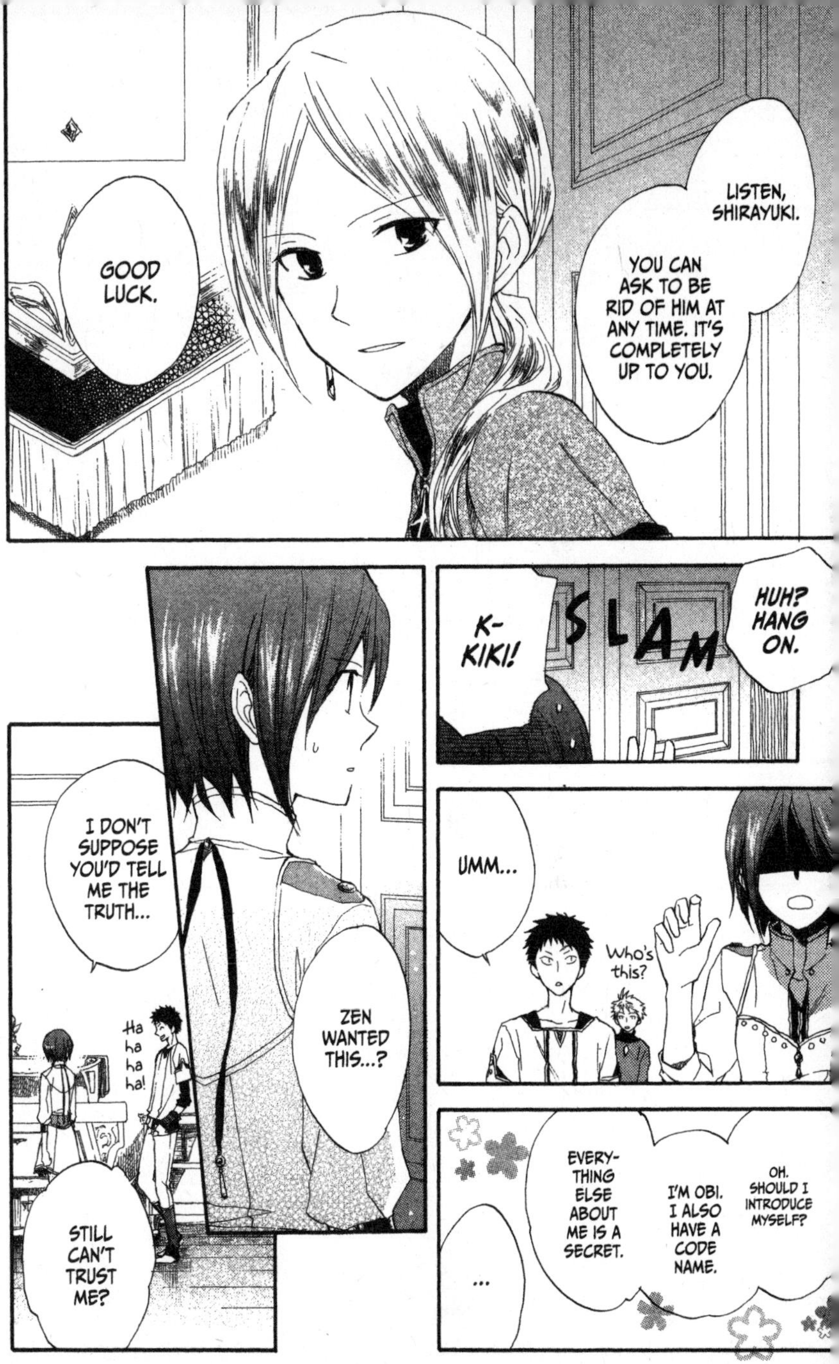
LISTEN, SHIRAYUKI.
YOU CAN ASK TO BE RID OF HIM AT ANY TIME. IT'S COMPLETELY UP TO YOU.
GOOD LUCK.
HUH? HANG ON.
SLAM
K-KIKI!
UMM...
Who's this?
OH. SHOULD I INTRODUCE MYSELF?
I'M OBI. I ALSO HAVE A CODE NAME.
EVERY-THING ELSE ABOUT ME IS A SECRET.
...
ZEN WANTED THIS...?
I DON'T SUPPOSE YOU'D TELL ME THE TRUTH...
Ha ha ha ha!
STILL CAN'T TRUST ME?

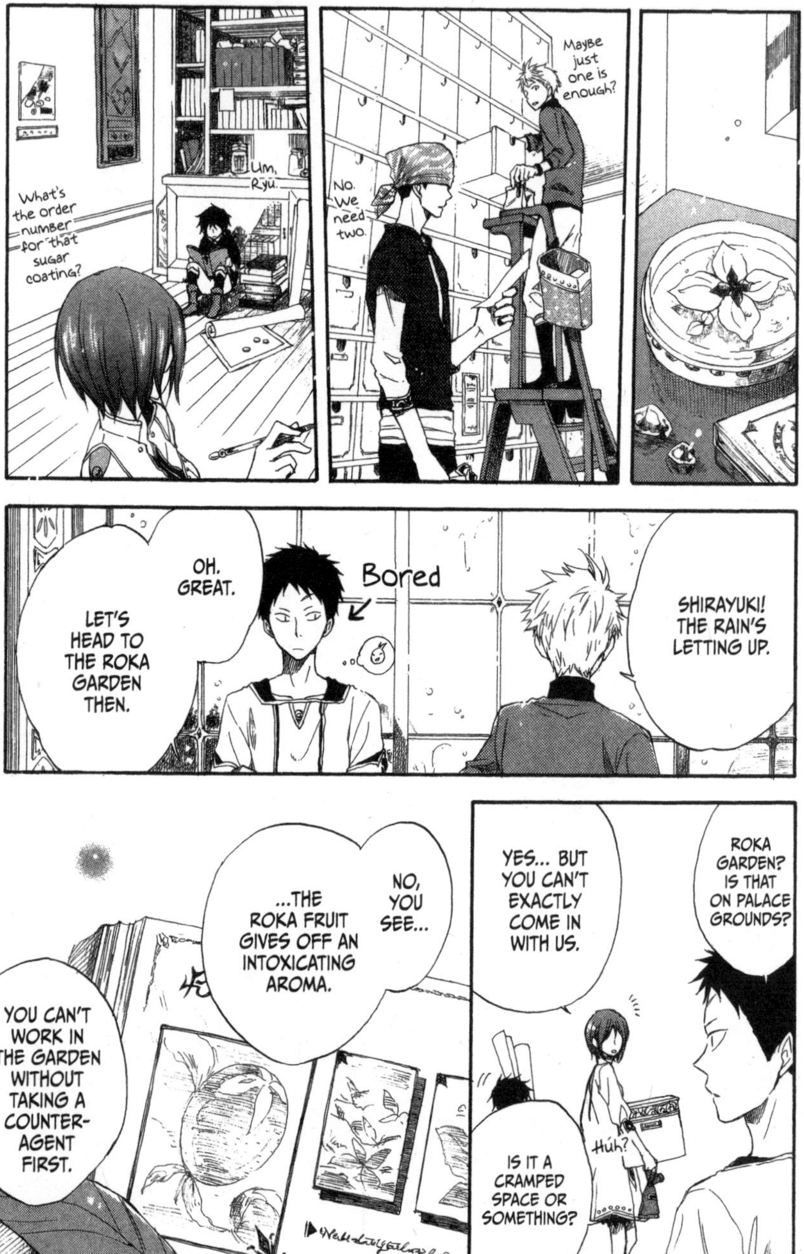
Maybe just one is enough?
No. We need two.
Um, Ryu.
What's the order number for that sugar coating?
SHIRAYUKI! THE RAIN'S LETTING UP.
Bored
OH. GREAT.
LET'S HEAD TO THE ROKA GARDEN THEN.
ROKA GARDEN? IS THAT ON PALACE GROUNDS?
YES... BUT YOU CAN'T EXACTLY COME IN WITH US.
Huh?
IS IT A CRAMPED SPACE OR SOMETHING?
NO, YOU SEE...
...THE ROKA FRUIT GIVES OFF AN INTOXICATING AROMA.
YOU CAN'T WORK IN THE GARDEN WITHOUT TAKING A COUNTER-AGENT FIRST.

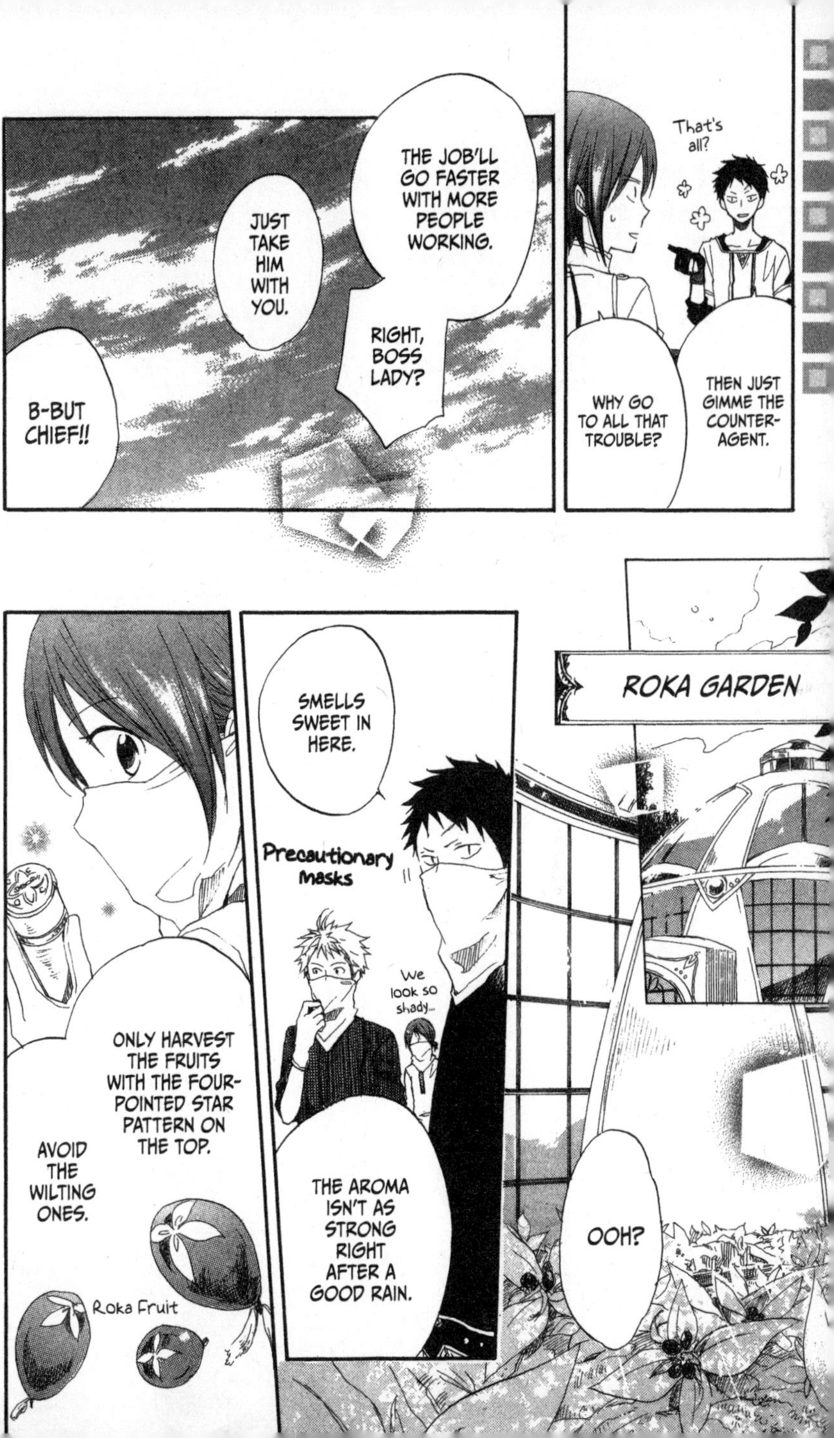
That's all?
THEN JUST GIMME THE COUNTER-AGENT.
WHY GO TO ALL THAT TROUBLE?
THE JOB'LL GO FASTER WITH MORE PEOPLE WORKING.
RIGHT, BOSS LADY?
JUST TAKE HIM WITH YOU.
B-BUT CHIEF!!
ROKA GARDEN
OOH?
SMELLS SWEET IN HERE.
Precautionary masks
We look so shady...
THE AROMA ISN'T AS STRONG RIGHT AFTER A GOOD RAIN.
ONLY HARVEST THE FRUITS WITH THE FOUR-POINTED STAR PATTERN ON THE TOP.
AVOID THE WILTING ONES.
Roka Fruit

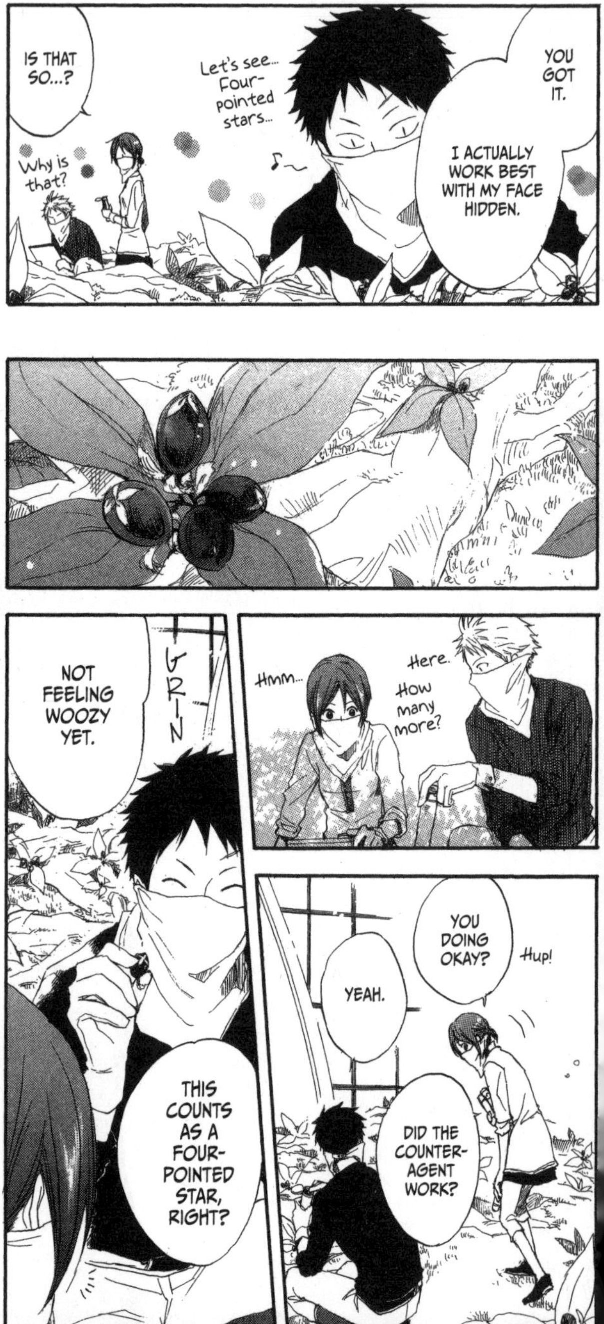
YOU GOT IT.
I ACTUALLY WORK BEST WITH MY FACE HIDDEN.
Let's see... Four-pointed stars...
IS THAT SO...?
Why is that?
Here.
How many more?
Hmm...
Hup!
YOU DOING OKAY?
YEAH.
DID THE COUNTER-AGENT WORK?
NOT FEELING WOOZY YET.
GRIN
THIS COUNTS AS A FOUR-POINTED STAR, RIGHT?

Character Spotlight

Unexpected Empty Page Space

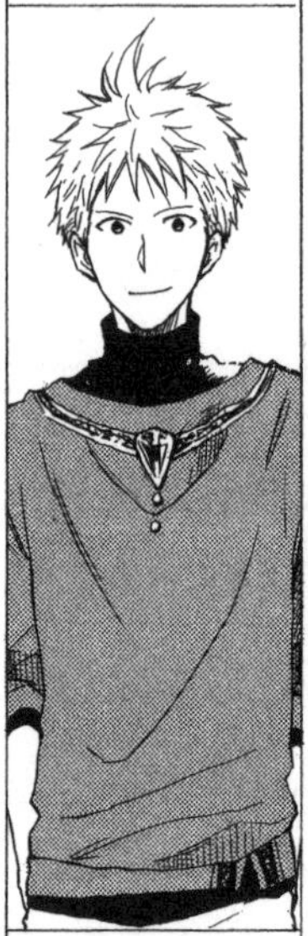

▸ Fellow Apprentice Guy

His name is Higata. He mostly works under Yatsufusa.

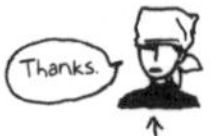
Thanks.
Yatsufusa

He keeps busy, managing the medicine stores and dealing with patients.

Thanks.

Higata is always very polite to Shirayuki even though he's actually older than her.

He's got a girlfriend he's known since childhood.

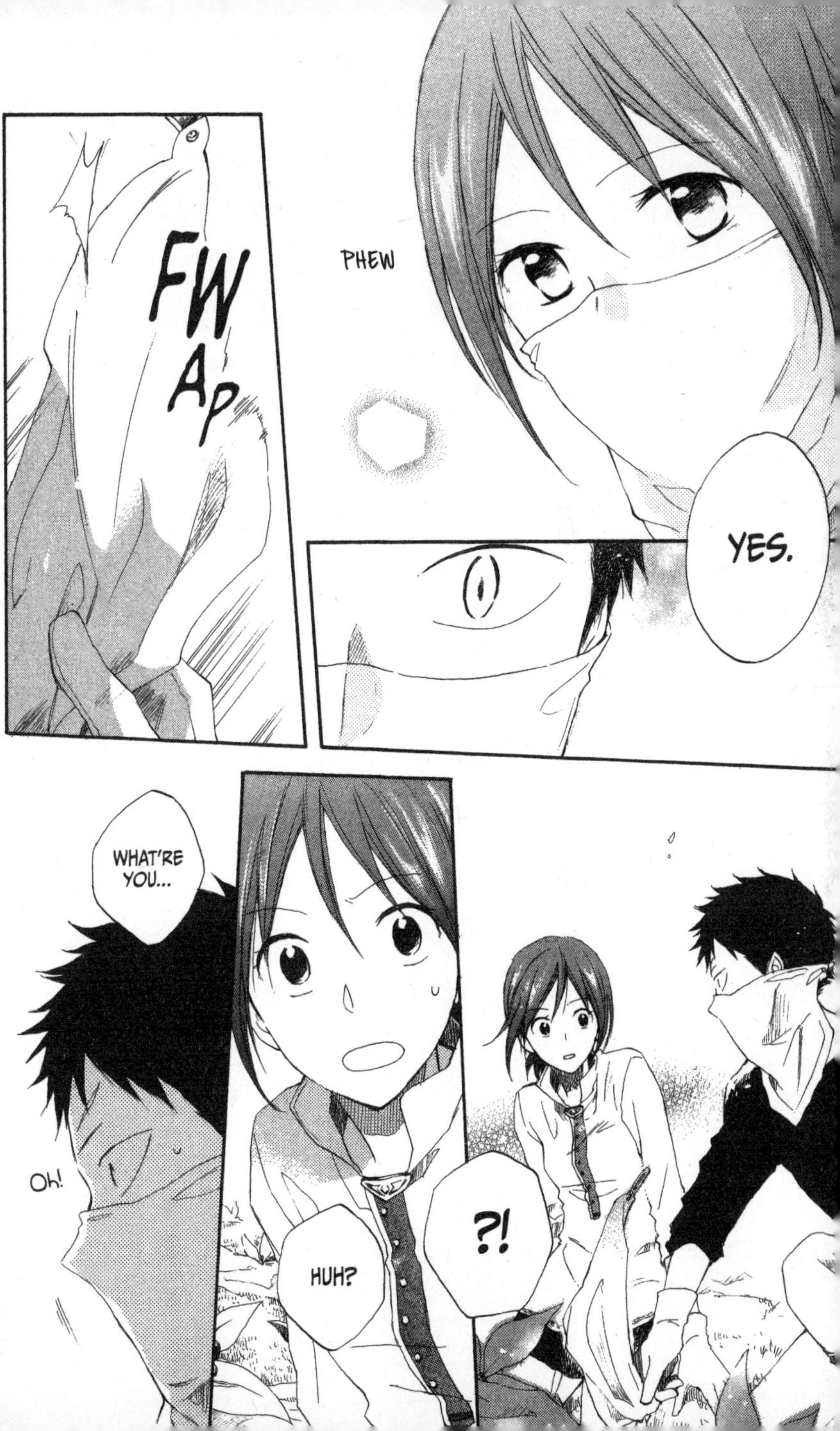
PHEW
YES.
FWAP
?!
HUH?
WHAT'RE YOU...
Oh!

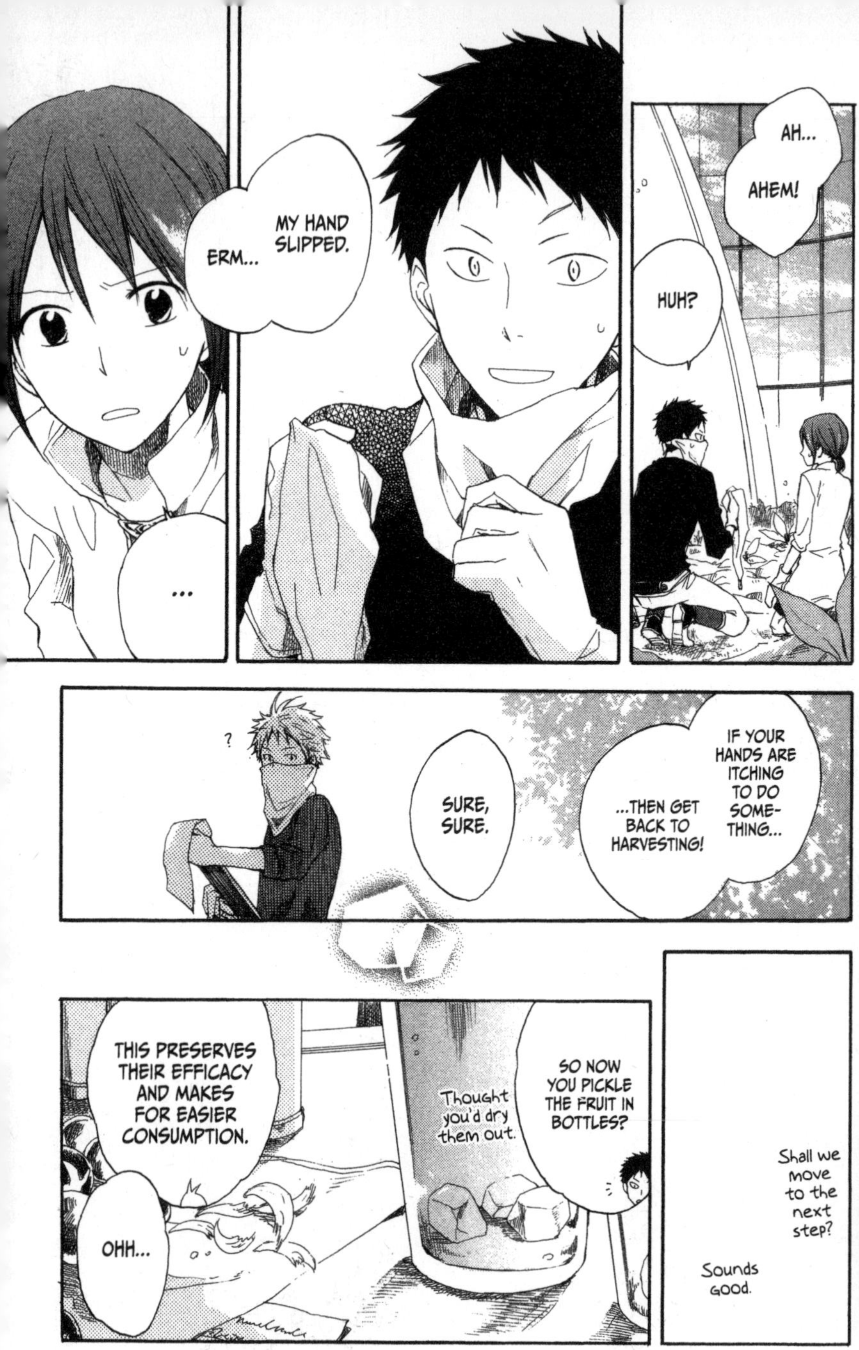
AH... AHEM!
HUH?
ERM... MY HAND SLIPPED.
...
IF YOUR HANDS ARE ITCHING TO DO SOME-THING...
...THEN GET BACK TO HARVESTING!
SURE, SURE.
?
Shall we move to the next step?
Sounds good.
SO NOW YOU PICKLE THE FRUIT IN BOTTLES?
Thought you'd dry them out.
THIS PRESERVES THEIR EFFICACY AND MAKES FOR EASIER CONSUMPTION.
OHH...

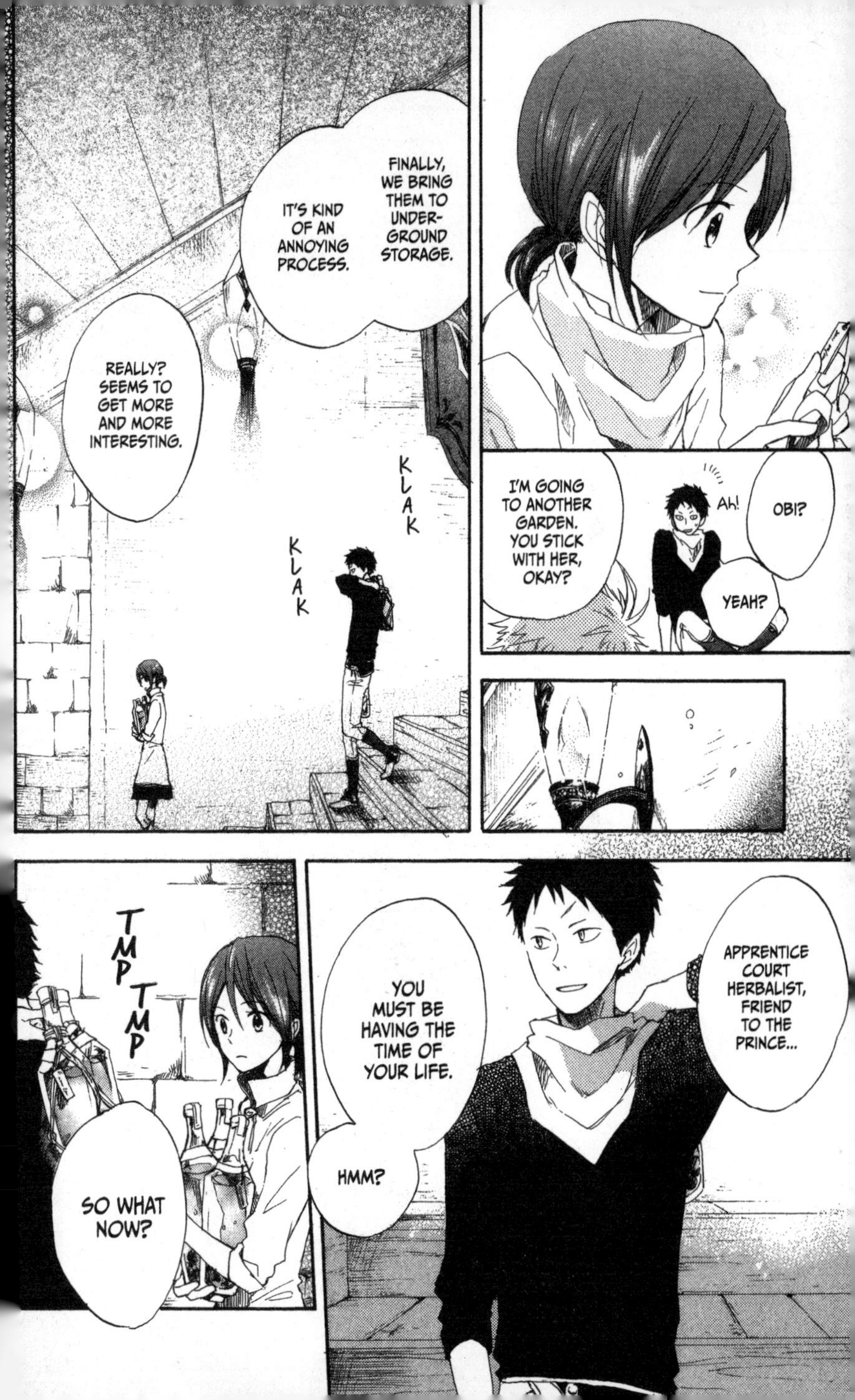
OBI?
Ah!
I'M GOING TO ANOTHER GARDEN. YOU STICK WITH HER, OKAY?
YEAH?
FINALLY, WE BRING THEM TO UNDER-GROUND STORAGE.
IT'S KIND OF AN ANNOYING PROCESS.
REALLY? SEEMS TO GET MORE AND MORE INTERESTING.
KLAK
KLAK
APPRENTICE COURT HERBALIST, FRIEND TO THE PRINCE...
YOU MUST BE HAVING THE TIME OF YOUR LIFE.
HMM?
TMP TMP
SO WHAT NOW?

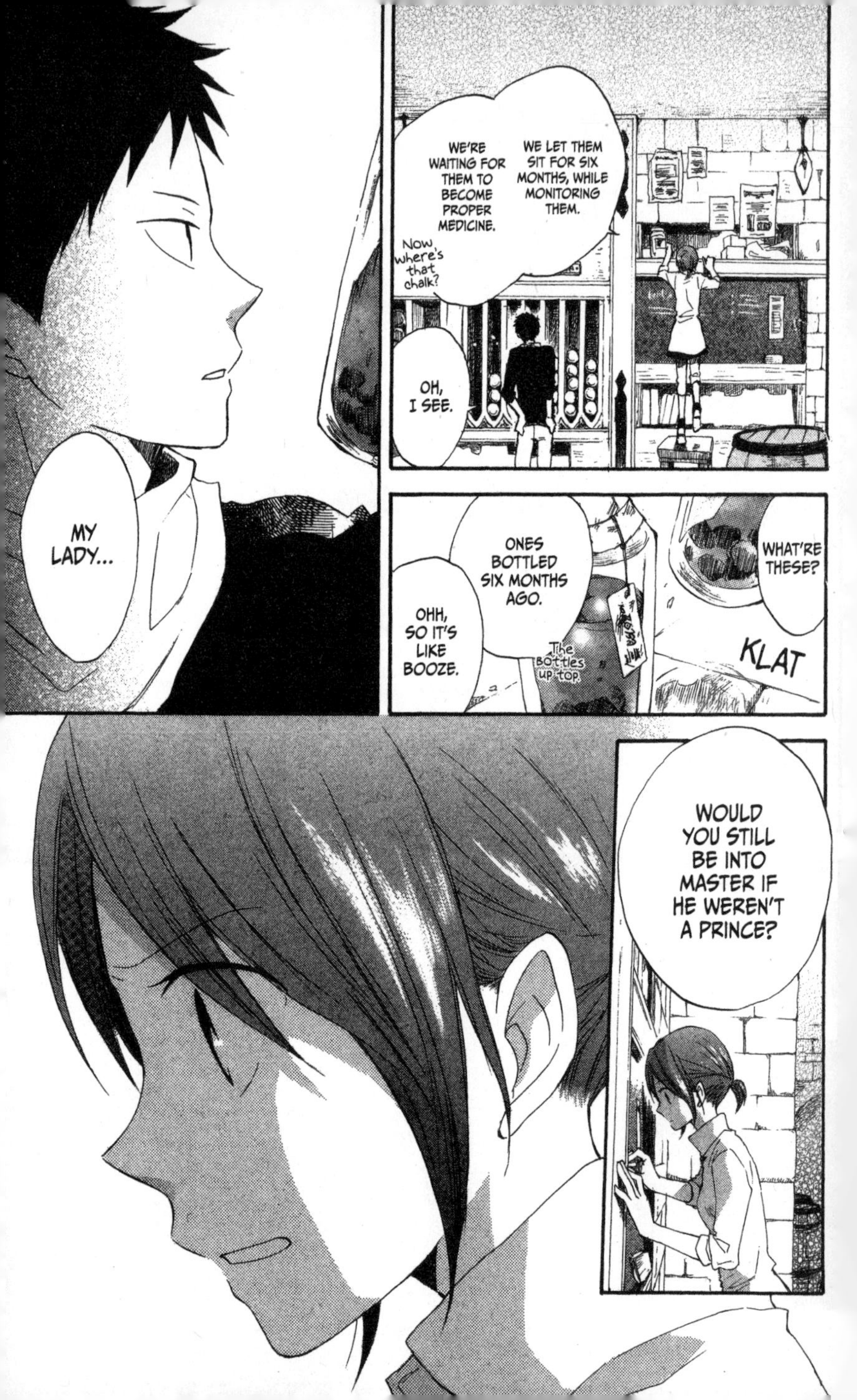
WE LET THEM SIT FOR SIX MONTHS, WHILE MONITORING THEM.
WE'RE WAITING FOR THEM TO BECOME PROPER MEDICINE.
Now where's that chalk?
OH, I SEE.
WHAT'RE THESE?
KLAT
ONES BOTTLED SIX MONTHS AGO.
The bottles up top.
OHH, SO IT'S LIKE BOOZE.
MY LADY...
WOULD YOU STILL BE INTO MASTER IF HE WEREN'T A PRINCE?

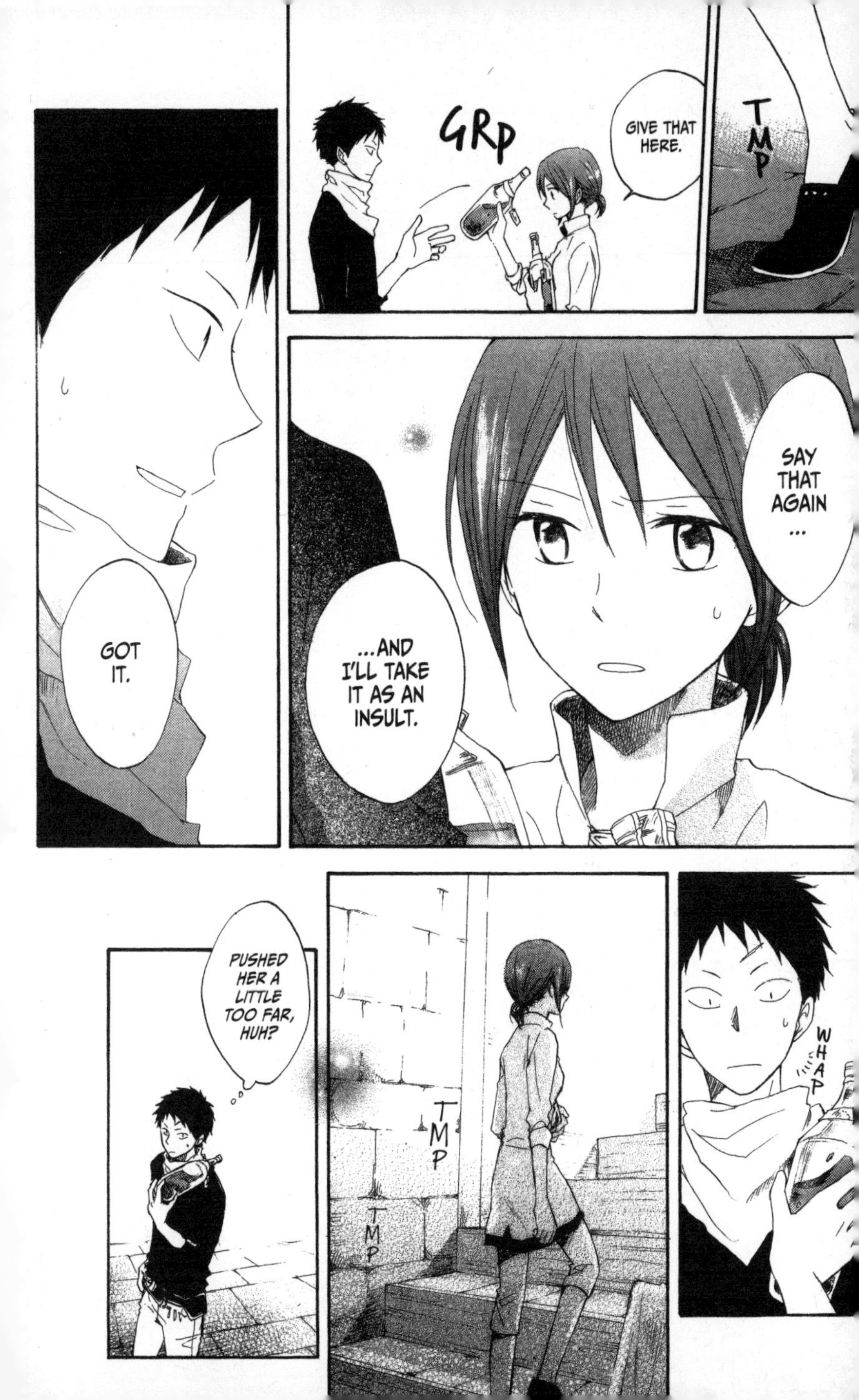
TMP
GIVE THAT HERE.
GRP
SAY THAT AGAIN ...
...AND I'LL TAKE IT AS AN INSULT.
GOT IT.
WHAP
TMP
TMP
PUSHED HER A LITTLE TOO FAR, HUH?

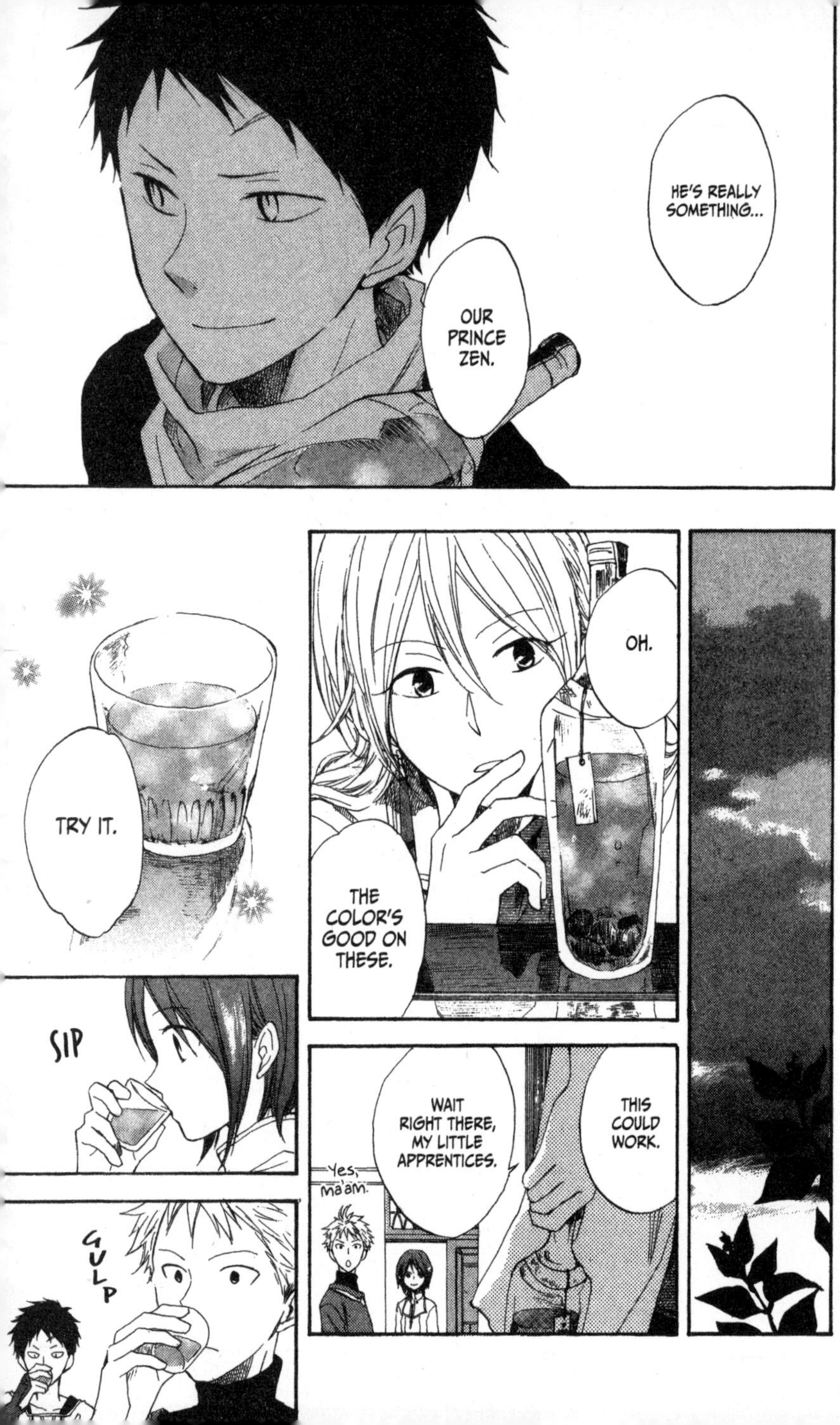
HE'S REALLY SOMETHING...
OUR PRINCE ZEN.
OH.
THE COLOR'S GOOD ON THESE.
THIS COULD WORK.
WAIT RIGHT THERE, MY LITTLE APPRENTICES.
Yes, ma'am.
TRY IT.
SIP
GULP

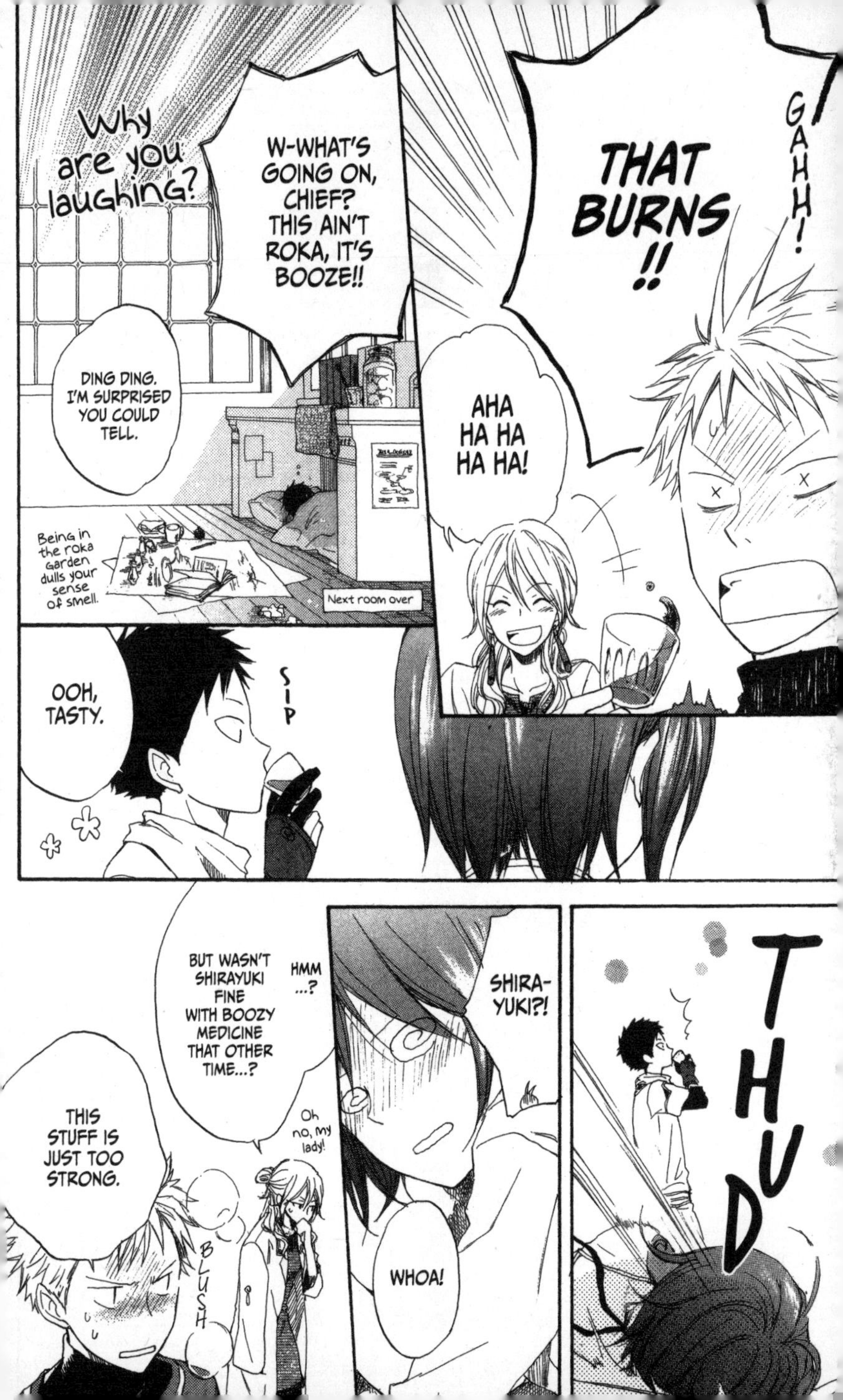
GAHHH!
THAT BURNS!!
AHA HA HA HA HA!
W-WHAT'S GOING ON, CHIEF? THIS AIN'T ROKA, IT'S BOOZE!!
Why are you laughing?
DING DING. I'M SURPRISED YOU COULD TELL.
Being in the roka garden dulls your sense of smell.
Next room over
SIP
OOH, TASTY.
THUD
SHIRA-YUKI?!
WHOA!
HMM ...?
BUT WASN'T SHIRAYUKI FINE WITH BOOZY MEDICINE THAT OTHER TIME...?
Oh no, my lady!
THIS STUFF IS JUST TOO STRONG.
BLUSH

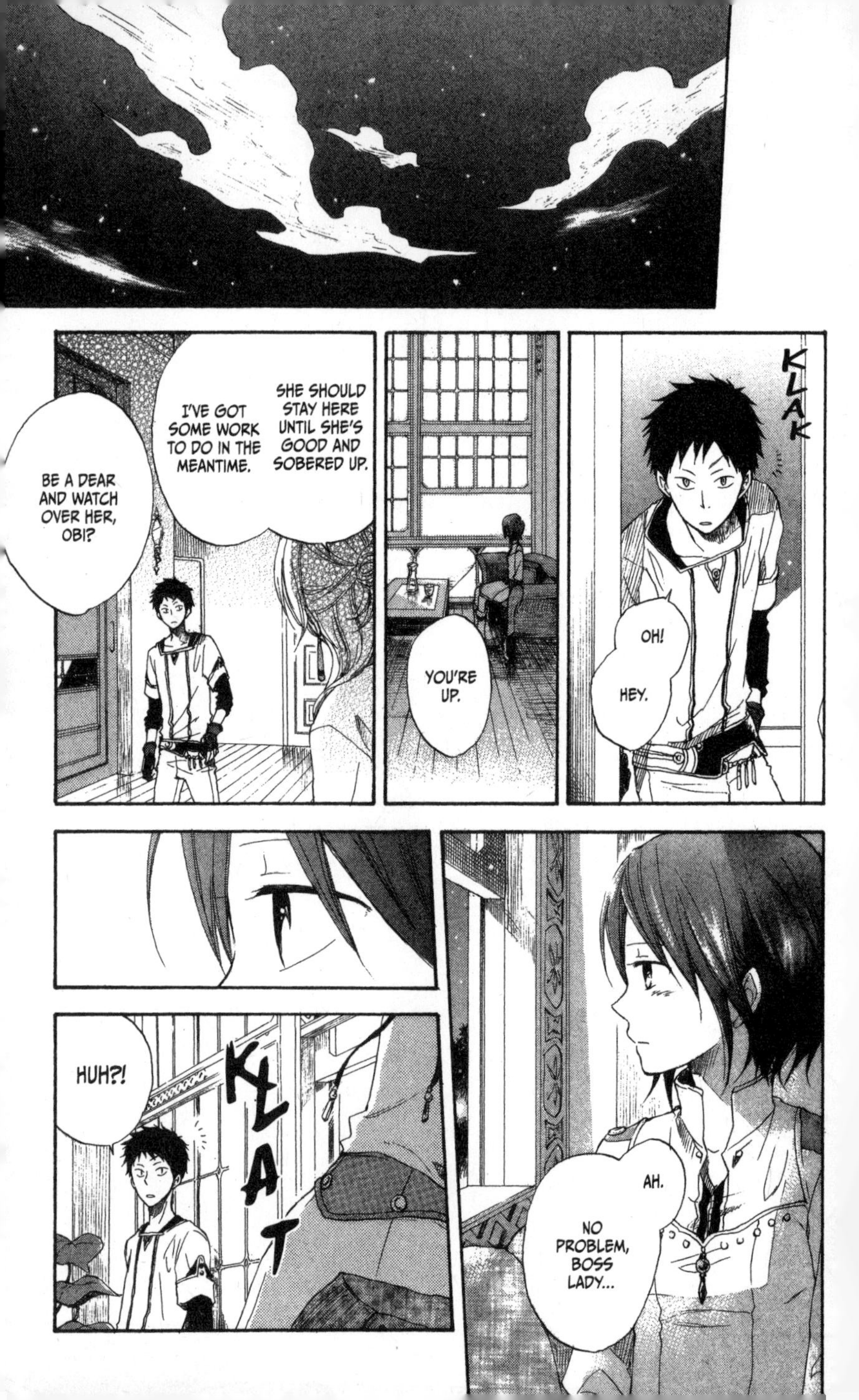
KLAK
OH!
HEY.
YOU'RE UP.
SHE SHOULD STAY HERE UNTIL SHE'S GOOD AND SOBERED UP.
I'VE GOT SOME WORK TO DO IN THE MEANTIME.
BE A DEAR AND WATCH OVER HER, OBI?
AH.
NO PROBLEM, BOSS LADY...
KLAT
HUH?!

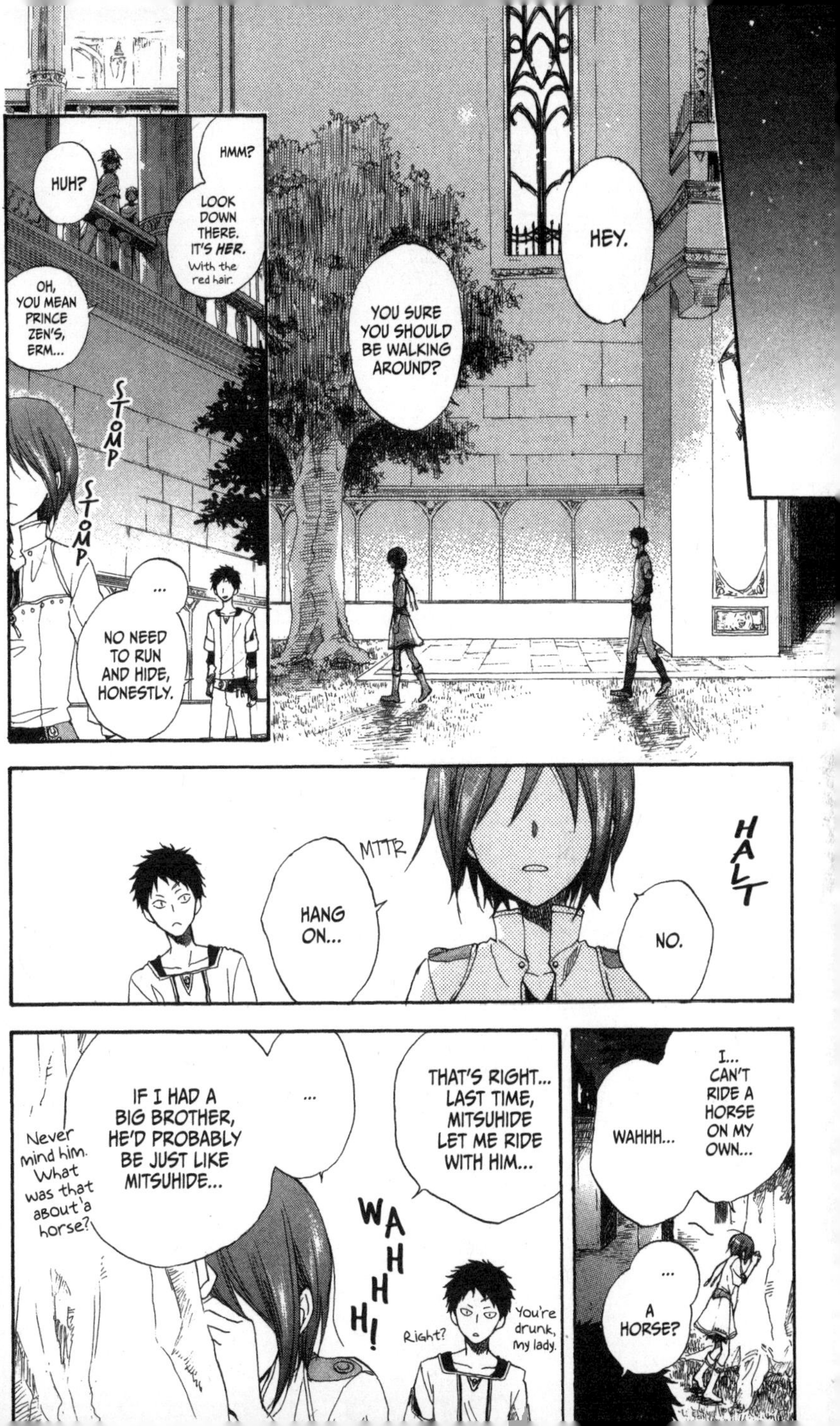

HEY.
YOU SURE YOU SHOULD BE WALKING AROUND?
HMM?
LOOK DOWN THERE. IT'S *HER*. With the red hair.
HUH?
OH, YOU MEAN PRINCE ZEN'S, ERM...
STOMP STOMP
...
NO NEED TO RUN AND HIDE, HONESTLY.
HALT
NO.
MTTR
HANG ON...
I... CAN'T RIDE A HORSE ON MY OWN...
WAHHH...
... A HORSE?
THAT'S RIGHT... LAST TIME, MITSUHIDE LET ME RIDE WITH HIM...
...
IF I HAD A BIG BROTHER, HE'D PROBABLY BE JUST LIKE MITSUHIDE...
Never mind him. What was that about 'a horse?
WAHHH!
You're drunk, my lady.
Right?

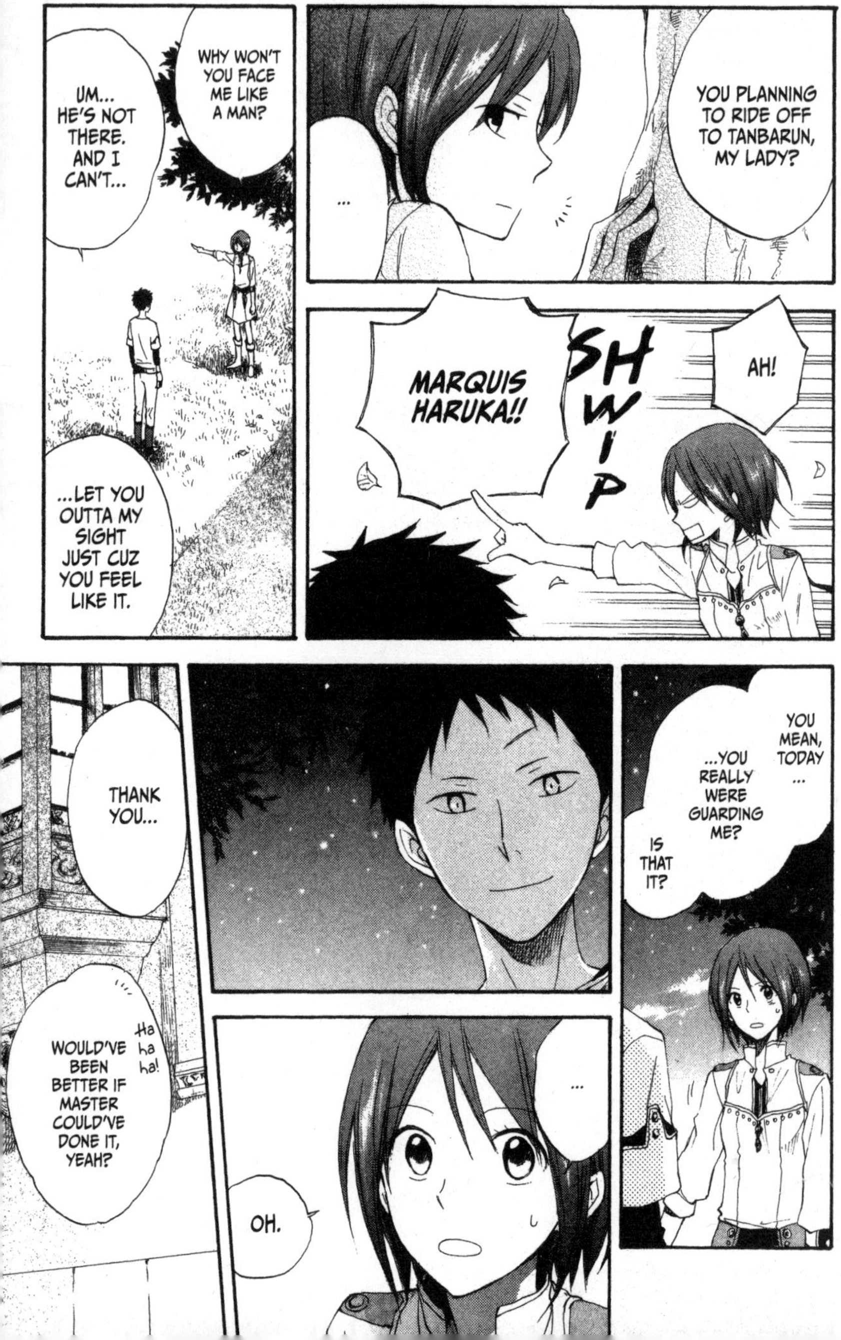
YOU PLANNING TO RIDE OFF TO TANBARUN, MY LADY?
...
AH!
SHWIP
MARQUIS HARUKA!!
WHY WON'T YOU FACE ME LIKE A MAN?
UM... HE'S NOT THERE. AND I CAN'T...
...LET YOU OUTTA MY SIGHT JUST CUZ YOU FEEL LIKE IT.
YOU MEAN, TODAY ...
...YOU REALLY WERE GUARDING ME?
IS THAT IT?
...
OH.
THANK YOU...
WOULD'VE BEEN BETTER IF MASTER COULD'VE DONE IT, YEAH?
Ha ha ha!

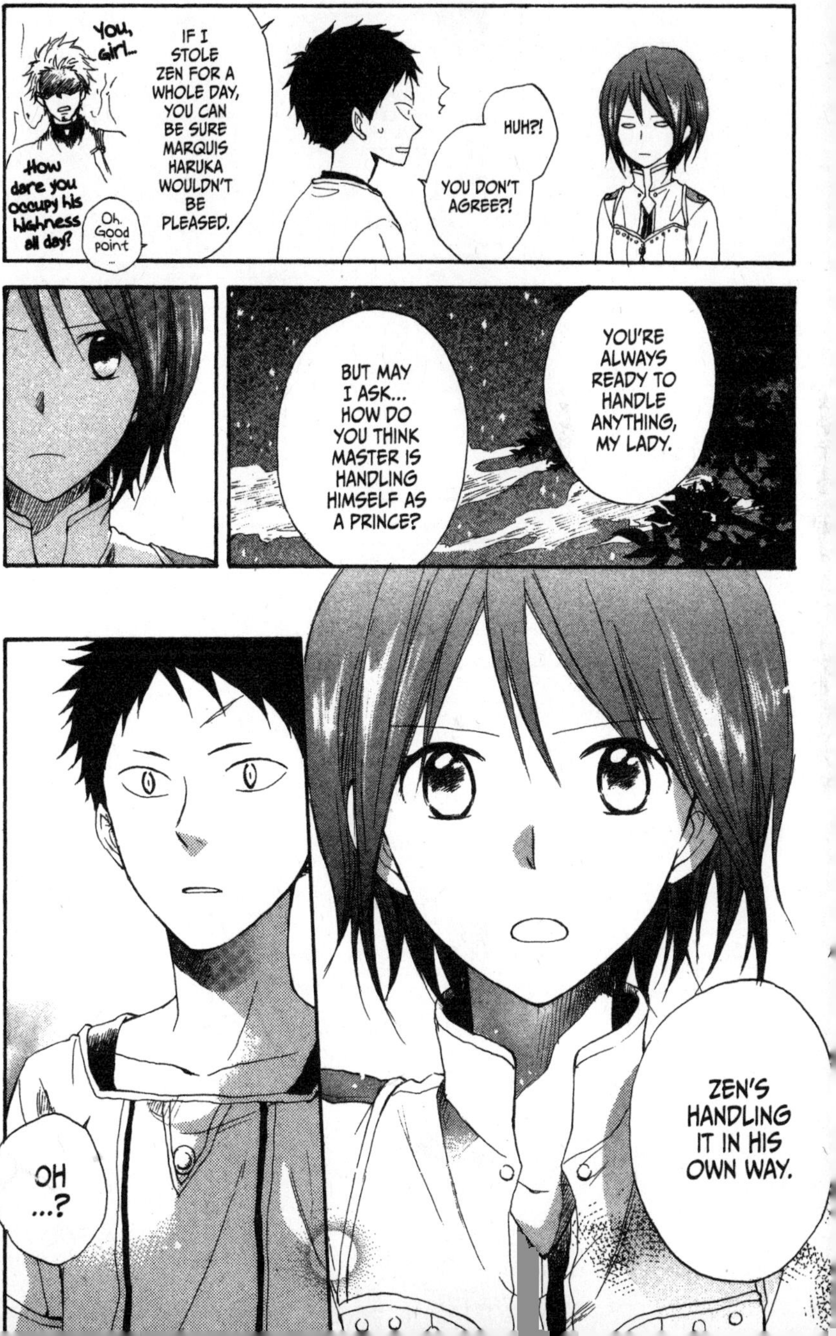
HUH?!
YOU DON'T AGREE?!
IF I STOLE ZEN FOR A WHOLE DAY, YOU CAN BE SURE MARQUIS HARUKA WOULDN'T BE PLEASED.
You, girl...
How dare you occupy his highness all day?
Oh. Good point...
YOU'RE ALWAYS READY TO HANDLE ANYTHING, MY LADY.
BUT MAY I ASK... HOW DO YOU THINK MASTER IS HANDLING HIMSELF AS A PRINCE?
ZEN'S HANDLING IT IN HIS OWN WAY.
OH ...?

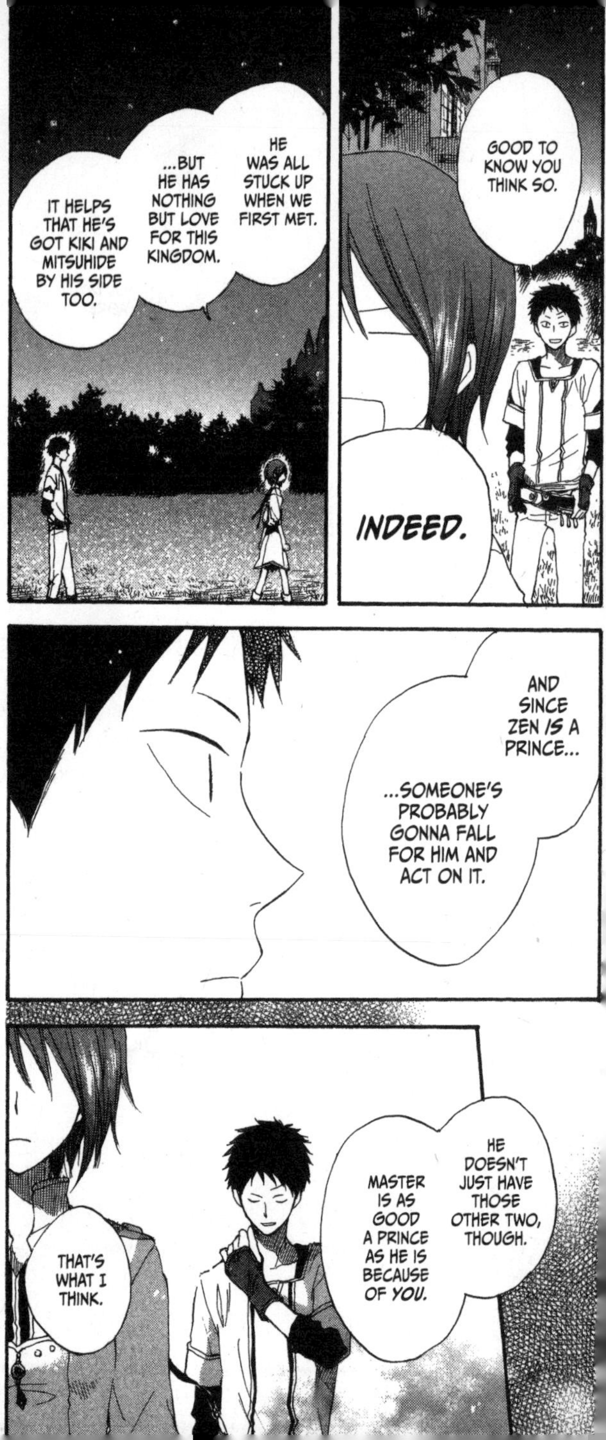
GOOD TO KNOW YOU THINK SO.
INDEED.
HE WAS ALL STUCK UP WHEN WE FIRST MET.
...BUT HE HAS NOTHING BUT LOVE FOR THIS KINGDOM.
IT HELPS THAT HE'S GOT KIKI AND MITSUHIDE BY HIS SIDE TOO.
AND SINCE ZEN *IS* A PRINCE...
...SOMEONE'S PROBABLY GONNA FALL FOR HIM AND ACT ON IT.
HE DOESN'T JUST HAVE THOSE OTHER TWO, THOUGH.
MASTER IS AS GOOD A PRINCE AS HE IS BECAUSE OF *YOU*.
THAT'S WHAT I THINK.

Spoilers Ahead

Chapter 11

This chapter is about viewing Shirayuki and Zen from Obi's perspective.

One night, when working on the rough draft, I was talking with my editor on the phone. Every comment from my editor was hilarious, and in the end my stomach hurt from laughing so hard.

Here's a gag version of the scene where Zen gives Obi his identification tag.

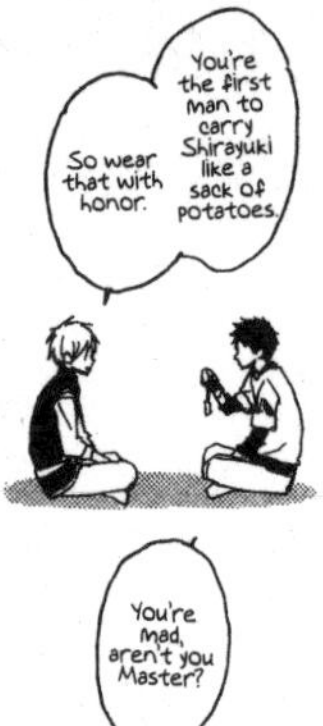
You're the first man to carry Shirayuki like a sack of potatoes.
So wear that with honor.
You're mad, aren't you Master?

Always so petty, Your Highness.

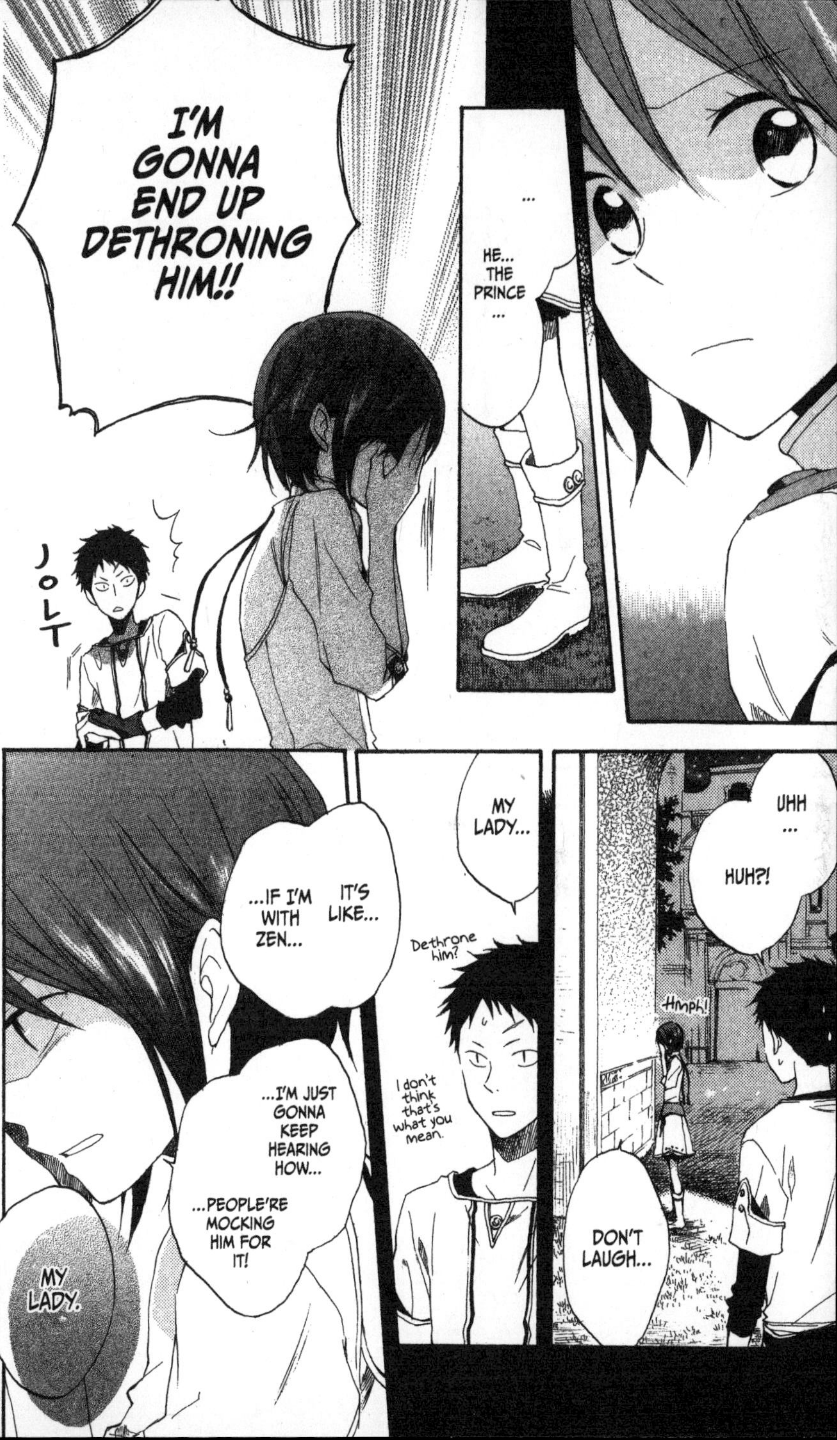
...
HE... THE PRINCE ...
I'M GONNA END UP DETHRONING HIM!!
JOLT
UHH ...
HUH?!
Hmph!
DON'T LAUGH...
MY LADY...
Dethrone him?
I don't think that's what you mean.
IT'S LIKE...
...IF I'M WITH ZEN...
...I'M JUST GONNA KEEP HEARING HOW...
...PEOPLE'RE MOCKING HIM FOR IT!
MY LADY.

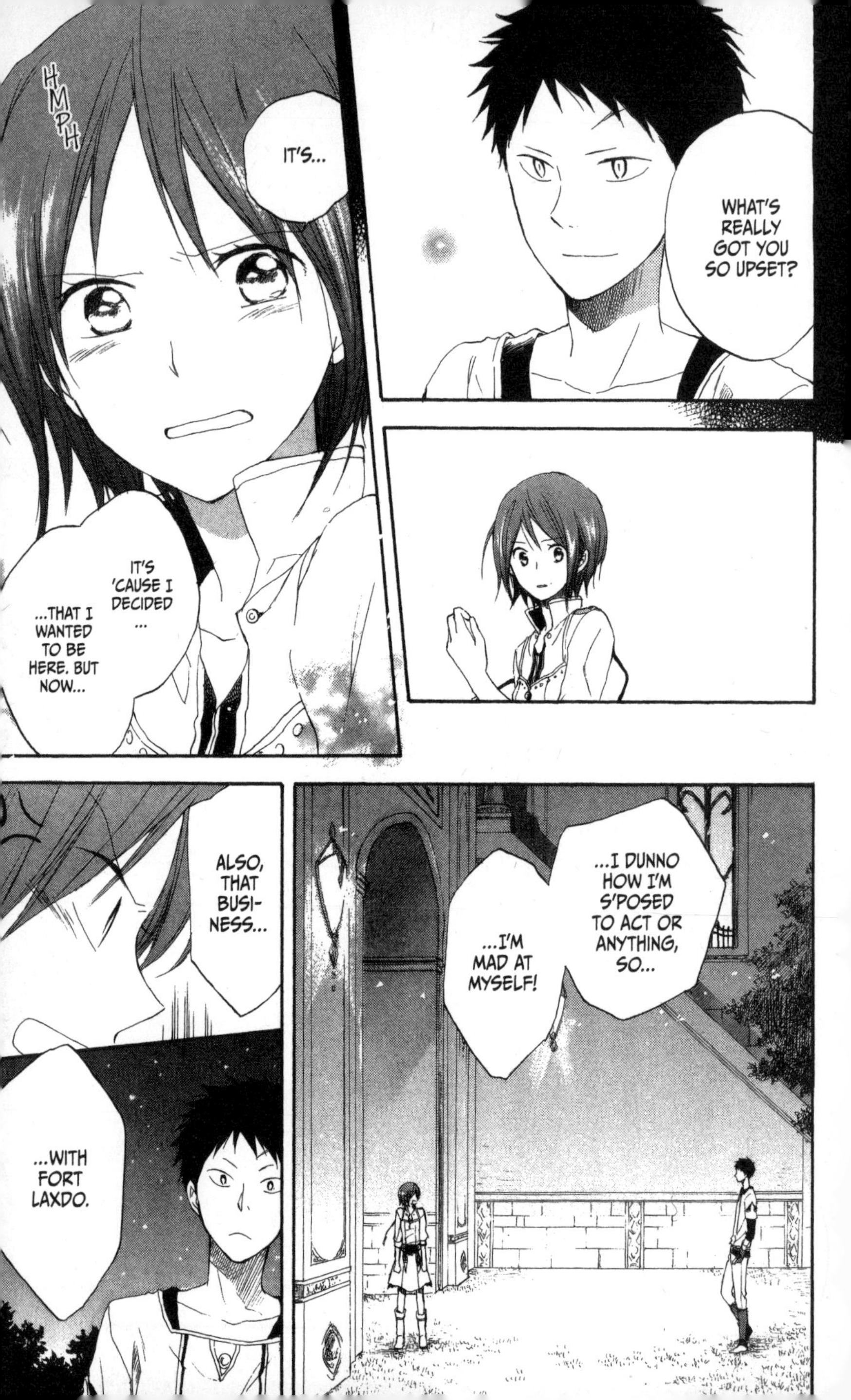
WHAT'S REALLY GOT YOU SO UPSET?
HMPH
IT'S...
IT'S 'CAUSE I DECIDED ...
...THAT I WANTED TO BE HERE. BUT NOW...
...I DUNNO HOW I'M S'POSED TO ACT OR ANYTHING, SO...
...I'M MAD AT MYSELF!
ALSO, THAT BUSINESS...
...WITH FORT LAXDO.

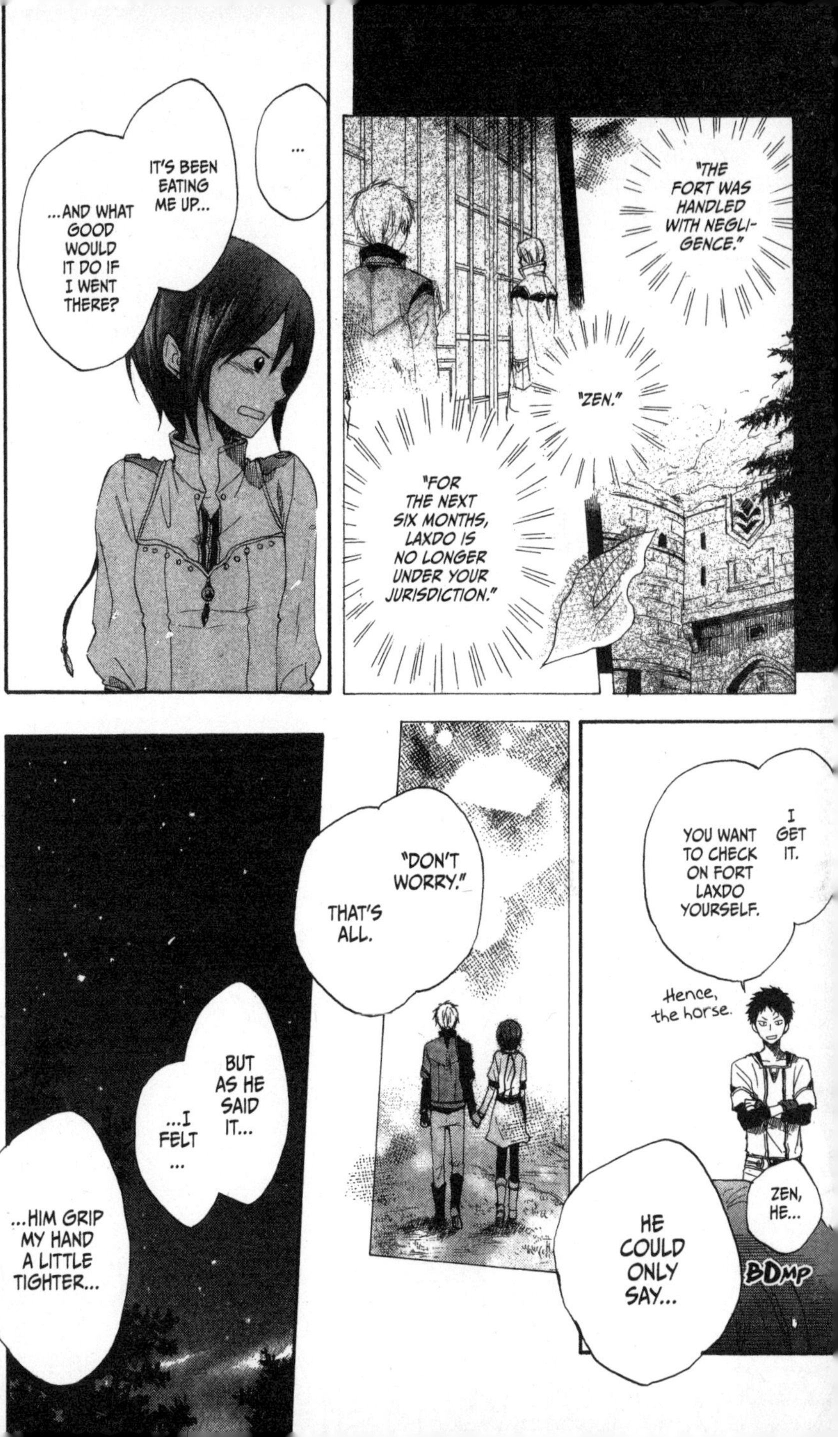
"THE FORT WAS HANDLED WITH NEGLIGENCE."
"ZEN."
"FOR THE NEXT SIX MONTHS, LAXDO IS NO LONGER UNDER YOUR JURISDICTION."
...
IT'S BEEN EATING ME UP...
...AND WHAT GOOD WOULD IT DO IF I WENT THERE?
I GET IT.
YOU WANT TO CHECK ON FORT LAXDO YOURSELF.
Hence, the horse.
ZEN, HE...
BDMP
HE COULD ONLY SAY...
"DON'T WORRY."
THAT'S ALL.
BUT AS HE SAID IT...
...I FELT ...
...HIM GRIP MY HAND A LITTLE TIGHTER...

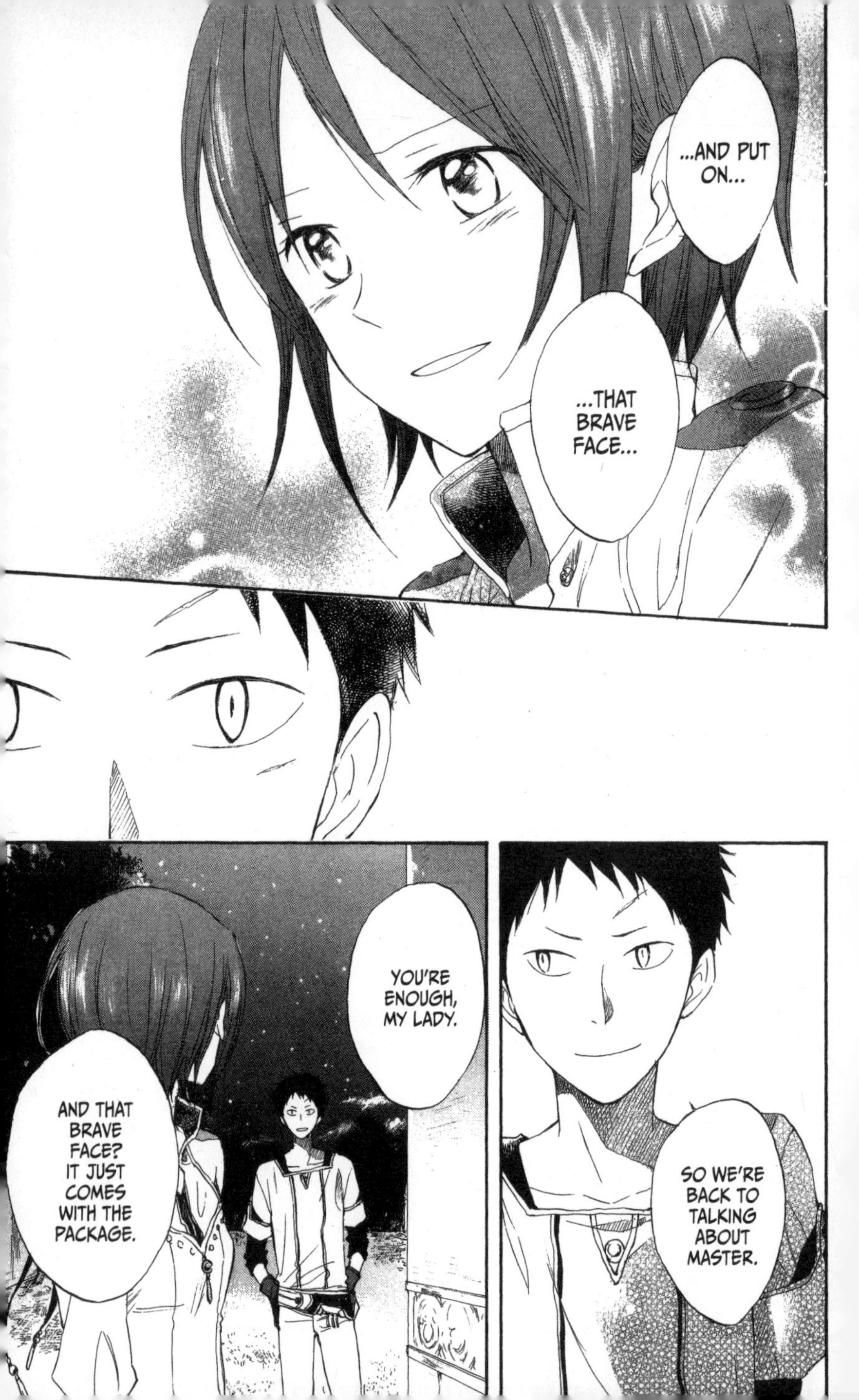
...AND PUT ON...
...THAT BRAVE FACE...
SO WE'RE BACK TO TALKING ABOUT MASTER.
YOU'RE ENOUGH, MY LADY.
AND THAT BRAVE FACE? IT JUST COMES WITH THE PACKAGE.

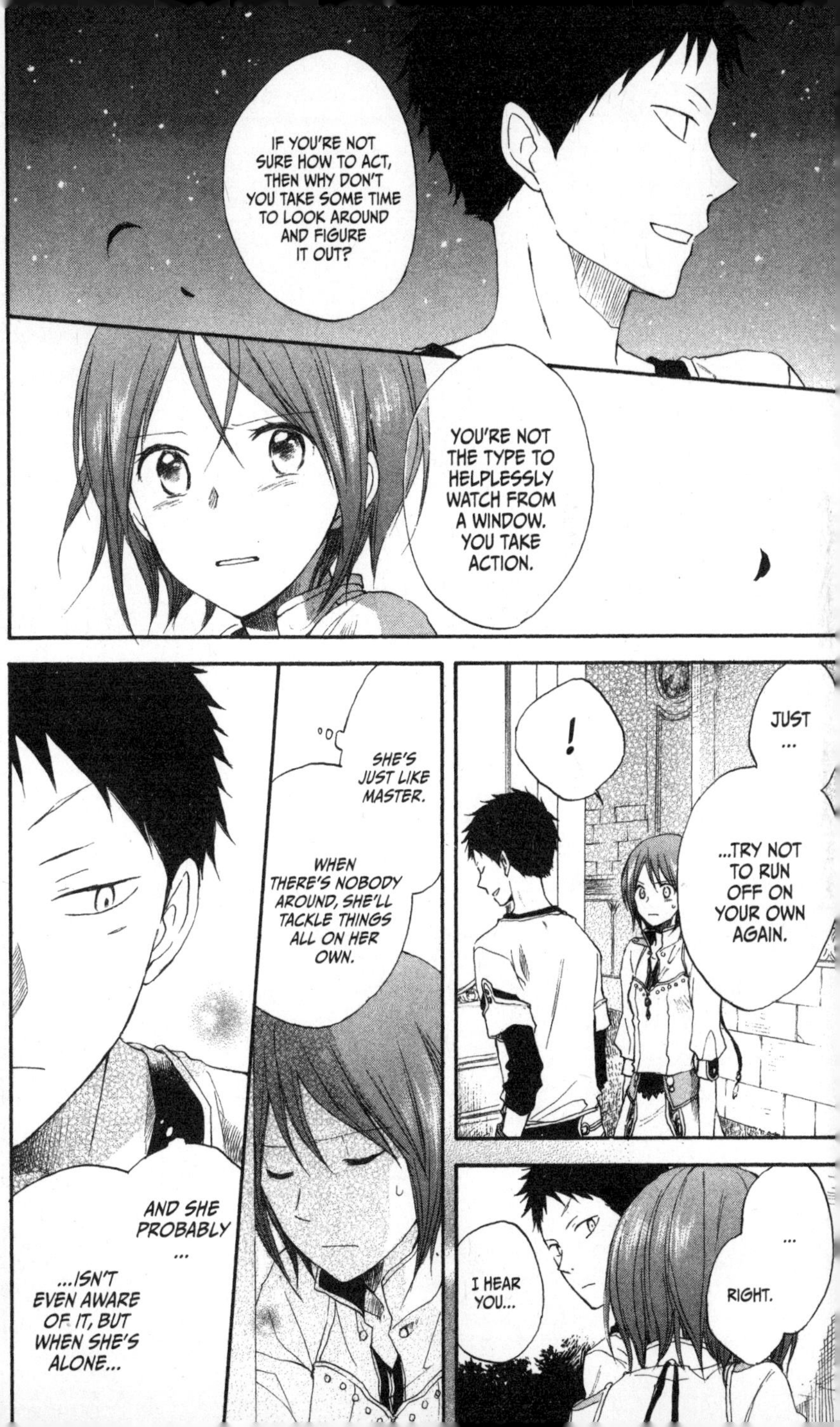
IF YOU'RE NOT SURE HOW TO ACT, THEN WHY DON'T YOU TAKE SOME TIME TO LOOK AROUND AND FIGURE IT OUT?
YOU'RE NOT THE TYPE TO HELPLESSLY WATCH FROM A WINDOW. YOU TAKE ACTION.
JUST ...
...TRY NOT TO RUN OFF ON YOUR OWN AGAIN.
!
...
RIGHT.
I HEAR YOU...
SHE'S JUST LIKE MASTER.
WHEN THERE'S NOBODY AROUND, SHE'LL TACKLE THINGS ALL ON HER OWN.
AND SHE PROBABLY ...
...ISN'T EVEN AWARE OF IT, BUT WHEN SHE'S ALONE...

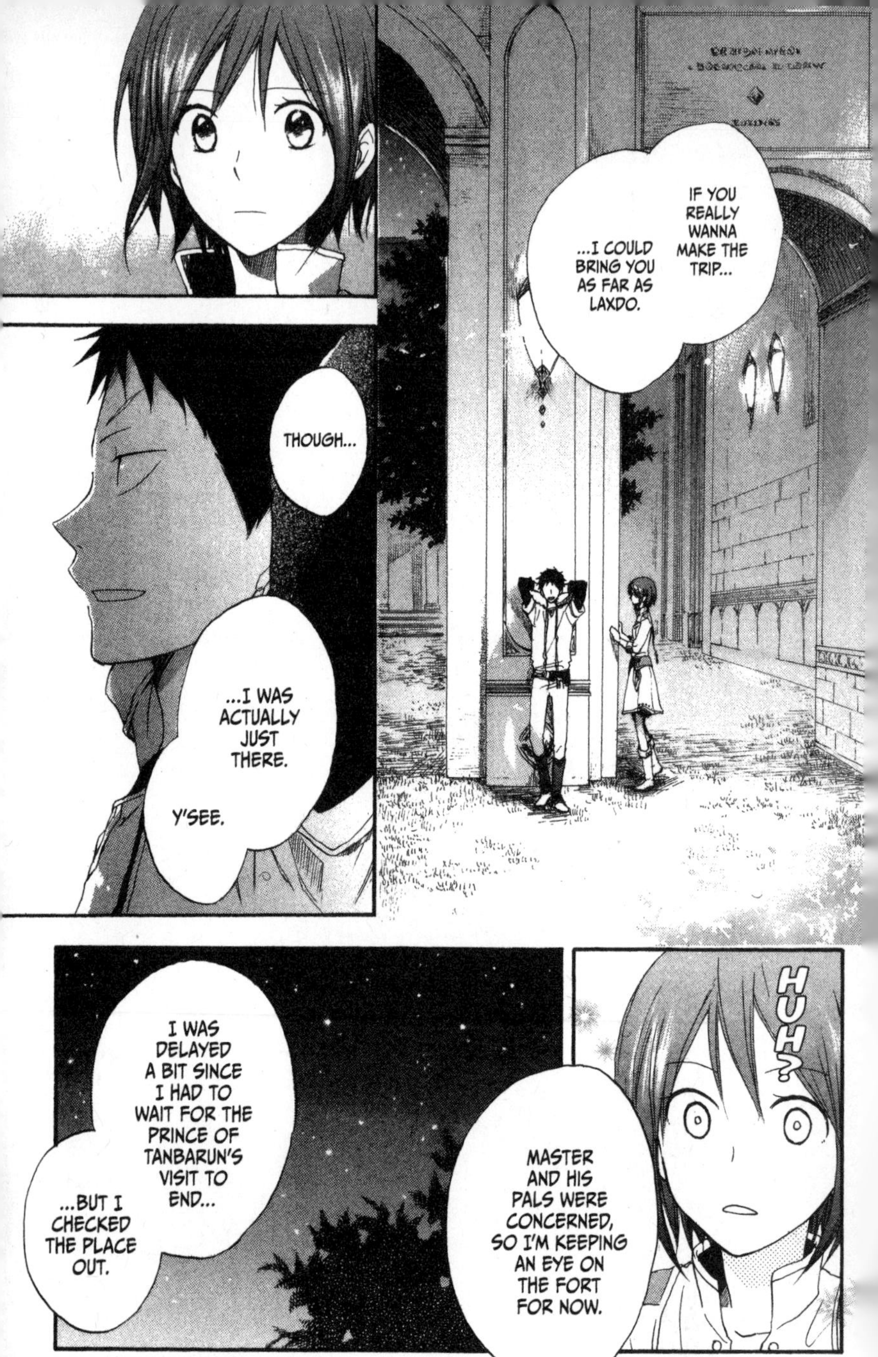
IF YOU REALLY WANNA MAKE THE TRIP...
...I COULD BRING YOU AS FAR AS LAXDO.
THOUGH...
...I WAS ACTUALLY JUST THERE.
Y'SEE.
HUH?
MASTER AND HIS PALS WERE CONCERNED, SO I'M KEEPING AN EYE ON THE FORT FOR NOW.
I WAS DELAYED A BIT SINCE I HAD TO WAIT FOR THE PRINCE OF TANBARUN'S VISIT TO END...
...BUT I CHECKED THE PLACE OUT.

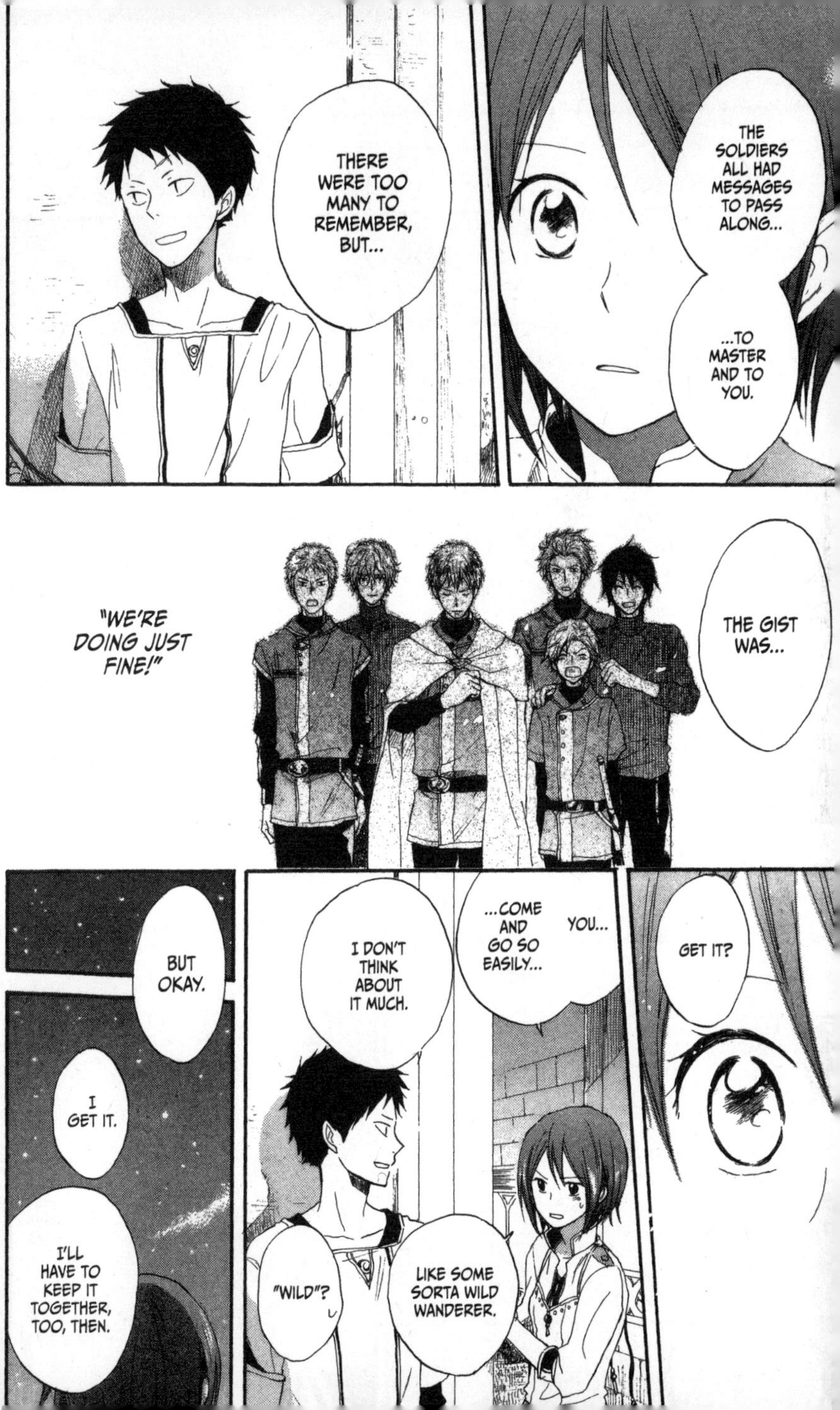
THE SOLDIERS ALL HAD MESSAGES TO PASS ALONG...
...TO MASTER AND TO YOU.
THERE WERE TOO MANY TO REMEMBER, BUT...
THE GIST WAS...
"WE'RE DOING JUST FINE!"
GET IT?
YOU...
...COME AND GO SO EASILY...
I DON'T THINK ABOUT IT MUCH.
LIKE SOME SORTA WILD WANDERER.
"WILD"?
BUT OKAY.
I GET IT.
I'LL HAVE TO KEEP IT TOGETHER, TOO, THEN.

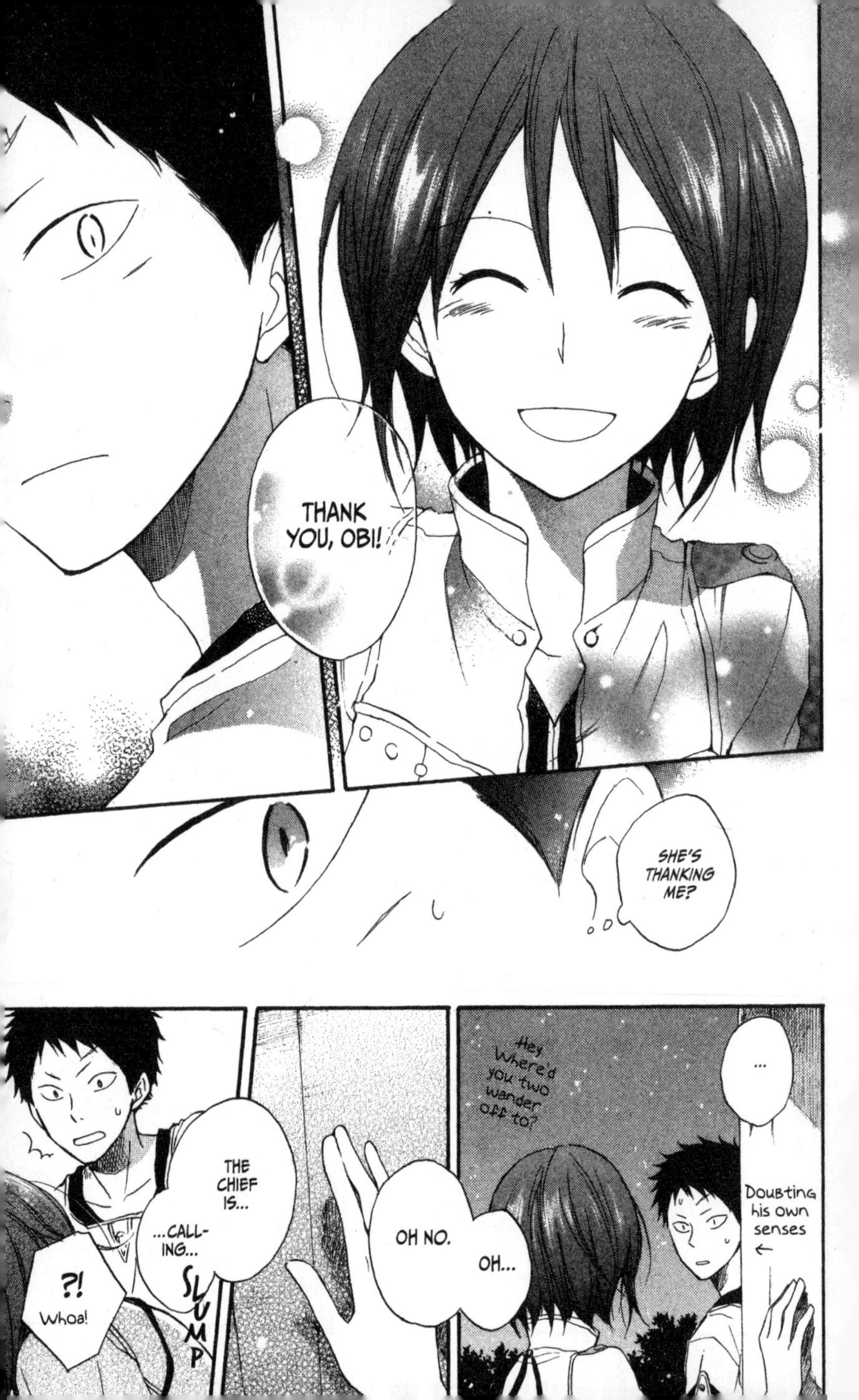
THANK YOU, OBI!
SHE'S THANKING ME?
...
Doubting his own senses ←
Hey Where'd you two wander off to?
OH...
OH NO.
THE CHIEF IS...
...CALL-ING...
SLUMP
?! Whoa!

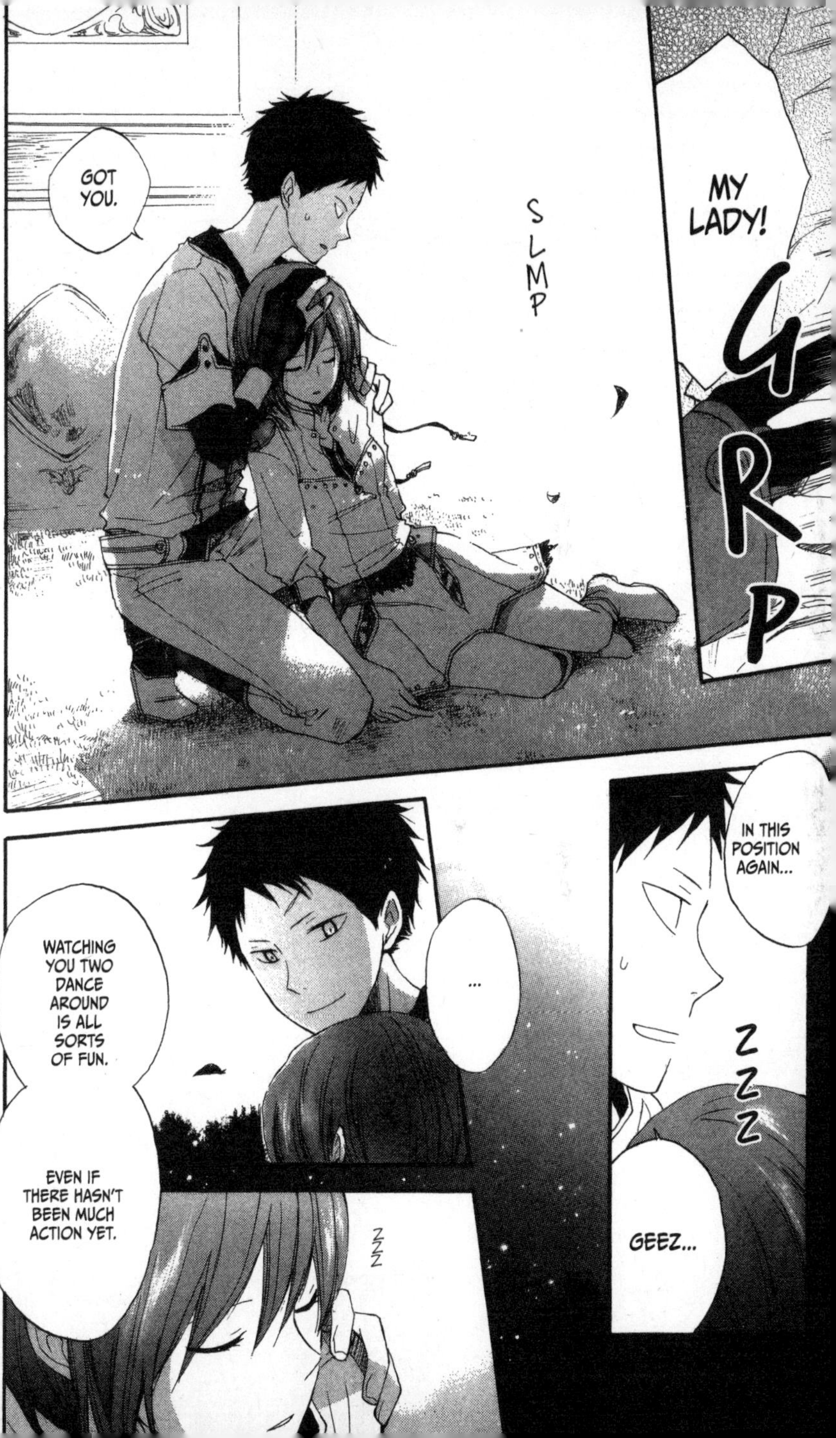
MY LADY!
GRRP
SLMP
GOT YOU.
IN THIS POSITION AGAIN...
ZZZ
GEEZ...
...
WATCHING YOU TWO DANCE AROUND IS ALL SORTS OF FUN.
EVEN IF THERE HASN'T BEEN MUCH ACTION YET.
ZZZ

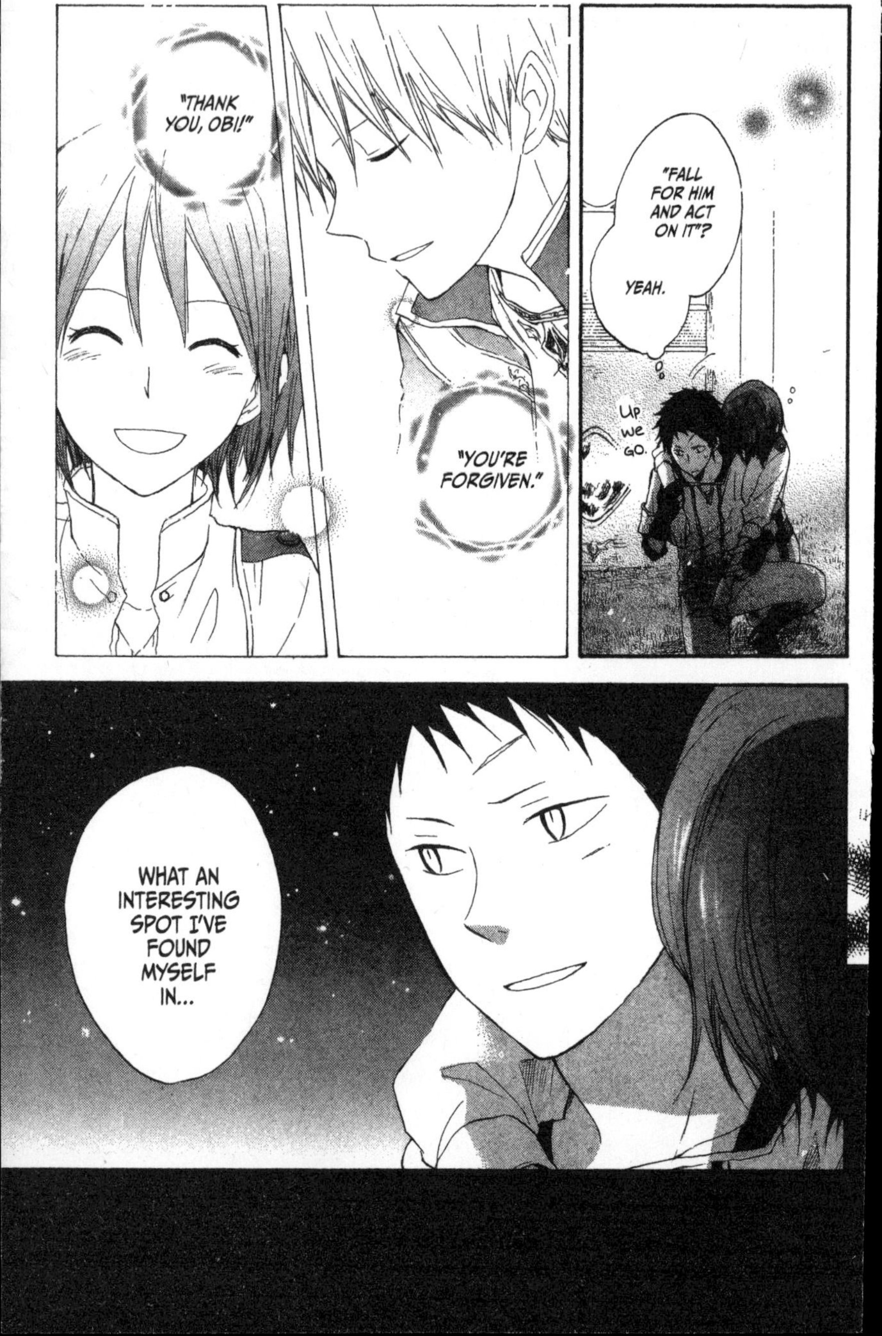
"FALL FOR HIM AND ACT ON IT"?
YEAH.
Up we GO.
"YOU'RE FORGIVEN."
"THANK YOU, OBI!"
WHAT AN INTERESTING SPOT I'VE FOUND MYSELF IN...

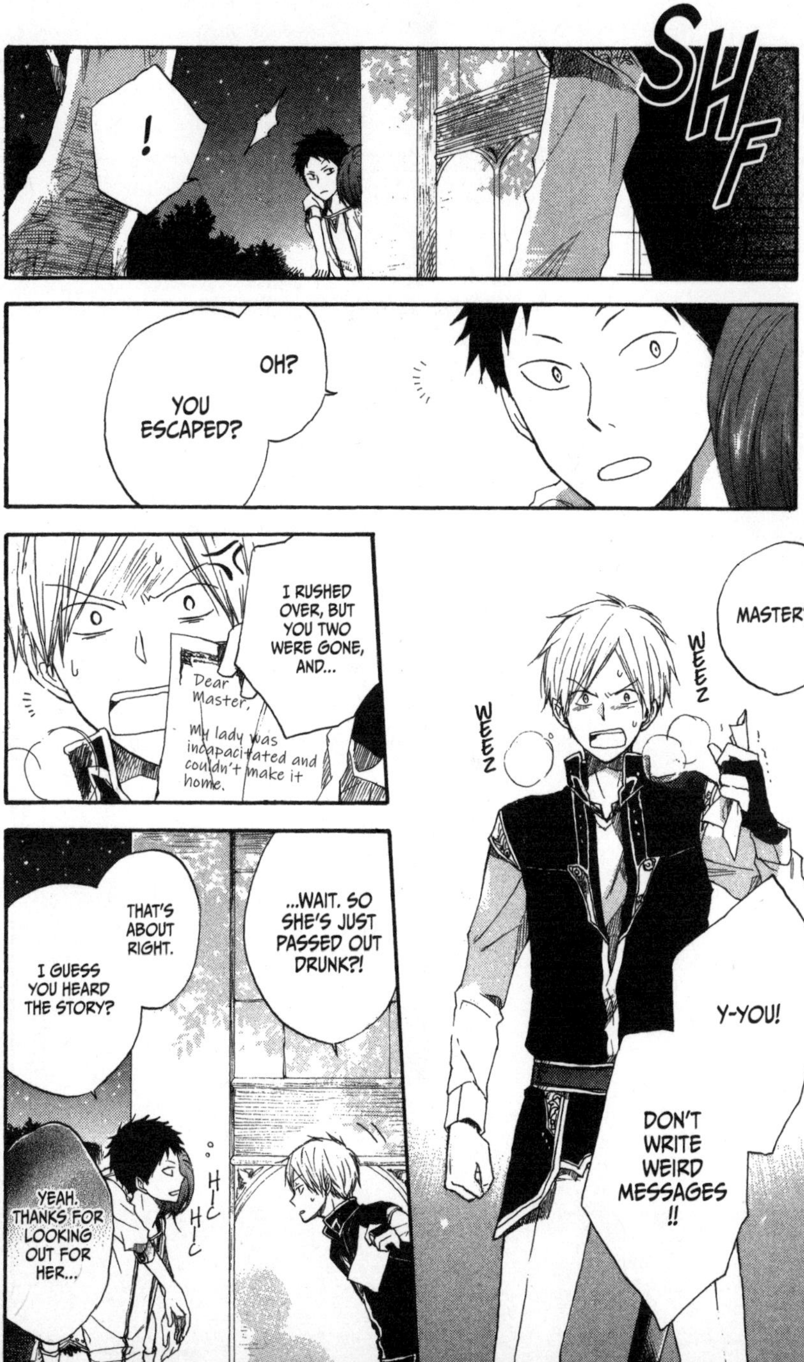
SHF
!
OH?
YOU ESCAPED?
MASTER?
WEEZ
WEEZ
Y-YOU!
DON'T WRITE WEIRD MESSAGES!!
I RUSHED OVER, BUT YOU TWO WERE GONE, AND...
Dear Master,
My lady was incapacitated and couldn't make it home.
...WAIT. SO SHE'S JUST PASSED OUT DRUNK?!
THAT'S ABOUT RIGHT.
I GUESS YOU HEARD THE STORY?
HIC
HIC
YEAH. THANKS FOR LOOKING OUT FOR HER...

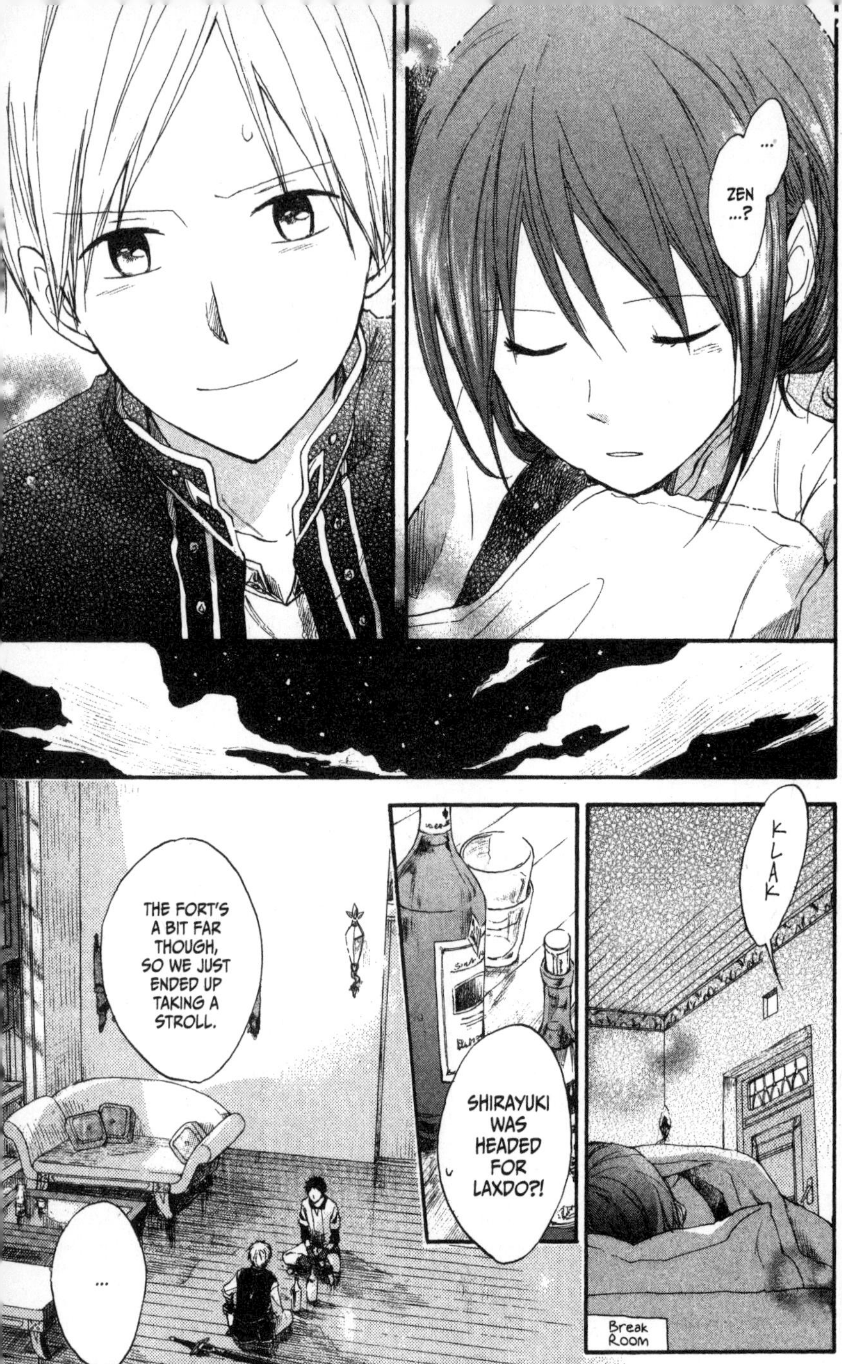
...
ZEN ...?
KLAK
Break Room
SHIRAYUKI WAS HEADED FOR LAXDO?!
THE FORT'S A BIT FAR THOUGH, SO WE JUST ENDED UP TAKING A STROLL.
...

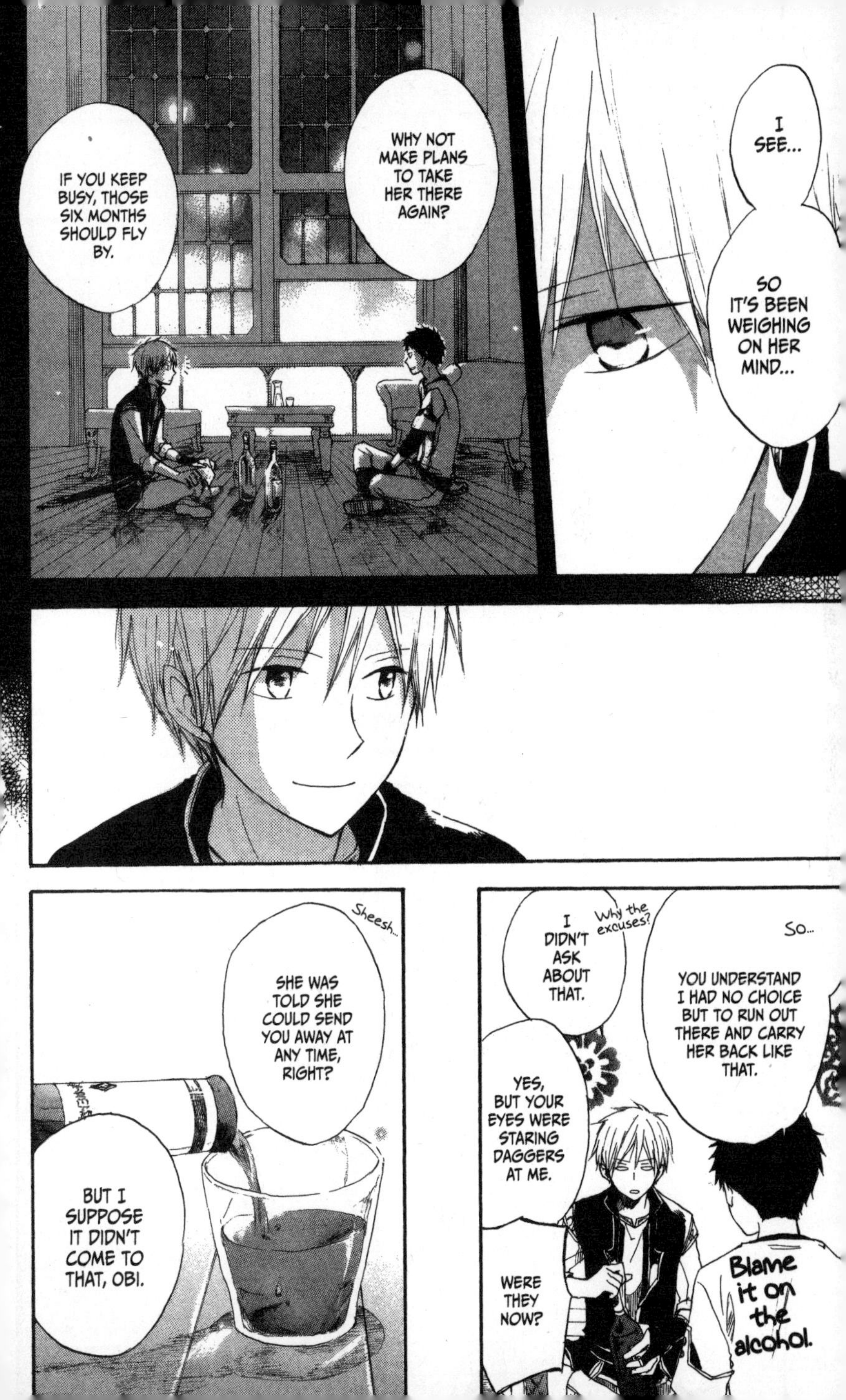
I SEE...
SO IT'S BEEN WEIGHING ON HER MIND...
WHY NOT MAKE PLANS TO TAKE HER THERE AGAIN?
IF YOU KEEP BUSY, THOSE SIX MONTHS SHOULD FLY BY.
So...
YOU UNDERSTAND I HAD NO CHOICE BUT TO RUN OUT THERE AND CARRY HER BACK LIKE THAT.
Why the excuses?
I DIDN'T ASK ABOUT THAT.
YES, BUT YOUR EYES WERE STARING DAGGERS AT ME.
Blame it on the alcohol.
WERE THEY NOW?
Sheesh...
SHE WAS TOLD SHE COULD SEND YOU AWAY AT ANY TIME, RIGHT?
BUT I SUPPOSE IT DIDN'T COME TO THAT, OBI.

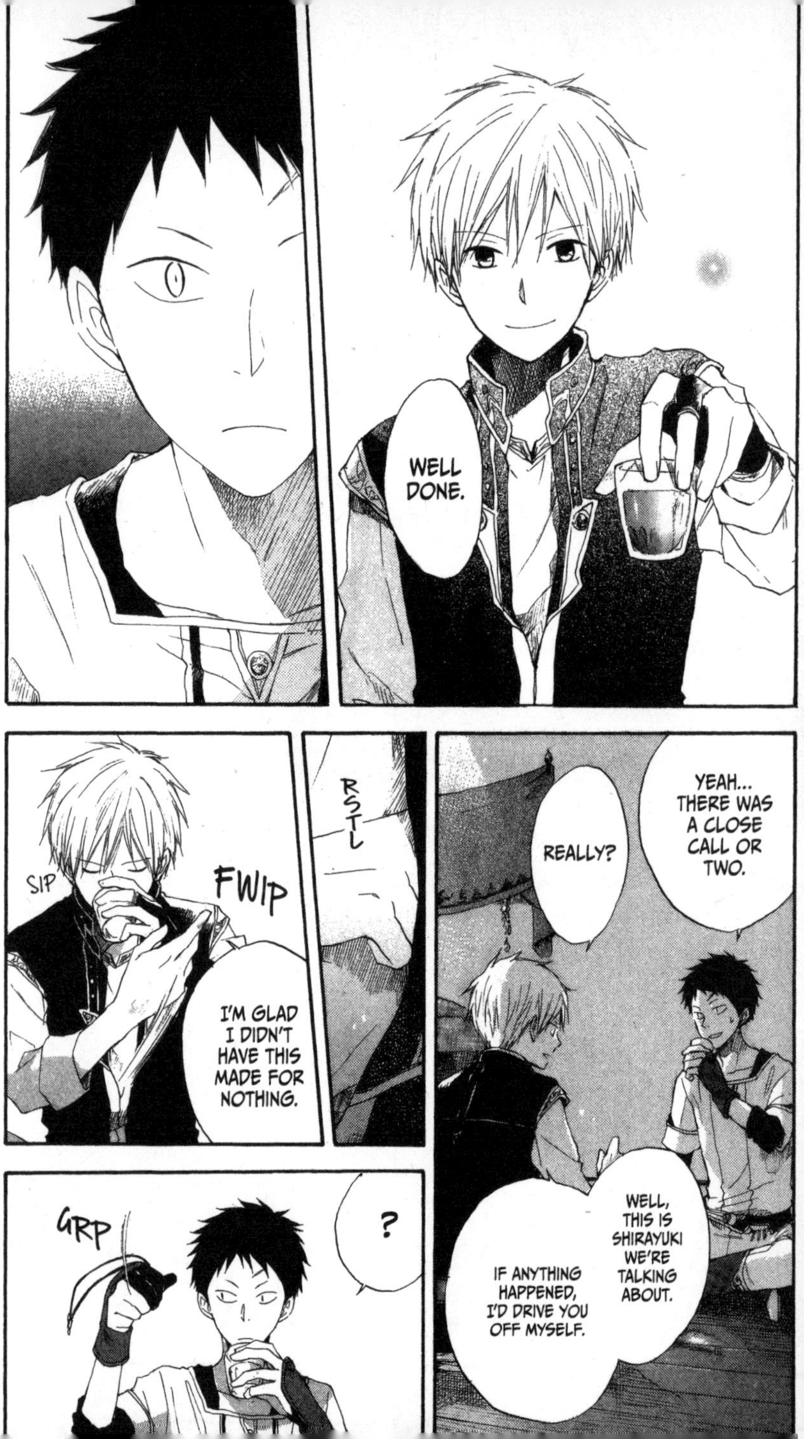
WELL DONE.
YEAH... THERE WAS A CLOSE CALL OR TWO.
REALLY?
WELL, THIS IS SHIRAYUKI WE'RE TALKING ABOUT.
IF ANYTHING HAPPENED, I'D DRIVE YOU OFF MYSELF.
RSTL
FWIP
SIP
I'M GLAD I DIDN'T HAVE THIS MADE FOR NOTHING.
?
GRP

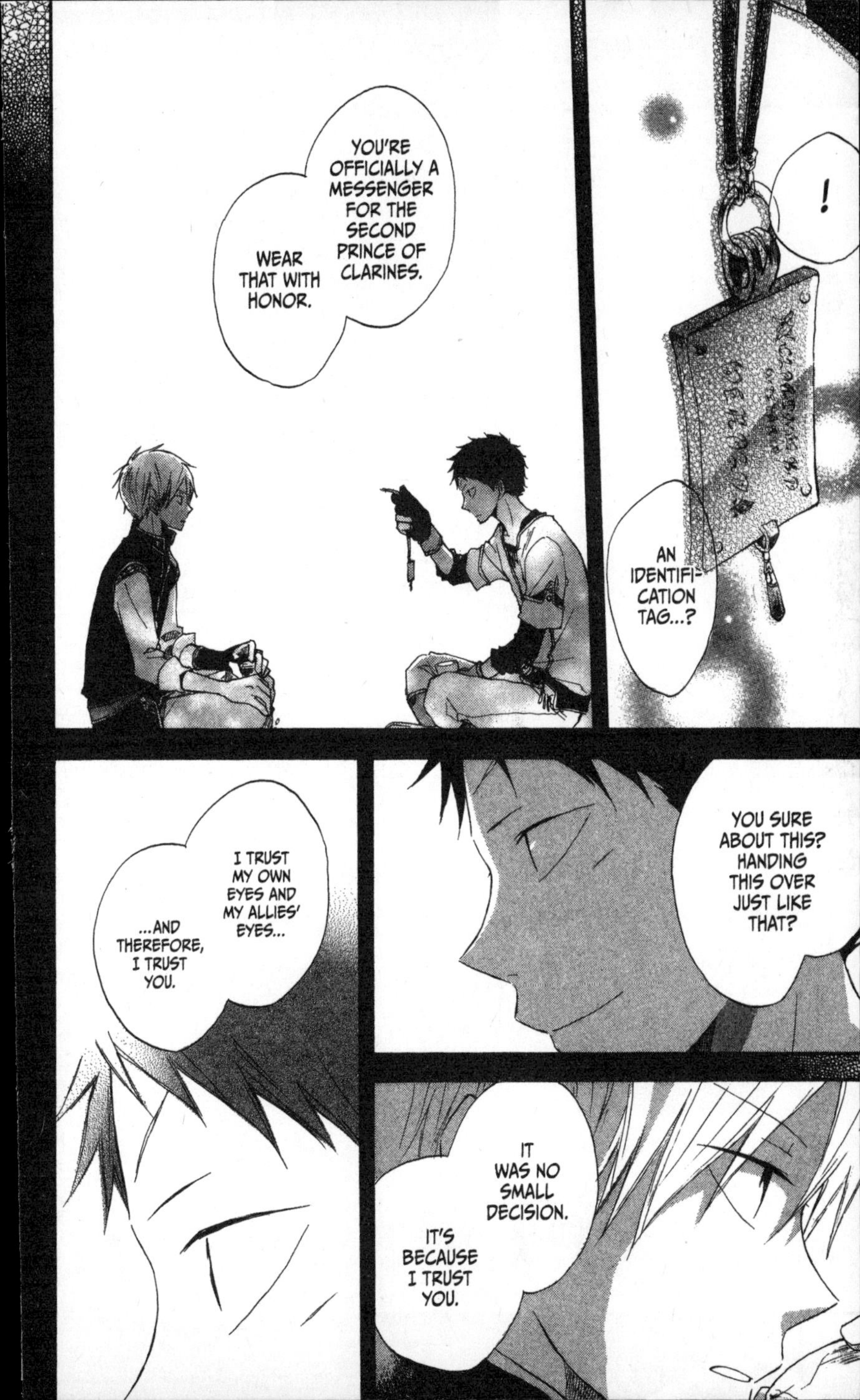
!
AN IDENTIFI-CATION TAG...?
YOU'RE OFFICIALLY A MESSENGER FOR THE SECOND PRINCE OF CLARINES.
WEAR THAT WITH HONOR.
YOU SURE ABOUT THIS? HANDING THIS OVER JUST LIKE THAT?
IT WAS NO SMALL DECISION.
IT'S BECAUSE I TRUST YOU.
I TRUST MY OWN EYES AND MY ALLIES' EYES...
...AND THEREFORE, I TRUST YOU.

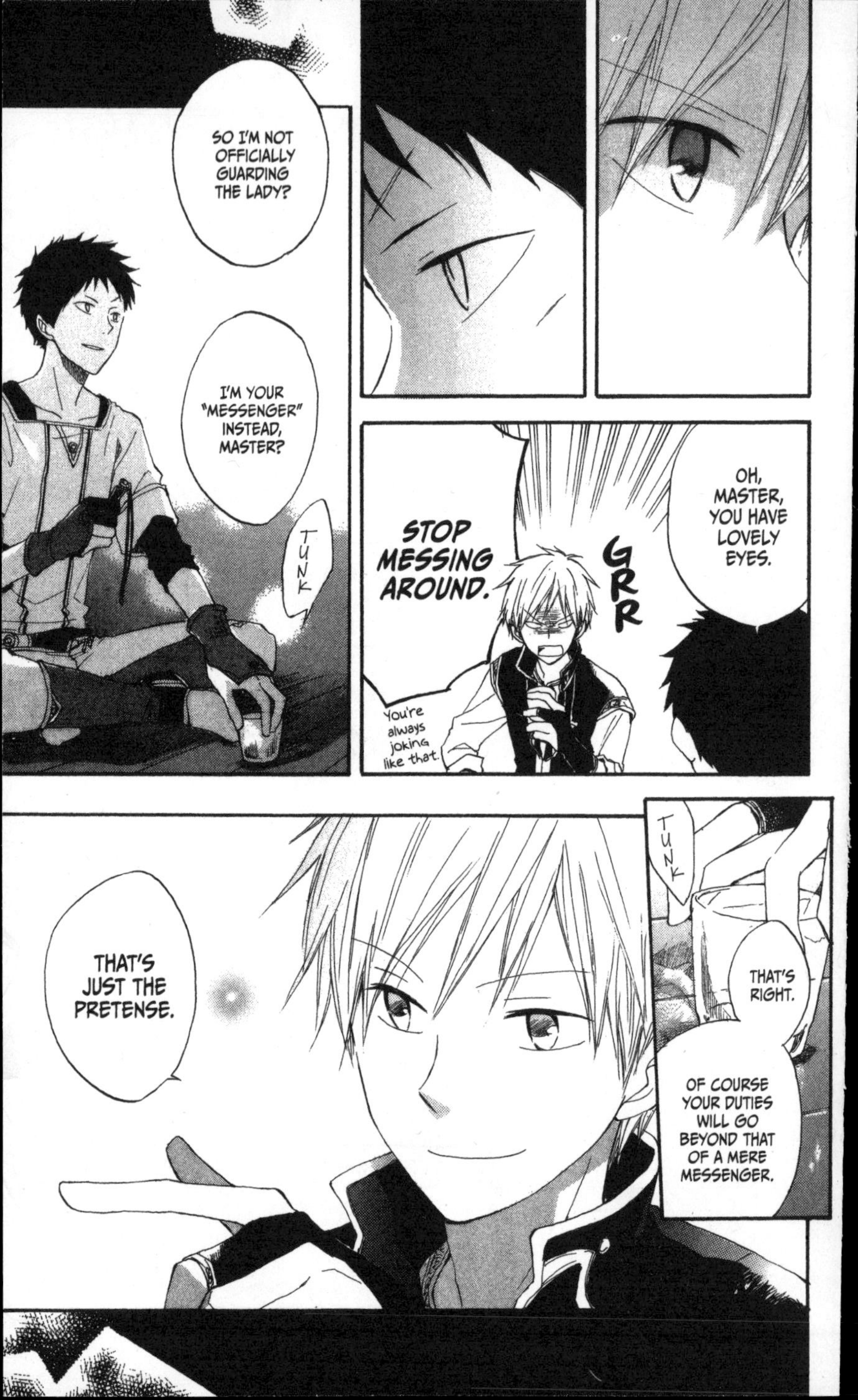
OH, MASTER, YOU HAVE LOVELY EYES.
GRR
STOP MESSING AROUND.
You're always joking like that.
SO I'M NOT OFFICIALLY GUARDING THE LADY?
I'M YOUR "MESSENGER" INSTEAD, MASTER?
TUNK
TUNK
THAT'S RIGHT.
OF COURSE YOUR DUTIES WILL GO BEYOND THAT OF A MERE MESSENGER.
THAT'S JUST THE PRETENSE.

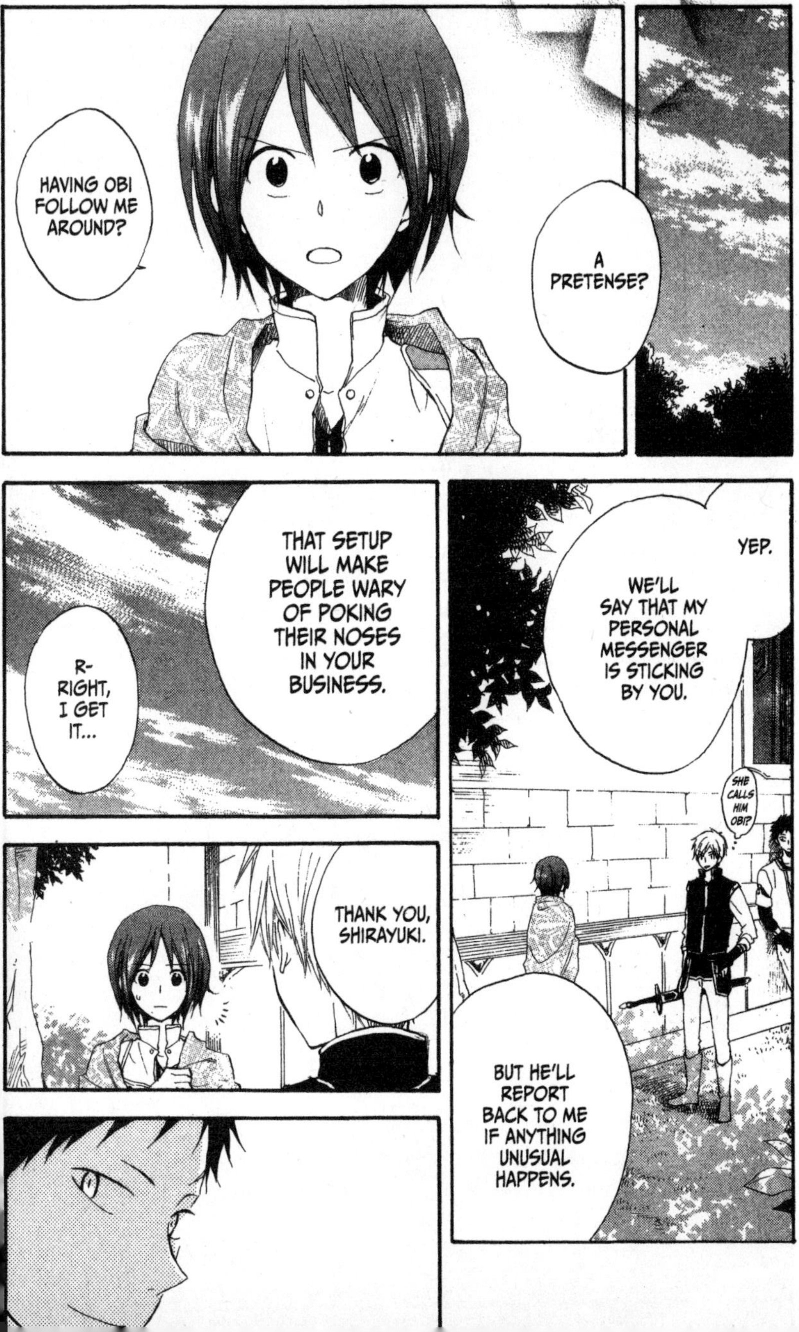
HAVING OBI FOLLOW ME AROUND?
A PRETENSE?
YEP.
WE'LL SAY THAT MY PERSONAL MESSENGER IS STICKING BY YOU.
SHE CALLS HIM OBI?
BUT HE'LL REPORT BACK TO ME IF ANYTHING UNUSUAL HAPPENS.
THAT SETUP WILL MAKE PEOPLE WARY OF POKING THEIR NOSES IN YOUR BUSINESS.
R-RIGHT, I GET IT...
THANK YOU, SHIRAYUKI.

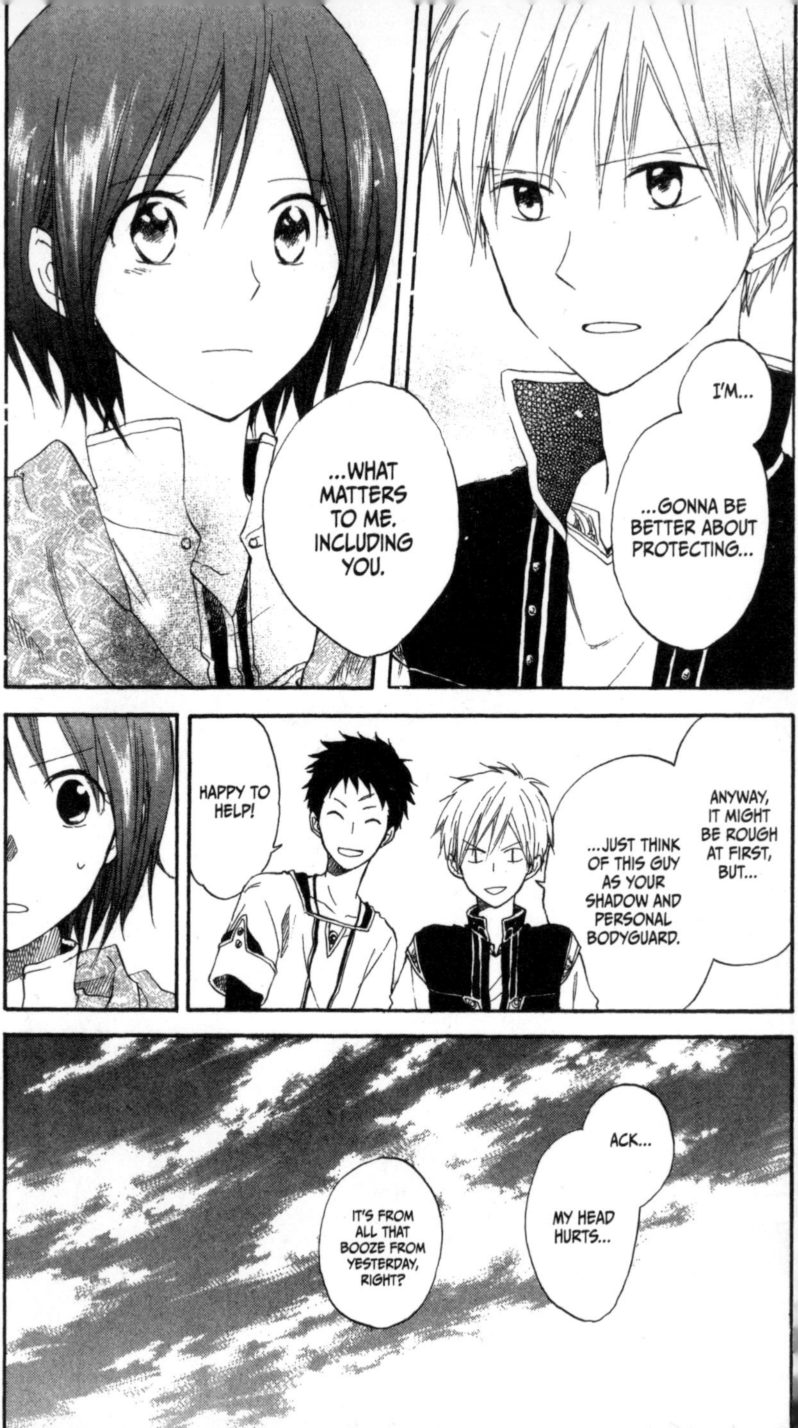
I'M...
...GONNA BE BETTER ABOUT PROTECTING...
...WHAT MATTERS TO ME. INCLUDING YOU.
ANYWAY, IT MIGHT BE ROUGH AT FIRST, BUT...
...JUST THINK OF THIS GUY AS YOUR SHADOW AND PERSONAL BODYGUARD.
HAPPY TO HELP!
ACK...
MY HEAD HURTS...
IT'S FROM ALL THAT BOOZE FROM YESTERDAY, RIGHT?

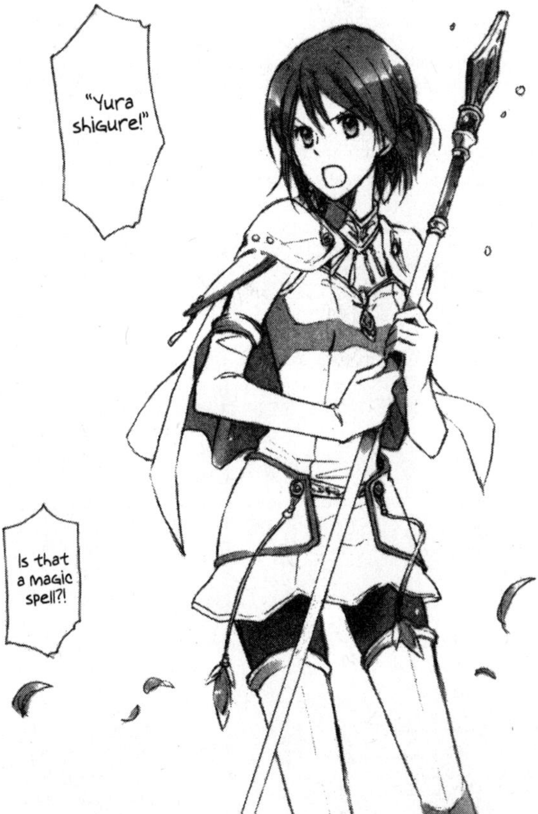
"Yura shigure!"
Is that a magic spell?!

Chapter 12

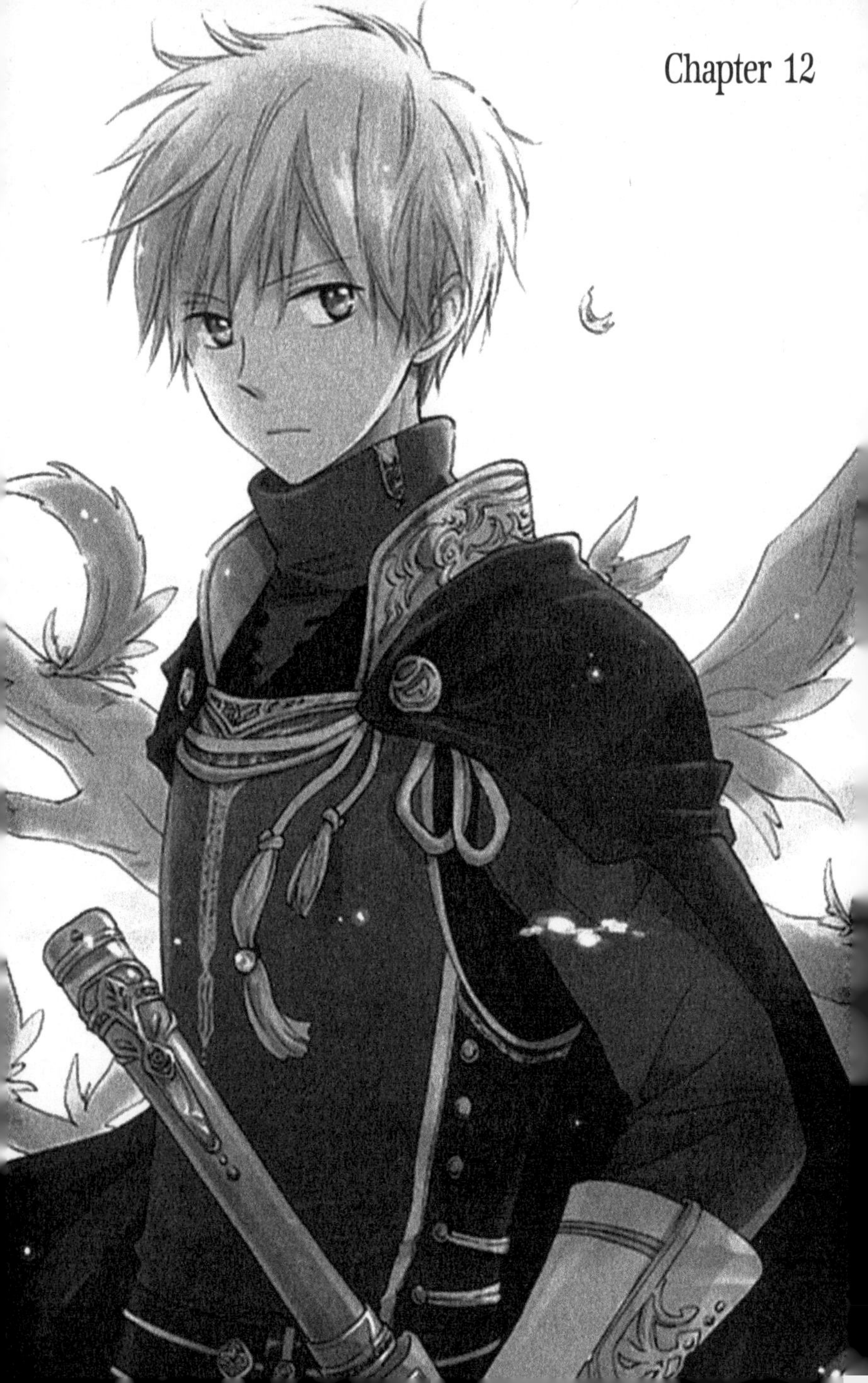

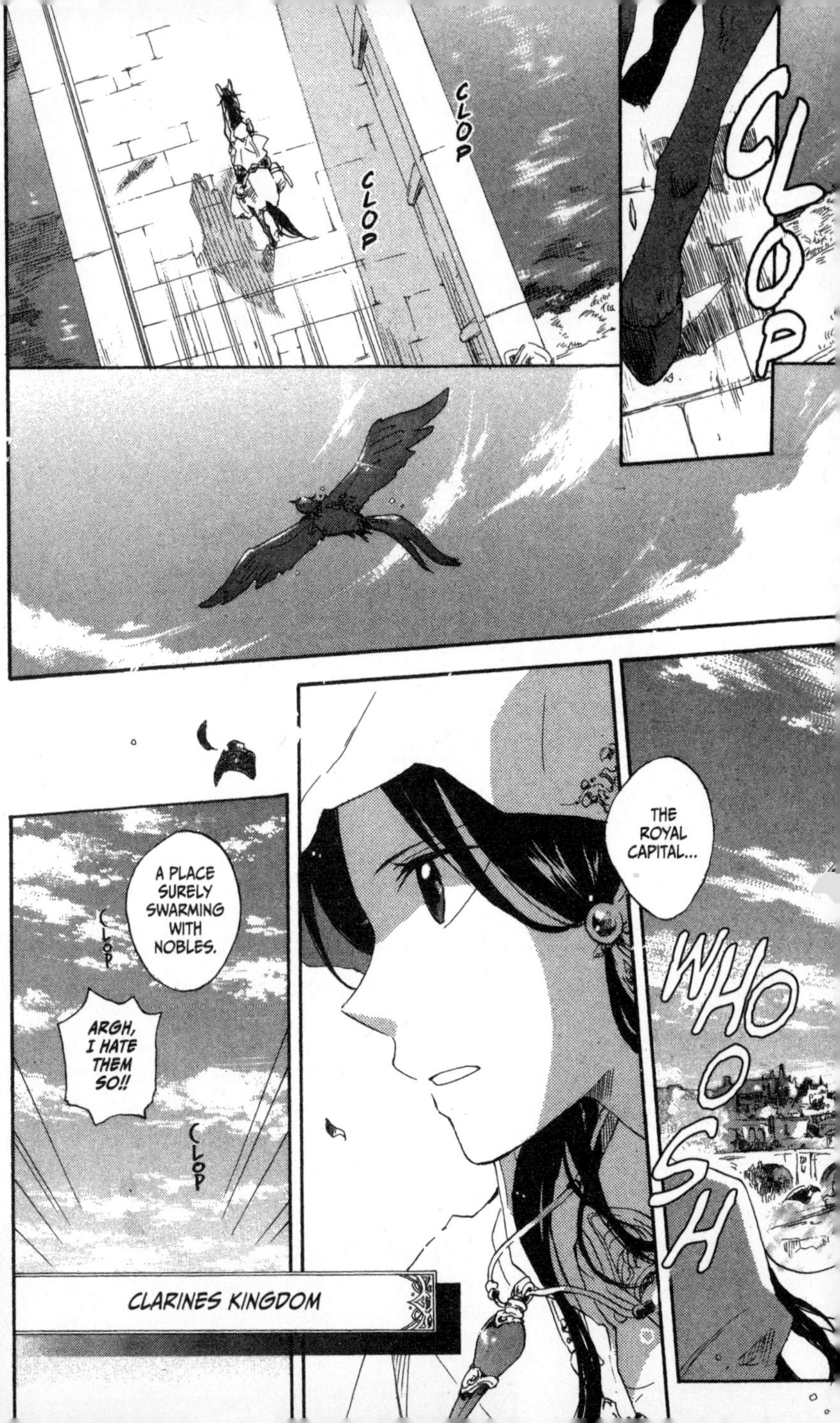
CLOP
CLOP
CLOP
THE ROYAL CAPITAL...
WHOOSH
A PLACE SURELY SWARMING WITH NOBLES.
CLOP
ARGH, I HATE THEM SO!!
CLOP
CLARINES KINGDOM

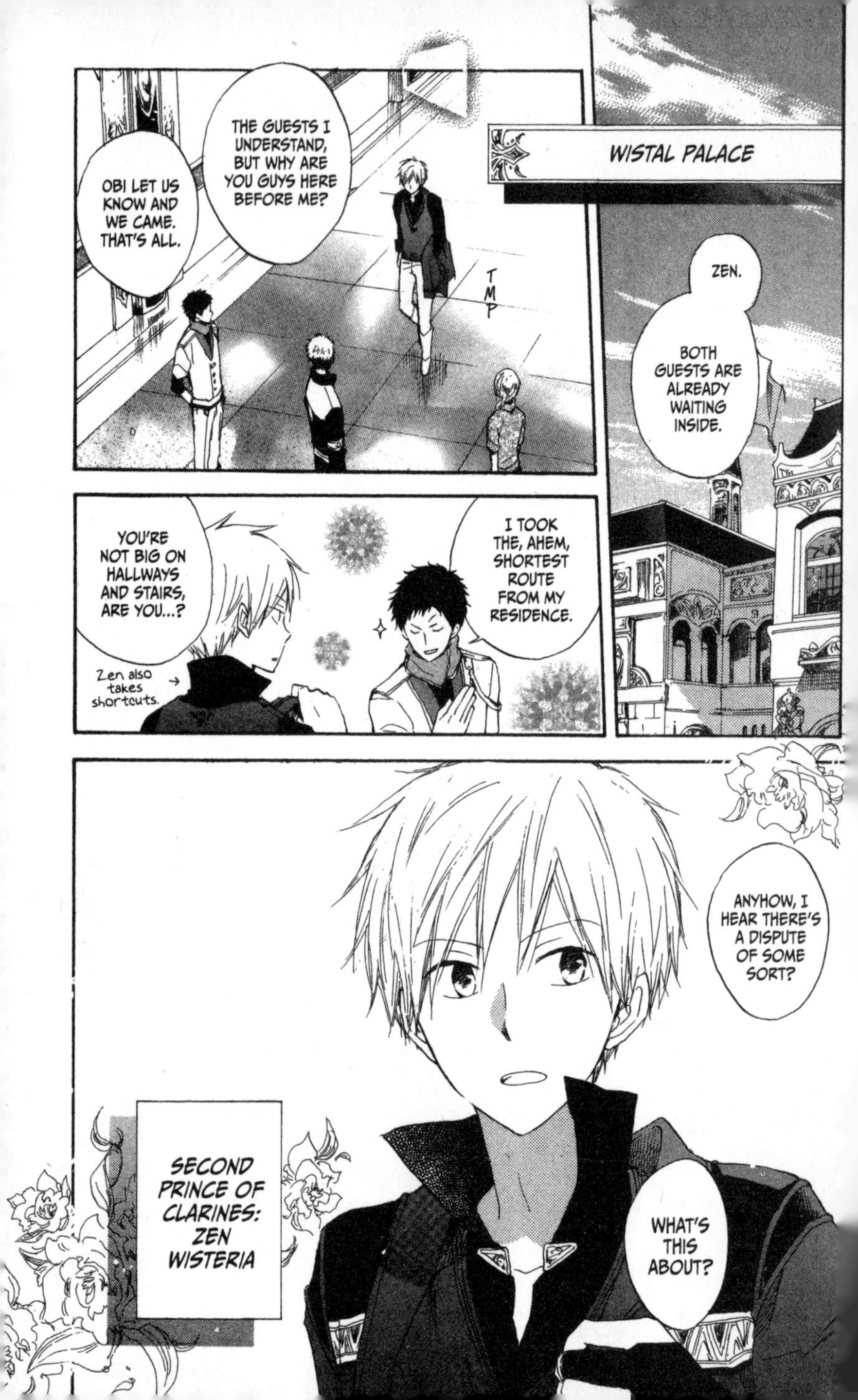
WISTAL PALACE
ZEN.
BOTH GUESTS ARE ALREADY WAITING INSIDE.
TMP
THE GUESTS I UNDERSTAND, BUT WHY ARE YOU GUYS HERE BEFORE ME?
OBI LET US KNOW AND WE CAME. THAT'S ALL.
I TOOK THE, AHEM, SHORTEST ROUTE FROM MY RESIDENCE.
YOU'RE NOT BIG ON HALLWAYS AND STAIRS, ARE YOU...?
Zen also takes shortcuts.
ANYHOW, I HEAR THERE'S A DISPUTE OF SOME SORT?
WHAT'S THIS ABOUT?
SECOND PRINCE OF CLARINES: ZEN WISTERIA

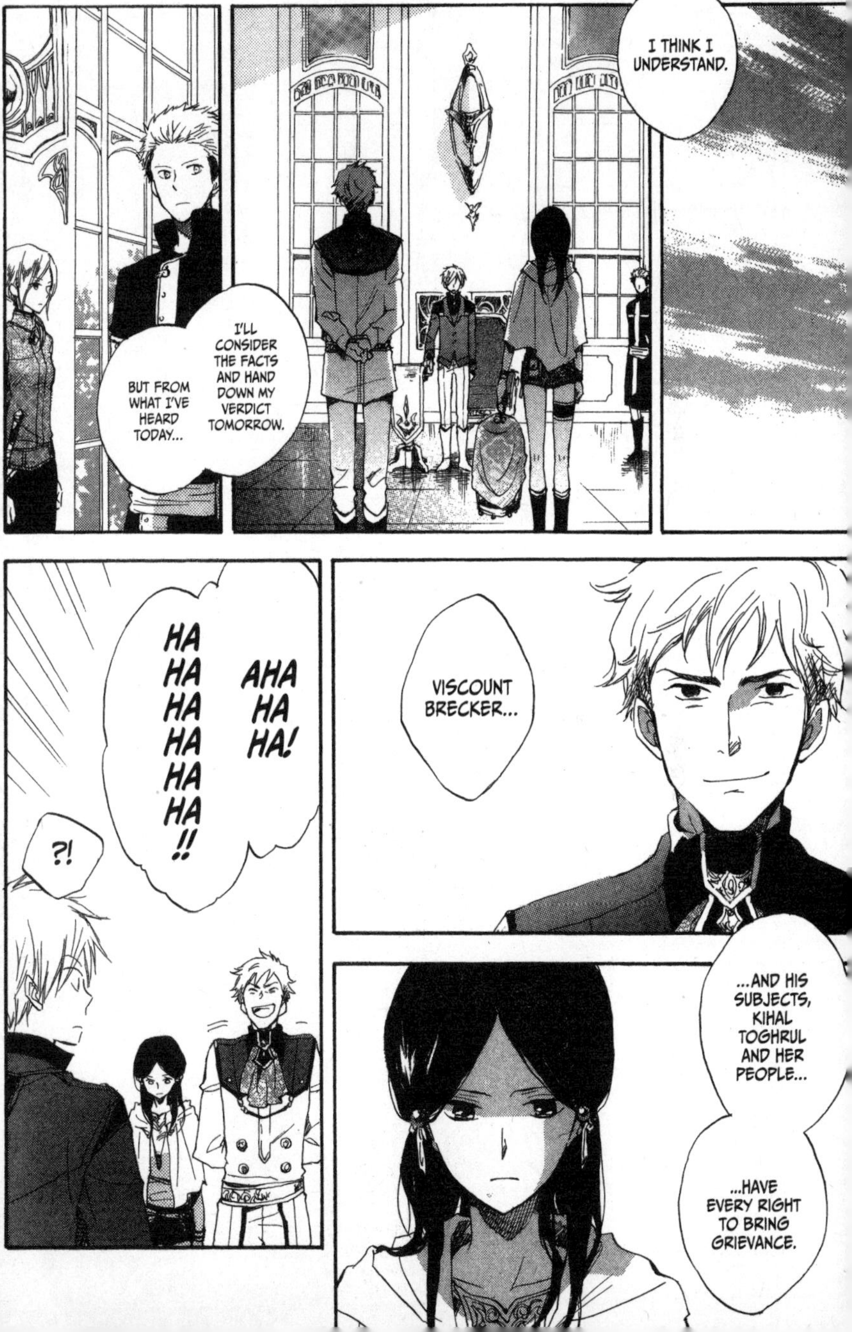
I THINK I UNDERSTAND.
I'LL CONSIDER THE FACTS AND HAND DOWN MY VERDICT TOMORROW.
BUT FROM WHAT I'VE HEARD TODAY...
VISCOUNT BRECKER...
...AND HIS SUBJECTS, KIHAL TOGHRUL AND HER PEOPLE...
...HAVE EVERY RIGHT TO BRING GRIEVANCE.
AHA HA HA!
HA HA HA HA HA HA!!
?!

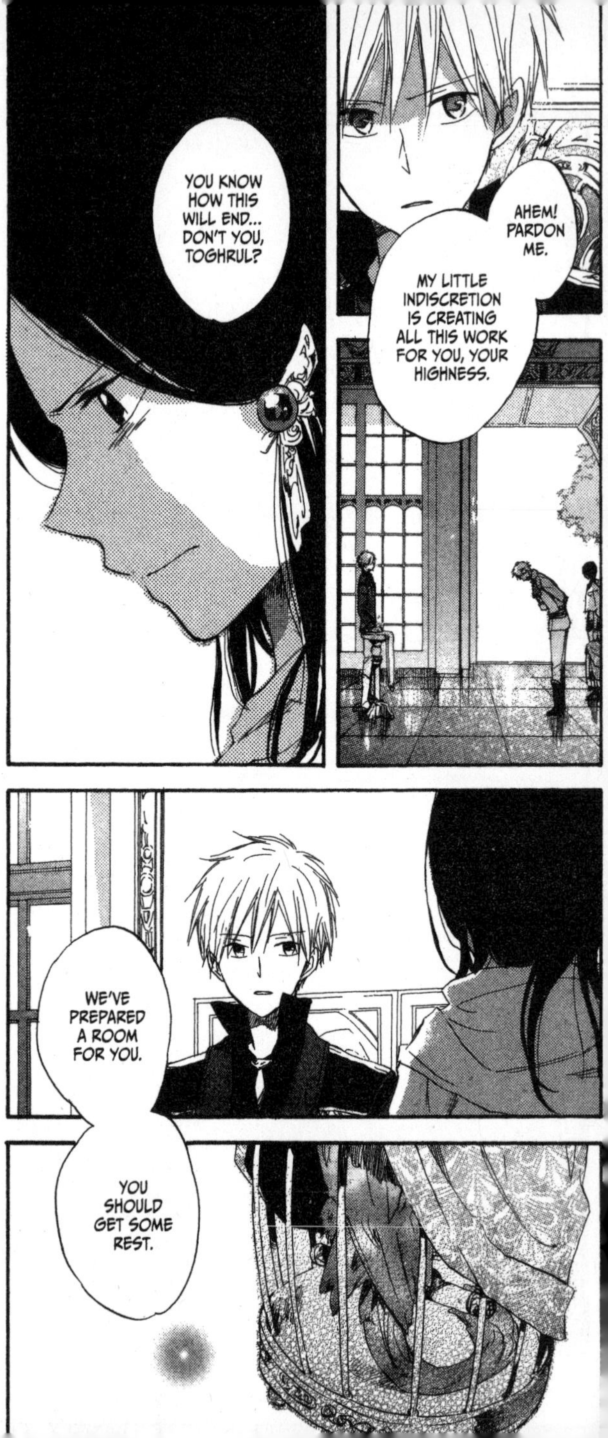
AHEM! PARDON ME.
MY LITTLE INDISCRETION IS CREATING ALL THIS WORK FOR YOU, YOUR HIGHNESS.
YOU KNOW HOW THIS WILL END... DON'T YOU, TOGHRUL?
WE'VE PREPARED A ROOM FOR YOU.
YOU SHOULD GET SOME REST.

Chapter 12

A new female character! When I draw Shirayuki and Kiki and Garak, I'm never really focused on the fact that they're girls (hang on, I'm going somewhere with this), but I was distinctly aware of that while drawing Kihal.

I-I mean it.

In palace interior scenes, I tend to include way more guards than maid staff, so maybe I should think about having Shirayuki interact with maids more often?

Or have her burst out with lines such as "Ooh! Prince Zen!" like a giddy schoolgirl.

Erm, absolutely not. Never mind.

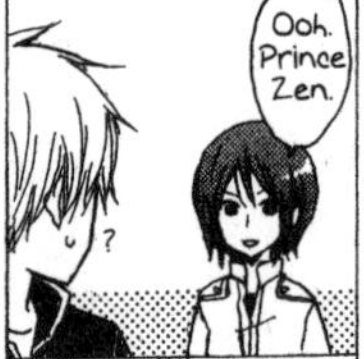
Ooh. Prince Zen.
?

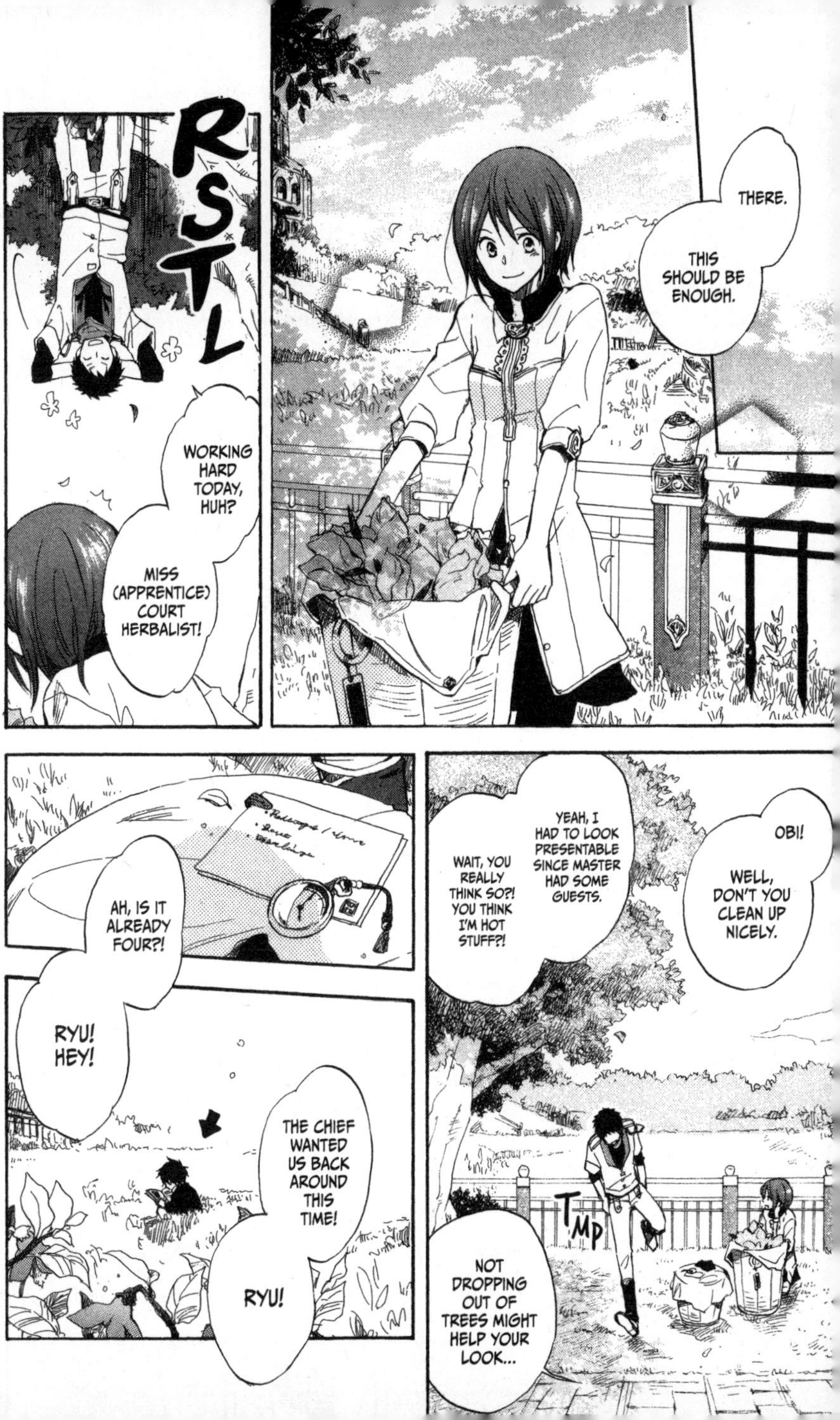
THERE.
THIS SHOULD BE ENOUGH.
RSTL
WORKING HARD TODAY, HUH?
MISS (APPRENTICE) COURT HERBALIST!
OBI!
WELL, DON'T YOU CLEAN UP NICELY.
YEAH, I HAD TO LOOK PRESENTABLE SINCE MASTER HAD SOME GUESTS.
WAIT, YOU REALLY THINK SO?! YOU THINK I'M HOT STUFF?!
TMP
NOT DROPPING OUT OF TREES MIGHT HELP YOUR LOOK...
AH, IS IT ALREADY FOUR?!
RYU! HEY!
THE CHIEF WANTED US BACK AROUND THIS TIME!
RYU!

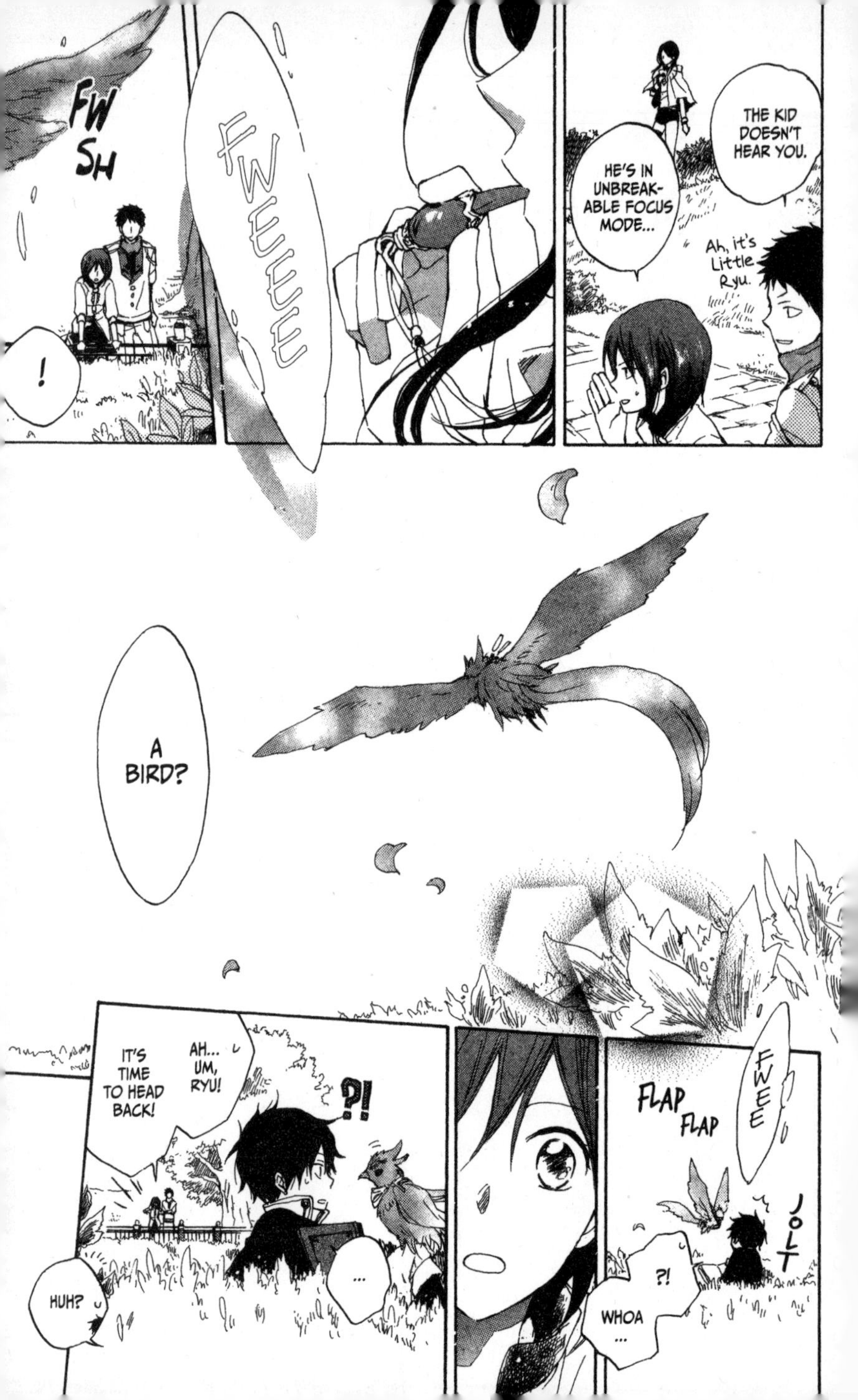
THE KID DOESN'T HEAR YOU.
HE'S IN UNBREAK-ABLE FOCUS MODE...
Ah, it's Little Ryu.
FWEEEE
FW SH
!
A BIRD?
FWEE
FLAP FLAP
JOLT
?!
WHOA ...
AH... UM, RYU!
IT'S TIME TO HEAD BACK!
?!
...
HUH?

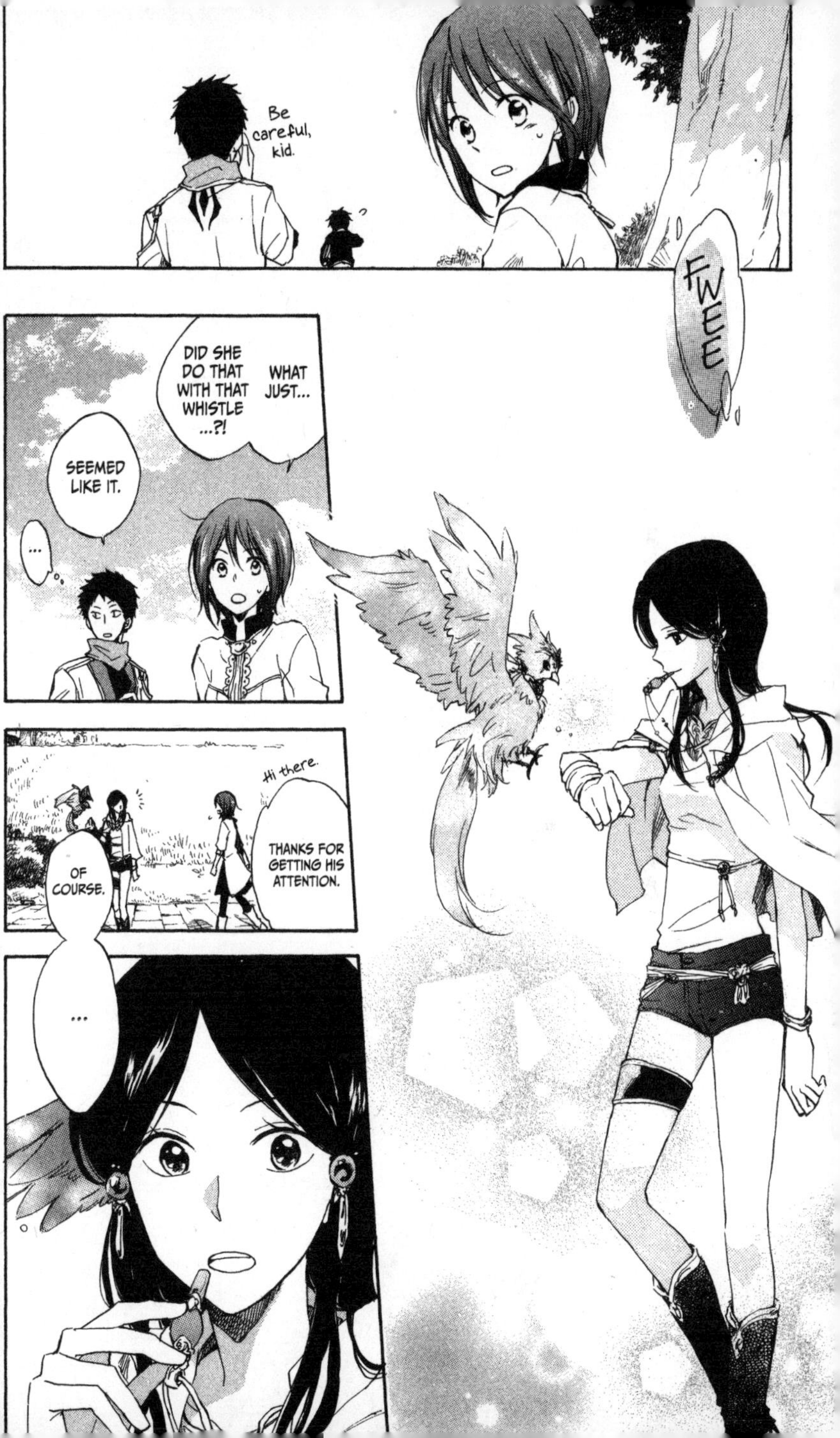
Be careful, kid.
FWEE
WHAT JUST...
DID SHE DO THAT WITH THAT WHISTLE ...?!
SEEMED LIKE IT.
...
Hi there.
THANKS FOR GETTING HIS ATTENTION.
OF COURSE.
...

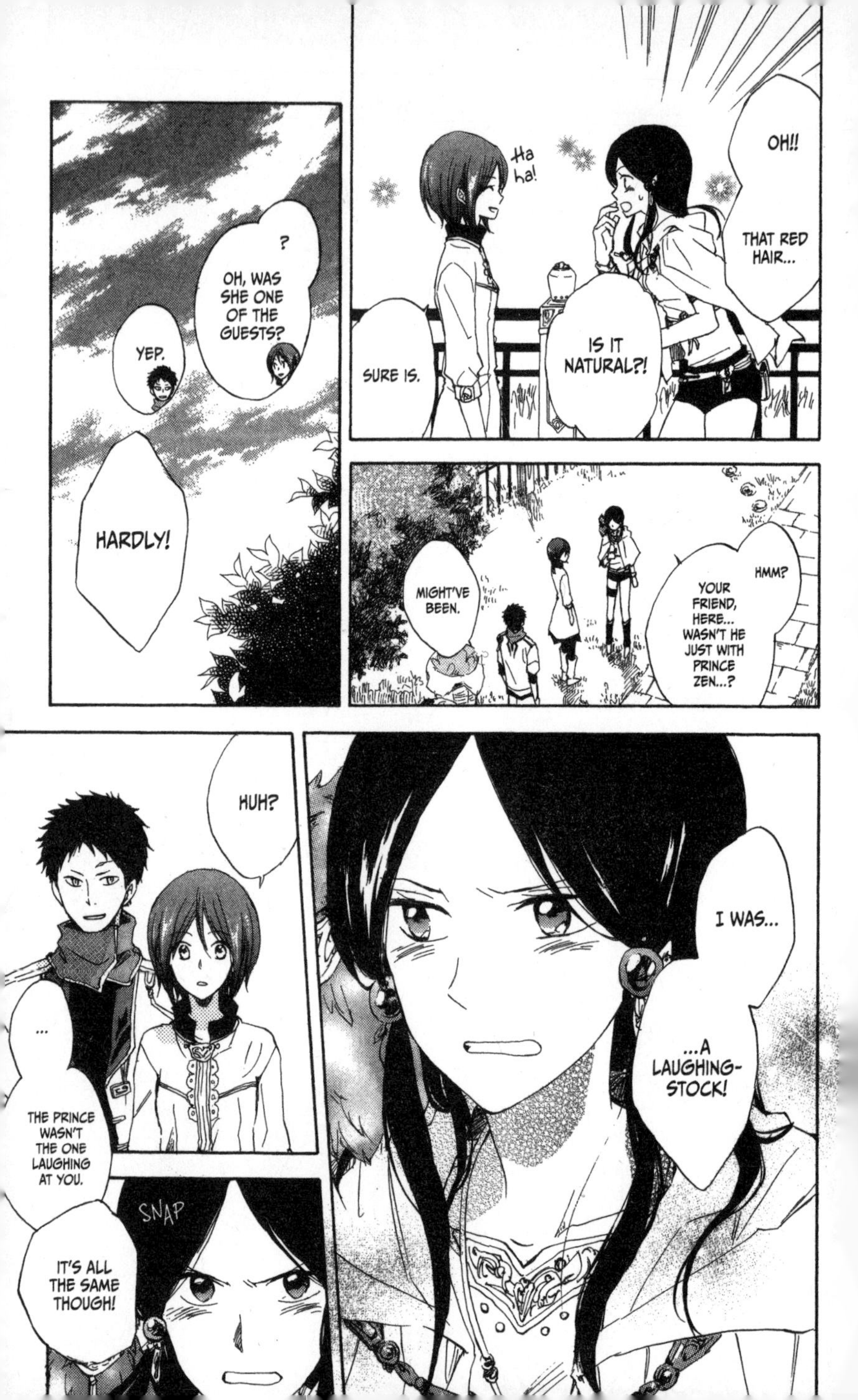
OH!!
THAT RED HAIR...
Ha ha!
IS IT NATURAL?!
SURE IS.
HMM?
YOUR FRIEND, HERE... WASN'T HE JUST WITH PRINCE ZEN...?
MIGHT'VE BEEN.
?
OH, WAS SHE ONE OF THE GUESTS?
YEP.
HARDLY!
I WAS...
...A LAUGHING-STOCK!
HUH?
...
THE PRINCE WASN'T THE ONE LAUGHING AT YOU.
SNAP
IT'S ALL THE SAME THOUGH!

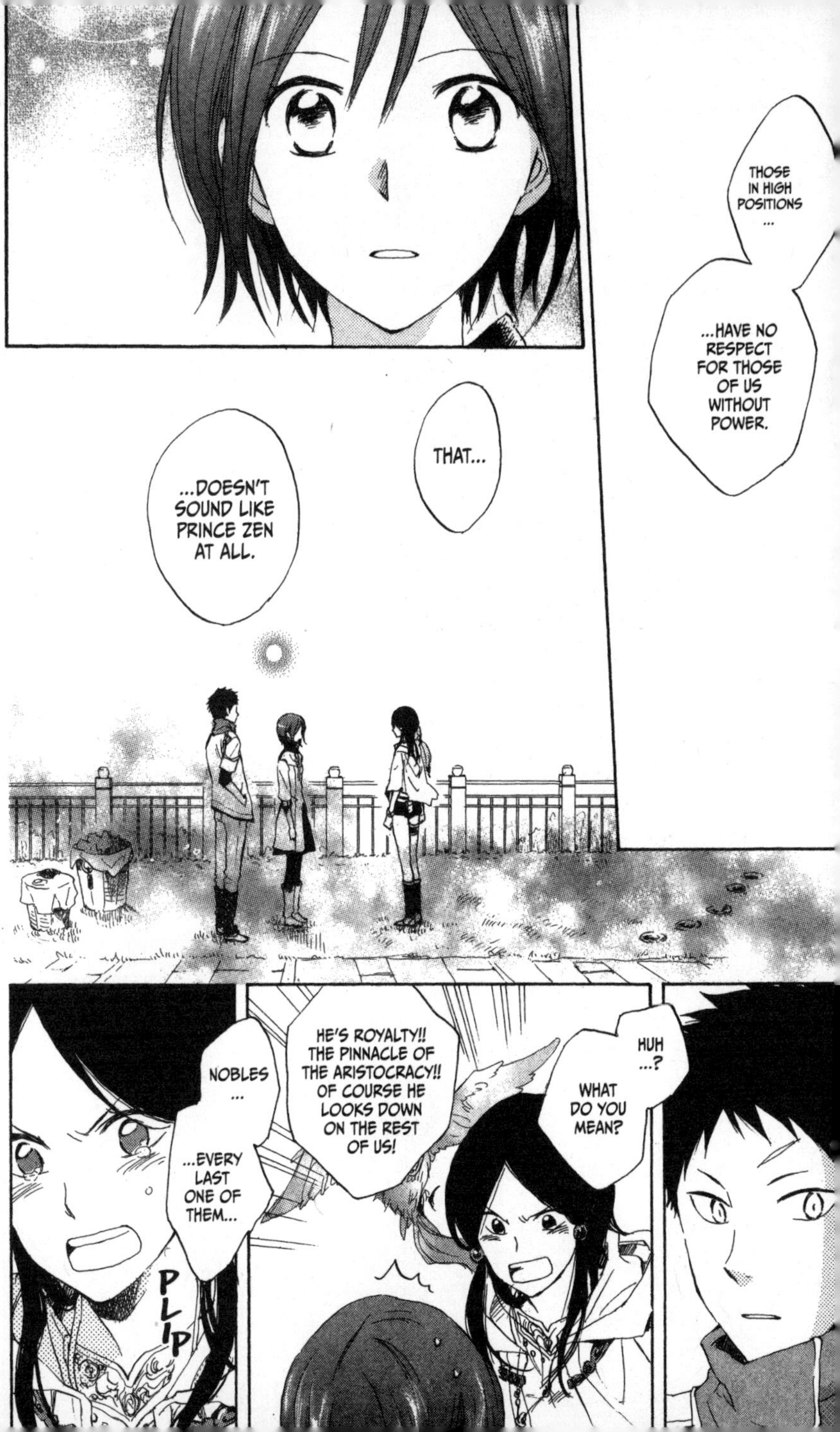
THOSE IN HIGH POSITIONS ...
...HAVE NO RESPECT FOR THOSE OF US WITHOUT POWER.
THAT...
...DOESN'T SOUND LIKE PRINCE ZEN AT ALL.
HUH ...?
WHAT DO YOU MEAN?
HE'S ROYALTY!! THE PINNACLE OF THE ARISTOCRACY!! OF COURSE HE LOOKS DOWN ON THE REST OF US!
NOBLES ...
...EVERY LAST ONE OF THEM...
PLIP

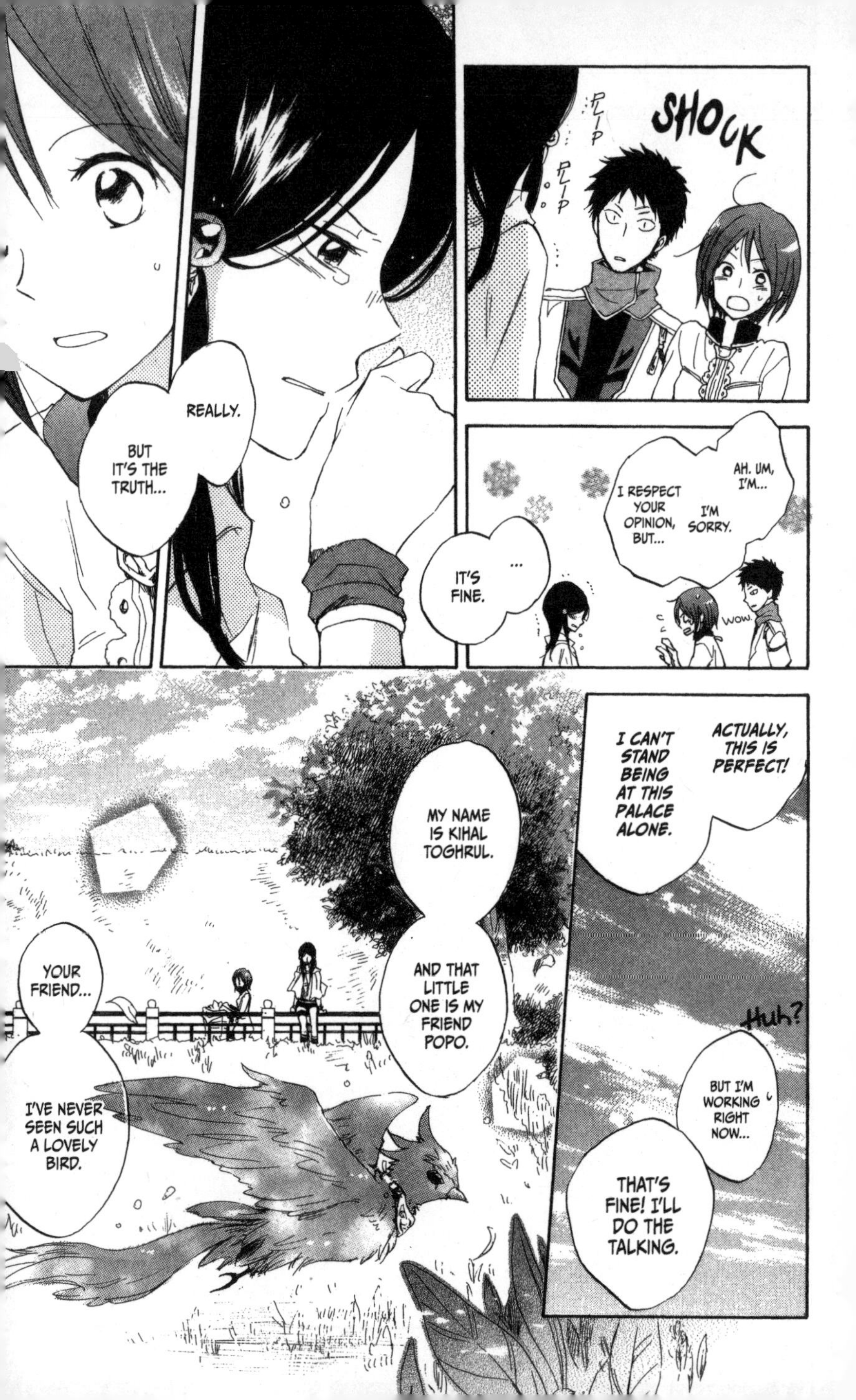
SHOCK
PLIP PLIP
AH. UM, I'M...
I'M SORRY.
I RESPECT YOUR OPINION, BUT...
...
IT'S FINE.
WOW.
REALLY.
BUT IT'S THE TRUTH...
ACTUALLY, THIS IS PERFECT!
I CAN'T STAND BEING AT THIS PALACE ALONE.
Huh?
BUT I'M WORKING RIGHT NOW...
THAT'S FINE! I'LL DO THE TALKING.
MY NAME IS KIHAL TOGHRUL.
AND THAT LITTLE ONE IS MY FRIEND POPO.
YOUR FRIEND...
I'VE NEVER SEEN SUCH A LOVELY BIRD.

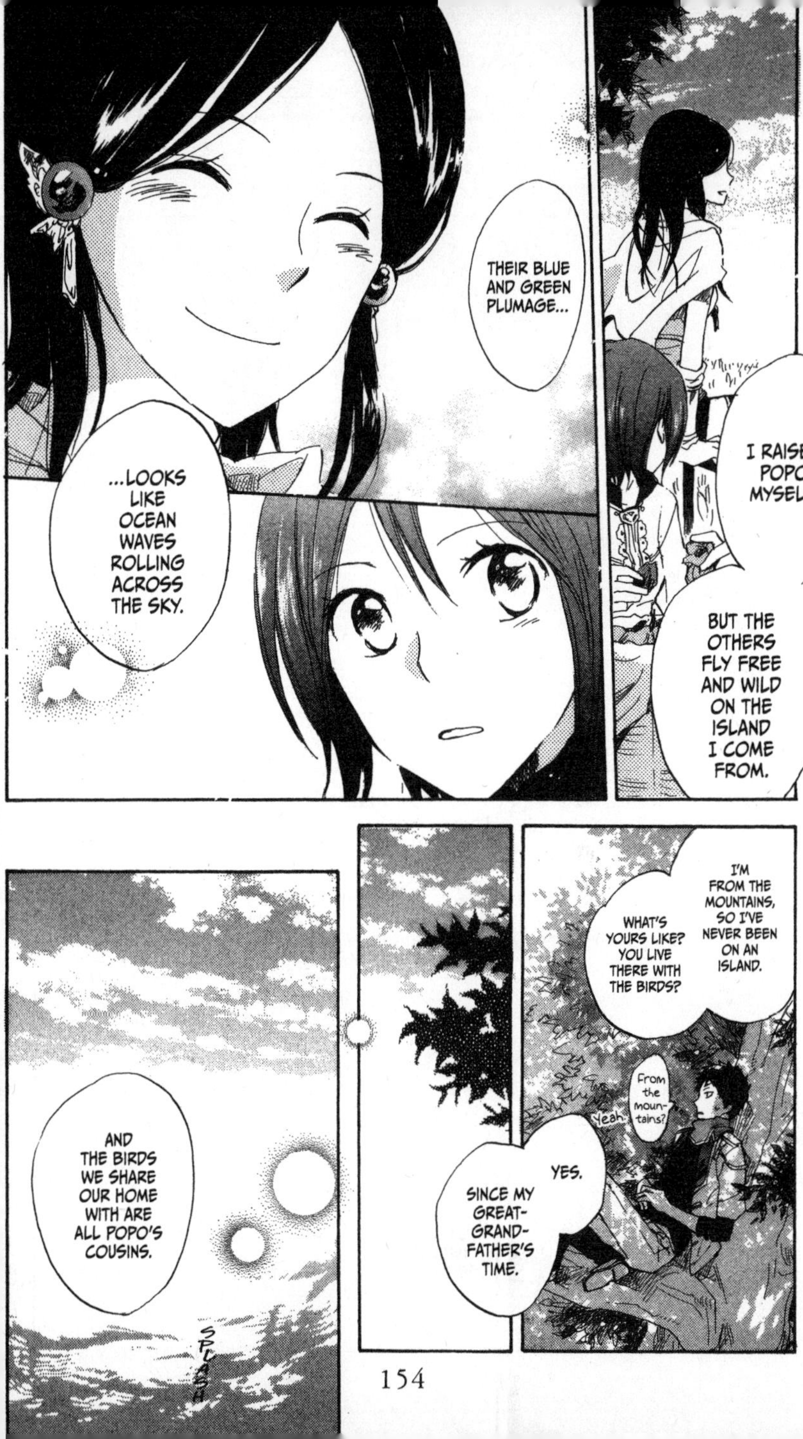
I RAISED POPO MYSELF.
BUT THE OTHERS FLY FREE AND WILD ON THE ISLAND I COME FROM.
THEIR BLUE AND GREEN PLUMAGE...
...LOOKS LIKE OCEAN WAVES ROLLING ACROSS THE SKY.
I'M FROM THE MOUNTAINS, SO I'VE NEVER BEEN ON AN ISLAND.
WHAT'S YOURS LIKE? YOU LIVE THERE WITH THE BIRDS?
From the moun-tains?
Yeah.
YES.
SINCE MY GREAT-GRAND-FATHER'S TIME.
AND THE BIRDS WE SHARE OUR HOME WITH ARE ALL POPO'S COUSINS.
SPLASH

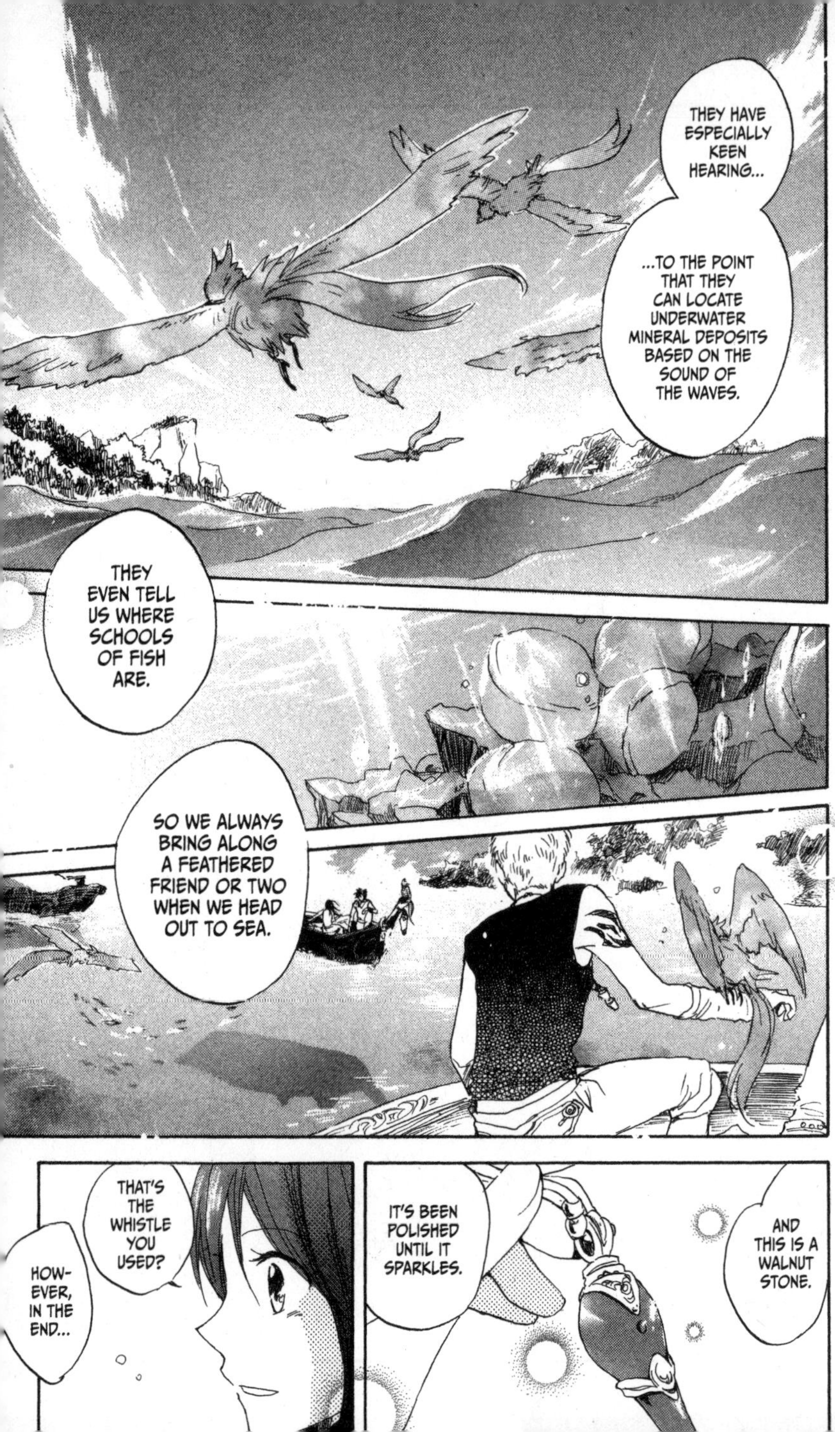
THEY HAVE ESPECIALLY KEEN HEARING...
...TO THE POINT THAT THEY CAN LOCATE UNDERWATER MINERAL DEPOSITS BASED ON THE SOUND OF THE WAVES.
THEY EVEN TELL US WHERE SCHOOLS OF FISH ARE.
SO WE ALWAYS BRING ALONG A FEATHERED FRIEND OR TWO WHEN WE HEAD OUT TO SEA.
AND THIS IS A WALNUT STONE.
IT'S BEEN POLISHED UNTIL IT SPARKLES.
THAT'S THE WHISTLE YOU USED?
HOW-EVER, IN THE END...

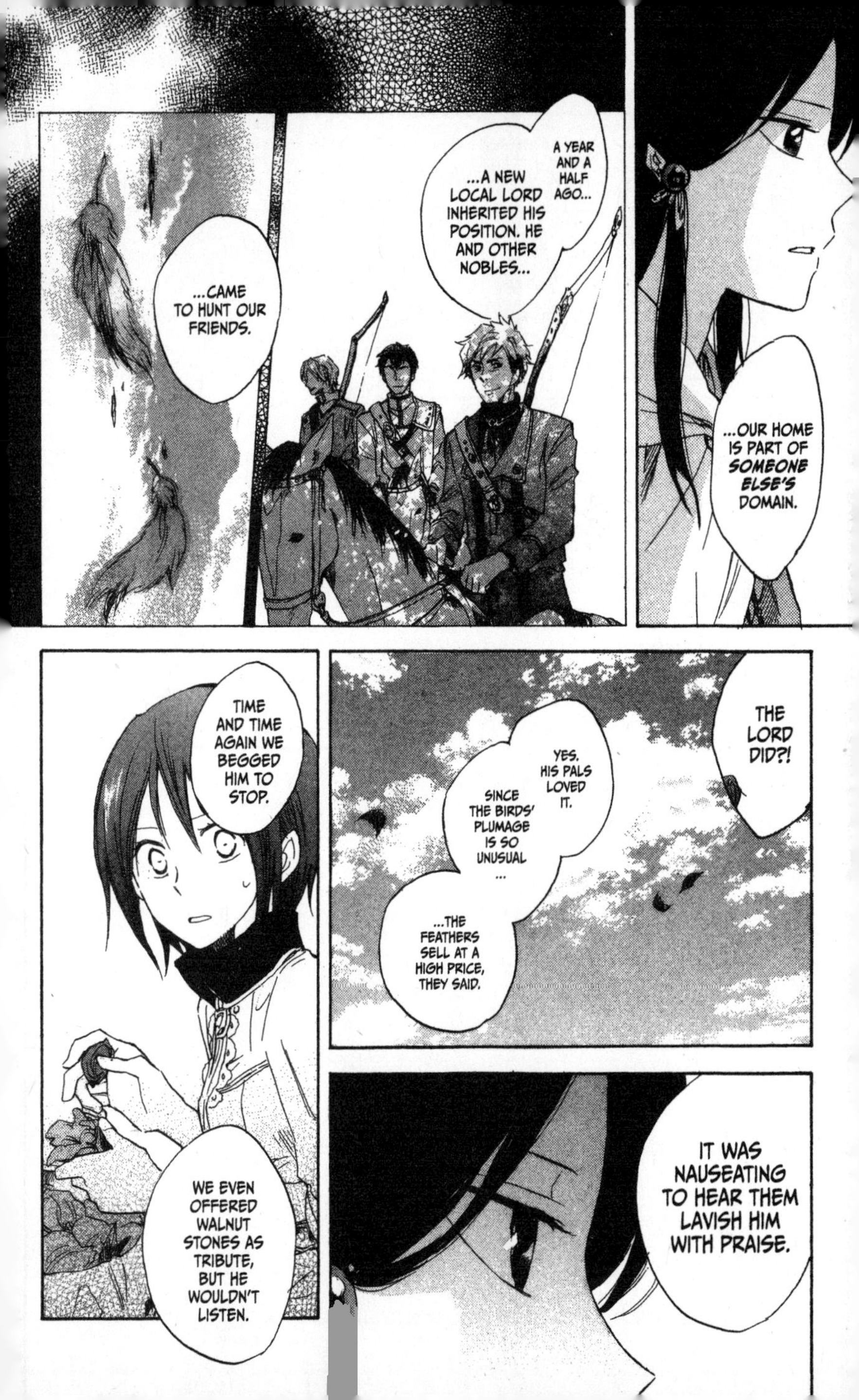
...OUR HOME IS PART OF SOMEONE ELSE'S DOMAIN.
A YEAR AND A HALF AGO...
...A NEW LOCAL LORD INHERITED HIS POSITION. HE AND OTHER NOBLES...
...CAME TO HUNT OUR FRIENDS.
THE LORD DID?!
YES. HIS PALS LOVED IT.
SINCE THE BIRDS' PLUMAGE IS SO UNUSUAL...
...THE FEATHERS SELL AT A HIGH PRICE, THEY SAID.
IT WAS NAUSEATING TO HEAR THEM LAVISH HIM WITH PRAISE.
TIME AND TIME AGAIN WE BEGGED HIM TO STOP.
WE EVEN OFFERED WALNUT STONES AS TRIBUTE, BUT HE WOULDN'T LISTEN.

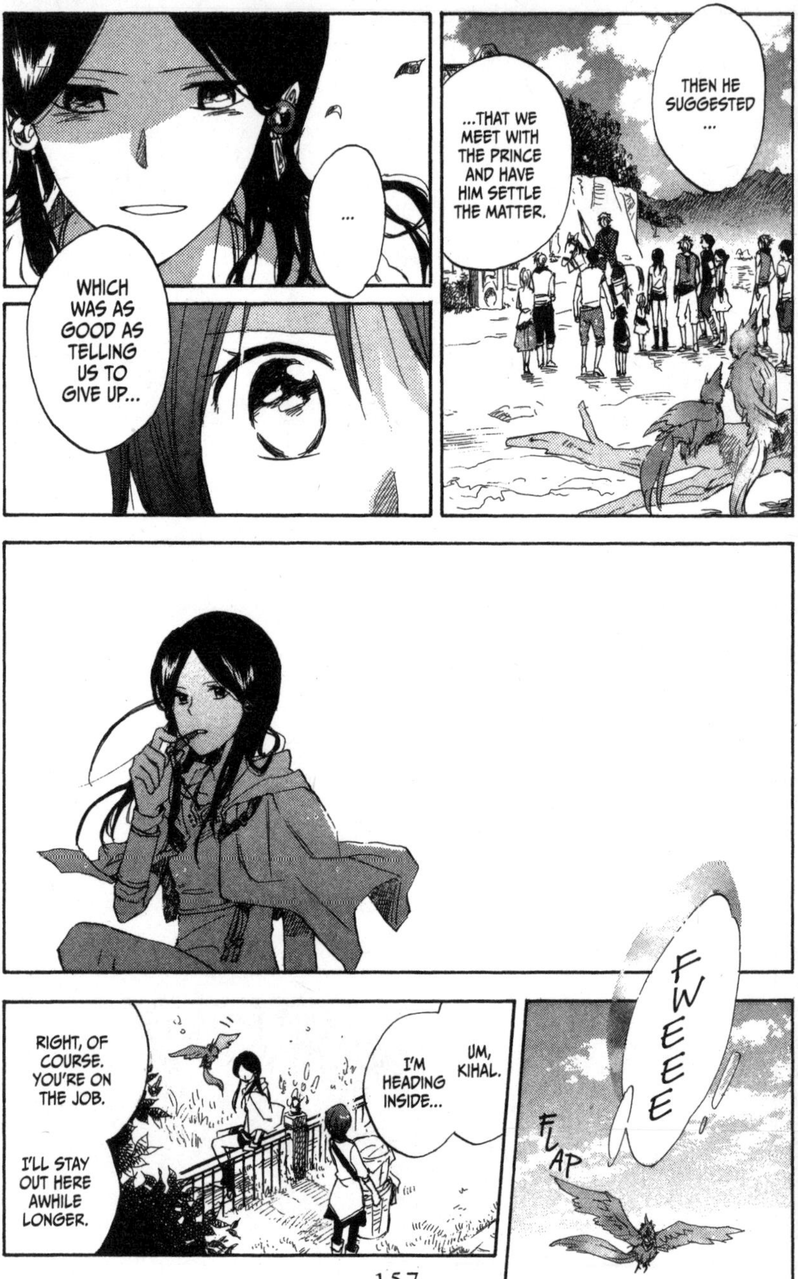
THEN HE SUGGESTED ...
...THAT WE MEET WITH THE PRINCE AND HAVE HIM SETTLE THE MATTER.
...
WHICH WAS AS GOOD AS TELLING US TO GIVE UP...
FWEEE
FLAP
UM, KIHAL.
I'M HEADING INSIDE...
RIGHT, OF COURSE. YOU'RE ON THE JOB.
I'LL STAY OUT HERE AWHILE LONGER.

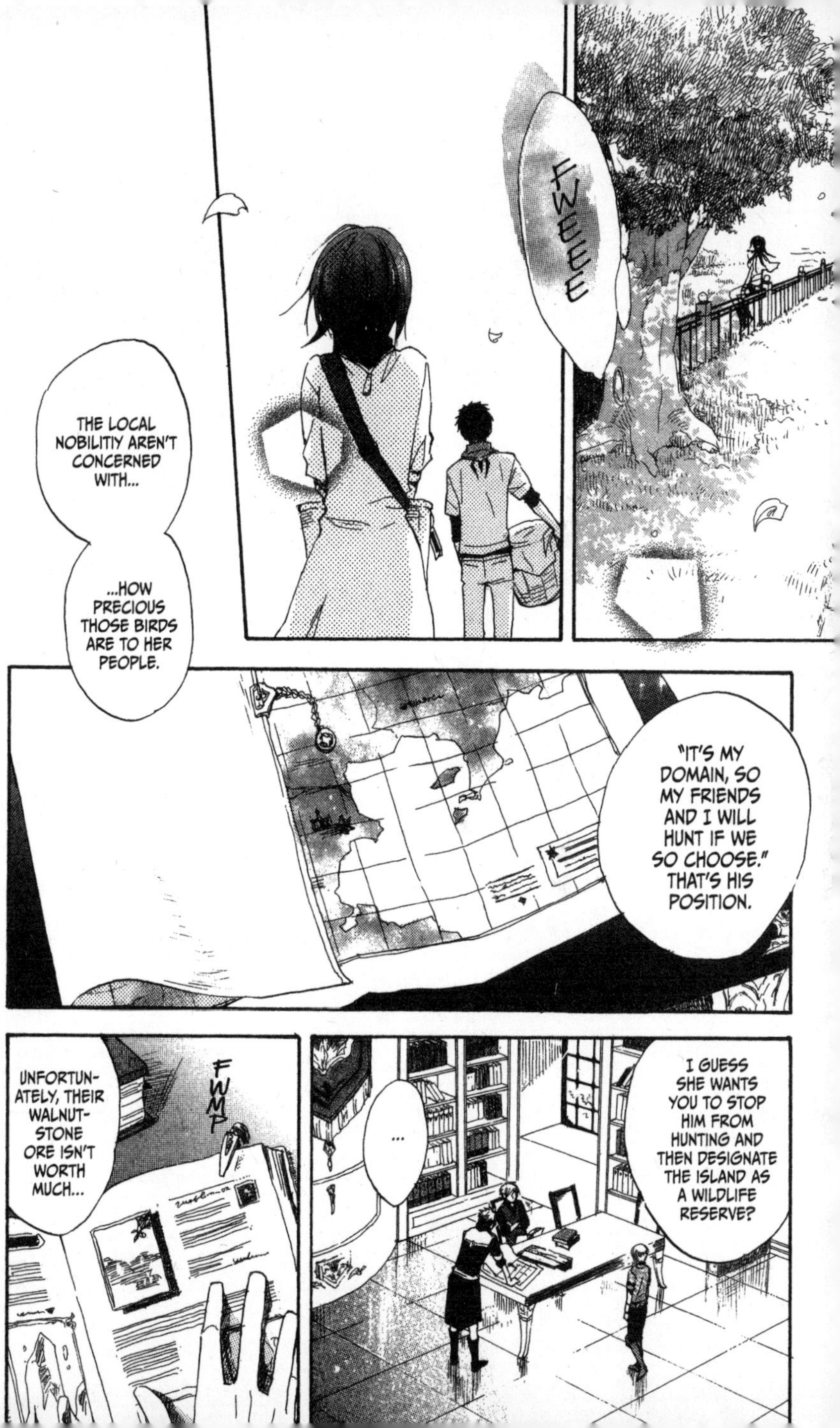
FWEEE
THE LOCAL NOBILITIY AREN'T CONCERNED WITH...
...HOW PRECIOUS THOSE BIRDS ARE TO HER PEOPLE.
"IT'S MY DOMAIN, SO MY FRIENDS AND I WILL HUNT IF WE SO CHOOSE." THAT'S HIS POSITION.
I GUESS SHE WANTS YOU TO STOP HIM FROM HUNTING AND THEN DESIGNATE THE ISLAND AS A WILDLIFE RESERVE?
...
FWMP
UNFORTUN-ATELY, THEIR WALNUT-STONE ORE ISN'T WORTH MUCH...

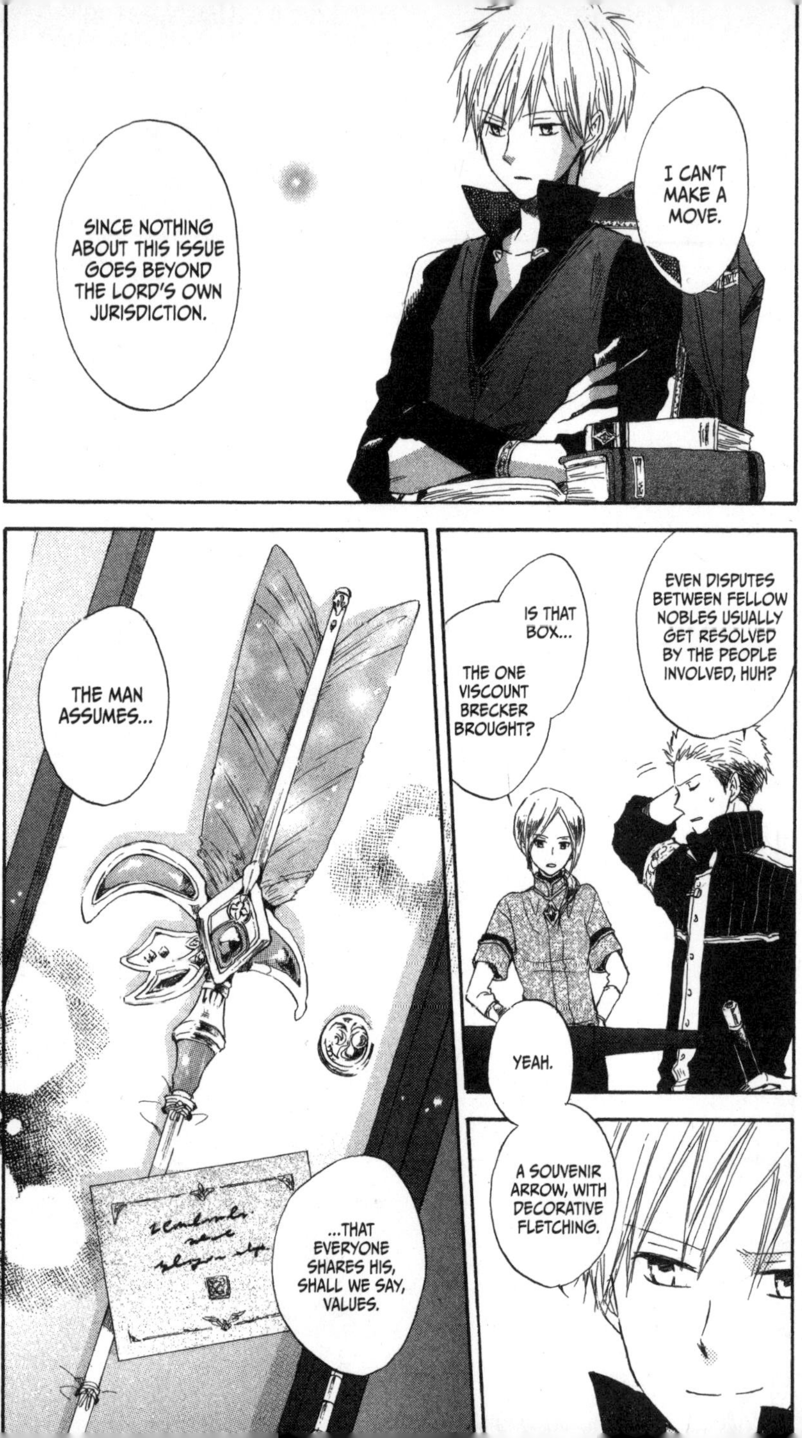
I CAN'T MAKE A MOVE.
SINCE NOTHING ABOUT THIS ISSUE GOES BEYOND THE LORD'S OWN JURISDICTION.
EVEN DISPUTES BETWEEN FELLOW NOBLES USUALLY GET RESOLVED BY THE PEOPLE INVOLVED, HUH?
IS THAT BOX...
THE ONE VISCOUNT BRECKER BROUGHT?
YEAH.
A SOUVENIR ARROW, WITH DECORATIVE FLETCHING.
THE MAN ASSUMES...
...THAT EVERYONE SHARES HIS, SHALL WE SAY, VALUES.

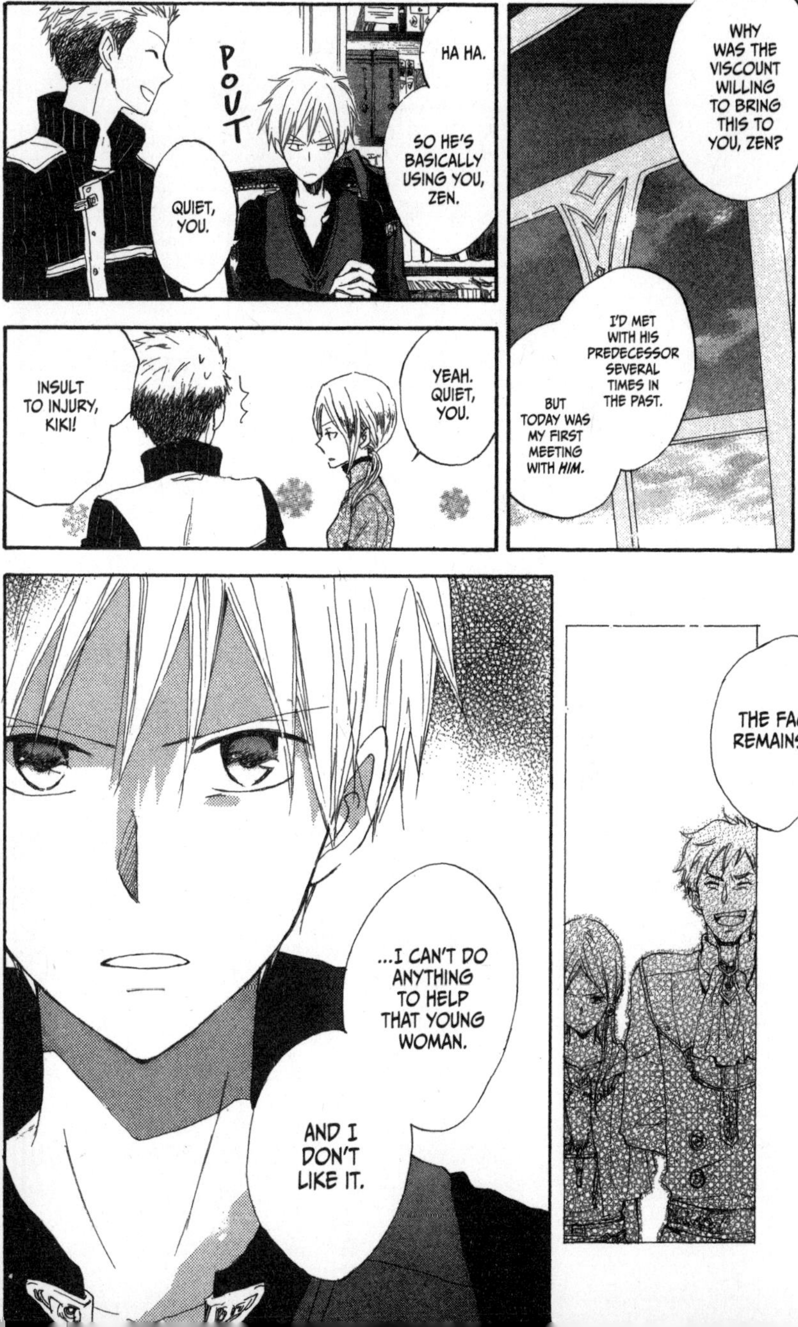
WHY WAS THE VISCOUNT WILLING TO BRING THIS TO YOU, ZEN?
I'D MET WITH HIS PREDECESSOR SEVERAL TIMES IN THE PAST.
BUT TODAY WAS MY FIRST MEETING WITH *HIM*.
HA HA.
SO HE'S BASICALLY USING YOU, ZEN.
POUT
QUIET, YOU.
YEAH. QUIET, YOU.
INSULT TO INJURY, KIKI!
THE FACT REMAINS...
...I CAN'T DO ANYTHING TO HELP THAT YOUNG WOMAN.
AND I DON'T LIKE IT.

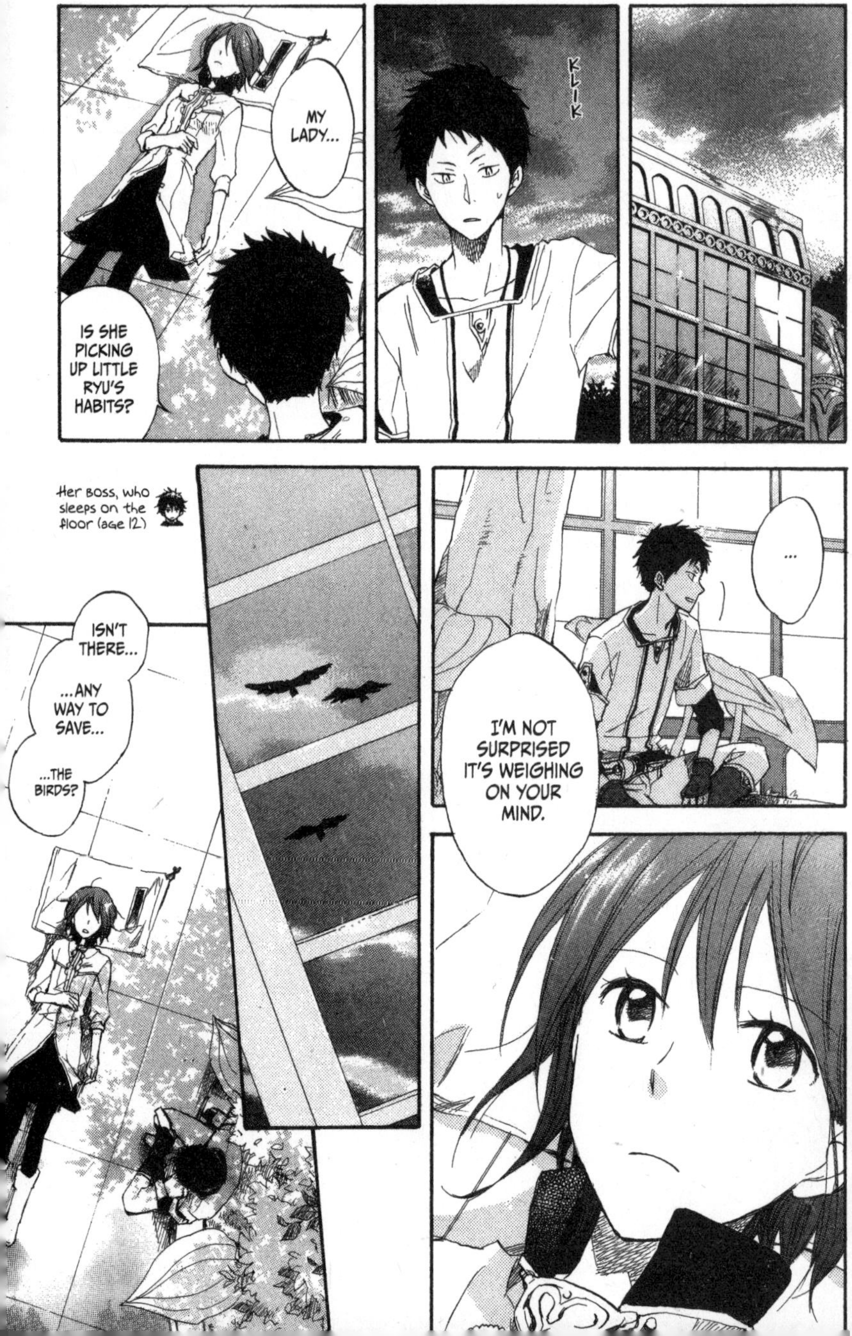
KLIK
MY LADY...
IS SHE PICKING UP LITTLE RYU'S HABITS?
...
I'M NOT SURPRISED IT'S WEIGHING ON YOUR MIND.
Her boss, who sleeps on the floor (age 12)
ISN'T THERE...
...ANY WAY TO SAVE...
...THE BIRDS?

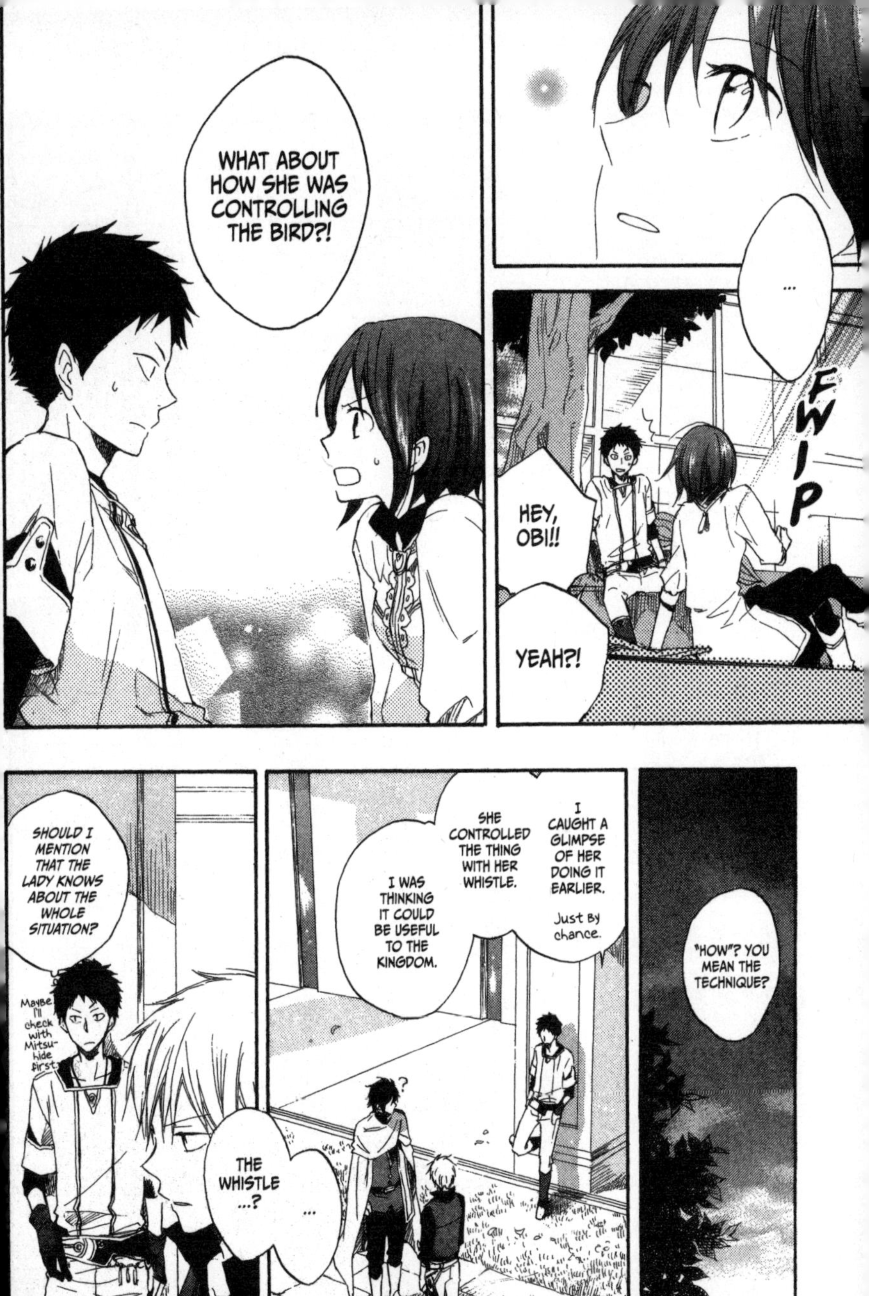
...
FWIP
HEY, OBI!!
YEAH?!
WHAT ABOUT HOW SHE WAS CONTROLLING THE BIRD?!
"HOW"? YOU MEAN THE TECHNIQUE?
I CAUGHT A GLIMPSE OF HER DOING IT EARLIER.
Just by chance.
SHE CONTROLLED THE THING WITH HER WHISTLE.
I WAS THINKING IT COULD BE USEFUL TO THE KINGDOM.
...
SHOULD I MENTION THAT THE LADY KNOWS ABOUT THE WHOLE SITUATION?
Maybe I'll check with Mitsuhide first.
THE WHISTLE ...?

NOW THEN, MISS TOGHRUL...
...SOMEONE WILL COME FOR YOU AT 10 A.M. SHARP.
FLAP
FLAP FLAP

When *Snow White with the Red Hair* volume 2 came out, my manga artist friend Toki Yajima sent me a homemade book cover.

The title? *My Neighbor, the Idiot Prince.*

My Neighbor, the Idiot Prince
Sorata Akiduki

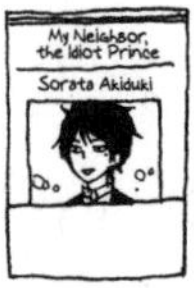

Raj on a cover? As the protagonist, no less?!

It was done in fine detail and was modeled on my cover for volume 1. Yajima even included the wrapper band at the bottom. I was so grateful, but also pretty amused...

-Plot Summary-

A hunter pursuing his destined love makes his debut in this fantasy romance. ★

Extra arcs, also included:
"Raj's Heartbreak"
"Raj's Timidity"
"Raj's Rise"

~Selections from *My Neighbor, the Idiot Prince*~

He even becomes king in these side stories!

Thank you, Yajima!!

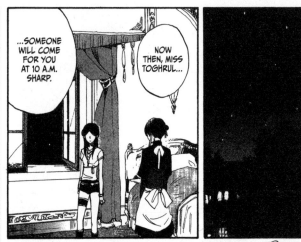

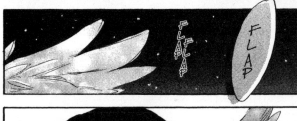

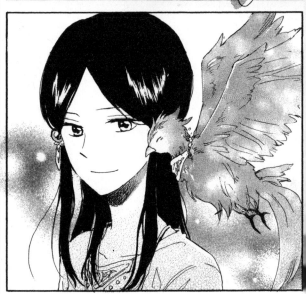

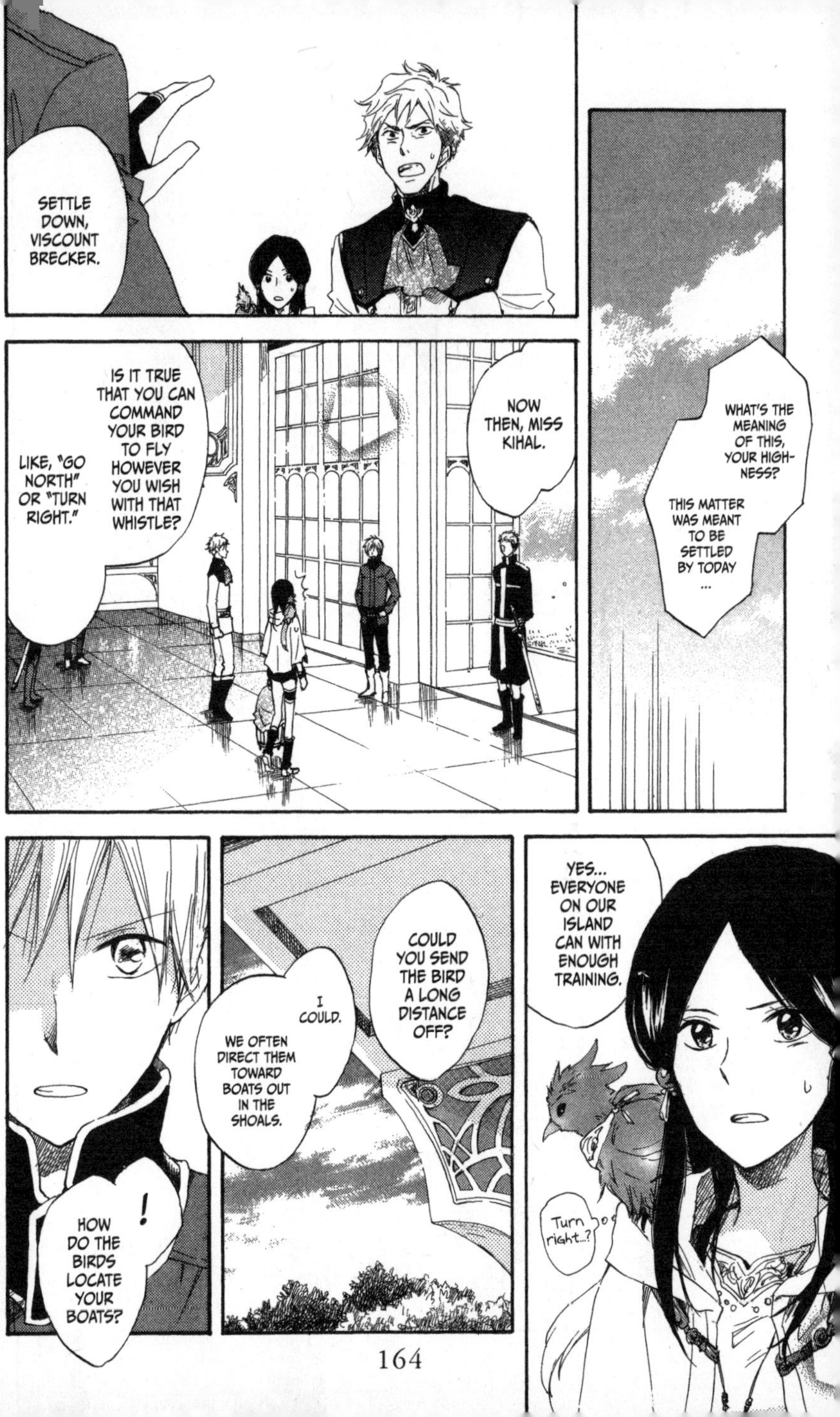
WHAT'S THE MEANING OF THIS, YOUR HIGHNESS?
THIS MATTER WAS MEANT TO BE SETTLED BY TODAY ...
SETTLE DOWN, VISCOUNT BRECKER.
NOW THEN, MISS KIHAL.
IS IT TRUE THAT YOU CAN COMMAND YOUR BIRD TO FLY HOWEVER YOU WISH WITH THAT WHISTLE?
LIKE, "GO NORTH" OR "TURN RIGHT."
YES... EVERYONE ON OUR ISLAND CAN WITH ENOUGH TRAINING.
Turn right...?
COULD YOU SEND THE BIRD A LONG DISTANCE OFF?
I COULD.
WE OFTEN DIRECT THEM TOWARD BOATS OUT IN THE SHOALS.
!
HOW DO THE BIRDS LOCATE YOUR BOATS?

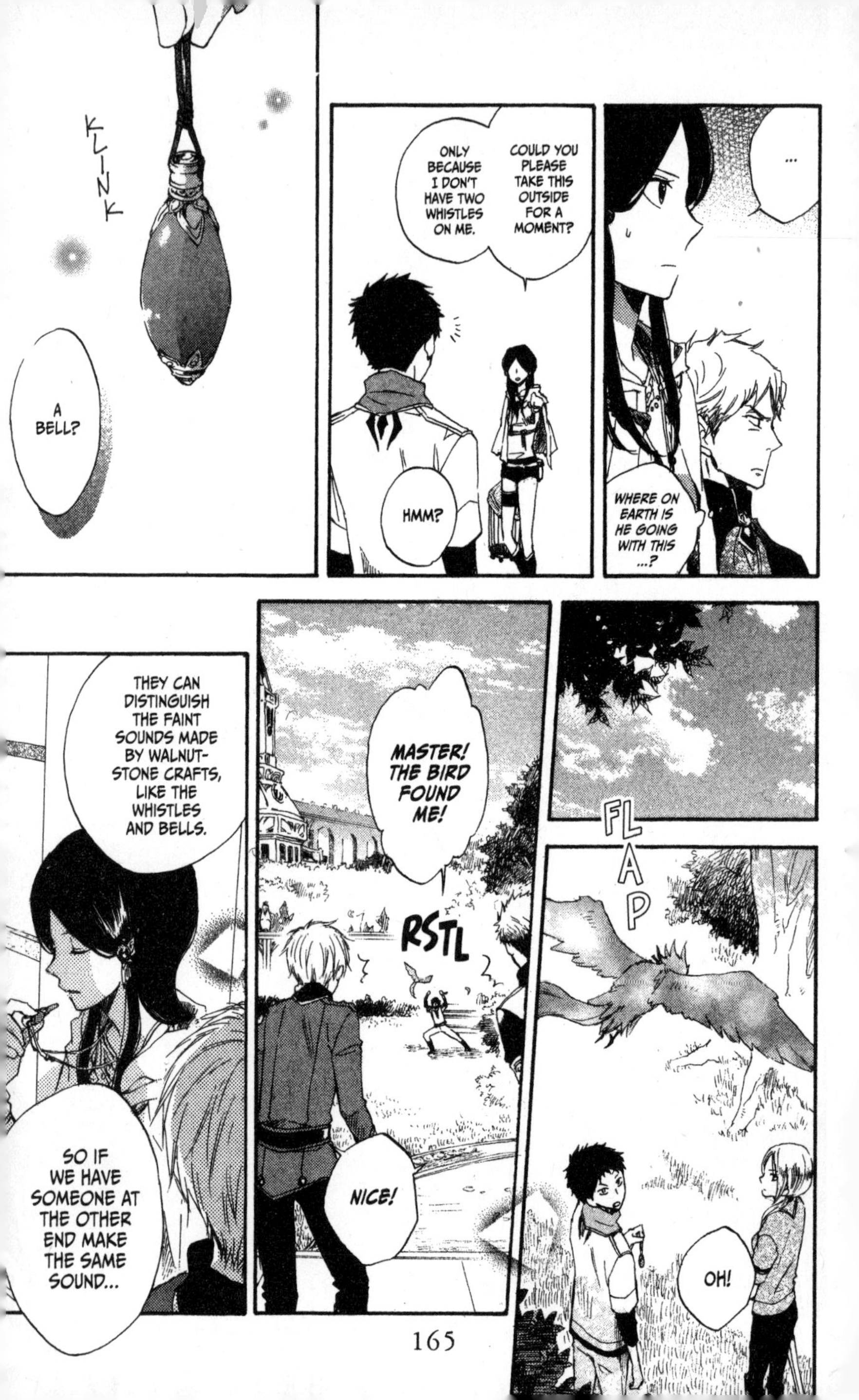
...
WHERE ON EARTH IS HE GOING WITH THIS ...?
COULD YOU PLEASE TAKE THIS OUTSIDE FOR A MOMENT?
ONLY BECAUSE I DON'T HAVE TWO WHISTLES ON ME.
HMM?
KLINK
A BELL?
FLAP
OH!
MASTER! THE BIRD FOUND ME!
RSTL
NICE!
THEY CAN DISTINGUISH THE FAINT SOUNDS MADE BY WALNUT-STONE CRAFTS, LIKE THE WHISTLES AND BELLS.
SO IF WE HAVE SOMEONE AT THE OTHER END MAKE THE SAME SOUND...

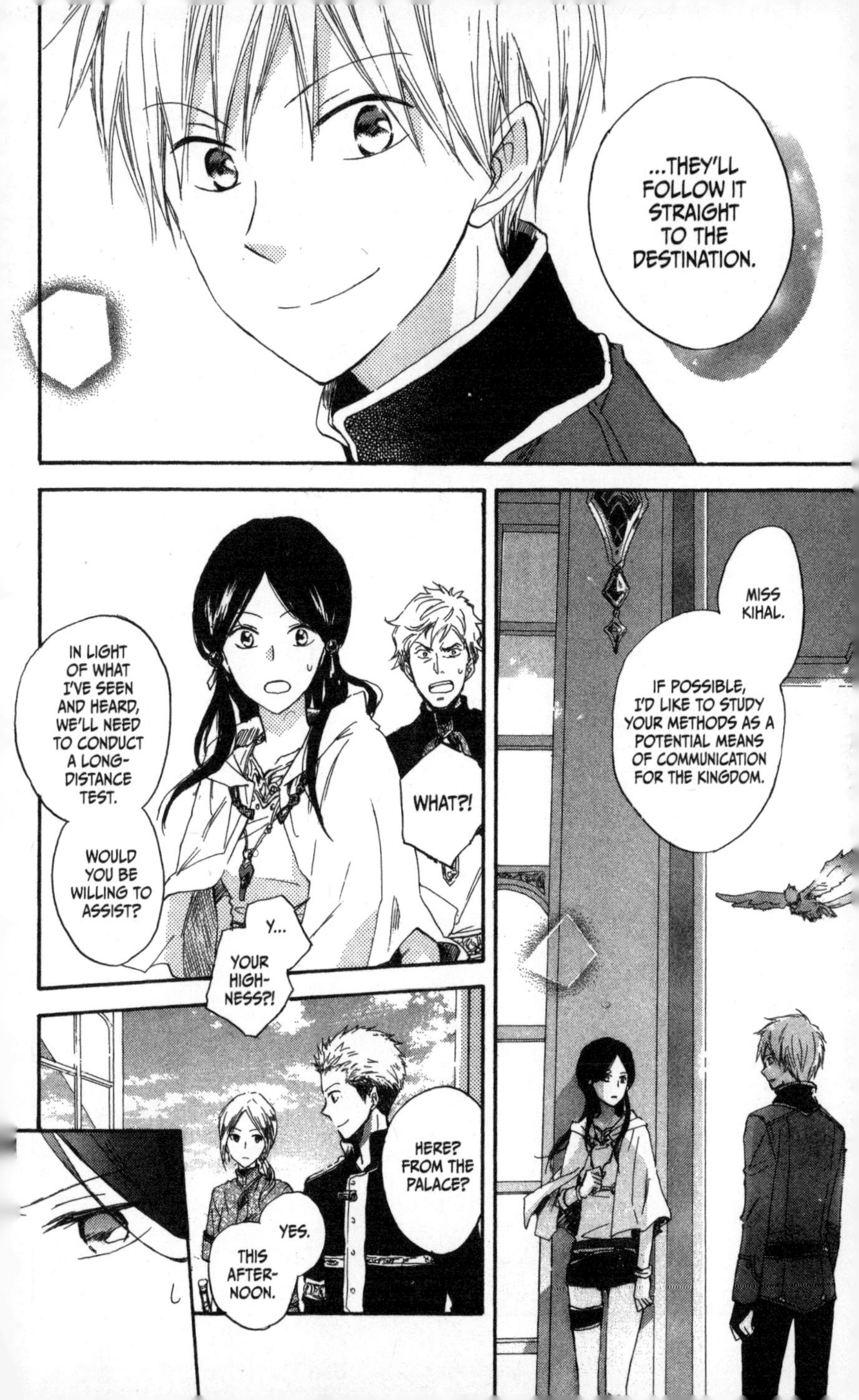
...THEY'LL FOLLOW IT STRAIGHT TO THE DESTINATION.
MISS KIHAL.
IF POSSIBLE, I'D LIKE TO STUDY YOUR METHODS AS A POTENTIAL MEANS OF COMMUNICATION FOR THE KINGDOM.
IN LIGHT OF WHAT I'VE SEEN AND HEARD, WE'LL NEED TO CONDUCT A LONG-DISTANCE TEST.
WOULD YOU BE WILLING TO ASSIST?
WHAT?!
Y... YOUR HIGHNESS?!
HERE? FROM THE PALACE?
YES. THIS AFTERNOON.

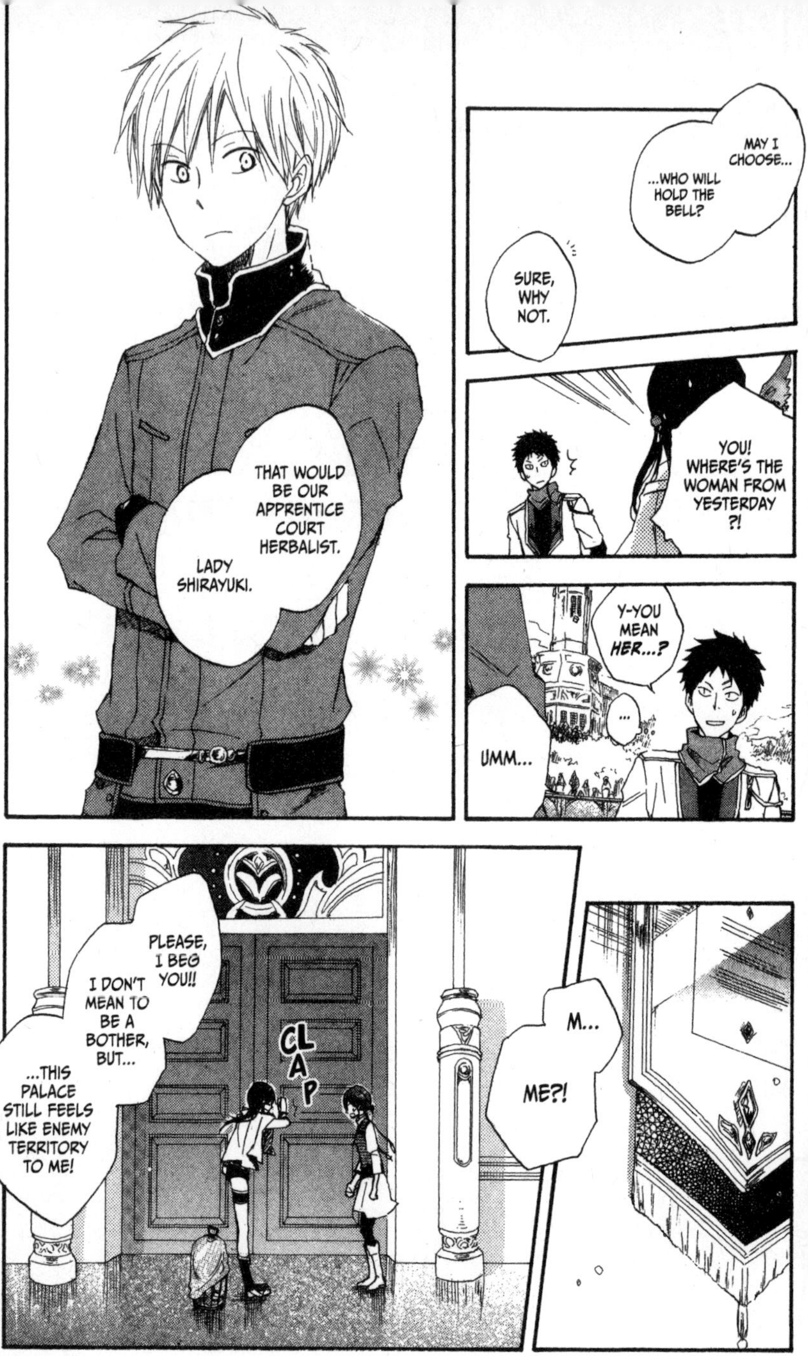
MAY I CHOOSE...
...WHO WILL HOLD THE BELL?
SURE, WHY NOT.
YOU! WHERE'S THE WOMAN FROM YESTERDAY ?!
Y-YOU MEAN HER...?
...
UMM...
THAT WOULD BE OUR APPRENTICE COURT HERBALIST.
LADY SHIRAYUKI.
M...
ME?!
PLEASE, I BEG YOU!!
I DON'T MEAN TO BE A BOTHER, BUT...
...THIS PALACE STILL FEELS LIKE ENEMY TERRITORY TO ME!
CLAP

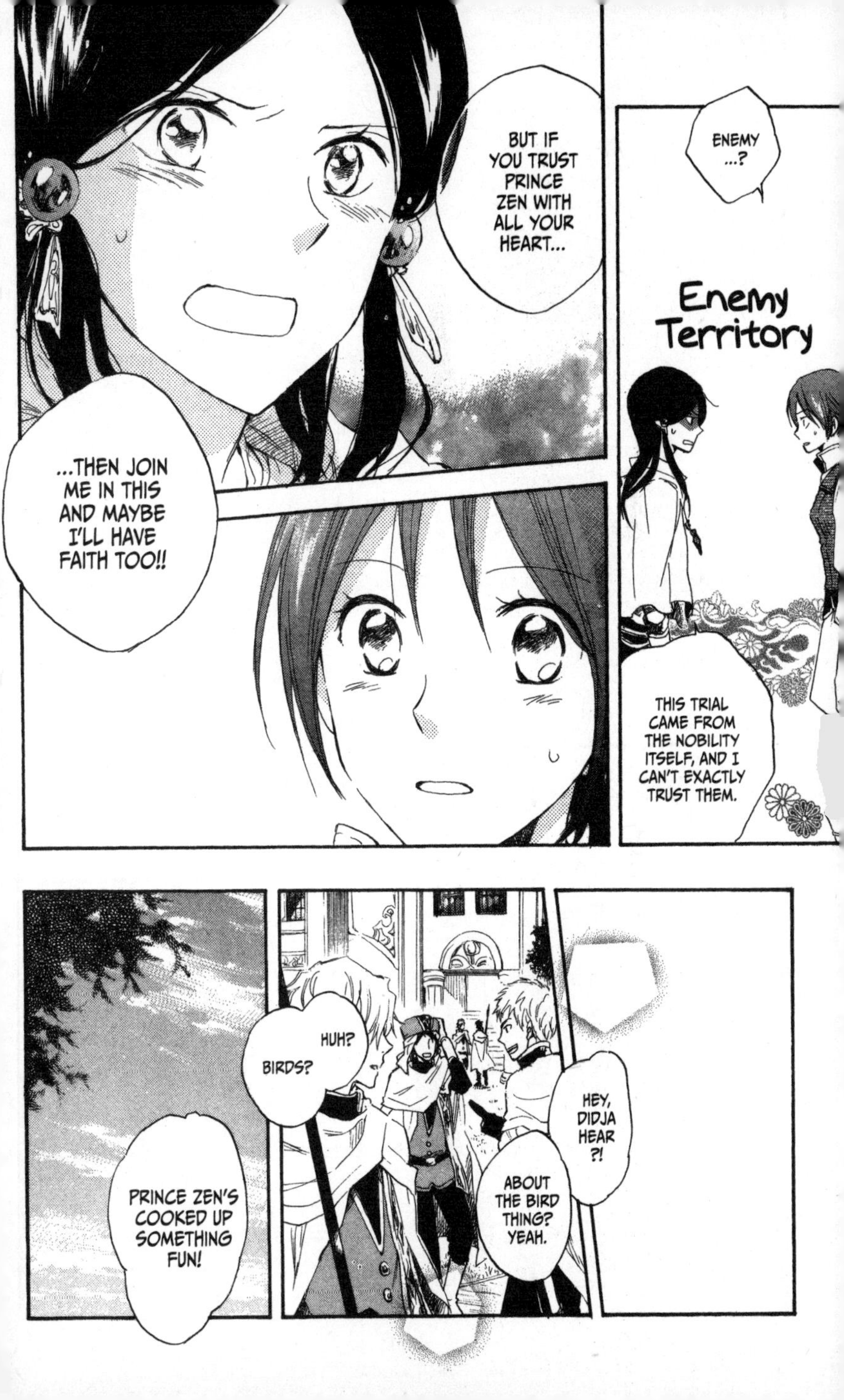
ENEMY ...?
Enemy Territory
THIS TRIAL CAME FROM THE NOBILITY ITSELF, AND I CAN'T EXACTLY TRUST THEM.
BUT IF YOU TRUST PRINCE ZEN WITH ALL YOUR HEART...
...THEN JOIN ME IN THIS AND MAYBE I'LL HAVE FAITH TOO!!
HEY, DIDJA HEAR?!
ABOUT THE BIRD THING? YEAH.
HUH?
BIRDS?
PRINCE ZEN'S COOKED UP SOMETHING FUN!

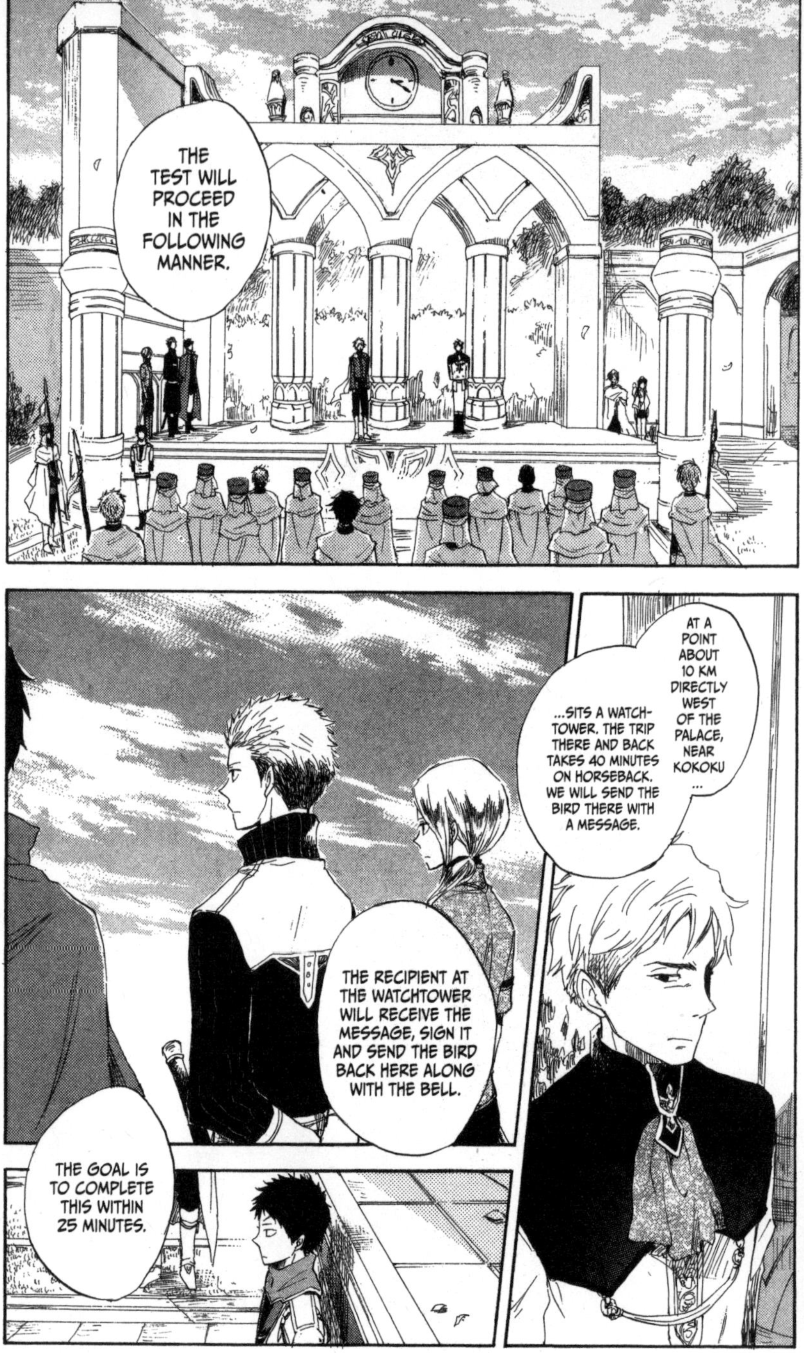
THE TEST WILL PROCEED IN THE FOLLOWING MANNER.
AT A POINT ABOUT 10 KM DIRECTLY WEST OF THE PALACE, NEAR KOKOKU ...
...SITS A WATCH-TOWER. THE TRIP THERE AND BACK TAKES 40 MINUTES ON HORSEBACK. WE WILL SEND THE BIRD THERE WITH A MESSAGE.
THE RECIPIENT AT THE WATCHTOWER WILL RECEIVE THE MESSAGE, SIGN IT AND SEND THE BIRD BACK HERE ALONG WITH THE BELL.
THE GOAL IS TO COMPLETE THIS WITHIN 25 MINUTES.

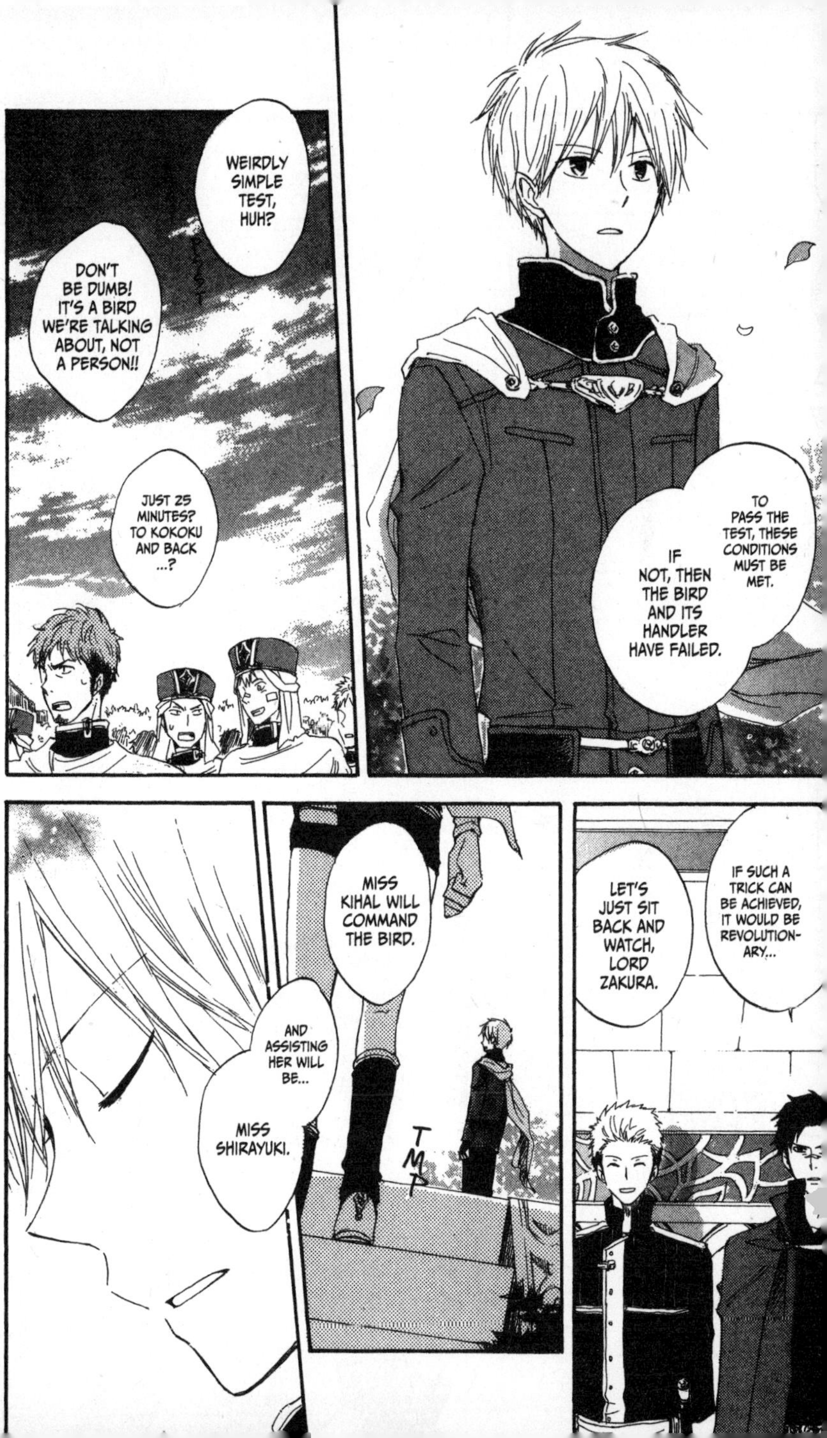
TO PASS THE TEST, THESE CONDITIONS MUST BE MET.
IF NOT, THEN THE BIRD AND ITS HANDLER HAVE FAILED.
WEIRDLY SIMPLE TEST, HUH?
DON'T BE DUMB! IT'S A BIRD WE'RE TALKING ABOUT, NOT A PERSON!!
JUST 25 MINUTES? TO KOKOKU AND BACK ...?
IF SUCH A TRICK CAN BE ACHIEVED, IT WOULD BE REVOLUTION-ARY...
LET'S JUST SIT BACK AND WATCH, LORD ZAKURA.
MISS KIHAL WILL COMMAND THE BIRD.
TMP
AND ASSISTING HER WILL BE...
MISS SHIRAYUKI.

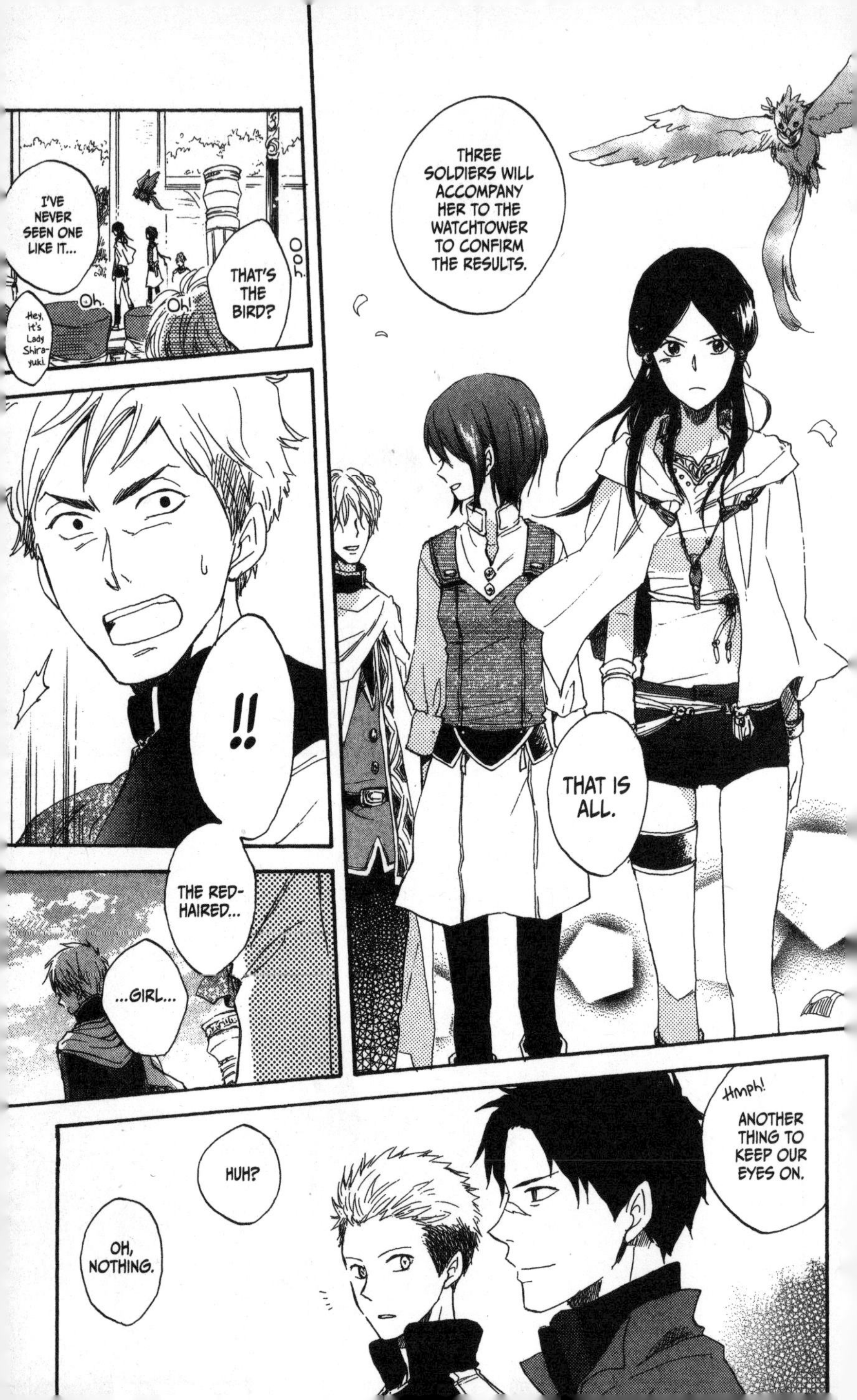
THREE SOLDIERS WILL ACCOMPANY HER TO THE WATCHTOWER TO CONFIRM THE RESULTS.
THAT IS ALL.
Ooh.
THAT'S THE BIRD?
Oh!
I'VE NEVER SEEN ONE LIKE IT...
Oh.
Hey, it's Lady Shira-yuki.
!!
THE RED-HAIRED...
...GIRL...
Hmph!
ANOTHER THING TO KEEP OUR EYES ON.
HUH?
OH, NOTHING.

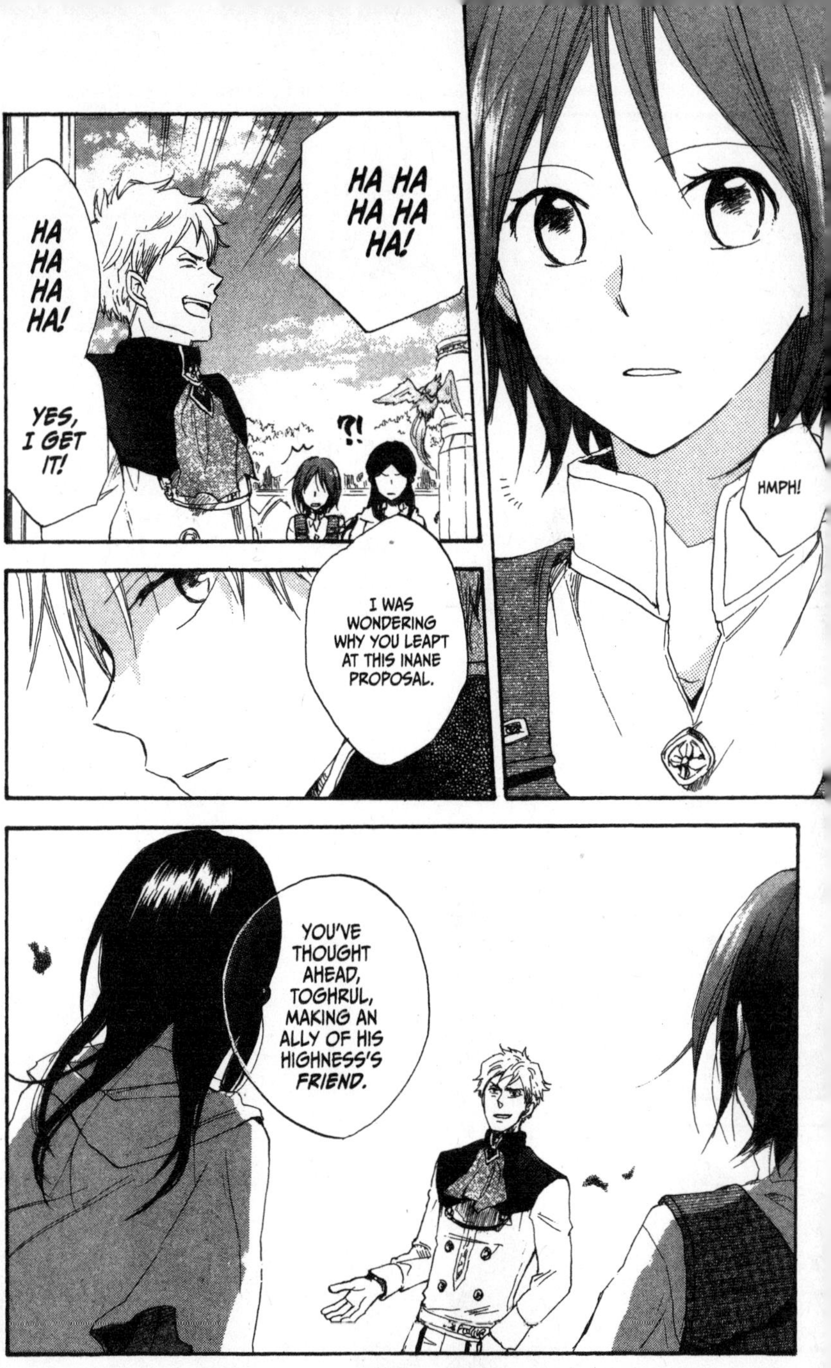
HMPH!
HA HA HA HA HA!
HA HA HA HA!
?!
YES, I GET IT!
I WAS WONDERING WHY YOU LEAPT AT THIS INANE PROPOSAL.
YOU'VE THOUGHT AHEAD, TOGHRUL, MAKING AN ALLY OF HIS HIGHNESS'S *FRIEND.*

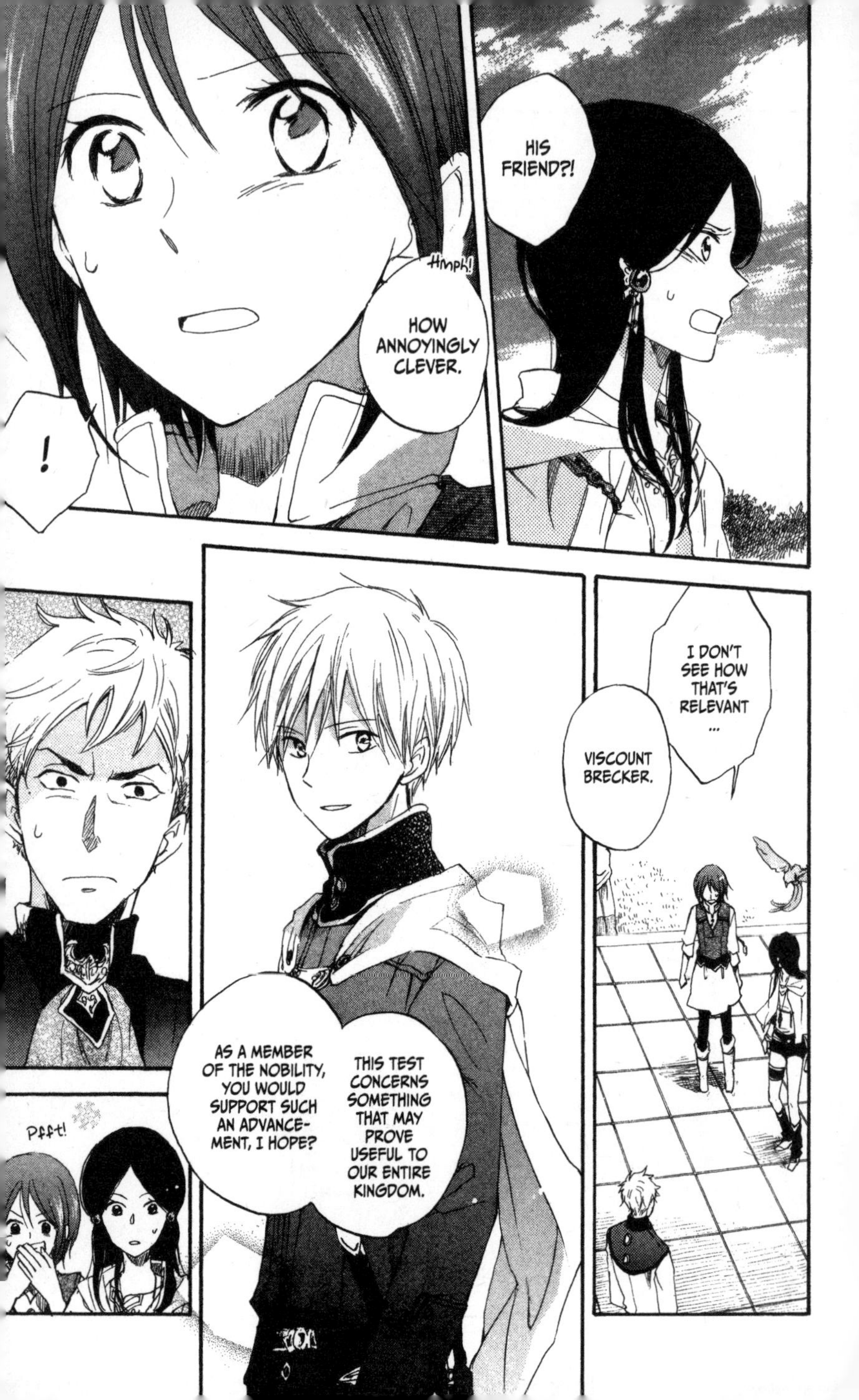
HIS FRIEND?!
Hmph!
HOW ANNOYINGLY CLEVER.
!
I DON'T SEE HOW THAT'S RELEVANT ...
VISCOUNT BRECKER.
THIS TEST CONCERNS SOMETHING THAT MAY PROVE USEFUL TO OUR ENTIRE KINGDOM.
AS A MEMBER OF THE NOBILITY, YOU WOULD SUPPORT SUCH AN ADVANCE-MENT, I HOPE?
Pfft!

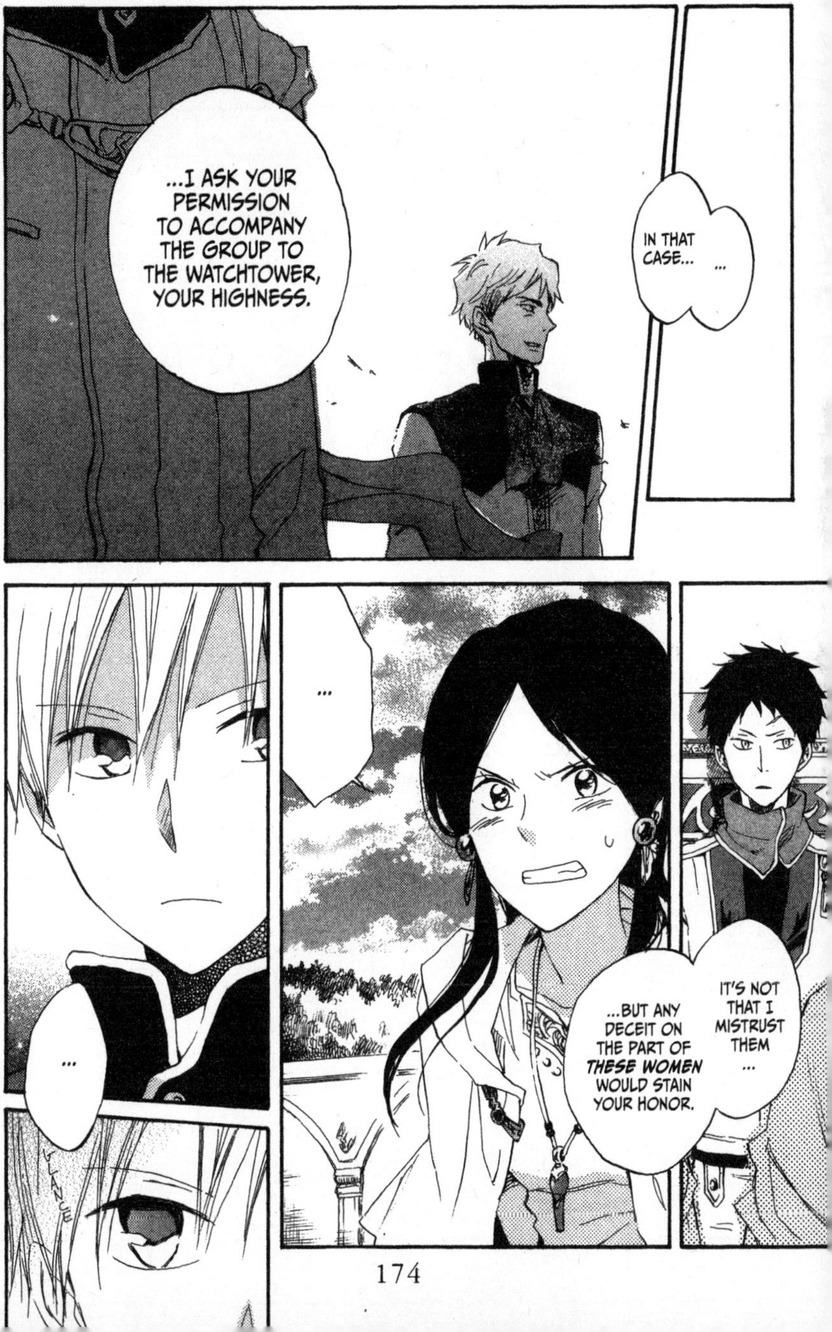

IN THAT CASE... ...
...I ASK YOUR PERMISSION TO ACCOMPANY THE GROUP TO THE WATCHTOWER, YOUR HIGHNESS.
...
IT'S NOT THAT I MISTRUST THEM ...
...BUT ANY DECEIT ON THE PART OF *THESE WOMEN* WOULD STAIN YOUR HONOR.
...
GLANCE

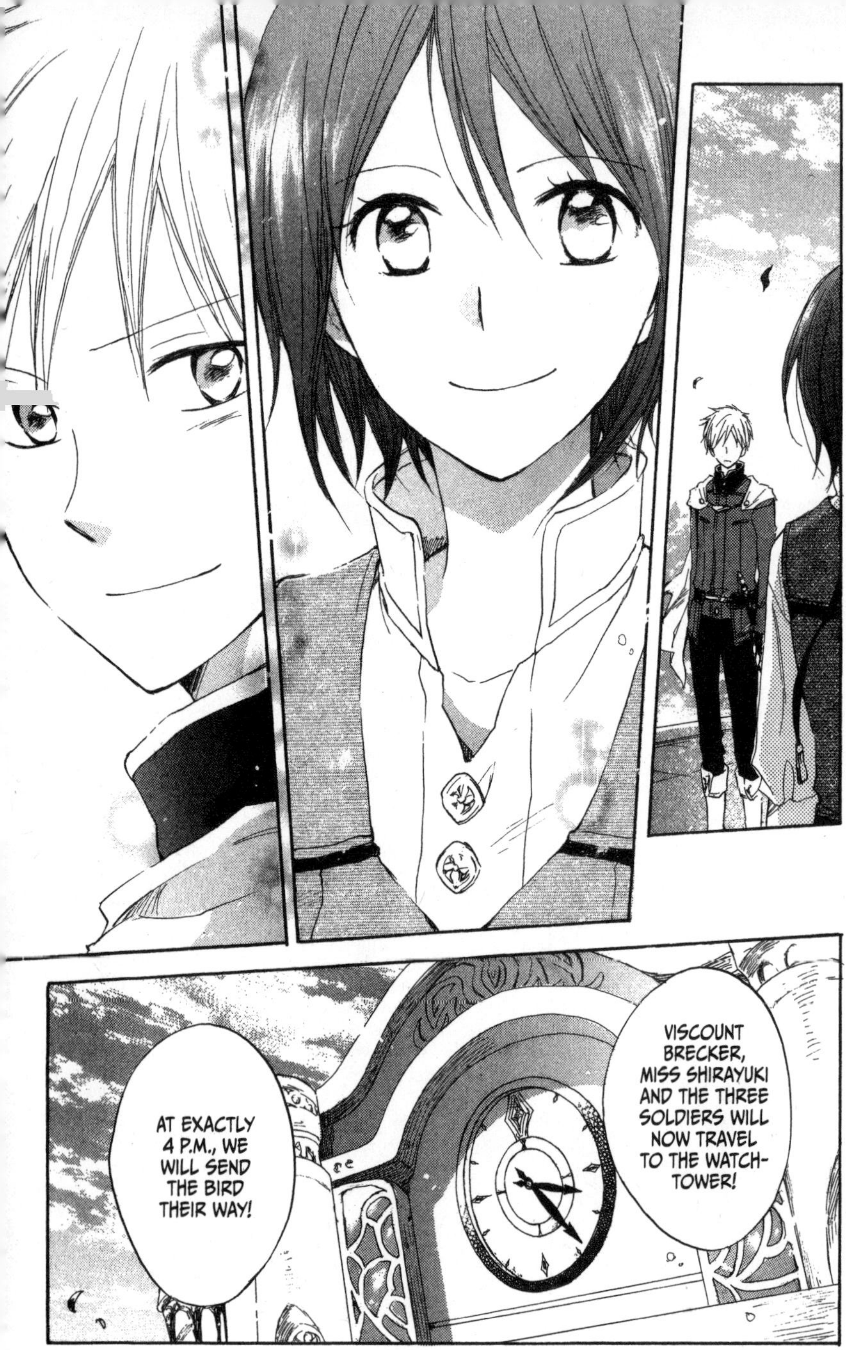
VISCOUNT BRECKER, MISS SHIRAYUKI AND THE THREE SOLDIERS WILL NOW TRAVEL TO THE WATCH-TOWER!
AT EXACTLY 4 P.M., WE WILL SEND THE BIRD THEIR WAY!

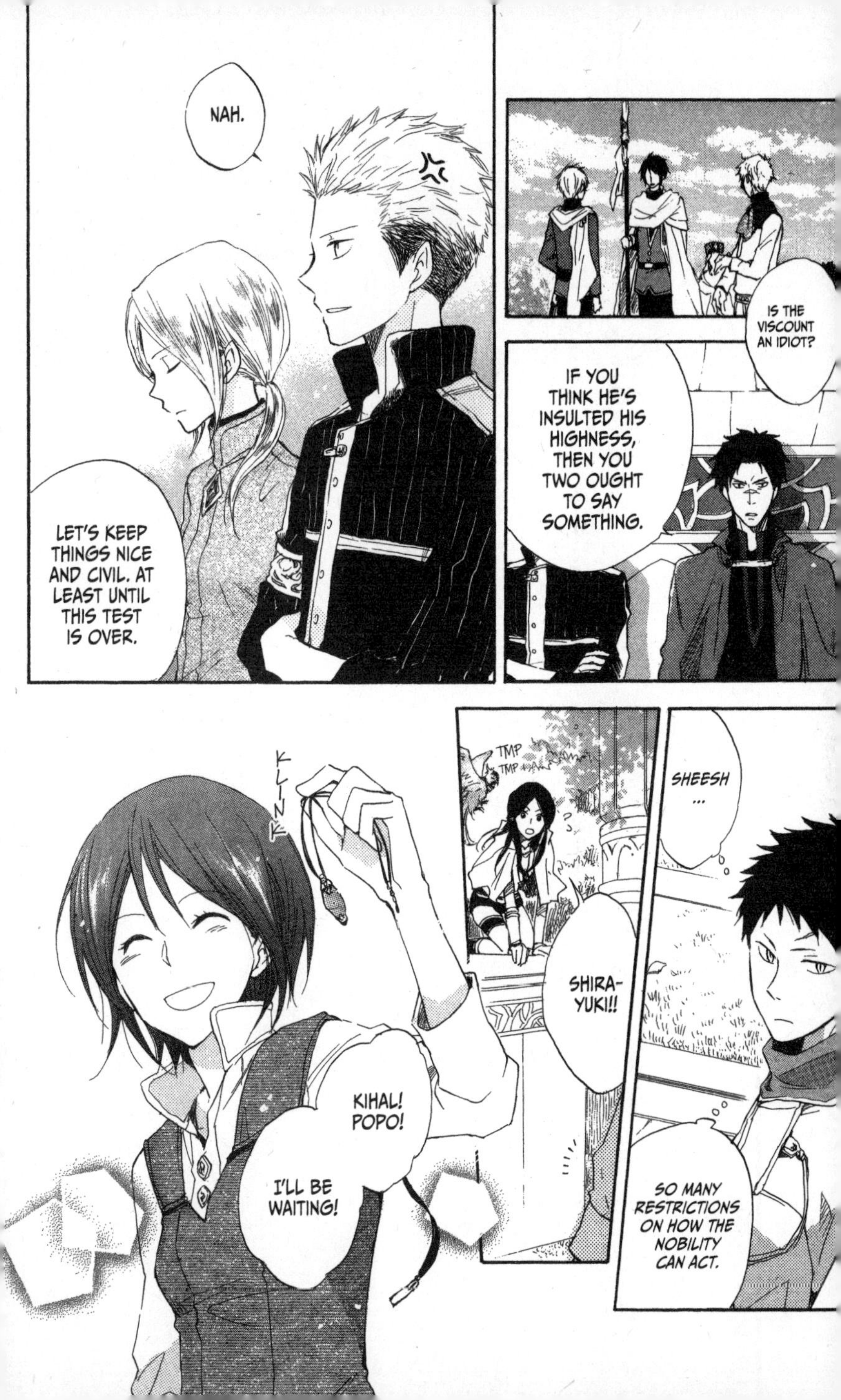
IS THE VISCOUNT AN IDIOT?
IF YOU THINK HE'S INSULTED HIS HIGHNESS, THEN YOU TWO OUGHT TO SAY SOMETHING.
NAH.
LET'S KEEP THINGS NICE AND CIVIL. AT LEAST UNTIL THIS TEST IS OVER.
SHEESH ...
SO MANY RESTRICTIONS ON HOW THE NOBILITY CAN ACT.
TMP TMP
SHIRA-YUKI!!
KLINK
KIHAL! POPO!
I'LL BE WAITING!

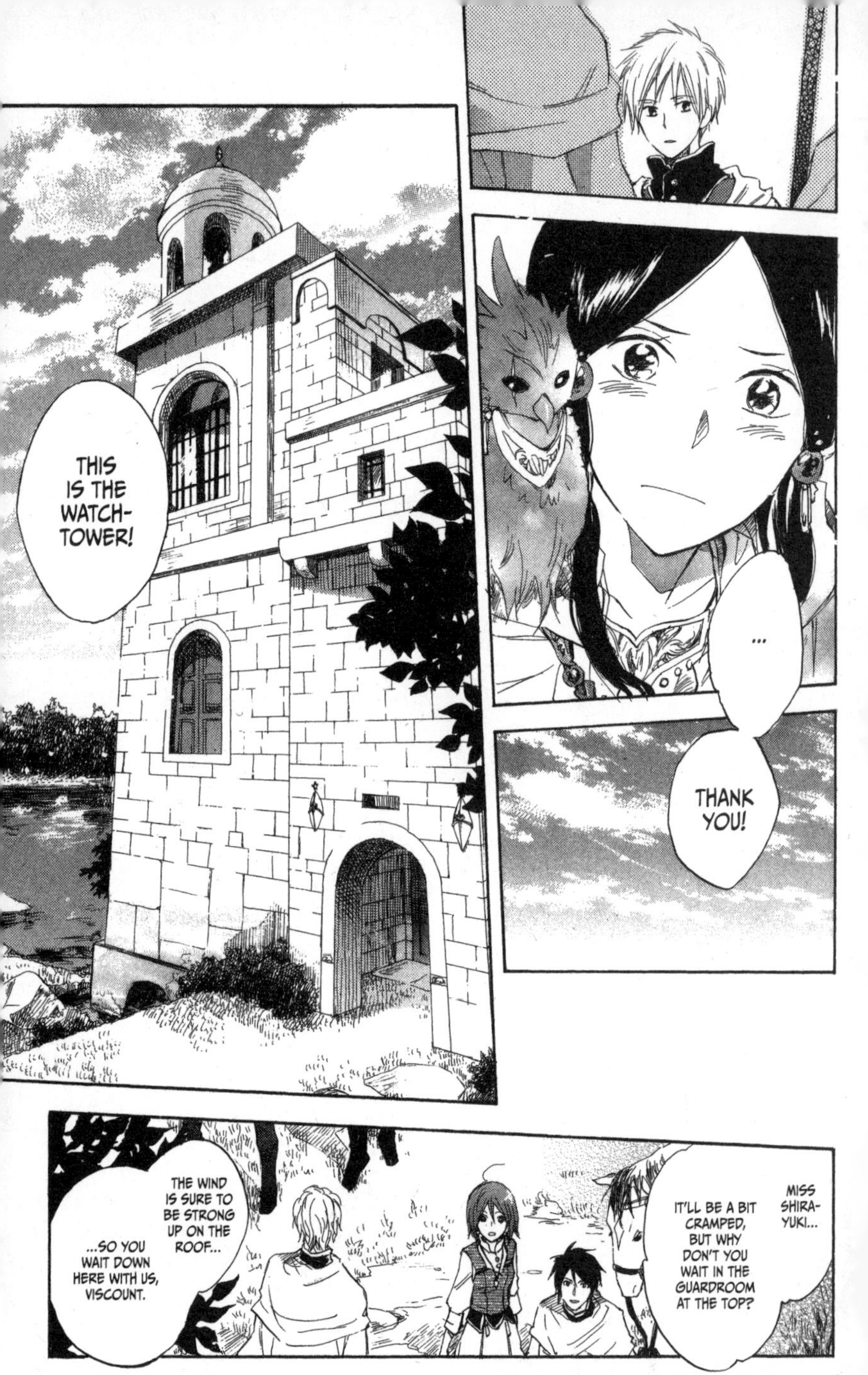
...
THANK YOU!
THIS IS THE WATCHTOWER!
MISS SHIRAYUKI...
IT'LL BE A BIT CRAMPED, BUT WHY DON'T YOU WAIT IN THE GUARDROOM AT THE TOP?
THE WIND IS SURE TO BE STRONG UP ON THE ROOF...
...SO YOU WAIT DOWN HERE WITH US, VISCOUNT.

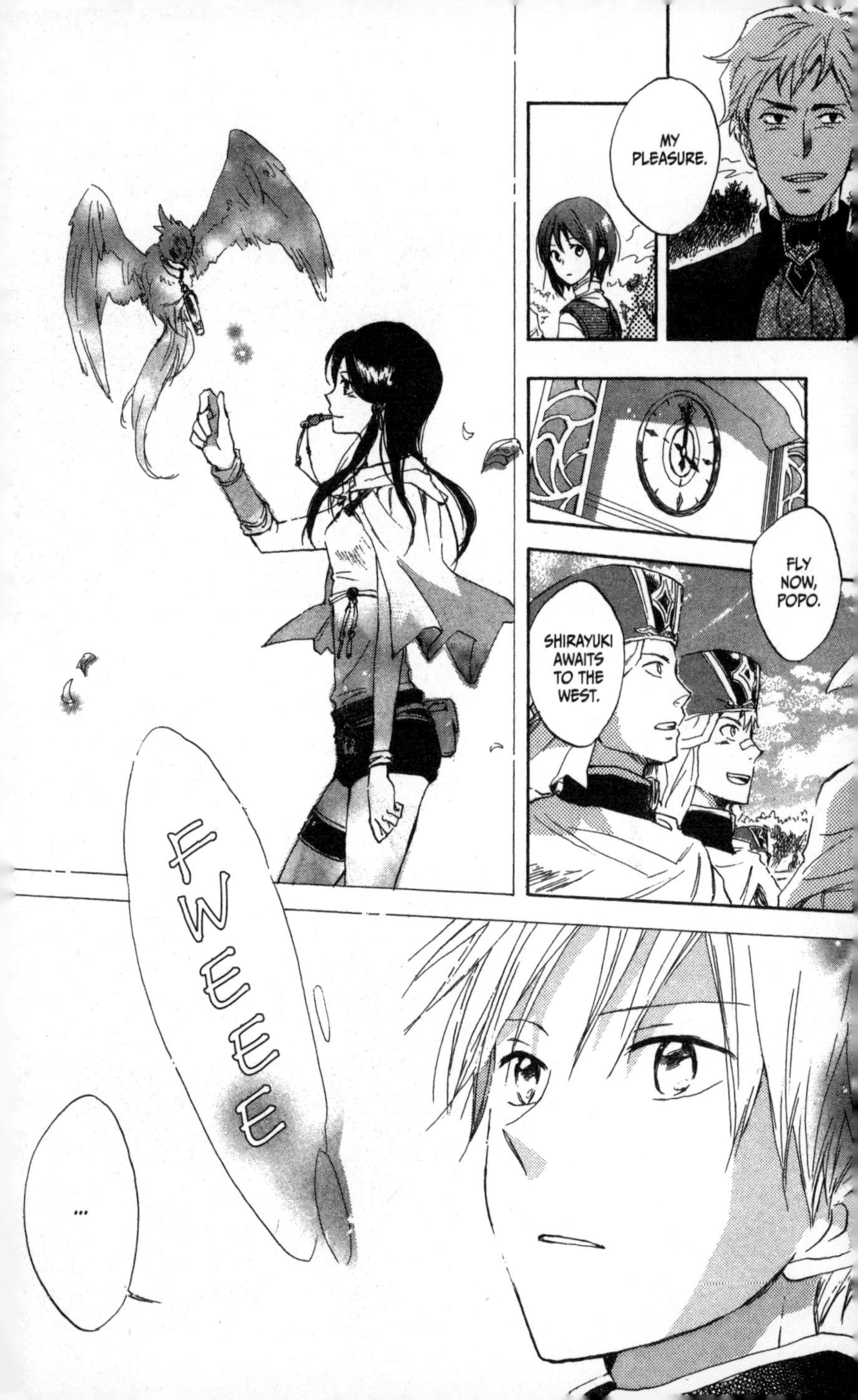

MY PLEASURE.
FLY NOW, POPO.
SHIRAYUKI AWAITS TO THE WEST.
FWEEE
...

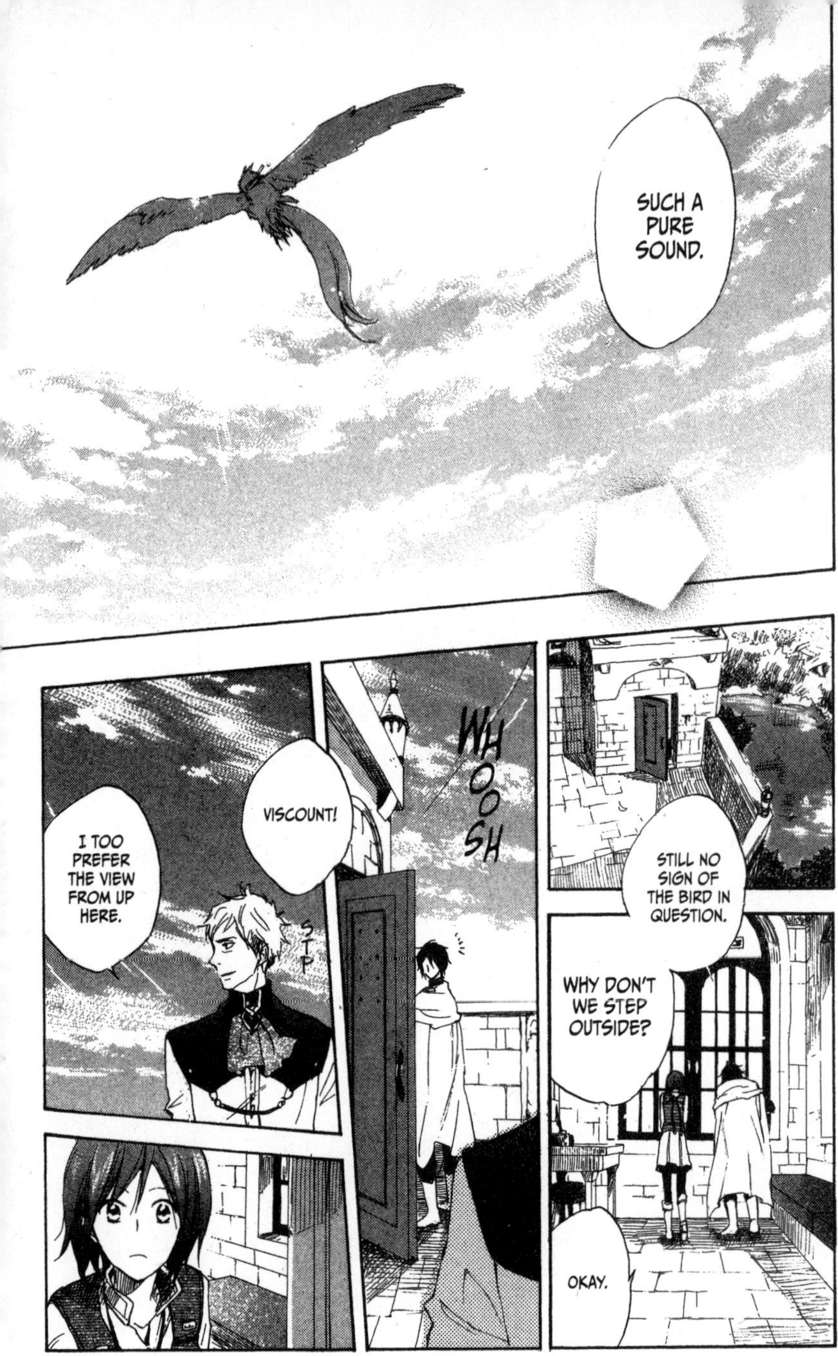
SUCH A PURE SOUND.
STILL NO SIGN OF THE BIRD IN QUESTION.
WHY DON'T WE STEP OUTSIDE?
OKAY.
WHOOSH
VISCOUNT!
STP
I TOO PREFER THE VIEW FROM UP HERE.

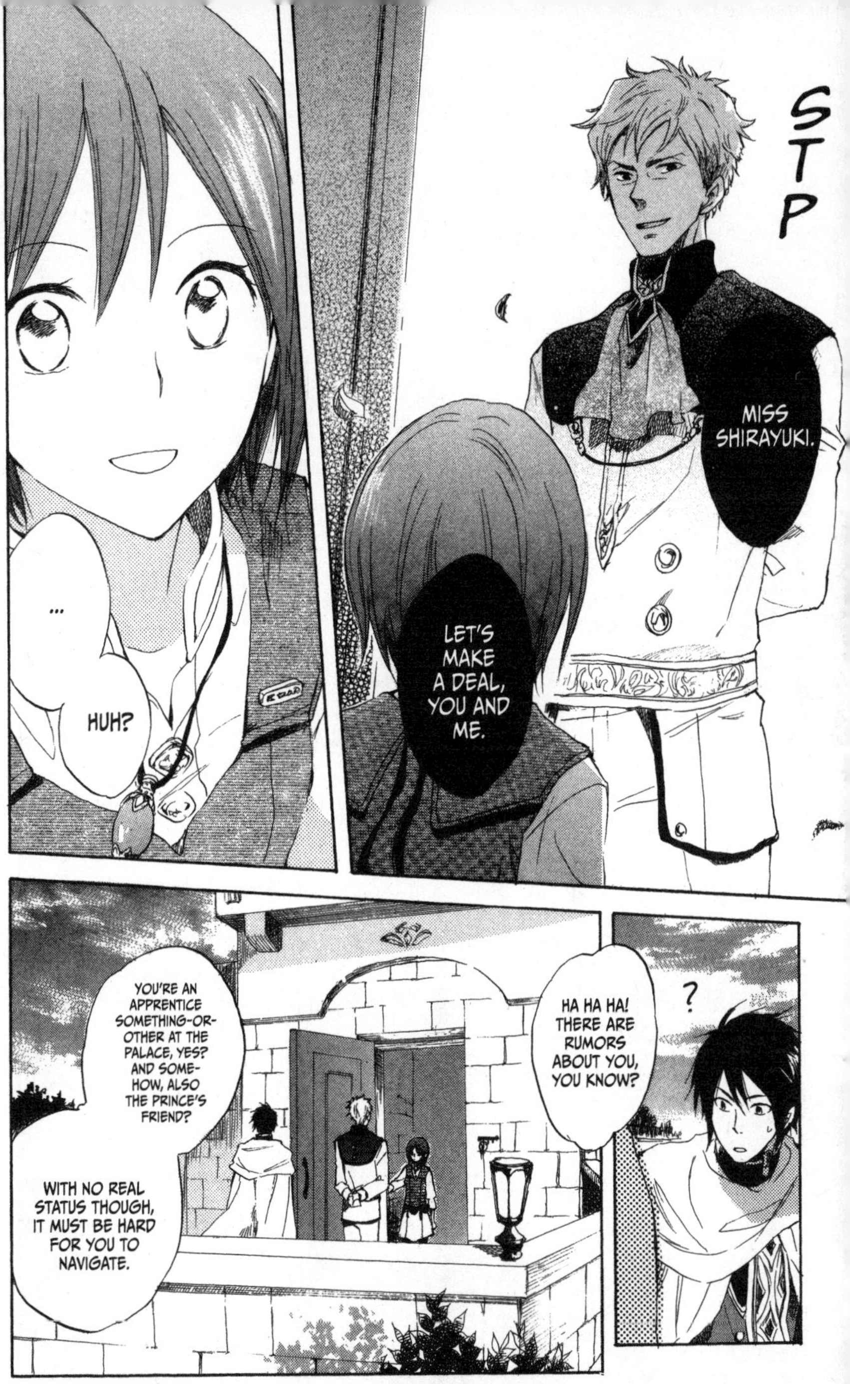
STP
MISS SHIRAYUKI.
LET'S MAKE A DEAL, YOU AND ME.
...
HUH?
?
HA HA HA! THERE ARE RUMORS ABOUT YOU, YOU KNOW?
YOU'RE AN APPRENTICE SOMETHING-OR-OTHER AT THE PALACE, YES? AND SOMEHOW, ALSO THE PRINCE'S FRIEND?
WITH NO REAL STATUS THOUGH, IT MUST BE HARD FOR YOU TO NAVIGATE.

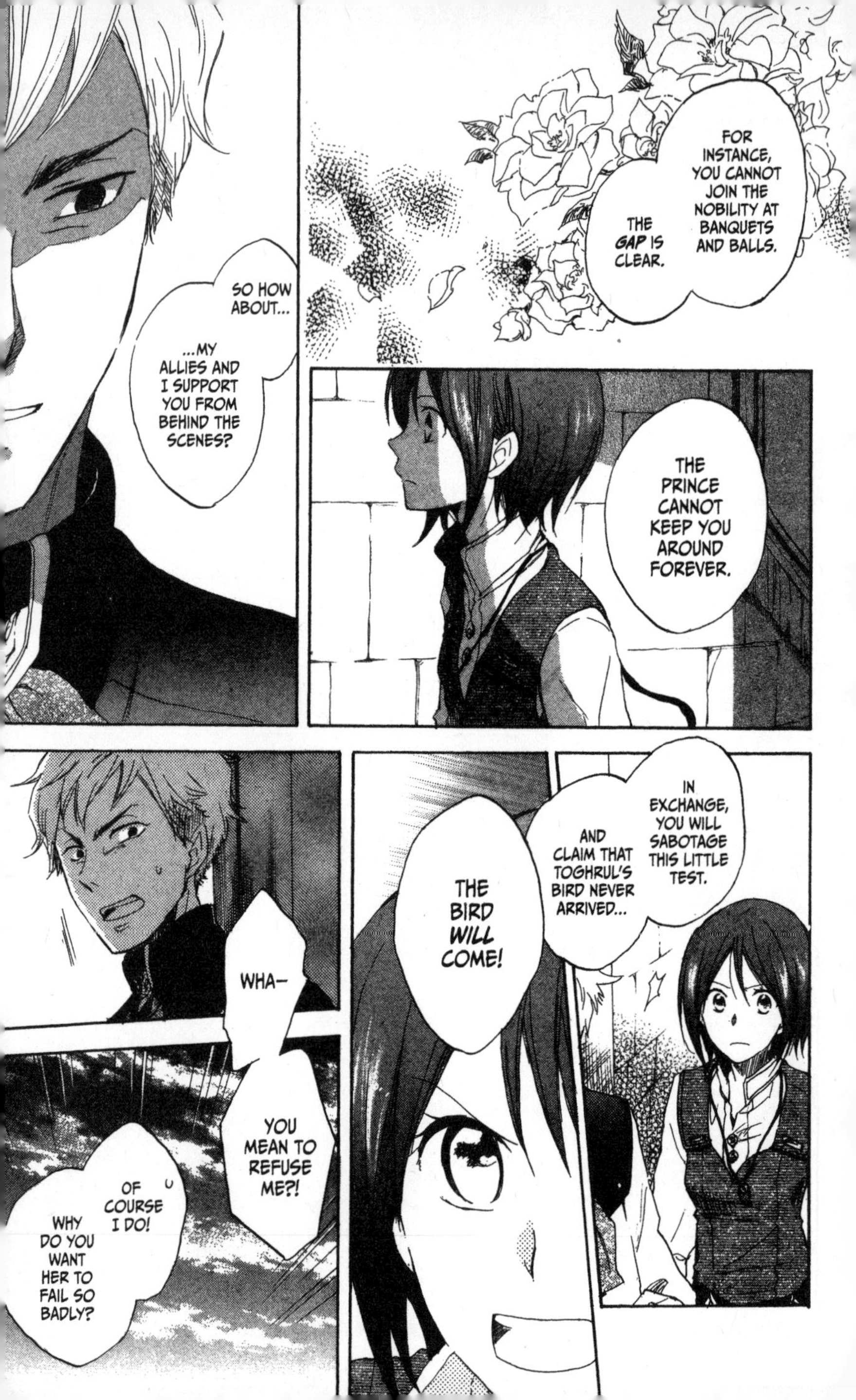

FOR INSTANCE, YOU CANNOT JOIN THE NOBILITY AT BANQUETS AND BALLS.
THE *GAP* IS CLEAR.
THE PRINCE CANNOT KEEP YOU AROUND FOREVER.
SO HOW ABOUT...
...MY ALLIES AND I SUPPORT YOU FROM BEHIND THE SCENES?
IN EXCHANGE, YOU WILL SABOTAGE THIS LITTLE TEST.
AND CLAIM THAT TOGHRUL'S BIRD NEVER ARRIVED...
THE BIRD *WILL* COME!
WHA-
YOU MEAN TO REFUSE ME?!
OF COURSE I DO!
WHY DO YOU WANT HER TO FAIL SO BADLY?

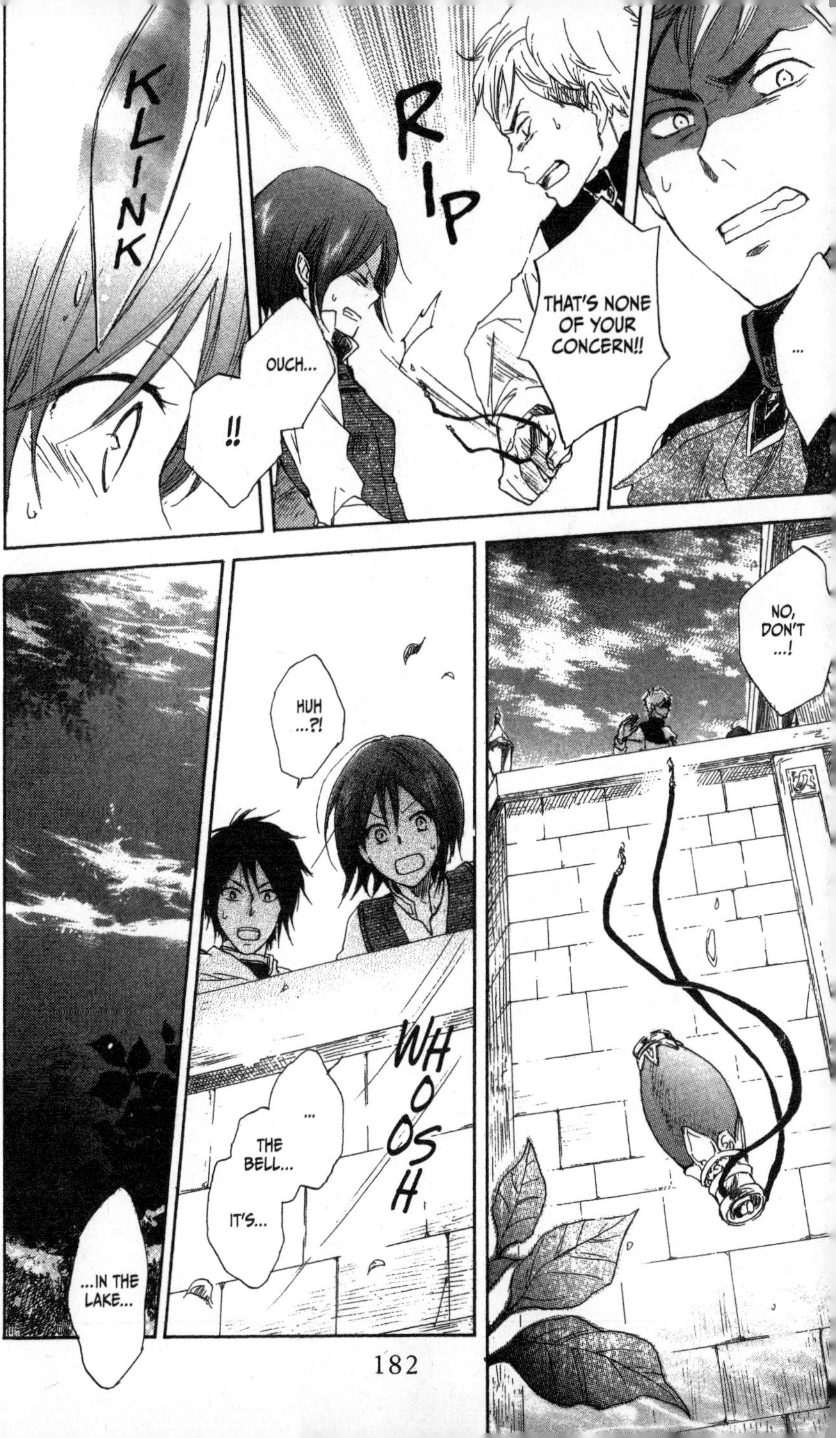
...
RIP
THAT'S NONE OF YOUR CONCERN!!
OUCH...
!!
KLINK
NO, DON'T ...!
HUH ...?!
WHOOSH
... THE BELL... IT'S...
...IN THE LAKE...

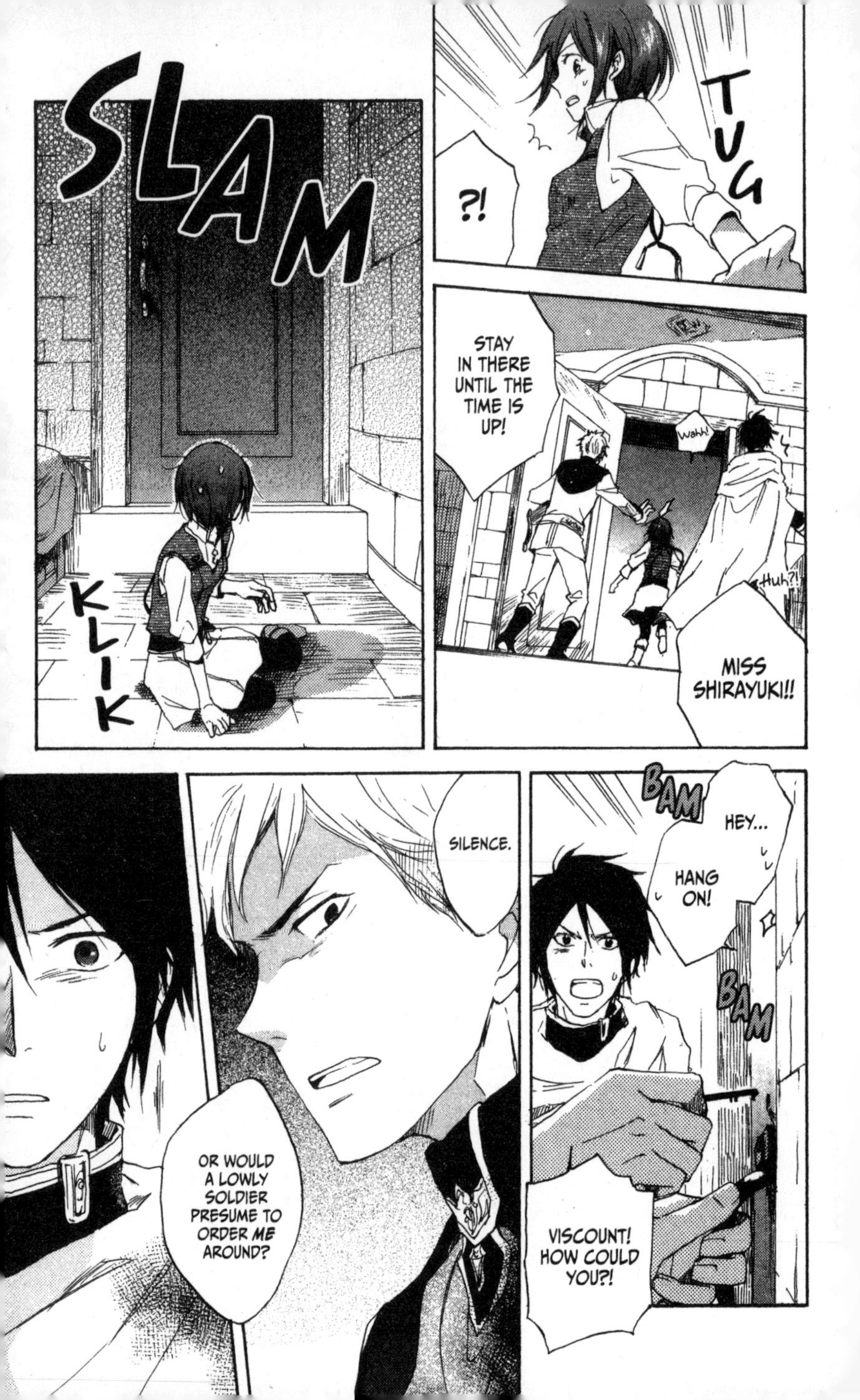
TUG
?!
STAY IN THERE UNTIL THE TIME IS UP!
Wahh!
Huh?!
MISS SHIRAYUKI!!
SLAM
KLIK
BAM
HEY...
HANG ON!
BAM
VISCOUNT! HOW COULD YOU?!
SILENCE.
OR WOULD A LOWLY SOLDIER PRESUME TO ORDER *ME* AROUND?

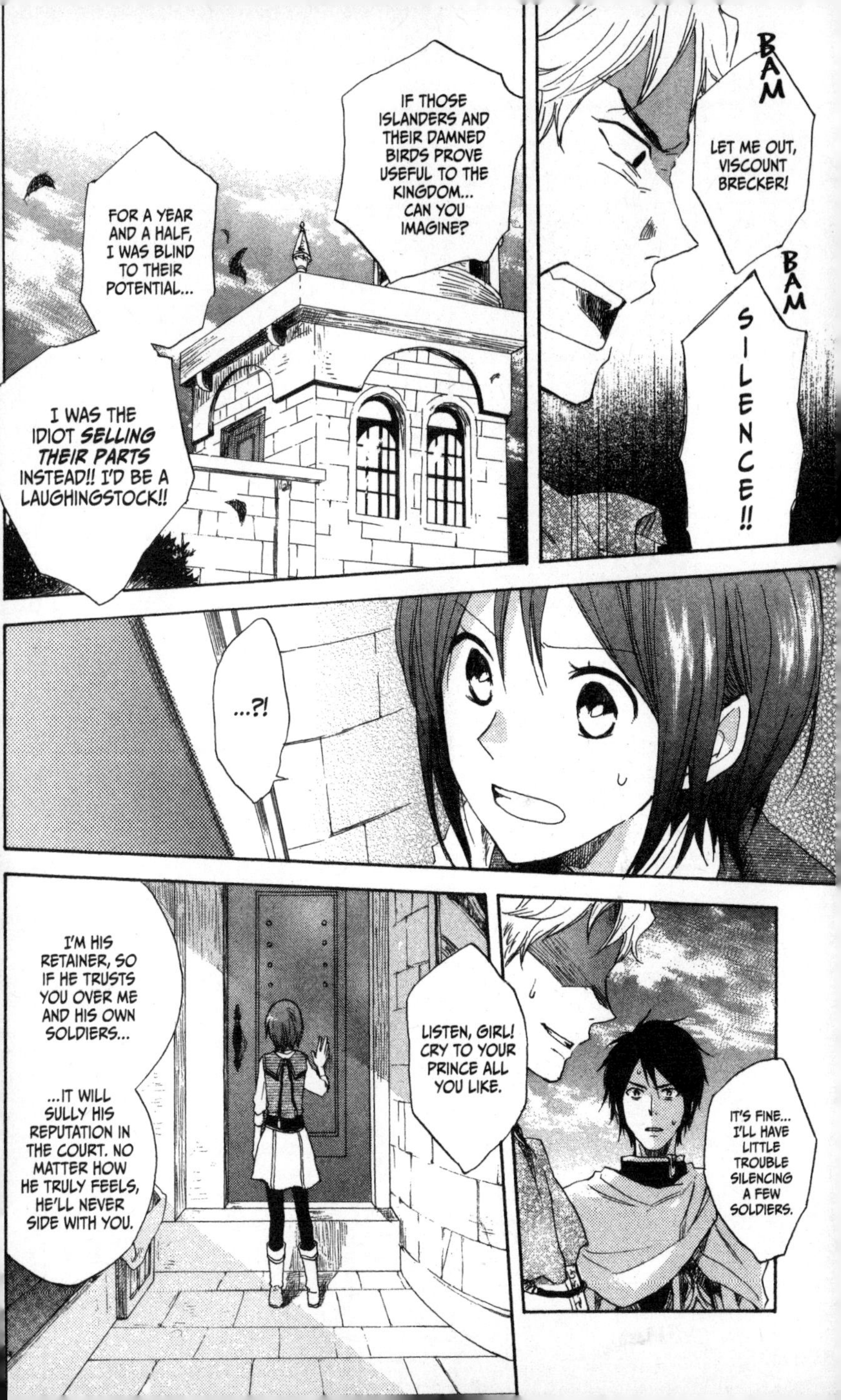
BAM
LET ME OUT, VISCOUNT BRECKER!
BAM
SILENCE!!
IF THOSE ISLANDERS AND THEIR DAMNED BIRDS PROVE USEFUL TO THE KINGDOM... CAN YOU IMAGINE?
FOR A YEAR AND A HALF, I WAS BLIND TO THEIR POTENTIAL...
I WAS THE IDIOT SELLING THEIR PARTS INSTEAD!! I'D BE A LAUGHINGSTOCK!!
...?!
LISTEN, GIRL! CRY TO YOUR PRINCE ALL YOU LIKE.
IT'S FINE... I'LL HAVE LITTLE TROUBLE SILENCING A FEW SOLDIERS.
I'M HIS RETAINER, SO IF HE TRUSTS YOU OVER ME AND HIS OWN SOLDIERS...
...IT WILL SULLY HIS REPUTATION IN THE COURT. NO MATTER HOW HE TRULY FEELS, HE'LL NEVER SIDE WITH YOU.

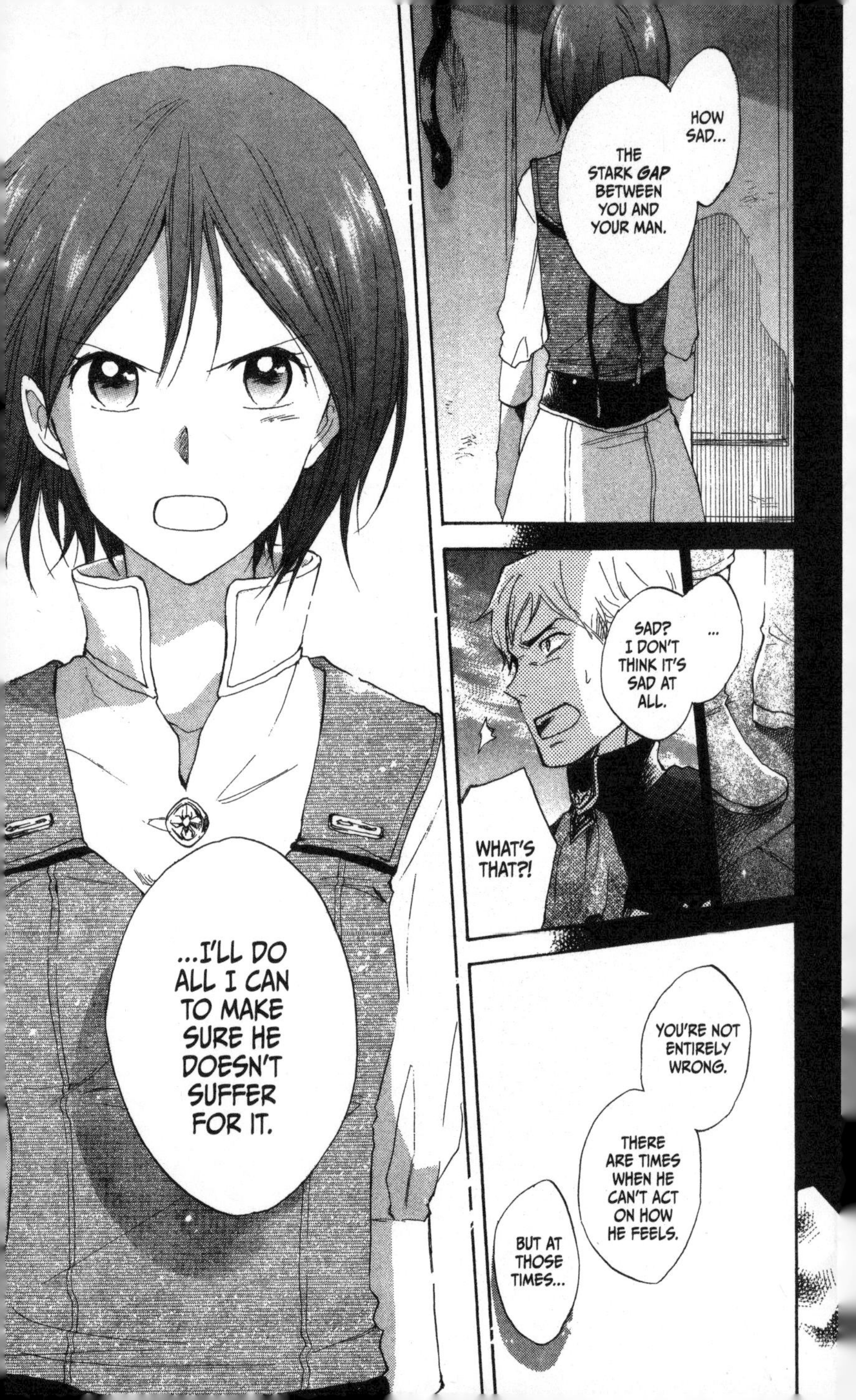
HOW SAD...
THE STARK GAP BETWEEN YOU AND YOUR MAN.
...
SAD? I DON'T THINK IT'S SAD AT ALL.
WHAT'S THAT?!
YOU'RE NOT ENTIRELY WRONG.
THERE ARE TIMES WHEN HE CAN'T ACT ON HOW HE FEELS.
BUT AT THOSE TIMES...
...I'LL DO ALL I CAN TO MAKE SURE HE DOESN'T SUFFER FOR IT.

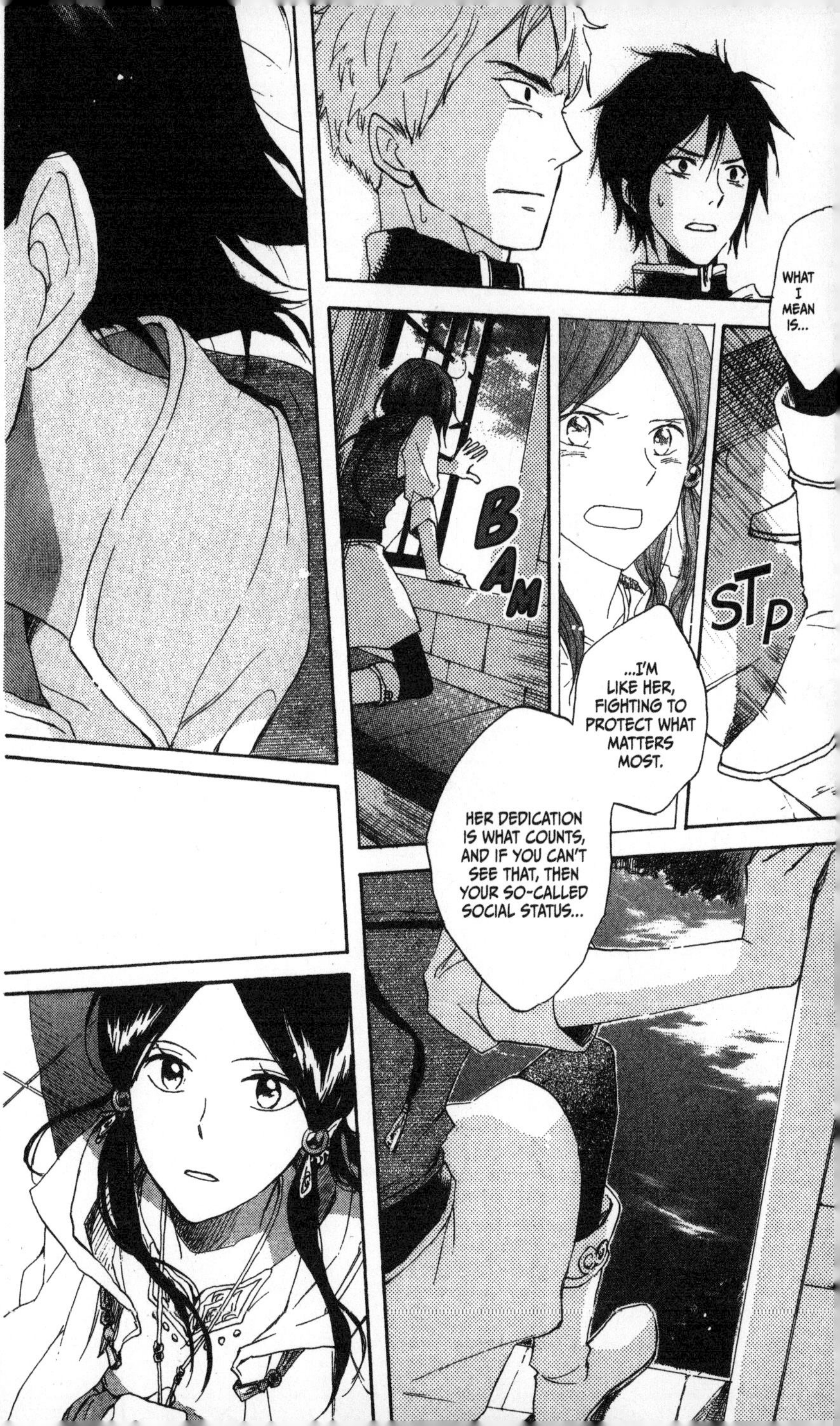
WHAT I MEAN IS...
STP
BAM
...I'M LIKE HER, FIGHTING TO PROTECT WHAT MATTERS MOST.
HER DEDICATION IS WHAT COUNTS, AND IF YOU CAN'T SEE THAT, THEN YOUR SO-CALLED SOCIAL STATUS...

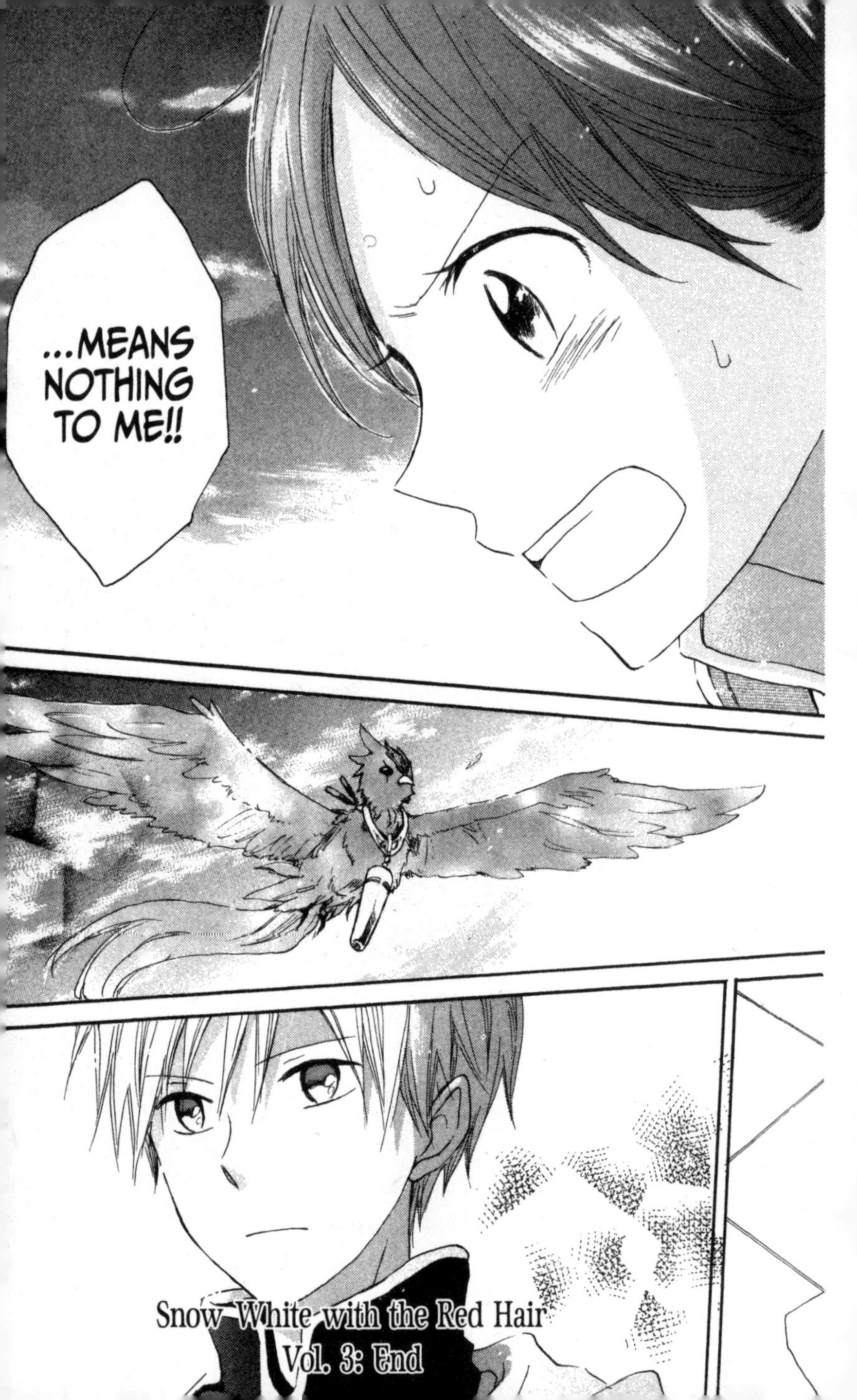
...MEANS NOTHING TO ME!!
Snow White with the Red Hair
Vol. 3: End

Bonus Pages

Nightcap

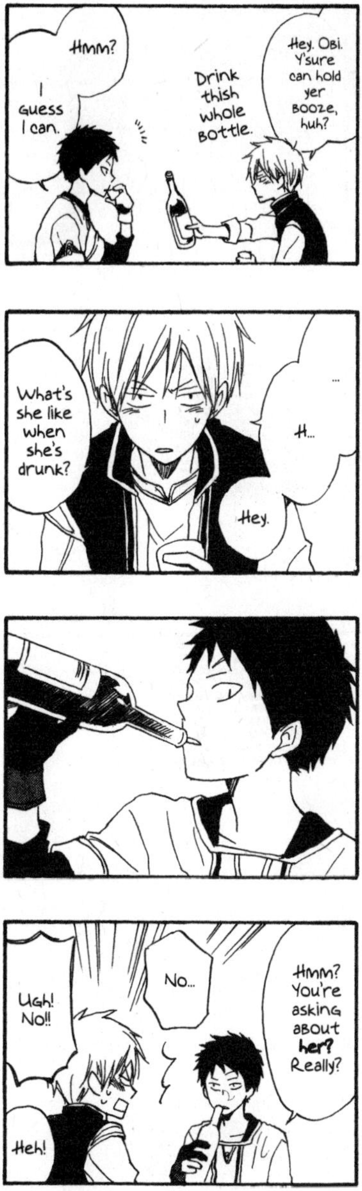
Hey. Obi. Y'sure can hold yer booze, huh?
Drink thish whole bottle.
Hmm?
I guess I can.
...
H...
Hey.
What's she like when she's drunk?
Hmm? You're asking about her? Really?
No...
Ugh! No!!
Heh!

Practical Joker

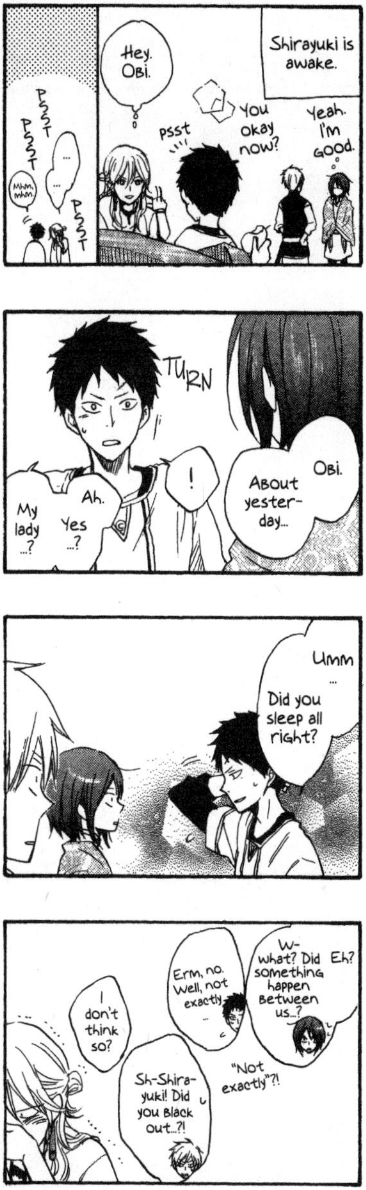
Shirayuki is awake.
Yeah. I'm good.
You okay now?
psst
Hey. Obi.
PSST PSST
...
...
PSST
Mhm, mhm.
Obi.
About yester-day...
!
TURN
Ah.
Yes ...?
My lady ...?
Umm ... Did you sleep all right?
Eh?
W-what? Did something happen between us...?
Erm, no. Well, not exactly ...
I don't think so?
"Not exactly"?!
Sh-Shira-yuki! Did you black out...?!

Poet's Gate Guard (The Right One): M.I.A.

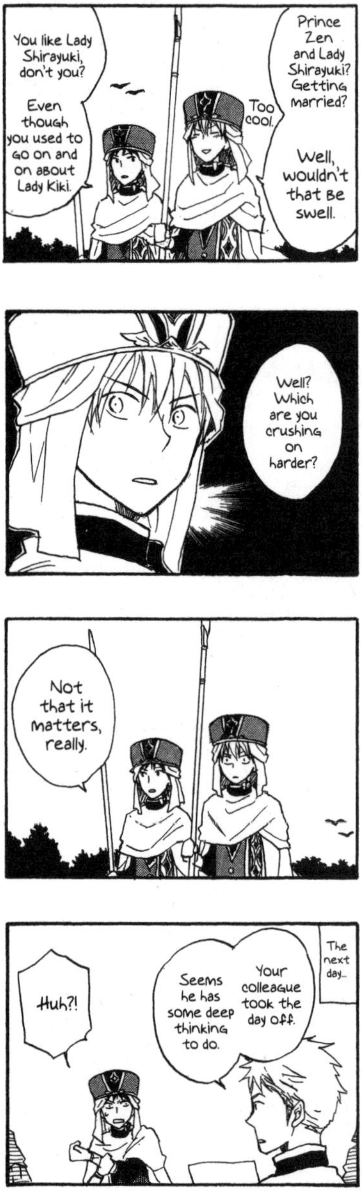
Prince Zen and Lady Shirayuki? Getting married?
Too cool.
Well, wouldn't that be swell.
You like Lady Shirayuki, don't you?
Even though you used to go on and on about Lady Kiki.
Well? Which are you crushing on harder?
Not that it matters, really.
The next day...
Your colleague took the day off.
Seems he has some deep thinking to do.
Huh?!

Day Off

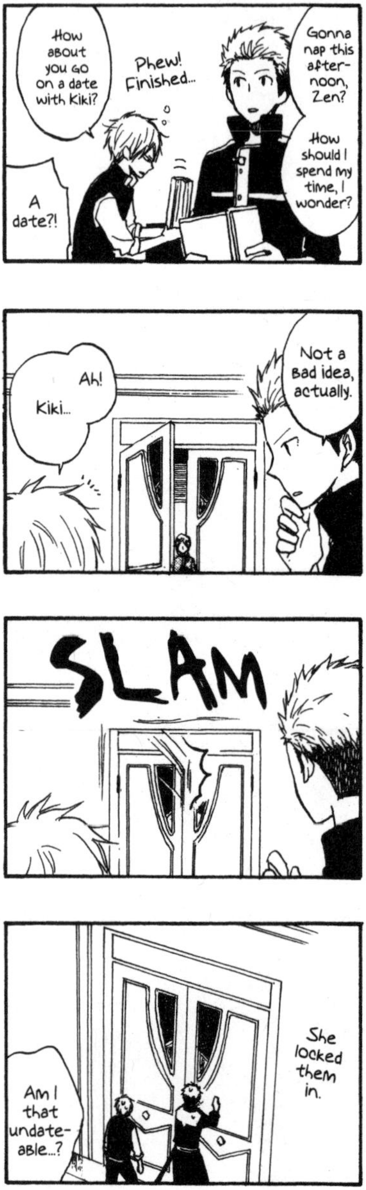
Gonna nap this after-noon, Zen?
How should I spend my time, I wonder?
Phew! Finished...
How about you go on a date with Kiki?
A date?!
Not a bad idea, actually.
Ah! Kiki...
SLAM
She locked them in.
Am I that undate-able...?

Bonus Pages: End

BIG THANKS TO:

My editor

Everyone in Editorial

Everyone in Publishing/Sales

Yamashita-san

My big sister, mother and father

Everyone who reads
and supports this series

Thank you!

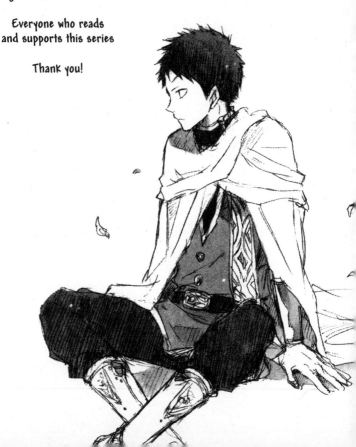

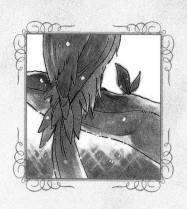

Sorata Akiduki was born on March 21 and is an accomplished shojo manga author. She made her debut in January 2002 with a one-shot titled "Utopia." Her previous works include *Vahlia no Hanamuko* (Vahlia's Bridegroom), *Seishun Kouryakubon* (Youth Strategy Guide) and *Natsu Yasumi Zero Zero Nichime* (00 Days of Summer Vacation). *Snow White with the Red Hair* began serialization in August 2006 in *LaLa DX* in Japan and has since moved to *LaLa*.

Snow White
with the Red Hair

3

SHOJO BEAT EDITION

STORY AND
Sorata A

TRANSLATION C
TOUCH-UP ART & LETTERI.
DESIGN **Alice Lewis**
EDITOR **Marlene First, Karla Clark**

Akagami no Shirayukihime by Sorata Akiduki
© Sorata Akiduki 2009
All rights reserved.
First published in Japan in 2009 by HAKUSENSHA, Inc., Tokyo.
English language translation rights arranged with HAKUSENSHA, Inc., Tokyo.

The stories, characters and incidents mentioned
in this publication are entirely fictional.

No portion of this book may be reproduced or transmitted in any form or
by any means without written permission from the copyright holders.

Printed in the U.S.A.

Published by VIZ Media, LLC
P.O. Box 77010
San Francisco, CA 94107

10 9 8 7 6 5 4 3 2 1
First printing, September 2019

PARENTAL ADVISORY
SNOW WHITE WITH THE RED HAIR is
rated T for Teen and is recommended
for ages 13 and up for mild language.

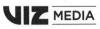

VIZ MEDIA
viz.com

Shojo Beat
shojobeat.com